SCANDAL!
Private Stories of Public Shame

D1190741

SCANDAL!

Private Stories of Public Shame

Colin Wilson and Damon Wilson

Published in 2003 by
Virgin Books
Thames Wharf Studios
Rainville Road
London W6 9HA

Copyright © Colin Wilson and Damon Wilson 2003

The right of Colin Wilson and Damon Wilson to be
identified as the Authors of the Work has been asserted by
them in accordance with the Copyright, Designs and
Patents Act 1988.

A version of this book previously appeared as *Scandal! An
Encyclopaedia* by Colin Wilson and Donald Seaman,
Weidenfeld and Nicolson, London 1986

www.virgin.com/books

Typeset by Phoenix Photosetting, Chatham, Kent
Printed and bound by CPD, Wales

1 85227 989 3

CONTENTS

ACKNOWLEDGMENTS

This book was suggested by the late Donald Seaman, and appeared under our joint authorship in 1986 with the title *Scandal: An Encyclopaedia*. In this new edition, Don's articles have been replaced by others by myself and my son Damon.

I would here like to acknowledge the help of my friend Paul Foot, in obtaining a copy of *The Liar*, the biography of Jonathan Aitken, by Luke Harding, David Leigh and David Pallister, and of Claire Armistead of the *Guardian* for tracking down one of the two remaining copies in a cupboard in her office.

I also want to thank the publishers of Kitty Kelley's biography of Frank Sinatra, *His Way*, for permission to quote from it.

Colin Wilson, Jan 2003

INTRODUCTION BY COLIN WILSON

This book was first suggested to me as a sequel to *An Encyclopedia of Modern Murder*, and I must admit that my reaction was unenthusiastic. Murder has always interested me because it is one of the extremes of human nature; by comparison, an interest in scandal seems a rather discreditable form of self-indulgence, like a passion for chocolate eclairs. Then I began to think about some of the classic scandals – the Duchess of Argyll, the Mayerling affair, the Dreyfus case, the Fatty Arbuckle 'rape,' the Profumo scandal – and saw that I was being narrow-minded. The great scandals afford the same opportunity to study the curious complexities of human nature as the famous criminal cases.

The next problem was to decide precisely what constitutes a scandal. A good starting point seemed to be Henry Fielding's remark: 'Love and scandal are the best sweeteners of tea.' That is to say, a scandal is any event that 'lets the cat out of the bag' and provides material for interesting gossip. That is why the best scandals seem to involve the downfall of some respectable person as a result of sexual or financial misdemeanours. The case of the rector of Stiffkey is probably the archetypal sexual scandal. But then, anyone who reads the story of the Reverend Harold Davidson will agree that this gentle and rather silly little man did not really deserve to be defrocked and – quite literally – thrown to the lions. On the other hand, the Reverend Henry Ward Beecher, that deafening foghorn of virtue, was undoubtedly a less-deserving case – at least it is known that he seduced the wives of two of his friends – and he succeeded in convincing his flock that he was a persecuted saint and remaining in his pulpit to the end of his days. If Harold Davidson deserved to be included, then Ward Beecher certainly did. So the element of 'downfall' had to be removed from our definition of scandal.

As I began to work on the book, I began to see an altogether more interesting common factor. When Professor Joad decided to save a few shillings by lying to a ticket collector about where he had boarded the train, he must have known that his career would be destroyed if he was caught. When Colonel Valentine Baker cast his eyes on Miss Rebecca Dickinson on the Portsmouth train and decided he wanted to possess her, he must have known that it could mean total ruin if she screamed. When Sir Gordon Cumming decided to cheat at cards when sitting at the same table as the Prince of Wales, he must have realized that detection would mean the end of his career as an 'officer and gentleman.' So why did they do it? Because they were dual personalities. Joad was a highly respected philosopher who wrote books about morals; another part of him was a greedy and dishonest adolescent who had a streak of meanness. Baker was a brave man and an honest soldier; but there was a part of him that regarded every girl as his legitimate prey (a feeling shared by his self-indulgent friend the Prince of

Wales). As to Sir Gordon Cumming, it will never be known why a wealthy landowner decided to add a few chips to his pile and so gain a small sum of which he had no need; there was obviously some fundamental split between the lieutenant-colonel of the Scots Guards and the gambler who felt a compulsion to cheat.

There is an ultimate stupidity about most criminals, even when they happen to be highly intelligent; they are a disturbing example of what William James calls 'a certain blindness in human beings'. With people involved in scandal, it is not so much blindness as a kind of astigmatism. They want the world to see them as respectable, but there is an element of childish egoism that they somehow feel they 'deserve' to indulge. The late Dr Rachel Pinney, a successful psychiatrist, told me that as soon as she found herself alone in someone else's house, she experienced an immediate compulsion to go and look in the drawers. She admitted that this dated back to childhood, when her parents went out and she was free to explore the 'forbidden' places of their bedroom. In *The Idiot*, there is a scene at a party where all the characters decide to tell one another the most shameful thing they have ever done – proof that Dostoevsky recognized this same 'split' as a fundamental part of human nature.

It is here that we can begin to grasp the deeper reasons for the fascination of scandal. Simone de Beauvoir remarked about Albert Camus that he often talked to her of an idea that obsessed him: that one day it had to be possible to write the Truth. 'The truth, as she saw it, was that in Camus the gap between his life and his writing was wider than in many others,' says Herbert Lottman, Camus's biographer. Camus was an incorrigible seducer who found girls irresistible; his marriage dissolved because of this problem and he spent much of his time living in hotels where he could entertain his mistresses more freely. It must have seemed ironic to this man, who knew he was regarded as one of the major intellectual figures of his time, to have to go through the usual trivial patter necessary to get a girl into bed. He knew he was not interested in her personally, that all he wanted was to get her to remove her clothes. Yet he was supposed to be a humanist who taught the importance of personal relationships. In a deeper sense, he undoubtedly believed in compassion and personal relationships. So how could it be possible to tell the exact truth about oneself?

The same point emerges in a story Lottman tells about Sartre and Camus getting drunk and staggering back home in the early hours of the morning. 'To think,' said Sartre, 'that in a few hours I'll be lecturing in the Sorbonne about the writer's responsibility.' He was not suggesting that there was something hypocritical about a 'serious' writer being drunk; only noting that the Sartre who stood up to speak to the students and the Sartre who was now weaving his way homeward were not quite the same person.

Now obviously, the simplest and crudest way of 'not being the same person' is to be a hypocrite, like Tartuffe. And that is why scandal intrigues us: because it suggests that truth has finally triumphed and the hypocrite stands exposed. But it is never quite as simple as that. The Reverend Harold Davidson did not believe for a moment that he was a hypocrite, which is why he fought so bitterly to reinstate himself in the church. Lord Byron and Oscar Wilde were certainly not hypocrites; in fact, they did their best to drop very broad hints about their 'secret sins' in their writings. (In the case of Wilde, I have always suspected some masochistic element that unconsciously connived in his own discovery and downfall.) H.G. Wells was not in the least hypocritical about his love life – indeed, he went out of his way to drop broad hints about it in many of his novels. Yet when confronted with a scandal – in the case of the young lady who tried to commit suicide on his carpet – he hastily contacted his friends on the newspapers and made sure nothing appeared in print. He had recognized – what becomes very clear in this book – that scandal is a kind of distorting mirror that obscures the truth just as much as it reveals it.

This is because scandal is based on wishful thinking. The public wants to be shocked in order to confirm its own sense of virtue.

Which explains why the universal love of scandal can be so dangerous. Fatty Arbuckle caused the accidental death of a young girl by landing on her with his full weight when she had a distended bladder. The simple explanation was not enough for the American public, and rumours began to circulate that he had raped her with a bottle, that his member was abnormally large, and so on. Arbuckle, being a naive and good-natured soul, totally failed to grasp what was happening, and was convinced that the public would once again take him to its heart if he was allowed the opportunity to make more films. What he failed to understand was that as a star of silent films, he had become a kind of myth. He was the archetypal clown, like Buttons in the pantomime. After the death of Virginia Rappe, he suddenly became a different type of myth – the ravening monster. (All fairy tales of monsters and beasts have sexual overtones. Think of Little Red Riding Hood.) He had become a victim of the psychological distortion mechanism.

Hollywood is, of course, one enormous distorting mirror – which is why the section on Hollywood scandal is the longest in this book. Robert Harrison, the publisher of Hollywood's most successful scandal magazine, *Confidential,* explained its success by saying, 'Americans like to read about things which they are afraid to do themselves.' But I am inclined to see this as an oversimplification. Would most people really have liked to launch the South Sea Bubble, or sodomize telegraph boys in cheap hotel rooms, or be involved in the bribery of politicians? Obviously not. What interests us is the contrast between myth and reality that becomes apparent when a scandal explodes.

Writers are particularly obsessed by this contrast because every writer sees it as his task to tell his own particular kind of truth. This occupation has its own dangers, as Graham Greene discovered when he reviewed a Shirley Temple film for a magazine in the 1930s and found himself in court on a libel charge. Evidently irritated by the sugary sweetness of the Shirley Temple image, Greene attempted to administer his own corrective by suggesting that her main appeal was to dirty old paedophiles; her studio was so enraged that they sued Greene on the grounds that he had accused them of procuring Miss Temple for immoral purposes. But why did the studio bother to sue the film critic of a small-circulation magazine? The answer must be that they felt that Greene was trying to prick the balloon, destroy the illusion, and their living depended on maintaining illusions.

This, then, is why we all enjoy reading about scandal: because we all enjoy seeing overinflated balloons explode. Yet this, as I have pointed out, is also a kind of illusion. Arbuckle was not really an overinflated balloon, even if he looked like one. Oscar Wilde was not really a monster of perversity. Harold Davidson was not really a satyr. Scandal specializes in half-truths.

This is why the range of this book is so wide and why some of its 'cases' – for example H.G. Wells and Bertrand Russell – do not, strictly speaking, qualify as scandals. Scandal lies in the nature of a human being rather than in the chain of events that caused a public commotion. Some scandals, when examined objectively, dwindle to microscopic proportions, and we realize that this is because they were never really scandals in the first place. This applies especially to political scandals, which are usually inflated out of all proportion by journalists and opposition politicians. When I was in Washington in 1966, I had dinner at the house of a Georgetown hostess who had been a close friend of President Kennedy. When I asked whether it was true that Kennedy had been a notorious womanizer, everyone looked shocked and reproachful and I was assured that there was absolutely no truth in the story. By the time the revelations of Judith Exner – and other of the president's ex-mistresses – began to appear, no one really cared any more. A recent paperback on Kennedy prints on its cover the story that when Jackie Kennedy came back from a journey, she found a pair of panties under the president's pillow; she tossed them at Kennedy with the comment, 'You'd better return these – they're not my size.' If Kennedy's opponents had got hold of that story in the early 1960s, it would have been blown up into a major scandal; Kennedy would have been branded a lecherous beast, a faithless husband, a danger to national security. Twenty years or so later, the same story provokes admiring chuckles; it proves that Kennedy was masculine and virile and willing to take risks – in fact, precisely the kind of man who ought to be president.

It seems even more puzzling that in spite of endless scandals about his alleged mistresses, Bill Clinton was then elected president for a second term, and that the Monica Lewinsky scandal, in which he was proved to have a taste for oral sex, apparently had no impact whatever on his popularity, and it seems highly probable that, if he had been allowed to stand for a third term, he would have been elected again.

Why should that have been so? The reason, I would suggest, is obvious: that Clinton was such an easygoing charmer that most people liked him – which is also why those who tried to bring him down, like Ken Starr and Linda Tripp, garnered so much unpopularity. And that, in retrospect, seems to be why Kennedy's sexual exploits were never revealed by some 'investigative journalist' – everybody liked him. And to make a maximum impact, the central character in a scandal must be disliked – or at least, regarded as a figure of unimpeachable reputation.

This is why the Jeffrey Archer story provided the British press with so many acres of moralizing editorials. Archer's rise to best-sellerdom and the House of Lords is certainly a remarkable success story. But the seeds of Archer's downfall lay in his love of publicity. He could not resist boasting about his own achievement and emphasizing that he was a millionaire. And there can be no doubt that the association of his name with that of Margaret Thatcher did him no good, since – whatever her real political achievements – she was seen as a headmistressy authority figure, whose ultimate downfall pleased as many Conservatives as Socialists.

This is why, when Archer was accused of paying a prostitute to leave the country in 1986, many people smiled grimly. Few – including myself – had the slightest doubt that he was guilty. So when he was not only acquitted – due in part to the asinine remarks of the judge about Mary Archer's 'elegance' and 'fragrance' – but also awarded staggering damages, most people seemed to feel that he had been far luckier than he deserved, and it was about time fate showed its impartiality by cutting him down to size. Under those circumstances, to stand as candidate for the mayor or London showed extraordinary tactlessness. Which explains why it caused such widespread satisfaction when, in 2000, he was found guilty of trying to pervert the course of justice, and sent to prison.

We could, of course, choose to look at all this from Archer's point of view. The original libel case came about because of a deliberate 'sting' by the *News of the World*, who persuaded the prostitute in question to telephone him and explain that she was being persecuted by the press. So when he found himself on the front page of the *News of the World*, Archer undoubtedly felt that he had been treated unfairly. His chances of winning the case were only 50/50 – particularly when a reputable journalist, Adam Raphael, testifed in court that Archer had told him that he *had* met Monica Coughlan – thereby contradicting Archer's own story. If it had not been for the judge's obvious bias in favour of Mary Archer and against the newspapers concerned, he probably *would* have lost.

It is easy to see why Archer felt justified in asking a friend to change the date on which he was supposed to have dined with him. This evidence was not, in fact, required in court. But when Archer received his enormous damages, he probably muttered, 'Serves 'em bloody well right.' And in altering a little of the evidence in his own favour, he *was* simply trying to serve them right.

It seems highly probable that the Archer case had an influence on the subsequent downfall of Jonathan Aitken. Aitken's remarks in Parliament about 'the cancer of bent and twisted journalism' have a ring of bitter sincerity. He had seen what happened to his colleague Jeffrey Archer, and must have been delighted to see the *News of the World* get its comeuppance. And he set out to give the press yet another black eye.

His mistake, we can now see, lay in overconfidence, and in not paying heed to the warning of the editor of the *Guardian* that he had proof that Aitken had not paid his own bill at the Ritz. Did it matter who had paid his bill? Probably not. Aitken's mistake lay in deciding to make an issue of it.

There is one more important point to be made. In the course of writing my half of this book, it became increasingly clear to me that most of the people involved in scandals have the same problem: an extremely powerful sex drive. A glance down the Contents page will demonstrate that most of the people in it are extremely highly sexed. This is natural, because they belong to what zoologists call 'the dominant five per cent,' and most dominant people are highly interested in sex. But we may also observe that most of these people also possessed a high degree of recklessness, and that it was their recklessness and lack of judgement that qualifies them for inclusion in *Scandal!* – an observation that adds a moral dimension to what would otherwise be a mere collection of gossip.

AITKEN, JONATHAN

A POLITICIAN'S SELF-DESTRUCTION

One of the most spectacular courtroom dramas of the 1990s ended in the downfall of the Conservative Cabinet Minister Jonathan Aitken, who had taken a libel action against the *Guardian* newspaper and Independent Television's programme, *World in Action*. Before he began his action, Aitken made a speech in Parliament in which he declared: 'If it falls to me to start a fight to cut out the cancer of bent and twisted journalism in our country with the simple sword of truth and the trusty shield of British fair play, so be it. I am ready for the fight!'

In fact, as Guardian editor Alan Rusbridger remarked after the trial: 'It was Aitken who was impaled on the sword of truth.'

Aitken had been an extraordinarily successful Conservative politician, who had made himself a fortune working as a 'fixer' for oil-rich Arabs – and in particular, for Prince Mohammed bin Fahd, the son of King Fahd of Saudi Arabia.

It might be said that the man who was ultimately responsible for Aitken's fall from grace was his great-uncle Max Aitken, better known as Lord Beaverbrook, millionaire proprietor of the *Daily Express* and minister in Churchill's wartime government. When Aitken was 21, in 1964, his great uncle told him that he had been making his will, and went on: 'I've been thinking about you. You're a very bright boy with a very bright future. In some ways you're the best of the bunch. I'm going to pay you the greatest compliment – I'm not going to give you a single cent.' Instead, he handed him £150: 'Now here's your fare back to Oxford.'

Aitken understood what he meant. His great-uncle was saying: 'I've made my own way in the world and I believe that's the way it should be done. If I give you too much help, it would only make you lazy.'

In fact, the young Aitken had a great deal going for him. Born on 30 August 1942, Jonathan William Patrick Aitken was the son of a Conservative Member of Parliament, Sir William Traven Aitken, and Lady Penelope Aitken, daughter of the 1st Baron of Rugby. His maternal grandfather was Lord Rugby, a distinguished colonial civil servant, who taught Jonathan Latin, French and poetry. Jonathan had started life badly, with tuberculosis of the lungs that spread to his bones. He spent three years in a plaster cast. In due course, he was sent to Eton. There, as the President of the Political Society, he acquired his skill in debating and in the judicious use of the English language. Unfortunately, the ritual beatings administered by prefects – whose ranks he eventually joined – also gave him a taste for flogging and being flogged.

At Christ Church College, Oxford, he read law. Although his father had quarrelled with Lord Beaverbrook, Aitken wrote to his great-uncle asking if he could come and see him, and Beaverbrook was impressed. As a result, Aitken came to know the Prime Minister Harold Macmillan, and became a part-time speechwriter to Selwyn Lloyd, the Chancellor of the Exchequer. And so, while still at Oxford, he got his foot on the bottom rung of the political ladder.

When Selwyn Lloyd was sacked by Macmillan in the famous 'Night of the Long Knives', Aitken went with Lloyd to Spain, helping him through a near-breakdown. As a result, he was appointed Lloyd's private secretary. He was soon mixing with all the senior Tories. When Selwyn Lloyd became Leader of the House, Aitken's prospects were greatly enhanced. Nevertheless, he turned down a suggestion by Randolph Churchill that he should contest a safe Tory seat at the age of twenty.

Aitken's father died in 1964, the same year as Lord Beaverbrook. Aitken was left only £5,000 and business interests in Canada (the original home of Lord Beaverbrook).

He joined the *Evening Standard*, which belonged to the Express Group, and proved to be a naturally brilliant journalist. He had already co-authored a travel book on America called *A Short Walk on the Campus*; now he went on to write a book called *Young Meteors*, about the up-and-coming younger generation, in which he singled out Roy Hattersley, and even mentioned David Frost and the Beatles. He also wrote a chapter about prostitution with some emphasis on sado-masochism. At his book launch, he met a girl named Jenny Fabian, who was also an author. She returned to his flat, where he asked her if she would like to be whipped with an electric cable, then tied her hands to the bedposts with a cord from his maroon silk dressing-gown. But then, Aitken found it easy to get women, having the looks of a matinée idol, and his sex life was interesting and varied.

He became a presenter for Yorkshire TV and, in that capacity, travelled to Nigeria to report on the civil war. It was because of this visit that he became embroiled in an affair that led to his first appearance in court, and caused him to lose the nomination for a Conservative safe seat in Yorkshire.

In December 1969, Aitken went to dinner with Major-General Henry Templar Alexander, the father of a girl Aitken had escorted to a dance. Alexander had served in Nigeria as a military observer, and was a supporter of the Federal forces who were fighting the rebel Biafrans. Alexander showed the young Conservative contender a document which revealed that Harold Wilson's Labour government was supplying arms to the Nigerian Federal forces. It was by a British official in the High Commission in Lagos, Colonel Robert Scott. Aitken photocopied this, sent it to his political mentor, Hugh Fraser, then sold the report to the *Sunday Telegraph*. The result was an article with the headline: SECRET BIAFRAN WAR PLAN REVEALED: MUDDLE, CORRUPTION, WASTE.

The consequence of this revelation was that Colonel Scott was expelled.

Alexander also found himself in trouble. Aitken lost no time in shifting the blame for the leak to Hugh Fraser, but the major-general had recorded the conversation in which Aitken explained that he was not to blame, and Aitken found himself in court for breaching the Official Secrets Act. Fortunately for Aitken, the judge, Mr Justice Caulfield, disliked both the Labour government and the Official Secrets Act and Aitken was acquitted.

But the trial cost him his 'safe seat.' The affair made him a lifelong opponent of the Official Secrets Act.

Aitken completed his betrayal of Hugh Fraser by having an affair with his wife, Lady Antonia Fraser. In their book *The Liar: The Fall of Jonathan Aitken*, Luke Harding, David Leigh, a TV producer, and David Pallister, a *Guardian* journalist, mention that Aitken's other conquests included Lady Charlotte Curzon, the daughter of Earl Howe, Elizabeth Harrison, former wife of actors Richard Harris and Rex Harrison, Arianna Stassinopoulos, Germaine Greer, Soraya Khashoggi, the ex-wife of the millionaire arms dealer Adnan Khashoggi, and (at the same time), Soraya's maid.

Aitken finally became a Conservative Member of Parliament at the age of 32, in 1974.

However, Mrs Thatcher failed to warm to Aitken, perhaps prejudiced by Aitken's remark to a Cairo newspaper that 'I wouldn't say she's open-minded on the Middle East so much as empty-headed. She probably thinks Sinai is the plural of sinus.' This was picked up by *Private Eye*, and the MP Airey Neave told Aitken to apologize.

He further alienated Mrs Thatcher by having a romance with her daughter Carol, who was ten years his junior. She went with him to knock on doors during his political campaign, as did his secretary Valerie Scott, with whom he was having an affair. Mrs Thatcher later referred to Aitken as 'the man who made Carol cry'.

His political advancement blocked, Aitken went into business and started a company to manage Unit Trusts. With his cousin, Tim Aitken, he formed a financial-services group, Aitken Hume. He soon ousted his cousin as chairman, and Tim Aitken was to tell friends that he had got 'a knife between his shoulder blades'.

Aitken was also associated with the immensely successful firm Slater-Walker, which was to collapse in 1974 as an indirect result of the Arab oil crisis.

The previous year, Aitken had attended a lunch in Paris and met a Saudi prince who loved everything British: Mohammed bin Fahd, son of the Crown Prince Fahd – the latter would become king in 1975 when his father, King Faisal, was assassinated. Mohammed and Aitken liked one another, with the consequence that Mohammed invited Aitken to call on him if he happened to come to Riyadh.

Mohammed's financial adviser and 'fixer' was a charming and good-looking young man called Said Ayas, who would play a major part in Aitken's rise – and fall.

If you were a Saudi prince – or a close friend of a Saudi prince – it was easy to become very wealthy. Saudi Arabia's wealth was based on oil, which had begun to flow in 1933. With its immense wealth, the country needed new towns, universities, railways, air transport, industrial machinery, a telephone system, and all the other appurtenances of modern civilization. The western companies that were called upon to supply these goods and services could make such enormous profits that they were perfectly happy to pay large bribes to anyone who could persuade the Saudis to accept their tender. (Bribery was endemic in the Middle East.) Prince Mohammed was the chief of these 'fixers'. and reckoned on making an income of $60 million per year in commissions. Ayas's income also ran to millions annually.

Jonathan Aitken made contact with the Saudis at about the time of the Yom Kippur war of October 1973, when Egypt and Syria united against Israel, and which ended in an Israeli victory. But as Israel expanded its territory the Arabs began to use the 'oil weapon', and it was their threat to cut off western supplies of oil that led the west to intervene and bring the war to an end. In fact, Colonel Gaddafi of Libya had already begun to raise oil prices shortly after his takeover in 1971.

In 1973, in the euphoria of the original successes of Egypt and Syria in the Yom Kippur war, the Organisation of Petroleum Exporting Countries (OPEC) doubled the oil prices, and then doubled them again that December. So Aitken came along when Saudi Arabia was literally awash with new wealth.

It was at the end of 1974 that Aitken flew to Riyadh and called at Said Ayas's house for dinner. Six months later, he discovered the way to Ayas's heart. Ayas's brother, Mimo, wanted to go to Cambridge, but only had an American degree that was not recognized by the university. Aitken pulled strings, and soon Mimo had been accepted at Downing College. It was the foundation of Aitken's friendship with Ayas – and of Aitken's fortune. Ayas introduced him to a rich Palestinian entrepreneur named Ramzi Sanbar who had made his fortune in the Saudi construction business. When the war between Muslim and Christian militias drove him out of Lebanon in 1975, Sanbar moved to London.

Soon, Aitken was installed in Sanbar's magnificent office in Park Lane. The authors of The Liar write: 'Sitting in a wood-panelled ground floor office, with his feet up on a mahogany desk, Aitken must have felt a cut above his parliamentary colleagues, making do with cramped offices in the Gothic labyrinth of the House of Commons.' There was a price, however, to this Faustian arrangement. From now on, Valerie Scott recalls, this junior Conservative back-bencher was obliged to do 'whatever made the Arabs happy'.

Aitken became Chairman of the British-Saudi Parliamentary Group in the Commons, which gave him access to free travel to Riyadh. He was to remark: 'I wish I had some interests to declare in this area, so fantastic are those opportunities.' Aitken soon had plenty of interests to declare – although, oddly enough, they were never declared in the newly drafted Register of MPs' Interests.

Aitken was given a magnificent blue Jaguar by his new employers; he admonished Valerie Scott not to tell anyone the prince had given him the car, adding that he was particularly anxious that his constituents (whom he described as 'peasants') should not find out. The authors of *The Liar* mention that 'gifts of expensive cars from princes to hangers-on were routine in those heady days. A joke going the rounds in Riyadh was that princely Cadillacs were dumped when the ashtrays were full.'

When the prince and his entourage came to Britain – which happened several times a year for a fortnight at a time – Aitken was there to do his bidding.

His white Rolls-Royce, upholstered in blue velvet, would pull up on the cobbled forecourt [of the Sanbar office]. A retinue of followers would throng into the rather sombre office. It was always a moment of high excitement for Sanbar's staff. The office butler had laid on sandwiches and the prince's favourite chocolate gateau from a local patisserie. At the end of each visit Said Ayas would get out the envelopes. Sometimes it was £250; if the prince was especially generous it might be £1,000 – the equivalent of three months' wages. The envelopes were handed out to everybody – the receptionist, butler and secretaries.

Aitken's envelope was assumed to contain very large sums indeed.

He worked for it. He learned Arabic, went along with the prince to various casinos – although gambling bored him – and came running whenever Mohammed beckoned.

Typical of Mohammed's activity was a deal he brokered with the Dutch Electronics firm, Philips. They were invited to place a bid to modernize the Saudi telephone system. The sum they quoted was £3.5 billion. The Saudi's own consultants estimated that it could be done for a little over half a billion. Other electronics firms – particularly in the US – protested, so that King Fahd felt obliged to put the contract out to the lowest bidder. Philips thereupon sent in a revised bid for £1.7 billion, and were given the contract in December 1977. Prince Mohammed's commission was $300 million, while Said Ayas collected $50 million. Presumably Ramzi Sanbar and his advisor Jonathan Aitken also collected commission.

In the summer of 1977, Aitken helped Prince Mohammed buy a jet plane. It was a Boeing 747 Jumbo which even had a fountain. It was Aitken who introduced Mohammed to Sir Kenneth Heath, the Chairman of Rolls-Royce, at the Paris air show. The plane cost £3.5 million – little more than small change to Mohammed. Pilots were supplied by British Caledonian and Aitken recruited some of the air-hostesses.

In the following year, Aitken's power increased when the prince dispensed with the services of Ramzi Sanbar, and got Aitken to buy a new office only fifty yards away from the old one in Mayfair. Aitken became managing director of the firm, which was called Al Bilad. Said Ayas was a director. Aitken purchased Rolls-Royces and Bentleys for the prince, and shipped them out to Arabia. The prince came to own a fleet of ninety.

But the chief business of Al Bilad UK was to act as the middleman for UK business contracts with Saudi Arabia. Its commission fees, charged to the British supplier, were 15 per cent. The authors of The Liar quote a businessman who met Aitken: 'a working man can quickly spot a spiv a million miles away. He was incredibly rude to people who worked for him and obsequious to the Arabs. He was like their messenger boy.'

Aitken had by then acquired himself a wife, Serbian born Lolicia Azucki, who later admitted that she had quite determinedly set out to marry him. At first her campaign was unsuccessful – Aitken would even refuse to take her telephone calls – but when she nursed him through typhoid at the end of 1977, he decided that, after all, he needed a wife.

In 1980, Aitken's contact with the Saudis enabled him to move into a four-storey Georgian town house in Connaught Square. It cost £183,000. A year later, they bought a Westminster house at 8, Lord North Street, close to the House of Commons and Conservative Central Office. In 1987, he was to buy the White House in Sandwich, in his Kent constituency, overlooking the Royal St George's golf course, which cost £500,000.

A sudden crisis in Britain's relations with Saudi Arabia brought new opportunities. Commercial television presented a drama, based on real life, involving the execution of a Saudi princess and her lover for adultery. The princess was executed by being shot in the back of the head. Officially, she was declared to have died in a swimming pool accident. The programme was broadcast in March 1980, and the Saudis were infuriated. The British Foreign Office apologized fulsomely through Lord Carrington, but Aitken benefited by the incident when the Saudis decided that they should try to acquire some influence by buying an interest in the British media. Aitken was part of a consortium that won the franchise for Breakfast TV. Peter Jay, the Chairman of TV-am later declared: 'I was given the impression [the money] came from cutting down a Beaverbrook forest in Canada.'

In fact, the Arab stake in TV-am contravened rules which prevented non-Europeans from controlling British TV stations. The answer was not to let it become known. When TV-am's ratings plummeted, Peter Jay was ousted in favour of Jonathan Aitken – who was also quickly ousted by the Independent Broadcasting Authority because, as a Conservative MP, he could not be regarded as politically impartial. It was a cartoon character called Roland Rat who rescued TV-am's ratings.

Aitken's cousin, Tim, who had apparently failed to learn from the 'knife between the shoulder blades' administered when he was ousted from the Chairmanship of Aitken Hume, had also joined the board of TV-am, but was once again dismissed. His place was taken by the Syrian entrepreneur Wafic Said.

Seven years later, Tim Aitken would tell the *Observer* newspaper about the Saudi financial backing organized by his cousin.

Mrs Thatcher's downfall came in 1990. John Major stepped into her shoes, and in 1992, Aitken was made Minister of State for Defence Procurement.

In fact, Mrs Thatcher had signed an arms deal with Saudi Arabia in 1986. It was worth £1.5 billion a year to the Ministry of Defence. For a Tornado Fighter-Bomber which cost £20 million to build, the Saudis were charged £35 million. The manufacturers then paid 26 per cent of the price in 'commission'. Helicopters, mine-sweepers and other arms sold to the Saudis were subject to a similar arrangement. Associates of Aitken did very well out of the deals. Wafic Said was able to afford a £9 million apartment in London, a town house in Regents Park, a Paris apartment, a villa in Marbella, a ski-lodge in Switzerland, and a flat in Monaco.

Although Aitken did not know it, the seeds of his downfall were sown in 1979 when an Alexandria-born entrepreneur named Mohammed al Fayed bought the run-down Ritz Hotel in Paris and set out to turn it into a home-from-home for the very rich. Jacques Chirac, then Mayor of Paris, presented al Fayed with the freedom of the city. But in London, this colourful Egyptian businessman was regarded with rather less favour by the British establishment.

According to the unauthorized biography by Tom Bower, al Fayed started out selling Coca-cola on the streets of his home town of Alexandria, got a job with arms dealer Adnan Khashoggi and married his sister, then, in the 1960s, persuaded the dictator Papa Doc Duvalier of Haiti to put money into various capital projects, from which the dictator failed to gain the expected returns.

In the 1970s, al Fayed and his brother met the remarkable businessman Tiny Rowland, who had made his fortune in Africa, and who was the head of a firm called Lonrho. For a while, the al Fayeds were on the board of Lonrho. But al Fayed disapproved of Rowland's methods, and there was a parting. In 1985, during a cash crisis, Rowland asked Mohammed al Fayed to buy some of his shares in the House of Fraser Group (which owned Harrods), which Rowland was hoping to take over. What followed was considered by Rowland to be a piece of appalling treachery – it was al Fayed who took over the House of Fraser. And the government, which had opposed Rowland's bid (Rowland had been the target of Mr Heath's comment about 'the unacceptable face of capitalism'), supported al Fayed and enabled him to take over the House of Fraser. Rowland was so furious that he spent the rest of his life trying to destroy al Fayed. Although he failed, and al Fayed was the eventual winner of their extremely public battle, the loquacious Egyptian did himself no good by saying uncomplimentary things about the British establishment. He was particularly incensed by a Department of Trade and Industry inspectors' report into his takeover of the House of Fraser which declared that al Fayed had lied about his origins.

In June 1993, al Fayed invited Peter Preston, the editor of the *Guardian*, to come and meet him in his office above Harrods. The *Guardian* had published a story about secret donations to the Conservative Party before the 1992 General Election, which led to the threat of a libel action. Al Fayed, who claimed indignantly that the government 'had shat on him', made accusations about Margaret Thatcher, her son, Mark, and business dealings with the Arabs. At the same time, he mentioned that he had been paying two Members of Parliament, Neil Hamilton and Tim Smith, to ask questions in Parliament that would help Fayed in his battle with Tiny Rowland.

As a result of that meeting, two *Guardian* reporters began investigating the matter of party funding.

But Fayed had come upon another story that he thought might interest the *Guardian*. And he told Preston about it on 16 October 1993. On the weekend of 17 September, Fayed had seen Jonathan Aitken in the Ritz Hotel in Paris together with Said Ayas, while Wafic Said was also in the hotel. According to Fayed, this amounted to seeing the Attorney General dining with Al Capone.

Moreover, said al Fayed, Aitken had not paid his own bill for that weekend. It had been debited to Ayas. And to prove his point, Fayed showed Preston a copy of the bill. It was for 8,010 French francs which, at approximately 8 francs to the pound sterling, was about £1,000. Since Aitken had not declared the benefits that came to him via Prince Mohammed in the MPs' Register of Interests, he was in breach of the Rules for Ministers.

Preston was not deeply interested. A mere thousand pounds seemed a fairly minor matter. After all, Aitken was known to be a millionaire. Nevertheless, David Pallister, a *Guardian* journalist who was an expert on Saudi affairs, wrote to Aitken about his weekend at the Ritz, and asked 'how it relates to your job in Government?'

Aitken's reply stated that the purpose of his visit to Paris that weekend had nothing whatsoever to do with Said Ayas, or Wafic Said. He was there, he said, to meet his wife and seventeen-year-old daughter, who were going to her new school in Switzerland that weekend. According to Aitken, he had had no 'social encounters' that weekend except with the godparents of his daughter Victoria.

Pallister happened to know that Said Ayas *was* Victoria Aitken's godfather. So Aitken's letter might be regarded as a deliberate evasion.

At this point, the affair certainly showed no sign of the storm that was brewing. Aitken had had his bill paid by his daughter's godfather, and he might have made a thousand excuses that would have satisfied Pallister's curiosity. Perhaps Ayas had accepted Aitken's hospitality in London, and was simply returning the favour. Or perhaps Aitken had simply left his credit card behind. Such excuses would have ended the affair there and then.

However, Preston happened to know Aitken personally, and since he had reporters investigating possible Tory financial irregularities, he asked if Aitken would like to explain himself more fully.

Aitken replied breezily that he felt that Preston had put two and two together and made about seven, and that the dinner in Paris was simply 'a casually arranged family affair'. It was nothing whatever to do with business.

But in that case, why had Ayas paid Aitken's bill?

Now, although Preston had seen a copy of this bill in al Fayed's office, al Fayed had refused to give it to him. But al Fayed was helpful about how the *Guardian* could obtain a copy. They merely had to fax a letter on Aitken's House of Commons notepaper asking if a copy of the bill could be sent to the fax number at the top of the letter – which was actually the *Guardian's* fax. Forty-eight hours later, the copy of the bill arrived. The ruse was not quite honest, of course, but then, its sole purpose was to keep al Fayed's name out of the story.

So now, on 11 January 1994, Preston wrote again to Aitken, saying that paying a bill for a thousand pounds had been 'an extraordinary act of generosity' on the part of Ayas, and asking him to explain it.

Aitken then made his fatal mistake. In his reply, he stated that Preston had been misinformed: 'Mr Ayas did not pay my hotel bill. . . the hotel bill was paid by my wife, with money given to her by me for this purpose some hours after I'd left Paris.'

Aitken had now committed himself to a lie, which he would eventually be forced to defend in court.

The truth was that Lolicia Aitken had not even been in Paris that weekend. She had gone to Switzerland to take her daughter, Victoria, to finishing school there, and had then flown straight back to Heathrow. In committing himself to a lie, Aitken was playing with fire.

Preston replied: 'I'm afraid I cannot easily accept your assurances about the Ritz bill. . .' The *Guardian* was in a position to *prove* that Aitken had not paid his hotel bill. Moreover, Aitken's assurance that his wife had paid the bill was rather mysterious in view of the fact that the bill showed that Aitken had been occupying a single room that weekend and, therefore, presumably, his wife was not there.

Soon, Aitken was phoning the *Guardian* to claim that he had now found his Ritz bill and had located 'an independent French witness' who confirmed that his wife Lolicia had paid it. Mr Ayas, he said, had now received a letter from the Ritz Hotel confirming that he did not pay the bill, and that Mrs Aitken did.

Since Aitken had invited Preston to refer the matter to Sir Robin Butler, the Cabinet Secretary, Preston sent the correspondence between himself and Aitken to Butler. Sir Robin asked Aitken whether he had paid his hotel bill, and Aitken assured him that he had. Thereupon, Butler wrote to Preston saying that Aitken had paid his own bill and so no breach of ministerial guidelines had taken place. Preston's response was to send the correspondence on to the Prime Minister, John Major.

The stakes increased in July 1994 when John Major appointed Aitken a minister, Chief Secretary to the Treasury. He could now call himself 'Right Honourable'.

In September 1994, al Fayed complicated the issue when he lost his temper after losing a case in the European Court of Human Rights. He had attempted to have the report by the Department of Trade and Industry into his Harrods takeover declared in breach of the Convention. Furious at what he saw as yet another betrayal by the British Government (who were also preventing him becoming a British citizen), al Fayed asked Preston to come and see him again. He was quite determined to cause the Government any embarrassment he could. This meant admitting that he had paid money to Neil Hamilton and Tim Smith to raise questions in Parliament.

When the *Guardian* printed this story, Tim Smith promptly resigned, and Hamilton was, in effect, sacked, insisting on his innocence.

Shortly thereafter, the *Guardian* printed an article about the Aitken affair, and the result was that the Shadow Chancellor, Gordon Brown, asked in Parliament whether any part of Aitken's bill had been paid by Mr Ayas. Aitken answered: 'I would very much welcome a chance to answer the question, not least because it is the first chance to clear myself of the scurrilous allegations that have been made.' And since the allegations against him now included the charge that he had lied to the Cabinet Secretary, Sir Robin Butler, he flourished a letter in which Sir Robin Butler declared that he did not regard Aitken as having lied to him. 'I hope that the House. . . will accept both my assurance and the Cabinet Secretary's assurance and put an end to the hysterical episode of sleaze journalism by the *Guardian*.'

Aitken had now lied to the House of Commons.

The story about the *Guardian's* fake letter to the Ritz had now also come out, having been leaked by the Downing Street Press Office. The Tories were furious, and demanded Preston's head. One Member of Parliament, Roger Gale, described Preston as 'the whore from hell'.

At the end of 1994, exhausted and depressed by the struggle, Preston resigned as editor, and Alan Rusbridger took over the post.

But as far as Aitken was concerned, the enemies were multiplying. The Independent Television programme *World in Action* had become interested in the affair, particularly in the fact that Aitken was taking part in the sale of arms to the Saudis at the time when he was Defence Procurement Minister.

Its producer, David Leigh, had built up a reputation for fearlessness, and now decided to start digging into Aitken's background.

The first thing he discovered was Aitken's enthusiasm for being whipped. This seemed to be widely known in London society. As to Aitken's dealings with the Saudis, David Pallister of the *Guardian* was the ideal ally.

Another interesting scandal that Leigh uncovered had to do with a 'Health Hydro', named Inglewood, that Aitken had run in the 1970s. Apparently many rich Arabs had taken advantage of its facilities, and had been supplied with call girls.

The result was a television programme called 'Jonathan of Arabia', which went out on the evening of 10 April 1995. And it was on that day, a few hours before the programme, that Aitken stood up in the House of Commons and made the speech which included his fighting declaration about the 'fight to cut out the cancer of bent and twisted journalism in our country with the simple sword of truth and the trusty shield of British fair play'. It was at this point that he seems to have decided that he had no alternative than to sue the *Guardian* and *World in Action* for libel.

A few hours after Aitken's 'sword of truth' speech, Alan Rusbridger went into conference with Geraldine Proudler, the *Guardian's* solicitor, and decided that they had better ask the famous barrister George Carman to defend them.

On the surface, it might seem that the defendants had an overwhelming case – based on the Ritz receipt. But then, Aitken certainly looked and sounded like an honest man. Besides which, he was a Conservative Cabinet Minister. He only had to convince the jury that there had been some slight misunderstanding, and that he really had paid his own bill, to have the defendants over a barrel.

The Ritz allegation, of course, was only a small part of the case. Aitken had been branded a pimp and a bribe-taker. If Aitken could somehow convince the jury that the 'gutter press' had done its best to damage his career, and force his resignation from office (which had happened in July 1995), he could receive enormous damages. British judges were not much in favour of Fleet Street, as the Jeffrey Archer libel case had shown.

At this point, Aitken made a serious mistake. For several years, he had carried on an affair with a woman called Paula Strudwick, who administered floggings with a birch twig. But in dragging the Paula Strudwick allegations into the case, Aitken was inviting the defendants to prove that they had a point. And the jury would hear an interesting story about adultery and sexual aberration that they might otherwise have been spared.

Before the trial, which began in June 1997, there were the May elections, which ended in a landslide victory for Labour. Jonathan Aitken was among the many who lost their seats, as was Neil Hamilton.

But before the libel case opened, Aitken and his team scored a notable victory. Aitken's counsel, Charles Gray, QC, went before the judge, Justice Sir

Oliver Popplewell, to suggest that the case was so complicated that it would only confuse a jury. The interests of justice would be better served if the judge heard the case by himself. The *Guardian* team was dismayed. They had been thinking in terms of convincing a jury of Aitken's many faults and misdemeanours; now they had to convince Popplewell alone. Since Popplewell was a Conservative, who probably regarded the *Guardian* as a left-wing rag, this meant that the going was likely to be more difficult than the defendants had hoped. For a while, there was even talk of a climb-down, although Rusbridger argued strongly against it.

So on Wednesday 4 June 1997, the Right Hon Jonathan Aitken entered the High Court with his wife Lolicia, prepared to do battle.

Gray began: 'Mr Aitken sues the *Guardian* over an article entitled "Aitken tried to arrange girls for Saudis". It is no exaggeration to say they have butchered his personal, political and professional reputation.' The *Guardian* had claimed that Aitken had 'pimped' for Arab clients and 'deliberately concealed' the fact that he was 'in the pockets of the Saudi Royal Family'. These allegations were 'false, utterly false', he told the court.

Aitken was in the witness box for eight days, and his performance was formidable. Carman's cross examinations failed to shake him.

Aitken scored a particularly good point when he described how, after reading the description of himself as a pimp, his twelve-year-old son had asked, 'What's a pimp, Daddy?' There was hardly a newspaper the next day that could resist the quote – the *Daily Telegraph* even made it a headline.

Over that weekend, Sir Justice Popplewell carefully studied the videotape of the *World in Action* programme. The following Monday he gave his judgement on it. It gave the impression that Aitken *had* known about certain forbidden arms shipments to Iran when he was Minister for Defence Procurement. And since this could not be supported by evidence to the contrary, Aitken had won an important point.

But, as Aitken attempted to explain away his weekend at the Ritz by expressing a suspicion that he had been 'set up', several journalists noticed that Lolicia Aitken, sitting on the front bench, was restless and dabbed her forehead and wrists with eau de cologne. The *Guardian* team had noted that, when Lolicia had been asked by journalists before the trial whether she had paid Aitken's bill, she had declined to confirm it. Why was she so nervous?

In fact, Aitken's version of events was about to hit a snag. On 6 April 1995, Aitken had been accosted by the *World in Action* team as he left home. He had been alone, but in one of his witness statements he had claimed that he had left the house with his daughter, Alexandra, and that she was 'visibly upset' by the television crew's 'aggressive behaviour' and had burst into tears. He and Alexandra had then escaped in his Jaguar, but they had been pursued in a dangerous 'Keystone Kops' chase by the Granada team driving a van, and were eventually forced to swap vehicles at the Spanish Embassy.

This was pure fiction and, in fact, the evidence was at hand to prove it. Quentin McDermott of the *World in Action* team recalled that the whole sequence had been recorded, but that it had ended up on the cutting room floor. He was able to recover it, and the videotape revealed that Aitken had left the house alone, clambered into his car, and driven off, while the journalists made no attempt to pursue him. When this was shown in court, Aitken looked deeply embarrassed at being caught out, but fortunately, the day's proceedings came to an end.

The next morning, Carman was ready to attack. 'Where on earth is your daughter in the film that we saw yesterday?'

Sitting on the front row, Lolicia mouthed at him the words: 'Another time.' Aitken quickly explained that he had been referring to another occasion – that they had been approached by camera crews several times that day. Once again he had escaped.

The case was accelerating towards its spectacular finish. A *Guardian* reporter, Owen Bowcott, was sent to the Swiss town of Villars, where Lolicia Aitken had delivered her daughter, Victoria, to the finishing school, Aiglon College. It seemed that the Hotel Bristol, where Lolicia Aitken had stayed during that weekend, had since gone bankrupt. Bowcott's job was to see whether he could get hold of the records of Lolicia's stay.

He found the caretaker, who introduced him to two men conducting a financial inventory of the hotel's contents. They agreed that the reception records were still in the basement, but were not authorized to allow anyone to examine them.

But Bowcott was in luck. The Hotel Panorama, a sister to the Bristol, had also gone bankrupt, and the manager there agreed to ring the head accountant in Lausanne and see if he would agree to allow Bowcott into the basement. The answer was no. But the manager agreed to give Bowcott the accountant's fax number, and Bowcott sent him a fax asking him to ring him at his hotel. In due course, the accountant rang back, and was fascinated by the story that Bowcott had to tell him. Finally, he agreed that Bowcott should be allowed to go into the basement.

It seemed an impossible task. It was piled high with boxes containing files, and there was almost no light. Eventually, after many hours' search, Bowcott came up with what he was looking for: a registration card for room 234 which stated: 'adultes: 2', and eventually he found the bill that stated that Mrs Aitken had arrived on Friday 17 September 1993, and stayed at the hotel that night with her daughter, and then stayed the following night alone – Victoria having apparently been delivered to school.

So now they knew that Lolicia Aitken had left the hotel on Sunday 19 September – the day when she was supposed to have paid Aitken's hotel bill in Paris. Of course, that did not prove that she had *not* gone to Paris – it was just possible for her to have caught a plane that would have got her to Paris in time.

When Bowcott's evidence was produced in court, Aitken was unphased. Did not these documents prove, Carman asked, that Lolicia Aitken spent Saturday evening in Switzerland, not in Paris? No, Aitken replied smoothly, he had phoned his wife at the Hotel Bristol at 10:15 on Sunday morning, and his wife had already left for Paris. And Aitken decided to compound the lie by declaring that Lolicia's mother had also been staying there in the Hotel Bristol with her. He was now playing a very dangerous game, since the documents could prove that he was lying.

More importantly, if Jonathan Aitken had spoken to someone in the Bristol Hotel at 10:15 in the morning, and that someone was not his mother-in-law, then his wife must have been still there at 10:15.

According to Aitken, his wife had arrived in Paris 'late to mid-morning' on the Sunday. A *Guardian* researcher soon proved that this was impossible. There was a plane at 11:15 am that would have taken her from Geneva to Paris just in time to pay the hotel bill. But since the journey from Villars to the airport was over an hour, she could not possibly have made that plane.

The *Guardian*'s lawyer, Geraldine Proudler, decided to subpoena British Airways to see whether Lolicia and Victoria had actually flown to Paris to have that meal with Victoria's godfather that Aitken had already admitted to. But BA wrote back saying that this would be an enormous task, which would take at least '33 man days to complete'. The airline appointed a senior British Airways criminal investigator named Wendy Harris to oversee the process. But she would not be available for another five days.

At the end of this period, on Monday 16 June, two of Geraldine Proudler's legal assistants turned up at Heathrow to aid the search. They found themselves in a vast, windowless warehouse full of spools of microfiche stacked on metal shelves.

The search was successful. The legal assistants found travel coupons showing that Mrs L Aitken and Miss V Aitken had flown directly from Heathrow to Geneva at 8:30 am on Friday 17 September 1993, and that Mrs Aitken had flown back alone from Geneva at 19.05 pm on Monday 20 September. Neither of them had been anywhere near Paris.

Geraldine Proudler was told of the discovery as she was leaving court later that day. She realized immediately what this meant – that Aitken had been proved a liar beyond all possible doubt, and that they had therefore won the case. Then she began to experience doubts. Would Aitken find a way of wriggling out of this?

In fact, Aitken had already decided that his wife and daughter would appear in court on his behalf, swearing to his story about the Ritz. Victoria had already written out her witness statement, in which she claimed that her Serbian grandmother had been present in the Hotel Bristol, and that she had telephoned the hotel on Sunday morning to be told that her mother had already left, but that her grandmother was still there.

Fortunately, Victoria Aitken would not be required to perjure herself in court.

Wednesday 18 June 1997, was the anniversary of the day Napoleon had been defeated at Waterloo. If Aitken was aware of this, he showed no sign of it as he strode purposefully into court.

Back in Switzerland, another researcher was looking through car-hire documents. He found some that revealed that Lolicia Aitken had hired a Volkswagen Golf at 12:02 pm on Friday 17 September 1993 at Geneva airport. According to Aitken, she had been in Paris at that time. She returned the car on Sunday evening.

At three o'clock that afternoon, Geraldine Proudler walked into court, and handed envelopes to David Leigh and David Pallister, and then handed another to George Carman. They contained Wendy Harris's statement about flights.

David Leigh was to write, 'Carman then rose to his feet for what he later described as the most dramatic moment of his distinguished career at the bar.' He told the judge that he was in a position to provide the plaintiff's solicitors and the judge with a signed witness statement from an employee of British Airways, after which he handed a copy of the statement to the judge, and another to Charles Gray. A few minutes later, the Rent-A-Car documents arrived.

Mr Justice Popplewell withdrew to his chambers to study the new evidence. Leigh writes:

the former Conservative minister was slumped in the front bench with the statement beside him. He sat in a crumpled diagonal posture, legs crossed, reading and re-reading every page. The press bench was buzzing. Aitken's barrister Charles Gray decided the best strategy was to pretend nothing had happened, although he later admitted he was fully aware of the significance of the document.

When George Carman had guided the judge through the car-hire documents, the judge remarked: 'Thank you very much. No doubt, Mr Gray, you will want to consider the position overnight.' Aitken slipped quietly out of the back of the court with his solicitor. He knew, as everybody else did, that his career was finished.

In fact, Aitken lost no time in slipping out of England and flying to California for a holiday with his son; the press did not succeed in tracing his address.

George Carman finally brokered an agreement with Charles Gray. Aitken would pay 80 per cent of the costs – a huge sum of more than £2 million – and the *Guardian* and Granada would pay 20 per cent of their own costs. This was not simple generosity on the part of the defendants. There was a second action – on the question of arms dealing – to be decided, and the judge might conceivably still find against the defendants.

Said Ayas was another victim of all the unwelcome publicity. Just before the case opened, he had returned to Saudi Arabia, where he was arrested on the orders of his former friend Prince Mohammed on a charge of having pocketed millions of dollars. Mohammed had apparently overspent and was half a billion dollars in debt to Saudi Arabian banks. Mohammed wanted some of it back.

After four months under house arrest, Ayas succeeded in escaping by dressing up as a woman and slipping past the guards outside his home. Back in his flat in London, he hired a bodyguard. Soon he learned that Prince Mohammed had lodged a writ demanding the return of £144 million. Under this pressure, Ayas finally explained – through his lawyers – what had actually been going on that weekend at the Ritz. It was indeed a massive arms deal, involving hundreds of millions of pounds. Ayas was likely to receive 'commission' of about $50 million.

This, apparently, explained why Aitken was so anxious to insist that it had merely been an innocent family gathering, with no business involved.

In May 1998, Aitken was charged with perjury, conspiring to pervert the course of justice and perverting the course of justice. Ayas was also charged with perverting the course of justice. On 19 January 1999, Aitken appeared at the Old Bailey to answer the charges. The result of the trial was that he was sentenced to eighteen months in prison. In fact, he served only seven months and emerged on 7 January 2000. He was obliged to wear an electronic tag on his ankle for two months. He proceeded to write a book declaring that the disaster had brought him to the feet of Christ.

For two years, Aitken made no attempt to pay the *Guardian's* costs, insisting that he was bankrupt. Eventually, the *Guardian* settled for £1.3 million of its £2 million; Aitken was obliged to sell his Lord North Street home.

Harding, Leigh and Pallister conclude in *The Liar* that:

The *Guardian* and Granada were, however, left with a consoling thought. The irony was that none of the arms deals which Aitken and Ayas had been so busily plotting in November 1993 ever came off – partly because Prince Mohammed's influence was fading fast, but more importantly because the *Guardian* investigated, then took the risky, and perhaps courageous, decision to publish.

ARBUCKLE, 'FATTY'

A STAR'S DISGRACE

The scandal that wrecked the career of film comic 'Fatty' Roscoe Arbuckle – and tarnished the image of Hollywood – occurred after a three-day drinking party in 1921.

Arbuckle was born on 24 March 1887 in Smith Center, Kansas, USA and named Roscoe Conklin Arbuckle. He worked as a plumber's assistant, then became a performer in carnivals and vaudeville – for all his enormous weight (330 lb or 21 stone) he was incredibly agile. At the age of 21 he was hired as an extra by the Selig Polyscope Company and he made his first one-reel comedy – *The Sanitarium* – in 1910. He was hired by Mack Sennett and made a dozen films in 1913 including *Fatty's Day Off* and *Fatty's Flirtation*. His attraction lay in his cherubic innocence – the good nature that he radiated was obviously genuine. Neither, for a Hollywood star, was he unusually sex-oriented; the girls he worked with found him protective and 'big brotherly'. His reputation was a great deal better, for example, than that of his co-star Charlie Chaplin. In 1917, he moved with Sennett to Jesse Lasky's Artcraft, and wrote and directed most of his own films. He gave Buster Keaton a start in life. When he made a film for Paramount, a banner over the gate read: Welcome To The Prince Of Whales. But an all-night party laid on in his honour by Jesse Lasky in Boston on 6 March in 1917, almost led to scandal. Twelve party girls were paid over $1,000 for their night's work. But some Boston resident who peered through the transom and saw Fatty stripping on a table with several girls called the police. It is alleged that Lasky, Adolph Zukor and Joseph Schenck ended by paying the district attorney and mayor $10,000 to overlook the incident.

In 1921, Arbuckle signed a contract worth $3 million and he decided to celebrate with a party in the St Francis Hotel in San Francisco. He arrived from Bay City on the evening of Saturday 3 September 1921, and took a suite, as well as three rooms on the twelfth floor, in the unlikely event that anyone should want to sleep. By the following afternoon, the party was in full swing, with about fifty guests, including such Hollywood cronies as Lowell Sherman and Freddy Fishback, and a number of pretty actresses. Arbuckle, separated from his wife, had asked his friend Bambina Maude Delmont to invite a girl he particularly admired – the starlet Virginia Rappe. The two women were staying at the nearby Palace Hotel, together with Virginia's agent.

Twenty-five-year-old Virginia Rappe was a model from Chicago, who had achieved public notice when her face appeared on the sheet music of 'Let Me Call You Sweetheart'. She was a pretty, fresh-faced girl, the type Hollywood liked to cast as a milkmaid – dressed in a check frock and sunbonnet she looked the essence of female innocence. According to film-maker Kenneth Anger (in *Hollywood Babylon*) this appearance was misleading. 'An offer came from

Sennett, and she went to work on his lot, taking minor parts. She also did her share of sleeping around, and gave half the company crabs. This epidemic so shocked Sennett that he closed down his studio and had it fumigated.' Arbuckle had been pursuing Virginia – without success – for five years. She found him unattractive and was later quoted as having said: 'I'd sooner go to bed with a jungle ape than have that fat octopus groping at me.' But since Arbuckle was now an influential figure in the film world and Virginia was still an unknown starlet, she was willing to make certain compromises to advance her career.

On Labour Day, Monday, 5 September 1921, the party was still going, and Virginia had come from the Palace Hotel, accompanied by a 'bodyguard'. Arbuckle was still dressed in pyjamas, carpet slippers and a bathrobe. Most of the other guests were in a similar state of *déshabillè*. Virginia refused champagne and accepted a gin and orange. She was drinking her third – and was anxious to get to the bathroom, which seemed to be constantly occupied – when Arbuckle grabbed her and steered her into a bedroom, winking at his friends and commenting: 'This is what I've been waiting for.'

A few minutes later, there were screams from the bedroom. Suddenly, the party noises died away. Maude Delmont went and tried the bedroom handle, calling, 'Virginia, what's happening?' There were more screams. Maude Delmont picked up the telephone and called down for the manager. The assistant manager, H.J. Boyle, rushed into the suite just as the door of bedroom 1219 burst open and Arbuckle appeared with Virginia's hat perched on his head at an absurd angle. He gave an innocent smile and did a little dance on the carpet. Back in the room, Virginia was making groaning sounds. Fatty's good temper seemed to slip and he said to Maude Delmont, 'Get her dressed and take her back to the Palace.' And when Virginia started to scream again he yelled, 'Shut up, or I'll throw you out of the window.'

Virginia was lying on the bed, almost nude, with her clothes scattered around her. She was moaning, 'I'm dying, I'm dying. He hurt me.' They tried to dress her, but her blouse was badly torn – it had obviously been ripped from her by force.

The house doctor was sent for and Virginia was moved to another room, still moaning. Arbuckle seemed to feel she was 'putting it on', perhaps to blackmail him into offering her a part, and snapped, 'Shut up. You were always a lousy actress.'

She was in pain for the next three days, often becoming unconscious. She was transferred to a nursing home, where she died. The doctor who performed the autopsy discovered that her bladder was ruptured. The result was death from peritonitis. What had happened seemed clear. Arbuckle had flung himself on her with his full weight when she had a full bladder and it had ruptured like a balloon. When it was reported to the coroner, police interviewed hospital staff to find out who was behind the accident. The next morning newspaper headlines all over the country talked about the orgy that had ended in rape and death.

An inquest found that Arbuckle was 'criminally responsible' for Virginia's death and recommended that he should be charged with manslaughter. Even before he went on trial in November, his career was in ruins. The fat, innocent man who made everybody laugh was really a 'sex fiend'. Rumours had it that his penis was so enormous that it had ruptured her bladder. But Arbuckle's friend Al Seminacher introduced a note of horror when he told people that Arbuckle had used a large piece of ice from the ice bucket to penetrate Virginia. Rumour added that he had first assaulted her by introducing a champagne bottle.

Church groups and women's clubs demanded that his films should be withdrawn from circulation, and that unreleased films should never be shown. It was hardly necessary. No one could laugh at Arbuckle when they remembered that this innocent, babylike character had torn off a girl's clothes and raped her. A 'Fatty lynching' mood swept the country: in Wyoming, cowboys shot up the screen of a cinema showing an Arbuckle short; in Hartford, Connecticut, women tore down the screen.

Arbuckle was released on bail. His trial began in November; he denied doing any harm to Virginia and his lawyers did their best to suggest that she was little better than a prostitute. After 43 hours deliberation, a jury was in favour of acquitting Arbuckle by ten to two but a majority verdict was not good enough and a mis-trial was declared. At his second trial, the jury found him guilty by ten to two and again they were dismissed. On 12 April 1922, a third jury found him innocent, and the foreman added: 'Acquittal is not enough. We feel a grave injustice has been done him and there is not the slightest proof to connect him in any way with the commission of a crime.' Outside the court, Arbuckle told newsmen, 'My innocence of the hideous charge preferred against me has been proved.' But it made no difference. Comedy depends upon a make-believe world in which no one does any real harm and everything is a joke. Fatty's 'rape' had introduced a brutal element of reality. This was the real reason why he remained unforgiven.

The $3 million contract was cancelled and his unreleased films were suppressed. It cost the studio $1 million. His friend Buster Keaton suggested he should change his name to Will B. Good. In fact, he directed a few comedy shorts under the name of William Goodrich. He toured America's backwoods in second-rate farces, but some of them were booed off the stage. In 1931 he pleaded in *Photoplay*: 'Just let me work . . . I think I can entertain and gladden the people that see me.' He seemed incapable of grasping that the case had somehow undermined the public's willingness to laugh at him.

He began to drink heavily: in 1931 he was arrested in Hollywood for drunken driving. Yet in 1933, his luck seemed to be turning. Warner Brothers took the risk of hiring him to make several short comedies. But after a celebration party in a New York hotel on 28 June 1933, he returned to his room and died of a heart attack. He was 46 years old.

ARCHER, JEFFREY

THE PERJURY SCANDAL

On Sunday 25 October 1986, the *News of the World* carried a headline: TORY BOSS ARCHER PAYS VICE GIRL. There was a picture of a prostitute named Monica Coghlan being offered an envelope at Victoria Station – an envelope, according to the newspaper, stuffed with £50 notes. The man handing it to her, Michael Stacpoole, was a close friend of the bestselling novelist Jeffrey Archer.

Monica Coghlan (known by her trade name of Debbie) operated in the West End of London. Six weeks earlier, on Monday 6 July 1986 an Asian lawyer named Aziz Kurtha had been to Monica Coghlan's room in the Albion Hotel, near Victoria Station, for sex, and was about to drive her back to Shepherd Market in Mayfair (where she picked up clients) when an expensive car flashed its lights at them. Debbie approached the driver, and Kurtha then recognized him as Jeffrey Archer. He beckoned to her and told her who it was. Then Debbie went back into the hotel with the man Kurtha believed he had recognized.

Kurtha had tipped off the *News of the World*, who tracked down Monica Coghlan and succeeded in persuading her – though rather against her will – to take part in a 'sting'. She had telephoned Archer, with a tape recorder at her side, and told him that she was the woman who had picked him up in Shepherd Market. She then said that she had been contacted by a man who had seen them together, and who was pressing her to give him evidence against Archer.

Archer protested that she must have the wrong number, and that he did not know her.

Coghlan went on to tell him that she was being 'hassled' by *Private Eye* and Kurtha and wanted them off her back.

Three weeks later, on 23 October, she rang him again, and said she was still anxious about being pressured by journalists. And Archer finally asked her: 'Would it help if you went abroad again?' Archer went on to suggest that he should 'help her financially' to go abroad. And it was then that Archer told her that if she would stand by platform 3 on Victoria Station at eleven o'clock the next morning, a friend of his would pass an envelope to her. She agreed, and said that she would make herself easy to recognize by wearing a green leather suit.

The following morning, a group of journalists were hanging around platform 3 at Victoria Station. Monica Coghlan had a radio microphone hidden in her clothes, and there were half a dozen cameramen carrying hidden cameras.

Stacpool at first approached the wrong woman, but when he located Coghlan and tried to give her the envelope, she refused to take it. He persuaded her to go with him for a drink to the Grosvenor Hotel next door, where he bumped into one of the news reporters he happened to know well, and confided to him that he was 'here to do a favour for a very important political friend'.

This was the story that appeared in the *News of the World*. It could be argued that whether or not Archer had sex with a prostitute was no business of the tabloid newspaper, but the *News of the World* would undoubtedly have replied that, since he was the deputy chairman of the Conservative Party, it was everybody's business.

The result was that Archer lost no time in resigning.

The following day, another London evening newspaper, the *Star* condemned the *News of the World*, declaring that 'it looks as if Archer has been the victim of a particularly nasty set-up job', and said that Archer had done the honourable thing in resigning so quickly. But the following Saturday, the *Star* came out with its own Archer story which claimed that 'Vice girl Monica talks about Archer – the man she knew.' It seemed that Monica Coghlan's nephew, a man called Tony Smith, had confirmed the story about Archer, and suggested that Monica and Archer had had sex – which the *News of the World* had been careful not to do. It also mentioned that 90 per cent of Coghlan's clients could demand 'a specialized field of sexual perversion.' 'One of them,' Tony Smith said, 'wanted to be dressed up like Little Red Riding Hood, complete with suspenders. He had to be trussed up, and Monica would whip him on the floor of his room.'

After the *News of the World* story, Archer's solicitor Lord Mishcon had lost no time in denying that his client had slept with the prostitute. Now, Archer issued libel writs against the two newspapers.

The libel action came to court early, as a special favour to Archer, who had protested that his political career was on hold until his name could be cleared. And by that time, Archer's lawyers had decided that the *Star* should be taken to court first, since it had gone further than the *News of the World*.

Meanwhile, Archer was causing his own legal team some headaches. Although his story was that he did not know Monica Coghlan and had never met her, he had told Adam Raphael, the political editor of the *Observer*, that he had met her 'very casually six months ago'. In his piece, Raphael had said that 'friends of Archer' had made this statement. In *Sunday Today* Rupert Morris had also stated that 'Archer has told friends that he did meet the woman once.' So here was an obvious contradiction, which an unsympathetic judge might take to indicate Archer's guilt.

The case came to trial on Monday 6 July 1987, and lasted for three weeks. Archer's QC, Robert Alexander, put Archer on the stand to say that he had only offered Monica Coghlan money because he deeply sympathized with her plight in being pressured by journalists. When the *Star*'s QC, Michael

Hill, asked Archer about telling Adam Raphael that he had met Coghlan 'only once, very casually, about six months ago', Archer flatly denied that he had said so, and claimed that 'among forty to sixty calls he got that evening' he could not precisely remember the conversation.

The essence of Archer's defence lay in an alibi. On Monday 8 September 1986, Archer insisted, he had been having dinner at Le Caprice in St Martin's Lane with his editor Richard Cohen and Cohen's wife Caroline. Cohen and his wife had left at 10:30 pm, but Archer had gone back into the restaurant to chat to other friends, including the businessman Henry Togna and his wife. By then, his film agent Terence Baker had arrived, and Archer said that he and Baker sat talking until around one o'clock in the morning – the time he was supposed to be in bed with Monica Coghlan. Then, said Archer, he had given Baker a lift back to his home in Camberwell.

Baker supported this, although the defence QC suggested that he and Archer had concocted the story between them. Baker admitted that he had no entry in his diary or even a chequebook stub to support his claim. The defence also asked why this account of the evening was so different from others in various newspapers – presumably traceable back to Archer. He had, according to the *Daily Express*, been 'in the presence of 40 other people at a function and then had other meetings . . .' These, it was implied, were all in connection with Archer's role in the Tory Party. But Archer simply insisted that the '40 people' had been the other people in the restaurant.

There were so many weak points in Archer's story that it looked very much as if he was going to lose his case.

The real turning point of the trial came when Mary Archer – his wife of more than twenty years – appeared in the witness box for the second time to refute a comment made by Monica Coghlan, to the effect that the skin on Archer's back was dry and spotty, something she noticed when he had undressed. Mary Archer testified that he had no spots on his back. Mary Archer had also testified earlier that her husband was not the kind of man to go to bed with prostitutes, and that he would probably 'run a mile' if he was approached by one.

Mary Archer certainly made a more effective witness than Monica Coghlan, who was forced to admit repeatedly that she had lied to Archer on the telephone, although on one occasion, she suddenly burst out at Robert Alexander: 'You're the liar and he's the liar. You're the one that's making vast amounts of money, not me. I'm penniless through all this. He can carry on. What's going to happen to me?'

But then, Coghlan did not help her own case by denouncing her nephew, Tony Smith, (quoted by the *Star*) as a compulsive liar and romancer.

The judge, Sir Bernard Caulfield, was obviously bowled over by Mary Archer's charm. His summing up included the following comments:

Remember Mary Archer in the witness box. Your vision of her probably will never disappear. Has she elegance? Has she fragrance? Would she have, without the strain of this trial, radiance? What is she like in physical features, in presentation, in appearance? How would she appeal? Has she had a happy married life? Has she been able to enjoy, rather than endure, her husband Jeffrey? Is she right when she says to you – you may think with delicacy – "Jeffrey and I lead a full life"?

And he went on to say that Archer obviously had no need of 'rubber-insulated sex in a seedy hotel round about a quarter to one after an evening at the Caprice. . .' Obviously, the judge was reflecting that Mary Archer was so much more attractive than Monica Coghlan that no one in his right senses would have had sex with the prostitute.

Finally, when the foreman of the jury was asked whether they found for Jeffrey Archer or the *Star* newspaper, the foreman replied: 'Mr Jeffrey Archer.' And when the foreman went on to say that Archer was being awarded £500,000 in damages, Archer was heard to gasp 'whew!'

It certainly looked as if Archer – who by any standards was one of the most successful men in England – had pulled off another triumph. But his position was not quite as secure as he thought. According to Nick Elliott, a producer at London Weekend Television, Archer's chief witness, Terence Baker – the man who claimed he had been driven back to Camberwell by Archer in the early hours of the morning – admitted to him in Le Caprice restaurant that he had lied in court, and that the truth was that he had simply left Archer outside Le Caprice at a late hour which would still have left Archer time to have sex with Monica Coghlan.

Archer's run of luck had certainly been remarkable. Jeffrey Howard Archer was born on 15 April 1940 in the City of London Maternity Hospital, the son of William Archer, aged 65, and of Lola, née Cook, aged 27. William Archer, it seems, was a charming conman and a crook – a fact first revealed by Michael Crick in his biography, *Jeffrey Archer, Stranger Than Fiction* (to which this chapter is indebted). According to Jeffrey Archer, his father was a colonel in the Somerset Light Infantry who received the DCM (Distinguished Conduct Medal) during the First World War. Archer also stated that his father had once served as British Consul in Singapore – obviously not a city that needs a Consul since it was a British colony.

Michael Crick stumbled on the truth about William Archer when, while be waiting in the New York Public Library for the librarian to bring a book, he happened to notice a biographical index to the *New York Times,* and tried looking up William Robert Archer. It spoke of a divorce suit in April 1919, in which Archer's wife Florence Brainerd was demanding the annulment of the marriage. Since Florence Brainerd was the daughter of a distinguished

Washington family, Crick was able to follow up the story in the Washington newspapers. And what he discovered was that Jeffrey Archer's father had not spent the First World War in the trenches, but in America, where 'he was exposed as a compulsive liar, an impostor and a conman, pursued by the police in three separate countries'. Archer's first marriage had been to Alice Linard, whom he married at the age of 25, in 1900; he proceeded to live so lavishly that by 1908 they had been forced to sell up – whereupon Archer deserted her. Two years later, Archer was declared bankrupt.

Thereupon Archer sailed to New York from which he returned as a salesman of chewing gum. When this also failed, Archer became a mortgage broker in London, and in October 1914 was charged at the Old Bailey with a series of fraud offences. Archer was allowed bail – of £200 – but absconded. He fled to France, got himself a passport in the name of 'William Grimwood' and went to America in 1916.

There he posed as a British Army surgeon who was recuperating from war wounds. He claimed to be a man of property, educated at Eton and Oxford. And he began collecting money for injured allied soldiers – which, predictably, never reached the soldiers.

Then Archer met 22-year-old Florence Brainerd, daughter of a wealthy businessman, and persuaded her to marry him. Immediately after their honeymoon, he resumed collecting money for charity – this time for artificial limbs for wounded soldiers.

Arrested in January 1917 on fraud charges, he was sentenced to three years in prison, but sent to an asylum, from which he was released after ten months. He then fled to Canada, where he soon appeared in a Toronto court for swindling a woman of $500 in war bonds with which he bought himself a car. Sentenced to a year in prison, he was instead deported back to Britain.

There he was promptly arrested for his earlier frauds, but escaped because one of the chief prosecution witnesses had died in the meantime. 'During his stay in America,' says Michael Crick, 'scarcely a day seems to have passed without his devising some brilliant new plot to rob someone.'

Jeffrey Archer's mother, Lola, was the daughter of a Bristol commercial traveller named Harold Cook, who sold 'fancy goods'. Her mother was a teacher. Lola got herself pregnant at the age of seventeen, and gave birth to an illegitimate daughter. This baby, Wendy, was given up for adoption. At the age of nineteen, Lola fell in love with the smooth and good-looking William Archer. Very soon, Lola was pregnant again, and in 1934, gave birth to a boy who was named Jeffrey Neville. Finally, because William Archer was so unreliable, Lola was forced to allow her son to be adopted. In 1938, Lola finally persuaded Archer to marry her, and so, two years later, Jeffrey Archer was born.

In 1942, the Archers moved to Somerset, then to Weston-super-Mare, where Lola began working as a journalist. At 67, William Archer must presumably have been receiving his old age pension. The rest of the burden of supporting the family fell on Lola. In May 1949 she became a journalist on the *Weston Mercury* and began a column called 'Over the Tea Cups'. In her first column, she talks about her son Jeffrey, and the problems of teaching him the value of money. Later she nicknamed him Tuppence. His regular appearances in her column may have given Archer his first taste for publicity. It may also explain why the young Archer was known among his school friends as a 'bighead'.

At the age of eleven he raised nearly £4 for the local scouts doing 'bob-a-job'. Fundraising would later become one of the young Archer's specialities.

In 1951, Archer won a scholarship to Wellington School, near Taunton, although to begin with he hardly distinguished himself, being something of a loner, and derided by other boys as 'the Pune' – because of his small stature.

In 1955, an interesting and possibly significant event occurred – Archer dived into the shallow end of the swimming pool, landed on his head, and dislocated his neck. According to one of his friends, Michael Taudevin, this completely changed his character. 'Suddenly he became a man with a burning ambition. I always maintained that it was because he fell on his head.'

He may be right. Augustus John was not a particularly good painter when he dived into the sea and knocked himself out on a rock; after that, he became a great painter. But then, it might also be observed that many sex criminals have started their careers with a bang on the head. This includes the 'Burning Car murderer' Alfred Rouse (hanged in 1931) and the more recent Gloucester mass murderer, Fred West. It is an interesting thought that Archer's dive into the swimming pool may have had something to do with his literary talent as well as with his sexual promiscuity.

Archer suddenly began to train obsessively, and to go in for weightlifting and gymnastics. He became a first class runner. And also began to take an interest in acting. He played parts in *Julius Caesar* and in Moliere's *The Miser*.

In 1956, his father finally died at the age of eighty – as Crick remarks: 'Dependent on others and in debt.' Archer says that his father's death came as a considerable blow to him, although the evidence seems to be that they were never close.

And in spite of his new prominence in sports and drama, Archer remained unpopular with the other boys – one former master says 'because of his cockiness and bumptiousness'.

It is not clear what Archer did after leaving school at the age of eighteen. Archer himself claims that he went to California and gained a BA degree and that he then went to Canada and raised half a million dollars for the YMCA. But the University of California apparently has no record of Archer being enrolled on any of its campuses. Later Archer downgraded his claims to attending a summer school at the University of California.

For a brief period Archer joined the army – The Duke of Wellington's Regiment in Yorkshire – then went on to Sandhurst. There seems to be no information on why he left after a few months. After that he became a police constable for a short time in London, but left in October 1960.

After these two false starts, he became a PE teacher at a private school on the edge of the New Forest, and there finally made his mark, being described by one colleague as 'the finest PE master I've seen or imagined. His energy was absolutely unlimited.' But the son of the school's owner describes him as 'an alert, pushy young man – very pushy'.

His next appointment was equally successful – as a PE master at Dover College where the headmaster, Tim Cobs, became his warm supporter. And it was partly because of Cob's help that Archer was able to move on to Oxford – not as a university student, but as a kind of trainee teacher trying to gain his diploma in education. Archer, of course, was not a graduate – he only had three O Levels – but because of Tim Cob's recommendation, was accepted for the teacher-training course.

At Dover College, Archer had used his talent for fundraising to good effect, and here at Oxford – the home of Oxfam – he made even more of a mark. Beginning with an attempt to raise £25,000 for a hospital in the foothills of the Himalayas, he soon switched his attention to a campaign called H£Million.

And it was here he showed his remarkable flair for publicity. He suggested to the organizers that they should get Oxford students involved in collecting for charity. Then, when he was introduced to the education correspondent of the *Daily Mail*, he asked him whether the *Daily Mail* might be interested in helping Oxford students to launch a campaign to raise half a million pounds. The correspondent said that it was unlikely whereupon Archer asked if it would help if he could persuade the Beatles to support it. The correspondent, understandably, thought it would.

Next, Archer sent a telegram to the Beatles' manager, Brian Epstein, signing it on behalf of 8,000 Oxford students. Epstein was only cautiously supportive. So Archer and the editor of the university magazine *Cherwell*, travelled up to Merseyside with Oxfam posters and collecting tins and went to the Empire Theatre where the Beatles were recording for the BBC's programme *Juke Box Jury*. Somehow, they got into the Beatles' dressing room, and persuaded them to pose for a photograph putting money into collecting tins and holding a poster reading:'WANTED £1,000,000'.

Epstein, who felt that they had been pushed into this, insisted that the Beatles would only 'lend their name' to the campaign. And at this point, Archer showed his talents as a pro by ringing Epstein and telling him that if the Beatles would agree to come to Oxford, Harold Macmillan – the ex-prime minister – would attend a dinner with them. And Epstein, who wanted to meet Macmillan, promptly agreed.

Oddly enough, so did Macmillan. But the meeting was never to take place. By some mix-up, the Beatles happened to be in Florida on the day when they were supposed to come to Oxford, so although Macmillan and the Beatles both dined at Oxford – on different dates – they never actually met. But with the help of the *Daily Mail*, the sum of a million pounds was finally achieved.

The following year, Archer had another brilliant idea – flying to Washington, and persuading President Lyndon Johnson to sign a set of records of Winston Churchill's war speeches, which would then be auctioned. Pan Am agreed to fly Archer to Washington free, and the result was another photograph, showing Archer in the Oval Office watching Johnson sign the record album.

The result of all this was that Archer's year at Oxford was finally extended to three, and he was elected to the Oxford Union executive committee. He spoke in several political debates, usually backing conservative issues but, by that time, his relentless careerism was earning him enemies, and he was not voted back onto the Union committee.

He also continued his career in sport, and was able to run the hundred yards in under ten seconds. He became a friend of the runner Chris Chataway.

It was also while at Oxford that he met a brilliant young biochemistry student called Mary Weedon, and persuaded her to marry him.

Archer's next venture into fundraising proved less successful. On leaving Oxford in 1965, he joined an organization called The National Birthday Trust, his job being to raise at least £10,000 a year. The purpose of the Birthday Trust was to help care for mothers and babies, and to research deaths of babies at the time of birth. Archer's sheer enthusiasm won him the job.

Unfortunately, enthusiasm was not enough, and after six months he had only succeeded in raising £1,374. And at the end of the year, Archer had actually cost the charity more than £6,000. Thereupon he resigned.

During that year, Archer finally managed to get his foot into Conservative politics. Through Chris Chataway and the Conservative central office, he became a Conservative candidate for the Greater London Council for the outer London borough of Havering. And Archer's energetic campaigning won him a seat on the GLC as Havering swung to the conservatives.

Archer was soon appointed to the Inner London Education Authority. Chris Chataway had been put in charge of ILEA, and Archer asked whether he could serve him in some way. When Chataway said yes, Archer moved himself into Chataway's office in County Hall and took over a desk. Asked why he had appointed Archer, Chataway replied 'I didn't; he appointed himself!'

Almost immediately he got himself into trouble with Tory colleagues. His first job was to appoint governors for several hundred schools and colleges; Archer's task was to find hundreds of Tories for the job. With only a few weeks to do this before each governing body chose a chairman, Archer hurled himself into it with such enthusiasm that people were soon ringing ILEA saying: 'Get this lunatic off our backs.' In council debates, Archer was a good speaker, but often so vitriolic that he made himself many enemies – particularly in Labour.

He also found an interesting new way of making money. He helped his fellow Tory councillors to claim expenses, which required endless paperwork. In exchange, he expected 10 per cent. Soon, he had become known as 'Mr 10 per cent'. But to the publishers of the first edition of Michael Crick's book about him, Archer indignantly denied that he had ever taken 10 per cent – which Crick was able to reveal as a lie.

Archer was still looking for full-time employment, and soon found a niche for his talents in the United Nations Association (UNA), a charity which acts as a support group to the UN. Its chairman, Humphrey Berkeley, signed on Archer as fundraiser. But Archer's first effort, a flag day, raised only a few hundred pounds more than in the previous year. However, his next attempt was more successful. Archer took charge of a fundraising dinner at 10 Downing Street. His job was to persuade business tycoons to come to dinner with the leaders of the Labour Party (Harold Wilson), the Conservative Party (Edward Heath) and the Liberals (Jeremy Thorpe). Archer went off to see Jack Cohen, founder of Tesco, and Olaf Kier, head of an engineering company, and returned with a cheque for £50,000 from Kier and a promise of the same amount from Cohen. (Archer would later make Cohen the model for the hero of his novel As the Crow Flies.) The dinner was a great success and raised over £200,000.

Although subsequent fundraising events – charity dinners and a film premiere in Leicester Square – raised far less money, Archer decided to start his own public relations business, which he called Arrow Enterprises. But the United Nations Association showed itself unwilling to pay the 10 per cent commission that Archer was asking.

On the other hand, the European Movement which campaigned for Britain to join the Common Market agreed to the commission, and Archer set out to raise £50,000. The result was another dinner, this time at the Guild Hall, but also with the three political party leaders, which led to him raising £450,000. Harold Wilson objected to the idea of giving Archer 10 per cent, but the European Movement gave him a flat fee which just happened to be £45,000. For 1969, that was a vast sum. It seems to have been the beginning of Archer's fortune.

From 1966 until 1969, Archer continued to try to get into parliament, and contested five seats.

On being turned down for a job as deputy to Douglas Hurd, Heath's political secretary, Archer remarked to another MP that he hadn't decided whether 'to become an MP or make a million'.

At the end of 1969, Archer finally gained his constituency – Louth, in Lincolnshire, not far from Grimsby.

Now a sudden embarrassment arose. His previous boss, Humphrey Berkeley, had apparently discovered that, while Archer was working for the United Nations Association, he was fiddling his expenses. He made the mistake of claiming that he'd given lunch to two millionaires in the Carlton Tower Hotel on the day when he happened to have had lunch with Berkeley and Chris Chataway. It proved that Berkeley had even paid the bill. The sums involved were not great, but Archer was obliged to repay £150. When a young reporter from *The Times* pressed Archer about this on a train, Archer burst into tears and begged him not to write the story. But what appeared was short and not too embarrassing. Archer, meanwhile, was suing Humphrey Berkeley for libel, but ended up by having to pay Berkeley's legal expenses – £17,000 – as well as his own.

As a Member of Parliament Archer did not make any great impact. He was in no hurry, feeling that he probably had a seat for life. His next aim was to make a lot of money – since he felt that serious politics requires a large bank balance.

Before he became an MP, he had been asked to go and see Earl Mountbatten of Burma who asked Archer for ideas to raise funds for the United World Colleges, over which he presided. Archer, always one to think big, suggested a concert of Bob Hope and Frank Sinatra, with Noël Coward compering. Archer went on to suggest a simultaneous show at the Royal Festival Hall with Richard Burton, Elizabeth Taylor, and Leonard Bernstein conducting. Noël Coward fell ill, and had to back out. As an alternative, Archer thought Princess Grace of Monaco would make a good replacement. Mountbatten rang her, and she immediately agreed.

The event – which was repeated twice in one evening – was a great success; it raised about £200,000, but Archer claimed to have been paid only a flat fee of £4,000.

Other events, including Bernstein conducting the Vienna Philharmonic Orchestra at the Albert Hall, and Marlene Dietrich singing at the Drury Lane Theatre, were altogether less successful; Archer lost badly on the latter deal. And an attempt to persuade Elvis Presley to come to England (Presley never did) and to bring the Beatles back together for a concert both fell through.

And then, Archer ran straight into the biggest disaster of his career.

The basic problem seems to have been greed. Archer was looking for a way to make a vast fortune, like his friend Jim Slater, who had made money by buying up moribund companies and then 'asset stripping'.

Archer decided to go into the stock market and make a quick killing.

He had become friendly with a banker named Michael Altmann, who worked at the First National Bank of Boston. Altmann happened to be staying in London, not far from Archer's home in The Boltons in West London, with a man called John Kennedy, and learned that Kennedy had agreed to pay a German inventor, Kurt Wymann, £25,000 for the rights to a remarkable anti-pollution device for cars, a valve that would cut carbon monoxide emissions and reduce petrol consumption. The company that would market this small device – about the size of a spark plug – was called Aquablast. Hearing about this, Archer was determined to get a slice of the action. He went on to invest large sums, some of them borrowed, in Aquablast. He ended by paying out £350,000.

Archer lost all this. Aquablast shares fell from 350 pence per share to 55 pence, and two men would later make an appearance in court in Canada on fraud charges, and receive prison sentences.

Archer made a desperate attempt to revive his fortunes by trying once more to persuade Elvis Presley to come to England for a concert – his 10 per cent would have cleared all his debts – but Presley's manager, Colonel Tom Parker, was adamantly against it. An attempt to rent the London skyscraper, Centre Point, and then let it out floor by floor, also came to nothing. The result was that on 17 May 1974, Archer was obliged to tell his wife Mary, who was seven months pregnant with their second child, that he was on the verge of bankruptcy.

The danger of bankruptcy made Archer decide to resign as an MP. But although Archer had no way of foreseeing it, his financial disaster was one of the best pieces of luck he ever had.

When he told a friend that he intended to write a novel to retrieve his fortunes, the friend commented 'Jeffrey, you can barely spell, let alone write.' 'That doesn't matter,' Archer replied, 'I can tell stories.'

Archer approached a friend, a TV producer named Ted Francis (who would later be instrumental in his downfall), and asked him to sit down while he read aloud from a sheaf of handwritten pages.

Archer's first plan was to write a film outline, and sell it to Hollywood or television. But when a film producer told him that it would stand a better chance if he wrote it as a novel, Archer went up to Oxford to stay with Sir Noel Hall, of Brasenose, and spent his days writing – a full morning's work, a brief pub lunch, then writing until six o'clock. In the evening, he would read what he had written to the Halls. At weekends he went back home, where his wife Mary carefully read what he'd written, and edited it.

Archer tells the story of Henryk Metelski, a Jew from New York's East Side. He becomes a messenger boy in Wall Street by cheating a friend out of a job. One day, in the washroom of a brokerage house, he picks up a cheque for $50,000. This has been dropped by a broker. And since it is Friday night, he knows that he has the weekend to turn the money into a larger sum. He uses a tip about an oil pipeline that he has heard during the day to buy himself shares in standard oil, then uses the shares to borrow the money to repay the lady who made out the cheque. The share prices rise, as he expected, and he makes over $7,000 profit.

In due course, Metelski, now calling himself Harvey Metcalfe (by coincidence, the name of the man who told Archer he could not write) goes on to become a multi-millionaire and a financial shark. As the novel begins, he has just bankrupted four 'suckers' who have invested money with him. The four get together, vowing to get their money back, 'Not a penny more, not a penny less,' and the remainder of the book tells the story of the 'sting' by which they do this. It is a remarkable, fast moving piece of writing, and reveals that, whether he can spell or not, Archer is a marvellously inventive storyteller.

Archer writes with the confidence of somebody who understands the stock exchange, and has read Gustavus Myers's *History of the Great American Fortunes*; the fantasy has a marvellous air of authenticity.

Archer's next piece of luck was to acquire himself a good agent – Debbie Owen, wife of the MP David Owen. Debbie Owen was about to pass Archer along to another agent when her husband happened to pick up the typescript, and began to chuckle as he read it.

Not a Penny More, Not a Penny Less did not, as is often claimed, turn Archer into an immediate millionaire. The American publisher Doubleday only paid an advance of $12,000. A number of foreign publishers bought the book from Doubleday for translation. But British publishers showed themselves less interested, and many turned it down. Finally, it was taken by Tom Maschler, of Jonathan Cape, who had been responsible for turning *Catch 22* and the novels of John Fowles into bestsellers. But Cape paid an advance of only £3,000. Then Warner Brothers bought the film rights of the book for £125,000. And at last, it began to look as if Archer was slowly fighting his way out of debt. (Typically, he claimed that it had made him a millionaire.)

Nevertheless, *Not a Penny More, Not a Penny Less* did reasonably well. Then a Canadian businessman who had heard the story of Archer's financial disaster telephoned him to offer him the use of his luxury home in Barbados, where he could begin to write his next novel. This was *Shall We Tell the President?* and was about a date in the future when Teddy Kennedy has become president, and there is a plot to assassinate him. Obviously indebted to Frederick Forsyth's *Day of the Jackal*, about a plot to kill General de Gaulle, *Shall We Tell the President?* has the same kind of feeling of authenticity as that novel. Archer obviously has an immense appetite for facts.

Nevertheless, neither of these first two novels had made him a fortune or become bestsellers. He decided to remedy this with his next novel, *Kane and Abel*, the story of two businessmen, born on the same day, William Kane, from Boston, and Abel Rosnovski, born in poverty in Poland. Published in England in September 1979, it reached the top of the *Sunday Times* bestseller list within two weeks, and went on to have the same kind of success in America, where it spent 29 weeks on the *New York Times* bestseller list. At last, Archer was wealthy.

He bought the Old Vicarage, Grantchester, associated with Rupert Brooke's famous poem, and there wrote a play based on a murder trial, although it was several years before it was produced. *Not a Penny More, Not a Penny Less* was serialized by BBC television in seven parts, with Archer as the narrator. At last, in 1981, *Not a Penny More, Not a Penny Less* reached the bestseller list.

Now he was rich again, Archer decided to get back into politics – but not as a lowly Member of Parliament. He became a very popular speaker at fundraising auctions and Tory dinners. But when Prime Minister Margaret Thatcher announced that Archer was one of her favourite authors, alongside John Le Carré and Frederick Forsyth, it was obvious that he was destined for better things.

One person who stood in the way of promotion – even a possible peerage – was the Tory Party's deputy leader, William Whitelaw, who remembered Humphrey Berkeley's report of 1969 and the libel trial that followed. Whitelaw is reported to have said that Archer would be promoted 'over his dead body'. But at this point, to everyone's astonishment, Berkeley himself showed a forgiving spirit, and wrote to Mrs Thatcher saying that if she decided to give Archer a job, he would certainly not object. And in September 1985, Margaret Thatcher telephoned Archer to offer him the post of Deputy Chairman of the Tory Party. This was obviously a major step on the way to a peerage.

In fact, Archer was not a particularly good Deputy Chairman. He was a little too frank, and prone to put his foot in it. He referred to Lord Gowrie, who had just resigned from the Cabinet, as a 'wally' and advised unemployed young men to 'get off their backsides and find a job', comparing their situation unfavourably with the determination that had rescued him from bankruptcy.

Another problem was his increasing reputation for promiscuity. According to Crick, 'Archer had started being unfaithful to Mary within a few years of their marriage in 1966. One friend recalls how in the early 1970s Archer would borrow his London flat for one-night stands. Then in the early 1970s, Archer began a lengthy affair with Andrina Colquhoun, who tried unsuccessfully to persuade him to leave his wife.' (To his credit, Archer replied 'No, marriage is for life.')

Then, in 1986, came the bombshell of the *News of the World* story about Monica Coghlan, and Archer offering her enough money to leave the country. And after Adam Raphael had admitted at the libel trial that Archer had told him that he *had* met the prostitute – although not slept with her – there were few people left who did not believe that Archer was guilty. And when Archer not only emerged triumphant, but with another half a million pounds, many people thought that his luck was just getting too good to last.

Nevertheless, it did. And when Mrs Thatcher ran into leadership problems in 1990 and was forced to resign, Archer appeared in her resignation honours list. Although Archer failed to get his peerage when the list was vetted by the Political Honours Scrutiny Committee, he was finally made Lord Archer in June 1992, when the new Prime Minister, John Major, made him a Conservative working peer. Archer chose the title Baron Archer of Weston-super-Mare of Mark.

In 1994, Archer found himself in the centre of another storm. This one was about shares in Anglia Television, of which his wife had been a director since 1987.

In November 1993, the National Heritage Secretary, Peter Brooke, announced that in 1984 companies could own two major ITV franchises, provoking sudden takeover fever.

On 13 January 1994, Archer telephoned a stockbroker named Simon Wharmby, and asked about buying some Anglia Television shares. Wharmby was able to buy him 25,000 shares at 485 pence. Apparently Archer had explained that he was buying the shares for somebody else. The following day Archer bought another 25,000 shares at the same price.

On Tuesday 18 January the media group MAI made a bid for Anglia Television, and the share price increased to 637 pence, a rise of 152 pence a share. Archer immediately instructed Wharmby to sell – the deal had made a profit of £77,219.

Since the timing looked just too convenient, the stockbroker had to refer it to his directors. And at a board meeting, a member of staff asked whether anyone realized that Mary Archer was director of Anglia Television.

Six days later, the man Archer claimed he was buying the shares for, Broosk Saib, deposited a cheque for the £77,000 profit into an account in west London.

The question, of course, was one of 'insider dealing' – the deliberate use of inside information to make a profit.

There was no reason why this story should ever have become public knowledge, except that a freelance journalist called Martin Tompkinson received a tip off and investigated the story, quickly discovering that Mary Archer was a director of Anglia, and that the company had recently been taken over by MAI.

The result was more bad publicity for Archer. Archer told a journalist who rang him about the story: 'It is completely untrue. I did not buy any shares.' He added 'That sort of accusation is libellous.' At that time, Archer was riding high, tipped to become the new Conservative Party Chairman.

When, in August that year, the full story of the buying of the Anglia shares finally emerged, Archer hastened to admit publicly that he had made a 'grave error'. He continued to insist that the deals had not been made with the help of any inside information from his wife, but admitted that it was a mistake to have bought the shares when his wife was a director. The Department of

Trade and Industry (DTI) had decided by then that no further action would be taken.

When, in 1997, the Blair Labour government decided that London should have a Lord Mayor, Archer's name was mentioned as a Conservative contender. Since Ken Livingstone was also regarded as a likely choice, most people did not think a great deal of Archer's chances. But Archer obviously felt that becoming Lord Mayor of London, like Dick Whittington, would be an appropriate climax for his political career.

It was at this point – in April 1998 – that Michael Crick, the author of the Archer biography, felt that Archer ought to be opposed. He writes: 'True, there had been plenty of damning details in the first edition of this book, but its scope had been restricted by the laws of libel. I knew there was plenty more about Archer's dishonesty and criminal behaviour that would inevitably emerge during a full election campaign.' So Crick wrote to his old friend William Hague, whom he'd known since university days, to say that 'In my view Archer is a much sleazier character than (Jonathan) Aitken or (Neil) Hamilton or any of the other miscreants of recent times.' Crick went on, 'I can think of at least half a dozen incidents in Archer's career when people have made serious allegations about his behaviour, but the evidence was insufficient for me to publish.'

Four weeks later, his letter having been politely brushed aside, Crick heard from Ted Francis, the television producer to whom Archer had read the first version of Not a Penny More, Not a Penny Less. Francis told Crick how, in January 1987, Archer had invited him for dinner at Sambuca, an Italian restaurant in Sloane Square and suddenly dropped into the conversation the comment: 'I want you to have had dinner with me here on 9 September.' Francis said that he laughed and said: 'Oh, all right Jeffrey, if you say so.' 'Then,' said Francis, 'he asked me: "Will you write a letter to my lawyer saying we had dinner on that evening and stayed quite late?" I said, "Hang on, Jeffrey, I might tell a fib for you but I'm not going to commit perjury. I won't stand up in a court and say this".'

But when Archer explained that he had, in fact, been having dinner with Andrina Colquhoun on that day, Francis happily agreed to the request as a personal favour. 'I knew for a fact that he and Mary had a falling out over Andrina and Mary said: "It's her or me."'

In due course Ted Francis wrote to Lord Mishcon explaining that Archer and he had eaten dinner together on Tuesday 9 September and that the dinner terminated at approximately 9:45 pm.

Early the following month, Archer agreed to lend Francis £25,000 for an Enid Blyton project. But when the contract came, the amount mentioned was only £20,000 – although Archer had made it clear that he would not expect this back. In fact, the amount that Francis finally received was only £12,000.

Another cause of resentment was that at one of Archer's parties, as Francis was talking to the actress Susan George, Archer walked up to them and said in a loud voice: 'Oh you wanna watch this fellow. I lent him £20,000 and I'm still waiting for it to come back.'

Michael Crick and Ted Francis met for lunch in a pub, and discussed how the story of the fake alibi might be used to destroy Archer's chances of becoming Mayor.

In fact, Francis seems to have decided to go it alone after that meeting. He rang up the publicist Max Clifford who contacted the News of the World. They agreed to pay about £17,000 for the story, of which £5,000 would go to two of Francis's favourite charities, £2,000 to cover his expenses, and the rest to buy a second-hand car.

What happened then was almost a repetition of the 'sting' with Monica Coghlan. Francis rang Archer with the News of the World reporter at his side taping the conversation. Francis declared that Crick knew all about the alibi story. Archer asked how, and Francis said: 'I've no idea.'

The following evening, Francis again rang Archer, claiming that Crick had got hold of a credit card receipt showing that Francis had, in fact, been staying at the Grand Hotel in Brighton on the night of Tuesday 9 September 1986 – the evening he was supposed to be eating with Archer at the Sambuca. Archer said that didn't matter because he had indeed been eating at the Sambuca that evening.

Forty minutes later, Francis rang back again. Archer said that he had now consulted his lawyer Lord Mishcon, and that 'He says as long as you say nothing, they've got nothing.'

By coincidence, on the Friday before the story was due to appear, the News of the World editor Phil Hall received a call from Jeffrey Archer inviting him to Archer's Christmas party. He said he would love to come, but asked whether he could go and see Archer immediately. At that meeting, Phil Hall told Archer about the story they were going to publish on Sunday. When Hall had finished explaining, Archer took off his glasses and said: 'Oh my God, this is going to be so damaging.'

It was at this point that Archer realized that he had to resign as mayoral candidate.

The Tory leader William Hague was told about Archer's troubles. He consulted with the Party Chairman, Michael Ancram, who agreed that Archer would have to resign. So when Archer rang Hague later that evening asking for another chance, Hague told him sternly that he would expect his resignation by the following morning.

Hague's own advisor, Stephan Shakespeare, reportedly told Archer: 'The establishment and the media hate you, but ordinary people won't condemn you.' This was undoubtedly a misjudgement. Shakespeare was under-estimating the extent to which most people felt impatient with Archer after the Anglia affair and other scandals, so there was a genuine widespread desire to see him get his 'comeuppance.' William Hague made it clear that his own patience was at an end. 'Jeffrey Archer has let the Party down and there can be no question of him continuing as our candidate.'

On the following Monday morning Hague summoned Archer to Central Office, and Archer was stripped of the Conservative Whip in the Lords. In fact, Hague had good reason for annoyance – the previous June, when the matter of Archer's candidacy for Lord Mayor was being discussed, Michael Ancram had asked him whether there were any 'substantial and damaging allegations' that were still outstanding, and had been assured that there were not. When reporters gathered around the gate at the Old Vicarage, Grantchester, it was Stephan Shakespeare who told them, 'He's extremely upset, extremely sorry, couldn't be more sorry. He's on the floor.' Mary Archer was quoted as saying: 'We are all human and Jeffrey manages to be more human than most.'

On 3 May 2001 Archer appeared at Bow Street Magistrate's Court to face five charges of perverting the course of justice and perjury. He was granted bail.

On 30 May the perjury trial began. Monica Coghlan, who was to have been called as a witness, had in fact been killed as a result of a car accident on 27 April 2001, when a fleeing robber, who had already hijacked two cars, collided with Monica Coghlan's car in Huddersfield, Yorkshire.

The accusation of attempting to pervert the course of justice arose from the fact that Archer had told his secretary, Angela Peppiatt, to make a bogus appointments diary that could be shown at the earlier libel trial. Peppiatt was so concerned that she made photocopies of the entries in the bogus diary and kept the original. She had been told to insert a list of appointments for the evening of 8 September 1986, the night he was supposed to have slept with Monica Coghlan. However, due to an error, Archer was accused of picking up the prostitute the following evening, Tuesday 9 September. The QC for the prosecution, David Waters, said, 'You may think it is not an exaggeration to say that had the jury seen that entry, putting it as its lowest, it would have had a significant impact on the outcome of the trial.'

The court was also told that during the first libel action, Archer was having an affair and was cheating on both his wife and his lover. The jury was told that Archer had a string of extra-marital affairs, including one that took place in Nigeria, and it was not unusual for him to ask friends to provide alibis to cover his infidelities from his wife. The jury was also told that Archer did not fulfil his promise to donate all of his £500,000 *Star* libel award to charity.

On 29 June, Lady Archer entered the witness box and flatly denied Mrs Peppiatt's allegation that she and her husband had been leading separate lives for some time before the period leading up to the libel trial.

Archer undoubtedly damaged his own case by deciding to remain silent at the trial, inevitably creating the impression that he was unable to produce an adequate defence against the charges.

Summing up on 7 July 2001, Archer's counsel Nicolas Purnell QC conceded that Archer may have been 'a bloody fool' for attempting to cover up his liaison with Andrina Colquhoun, but he was not a criminal.

On 13 July, Archer received the news that his mother Lola had died, aged 87. On the same day, the jury retired to consider its verdict on two counts of perjury and three counts of perverting the course of justice.

On Thursday 19 July 2001, Archer was found guilty of perjury and perverting the course of justice, and sentenced to four years in prison. He was ordered to pay £175,000 costs.

Archer began his sentence at Belmarsh jail in south London, was subsequently transferred to Wayland Prison in Cambridgeshire, a category C jail, and then to North Sea Bank, an open category D prison near Skegness, in Lincolnshire. Where, the newspaper reports said, 'He will have a key to his cell and the tang of sea air in his nostrils.'

Another newspaper report of the time stated that Archer would repay the £500,000 libel damages he received from the *Star*, plus interest, bringing the sum up to very nearly £3,000,000. Another report said that Archer would be repaying the *News of the World* the £50,000 damages and £30,000 costs it incurred at the libel trial.

Sir Bernard Caulfield, the judge whose lyrical outburst about Mary Archer had probably swayed the jury in Archer's favour in 1987, was spared the embarrassment of seeing the novelist's downfall – he had died in October 1994.

THE BACCARAT SCANDAL

THE TRANBY CROFT CASE

His Highness Edward Albert, Prince of Wales – the son of Queen Victoria – seems to have been in many ways a rather unsavoury character. He was an incorrigible seducer of women, who spent most of his time drinking, playing cards, and indulging in slightly sadistic forms of horseplay. At least one of his friends – Christopher Sykes – ruined himself trying to keep up with the Prince's extravagant way of life. Another, Sir William Gordon Gordon Cumming, Bart, a Scottish landowner, also owed his ruin – although in a slightly less direct manner – to his spoiled and unreliable friend.

Gordon Cumming seems to have been rather a disagreeable character, noted for his rudeness and boorishness; the *Sporting Times* described him as 'possibly the handsomest man in London, and certainly the rudest'. On meeting a medical acquaintance in the courtyard of Buckingham Palace he is said to have enquired: 'Hello, is one of the servants sick?'

On 8 September 1880, the Prince of Wales was a guest at Tranby Croft, the house of Arthur Wilson, a rich Hull shipowner. By his special request, Gordon Cumming had also been invited to Tranby Croft. Cumming was at the time a lieutenant-colonel in the Scots Guards.

After a late dinner, the guests listened to some music, then settled down to play baccarat – a card game which has something in common with both roulette and bingo. A dealer hands out a card, face-downwards, to two sets of players who sit on either side of him. The aim is to get a score of eight or nine. The dealer looks at his own two cards, and he may 'declare'. Or he may offer another card to the two lots of players. When either a player or the dealer has eight or nine, he has won. It is a game of chance. The players may stake what they like on the game, and the dealer, like the croupier in roulette, either wins or loses.

The players must sit with their money – or counters representing money – in front of them. The cheating of which Gordon Cumming was accused consisted in quietly adding a few counters to his stake after the cards had been declared in his favour. It was the son of the house, Arthur Stanley Wilson, who thought he saw Gordon Cumming doing this. He quietly drew the attention of another guest, Berkeley Levett, to this. Levett watched carefully and was soon convinced that he had also seen Gordon Cumming add to his stake after he had won, so increasing his winnings. Later that evening, when the game was finished, he told his mother, and his brother-in-law, Lycett Green, what he had seen. It was decided that the best thing to do was to watch Gordon Cumming carefully the next evening to see if he cheated again.

They did this on the evening of 9 September and five of them – Lycett Green and his wife, and the two Wilson parents and their son – were all convinced they saw Gordon Cumming cheating.

Now this was a serious business – not because of the money involved – for Gordon Cumming had only won £228 in two nights' play but because he was there at the invitation of the Prince of Wales. Edward Albert – later Edward VII – already had a bad reputation as a gambler and ladies' man, and was often pilloried in the Press. The first thought of his hosts – and they seem to have been social climbers – was to save the Prince from scandal.

Other guests were let into the secret, including Lord Coventry and his assistant General Owen Williams, a close friend of Gordon Cumming. The Prince was told by Coventry that Gordon Cumming had been seen cheating at baccarat, then Coventry and General Williams went to Gordon Cumming, who was in the smoking room, and told him that he had been accused by Lycett Green and young Wilson of cheating at baccarat. Gordon Cumming was indignant and said, 'Do you believe the statements of a parcel of inexperienced boys?' After dinner, Coventry, Williams and the Prince of Wales all confronted Gordon Cumming, who continued to insist on his innocence. And later, a document was presented to Gordon Cumming, which he was asked to sign. It declared that, in exchange for the silence of the witnesses against him, Gordon Cumming would solemnly undertake never again to play cards. If he did not sign it, he was told, he would have to leave the house immediately and be proclaimed a cheat on every racecourse in England. Gordon Cumming decided to sign.

Far from 'hushing up' the scandal, all this secrecy only made it a better subject for gossip. By the next day it was being openly discussed on Doncaster Racecourse. And three months later, on 27 December 1890, Gordon Cumming received an anonymous letter from Paris saying that the scandal was being discussed in Paris and Monte Carlo. Belatedly, he decided to sue. He was demanding an apology from the Wilsons, the Lycett Greens, and Berkeley Levett. Understandably, they refused. Gordon Cumming's solicitors issued a writ for slander.

Sir Edward Clarke was briefed for the prosecution and Sir Charles Russell for the defence – Russell had a reputation of being quite as rude and arrogant as Gordon Cumming. The judge was the Lord Chief Justice himself, the Right Honourable John Duke Bevan Coleridge, a close friend of Russell.

The case opened on 1 June 1891. The defence was one of justification – that Gordon Cumming had not been slandered because he really had cheated. There were no spectacular revelations and no dramatic surprises. The Prince of Wales appeared in the witness box but his evidence was neither for nor against Gordon Cumming. The prosecution failed to shake the witnesses who thought they had seen Gordon Cumming cheat, although he scored a few good points. Gordon Cumming explained that he signed the paper 'because it was the only way to avoid a terrible scandal'. Clarke's final speech was so brilliant that it looked for a while as if Gordon Cumming had won after all. But the judge's summing up was against Gordon Cumming, his central point being that surely an innocent man would not have signed a paper virtually admitting his guilt. One writer on the case has described the summing up as 'polished, skilful and fiendishly unfair'. The jury took only thirteen minutes to find the defendants not guilty. They were awarded their costs. Gordon Cumming – now a socially ruined man – slipped out of court immediately after the verdict. The crowd hissed the jurors, and even tried to attack the defendants as they left the court; this was probably due less to a conviction that Gordon Cumming was innocent than to an intense dislike of the Prince of Wales.

The following day, Gordon Cumming married his 21-year-old fiancée, an American heiress named Florence Garner, who had stuck to him throughout his ordeal. She remained convinced to the end of her life that her husband had been deliberately 'framed' by the Prince of Wales because of a disagreement about a lady. It is true that 'Bertie' (as the Prince was known) was a petty and vindictive man – he continued to persecute Gordon Cumming for the rest of his life – but there seems to be no evidence for Lady Gordon Cumming's assertion. The Gordon Cummings spent most of their lives on their Scottish estate and seem to have been reasonably happy together.

BAKER, COLONEL VALENTINE

ATTEMPTED RAPE ON A TRAIN

The attempt of Colonel Valentine Baker to rape a young lady on a train was one of the most widely publicized scandals of the 1870s.

On the afternoon of 17 June 1875, a 21-year-old girl named Rebecca Kate Dickinson boarded the Portsmouth to London train at Midhurst, in Sussex. She was alone in the compartment when 49-year-old Colonel Valentine Baker, until recently commanding officer of the 10th Hussars, entered the train at Liphook. Miss Dickinson was a pretty, self-possessed young lady who was on her way to Switzerland for a holiday. Colonel Baker was Assistant Quartermaster-General at Aldershot, a highly distinguished soldier who was an intimate friend of the Prince of Wales. He was also a married man, with two young daughters.

Baker made polite conversation for the first fifty minutes of the journey, apparently the ultra-respectable English gentleman exchanging common-places with a girl young enough to be his daughter or even granddaughter. But when the train pulled out of Woking, and London was half an hour away, he suddenly asked her if she often travelled alone. When she said she didn't, he asked her if they could meet on the train at some future time. She said no. He asked her name and she declined to tell him. He asked if he could write to her and she said no. He then closed the window and sat down next to her. When she asked him to sit further away he said, 'Don't be cross', and put his arm round her waist. 'You must kiss me, darling.' She struggled to her feet but he forced her down again and held her down with his weight while he kissed her again and again on the lips. 'If I give you my name will you get off?' she asked. Instead of replying he sank in front of her, thrust one hand up her dress and began to fumble with his flies with the other.

She struggled to her feet and tried to smash the window with her elbow; then she lowered it and screamed. Baker pulled her back so violently that she was half suffocated. She twisted the door handle and began to climb out backwards. 'Get in, dear!' said the colonel in great alarm. And he offered to get out of the other door in an effort to calm her. But she knew the other door was locked.

She could see two men looking out of the window of the next compartment as she balanced on the running board and she shouted, 'How long before the train stops?' But their answer was carried away by the roar of the engine and the wind.

At 4:45 the train passed through Walton station and a bricklayer called William Burrowes saw a young lady standing on the running board, clinging to the handle of the door; someone inside the compartment seemed to be preventing her from falling by holding onto her other arm. The stationmaster signalled to Esher and there the train stopped. As it began to slow down, Baker said urgently, 'Don't say anything – you don't know what trouble you'll get me into. Say you were frightened.'

Railway officials at Esher wanted to know what had happened but she was too upset and exhausted to say much. Baker was told to go into another compartment. A clergyman named Baldwin Brown got in with Miss Dickinson and travelled with her to London.

At Waterloo, Miss Dickinson, Colonel Baker and the Reverend Brown were taken to the Inspector's office. Baker must have been relieved when she declined to go into details about her complaint. She gave her name and address; so did Baker. And then the Reverend Brown escorted her to her brother's house – he was a doctor living in Chesterfield Street. At this point, Rebecca Dickinson apparently wanted to forget the whole thing but her brother pointed out that Baker might do the same thing to other girls. So, reluctantly, she agreed to report the matter to the police.

The news items about the case caused widespread interest and astonishment. Valentine Baker was the kind of soldier who had created the British Empire; he was also the author of a number of books on cavalry tactics. He was the younger brother of the explorer Sir Samuel Baker, who had journeyed to the source of the Nile. It was true that he was the son of a merchant, not a 'gentleman', but the Victorian era was the age of opportunity, and no one held this against him, least of all the future King Edward VII, his close friend. Surely there must be some mistake? Why should such a man risk his career and reputation to assault a girl on a train?

Three days after the assault, Baker was arrested at Guildford. His trial took place at Croydon Assizes on 2 August 1875, a Bank Holiday Monday. Huge crowds gathered outside the courtroom long before the trial was due to start at 10:30 am. Two well-dressed ladies even tried to get in through a window. Many peers were in court, including Lord Lucan and the Marquess of Tavistock. A rumour was going about that those in 'high places' had arranged for the whole thing to be dropped, so there was some relief when the Grand Jury found a True Bill and Mr Justice Brett refused to postpone the trial. There was so much noise coming from the crowds outside – disappointed at being unable to get in – that the case had to be adjourned for ten minutes while the police tried to restore order. Then Mr Sergeant Parry, QC, for the prosecution, called Miss Dickinson into the witness box. But he declined to increase her distress by asking her a single question. So the defence lawyer, Henry Hawkins, cross-examined her. He elicited the interesting fact that part of the conversation between Liphook and Woking had been about hypnotism and that Colonel Baker had told Miss Dickinson that he thought she could be mesmerized. She also detailed other topics they had discussed, including the murder of a certain Mr Walker. The defence was obviously trying to establish that Miss Dickinson's openness, her willingness to engage in animated conversation, had probably convinced the Colonel that a kiss might not be rejected.

But the evidence against the colonel was serious. He had fairly certainly intended rape – otherwise, why had he unbuttoned his flies? The guard had noticed that they were undone at Esher. And so had the two gentlemen in the carriage that Baker transferred into. He had also put his hand up her skirt, although it had apparently gone no further than above the top of her boot.

The judge's summing up emphasized that Baker's chief concern had apparently been to save Miss Dickinson from falling from the running board and he indicated that he could see no evidence that there was 'intent to ravish'. This was on the grounds that Baker had hoped to win the girl's consent to intercouse by 'exciting her passions'. The jury took the hint. Baker was found not guilty of intent to ravish but guilty of indecent assault and common assault. The judge then told Baker sternly that, 'Of all the people who travelled in the train that day, you were the most bound to stand by and defend a defenceless woman. Your crime is as bad as it could be.' And he sentenced Baker to a year in jail – without hard labour – and a fine of £500.

The press, on the whole, felt it was a just verdict – most people had believed that this friend of royalty would be acquitted. But the general public seemed to feel that Baker had got off too easily – a mere year in 'honourable detention', then back to the old life.

But Baker was disgraced. He tried to resign his commission and was told that he was to be cashiered. It was widely believed that this was due to Queen Victoria's intervention. (The Queen was not fond of her rakish son – or his friends.) It is true that, in Horsemonger Lane jail, Baker was treated with due consideration, allowed to wear his own clothes, to send out for his food and to receive his friends more or less as he wished. But the knowledge that he had involved his family in the most degrading kind of public scandal was enough to turn him into a psychological wreck. Three months after his imprisonment, it was reported that he was critically ill. *The Times* published a letter from his wife assuring his 'many friends' that he was no longer in danger of his life but admitting that his condition caused her much distress.

He served his full term; then, with his wife and two young daughters he left England. He became a lieutenant-general in the Ottoman army and fought bravely during the Russo-Turkish war. Then he went to Egypt and accepted an appointment as a commander of police. He attempted unsuccessfully to relieve Tokar during the Sudan war but his poorly trained force was destroyed. He himself was seriously wounded in a later action. When he came back to London to recuperate, a cheering crowd greeted him at Victoria Station. His friends tried hard to get him reinstated in the British army. But their efforts were a failure – almost certainly due to Queen Victoria's determination that the would-be rapist would never again become a soldier of the queen. Baker died of heart failure, after an attack of typhoid, on 12 November 1887, twelve years after the Dickinson case. The Queen finally relented and cabled that Baker was to be buried in Cairo with full military honours.

The mystery remains: why did Baker do it? In court he swore solemnly that the facts were not as Miss Dickinson represented them. His supporters took this to mean that she had given him some encouragment. He also spoke of her 'exaggerated fear'. Did he mean that he believed she had been willing to be kissed but had become alarmed when he had shown signs of being carried away?

But the theory that Baker gave way to an 'irresistible impulse' will not hold water. He was a highly disciplined soldier and discipline means the ability to resist 'impulses'. Yet this in itself suggests another explanation. Baker was a close friend of the Prince of Wales who spent much of his time bedding attractive women. So it is easy to understand that Baker may have regarded Rebecca Dickinson as a challenge, the natural prey of a dashing cavalry officer. But when he asked her if he might see her again, he was promptly rebuffed. For a man who is accustomed to giving orders and having them obeyed – and probably dominating his own wife and daughters with the natural authority of a sultan – this must have seemed an intolerable humiliation. He might have withdrawn stiffly into his shell and passed the rest of the journey to London in sulky silence. But he was not that kind of a man; he was used to pressing on in the face of odds. He asked her name and again was rebuffed. The distinguished soldier, the friend of royalty, was being snubbed by a mere 'chit of a girl'. By this time he was probably burning with humiliation – and with the feeling that perhaps, after all, he was making a fool of himself. The author of a book on cavalry tactics had mistimed his charge. If he drew back now, he would remember this for the rest of his life with a shock of outraged vanity. The soldier had to act. He stood up and closed the window . . .

BEECHER, HENRY WARD

THE PREACHER AND THE ADORING DISCIPLES

Beecher was one of the most celebrated preachers of the nineteenth century. He was almost ruined by a scandal in which he was accused of adultery with one of his flock.

Henry Ward was born in Litchfield, Connecticut, USA in June 1813, the eighth of thirteen children of the Reverend Lyman Beecher. He had been a shy child with a stammer and his scholastic performance had been abysmal until he went to Amherst College at the age of seventeen. At 24 he became minister to a small congregation at Lawrenceburg, Indiana, and began to develop his preaching talent. He was fundamentally an actor: he preferred to stand or sit on a platform rather than in a pulpit and told anecdotes with a wealth of gesture and facial expression that made his audience feel they were in a theatre. On one occasion, he mimed catching a fish so perfectly that a man in the front row jumped up crying, 'By God, he's got him!' Physically speaking, Beecher was not unusually attractive, with a round face, thick lips, a fleshy nose and shoulder-length hair. But his congregation found him magnetic and women adored him. A book of his called *Seven Lectures to Young Men* appeared in 1844 and became something of a bestseller. Yet for many years he was regarded simply as one of the preacher-sons of the far more famous Lyman Beecher. In 1847, he was persuaded to move east by Henry C. Bowen, a Brooklyn businessman, whose young wife was an admirer of Beecher. Within three years, his sermons were attracting audiences of more than 2,000, and he had the largest congregation in America.

As he grew older, Beecher gradually changed his stance from that of a narrow, hell-fire revivalist preacher to a liberal who advocated women's rights and Darwinian evolutionism, and opposed slavery. In 1861, Bowen made Beecher the editor of his newspaper *The Independent*. A young man named Theodore Tilton, who passionately admired Beecher, had been given the job of managing editor, largely due to Beecher's insistence. In 1855, Beecher had married Theodore Tilton to a pretty, dark-eyed young woman named Elizabeth Richards who, like her husband, regarded Beecher with adoration. *The Independent* became one of America's most widely read newspapers, largely due to Beecher's regular contribution, 'The Star Papers'. It was partly through the influence of Theodore Tilton that Beecher preached liberal doctrines.

In 1862, the attractive and popular Lucy Bowen died at the age of 38; she had borne ten children. On her death bed she beckoned her husband to move closer and whispered into his ear a confession that stunned him. She had been committing adultery with Henry Ward Beecher. Henry Bowen was in a difficult position. He was convulsed by jealousy and resentment: the man he had brought from Indiana and made editor of his newspaper had been his wife's lover. Beecher's column ceased to appear in *The Independent* and not long after Beecher himself left for England to preach the doctrines of anti-slavery. It was many years before he and Bowen renewed their friendship. When Beecher returned from England, Tilton insisted that he should become a regular visitor at his house; he wanted to share his friend with his wife. If anyone had told him that this would one day involve sharing his wife with his friend, he would have been furiously indignant; no one believed more deeply than Tilton in Beecher's total honesty and integrity.

Theodore Tilton, like Henry Ward Beecher, had started life as a highly orthodox young man who would 'rather have had my right hand cut off than have written a letter on the Sabbath.' Yet when he had met the seventeen-year-old Elizabeth Richards – known to all as Libby – their passion had been so intense that they consummated their love before Beecher joined them in wedlock. Ten years after their marriage, Tilton began to experience 'doubts' – about Christ's divinity, the absolute authority of the Bible, and other such weighty matters. Libby was horrified and Beecher had to comfort and soothe her. While her husband was away lecturing, Libby wrote him long letters in which she spoke freely of her love for Beecher. Neither she nor her husband experienced any misgivings; both believed implicitly that the highest form of love is wholly spiritual, and that such love casts out carnal desire. So Libby went on playing with fire, assuring herself that she was part of a 'blessed trinity' rather than an eternal triangle. In 1867, Beecher signed a contract to write a novel for which he was to receive the record sum of $24,000. (His sister was Harriet Beecher Stowe, author of *Uncle Tom's Cabin*.) He would bring the novel – *Norwood* – to Libby's house to ask her advice.

In August 1868, the Tiltons' baby son, Paul, died of cholera. Soon afterwards, Theodore Tilton set out on another of his lecture trips. On 9 October Libby went to hear Beecher deliver a speech at the Brooklyn Academy of Music and was overwhelmed with admiration. On the following day, Libby called on him at his home. That afternoon the inevitable happened: Libby became his mistress. It seems to have been Beecher who took the lead, since she later explained that she had 'yielded to him' in gratitude for the sympathy he gave her on the death of her child. Beecher had apparently assured her that their love was divine and that having sexual intercourse was its proper and valid expression, like a handshake or a kiss. He insisted that she should guard their secret – he called it 'nest hiding', borrowing the terminology from bird-watching. Not long after this, Beecher called on Libby at her home at 174 Livingston Street in Brooklyn, and once again they made love. After that, they made love on a number of occasions, at their respective homes, and in 'various other places'.

But the delicate, romantic Libby was not made for adultery. It began to prey on her mind. Beecher enjoyed sex much more than she did and wanted to make love every time they were alone. He obviously enjoyed it so much that Libby began to wonder whether it could be true that their relationship was blessed by God. In the summer of 1870, Libby went to pass the hot months – as was her custom – at Schoharie, New York. But on 3 July, tormented by conscience, she returned to Brooklyn and confessed everything to her husband.

Tilton was deeply shaken. His initial reaction, understandably, was to denounce the 'whited sepulchre', but his wife had preceded her confession with the demand that he would not harm the person implicated. His mind was still in confusion the next day when he went to his office. He admitted later that his chief desire was to find some excuse for his wife. He decided that '. . . she sinned as one in a trance. I don't think she was a free agent. I think she would have done his bidding if, like the heathen-priest in the Hindoo-land, he had bade her fling her child into the Ganges . . .' In this he showed a great deal of insight – there can be no doubt that Lib Tilton regarded herself as Beecher's slave, to do with as he would. Tilton then decided that he would not denounce Beecher, but that his punishment would be that Lib herself would go and tell him that she had confessed to her husband. Having decided 'in my secret self to be a conqueror', Tilton exerienced a kind of ecstasy; for the next two weeks, 'I walked the streets as if I scarcely touched the ground.' Then human nature asserted itself. He had to tell somebody. One evening three prominent figures in the feminist movement came to the house and Tilton unburdened himself about the 'lecherous scoundrel who has defiled my bed'. When he came back from seeing two of the ladies home, the third – a woman named Sue Anthony – had to interpose herself between Tilton and his wife as he railed at her. She was later to allege that Libby Tilton then confessed in detail to her adultery with Beecher.

Libby then made the immense mistake of telling her mother – a psychotic and an impossible lady named Mrs Nathan B. Morse – about her affair. Mrs Morse had separated from her second husband after trying to strangle him to death. She hated Tilton and adored Beecher. Now she glimpsed the marvellous possibility that Libby might divorce Tilton and marry Beecher; she set about promoting this end by gossiping all over Brooklyn about the scandal, writing abusive letters to her son-in-law, and insinuating letters to Beecher that began 'My dear son . . .'

On Christmas Eve that year, Lib Tilton suffered a miscarriage; she later referred to it as 'a love babe' and there seems no doubt that she believed the child to be Beecher's. She was in a state of agonized misery. Her husband hardly ever spoke to her – he spent much of his time at the house of a friend called Frank Moulton, who became his confidant – and on one occasion, she went to the graveyard and lay down on the grave of her two dead children until a keeper made her move on.

Mrs Morse's gossip finally reached the ears of Henry Bowen, the other man Beecher had cuckolded. He immediately saw it as a marvellous opportunity to get his own back on Beecher without compromising the reputation of his dead wife (he had now remarried). Bowen asked Tilton to go and see him and then proceeded to accuse Beecher of being an inveterate seducer. According to Bowen, Beecher was even a rapist – he had thrown down a well-known authoress on the sofa and taken her by force. The story of Beecher's seduction of the former Mrs Bowen was repeated. Finally, Tilton was persuaded to write a letter to Beecher, ordering him to renounce his ministry and quit Brooklyn 'for reasons he well understood'. Bowen promised to deliver this. But Bowen was playing a double game. He was too much of a coward to want to confront Beecher openly. What he wanted to do was to pretend he was the friend of both parties, while setting them at one another's throats. He went to Beecher, gave him the letter, then assured him that he was on his side and that Tilton was himself a seducer of many women. (This seems to be true – Tilton apparently admitted to one of Bowen's employees, Oliver Johnson, that he had even slept with one of his mistresses in his own home.) Meanwhile, Tilton decided to use Frank Moulton as a go-between; he made his wife write a confession of her adultery, then sent Moulton to tell Beecher about it. This was the first Beecher knew about Libby's confession of adultery.

Beecher now went to see Libby, who was still in bed after her miscarriage. And he succeeded in persuading her to write a letter in which she declared that her confession had been untrue, wrung out of her by her husband's jealousy. There followed more to-ing and fro-ing between the various parties which ended finally in an uneasy truce between Beecher and the wronged husband. Beecher heaved a sigh of relief; it looked as if his sins would not find him out after all.

But he had reckoned without an extraordinary lady named Victoria Woodhull, an ardent 'women's libber' of the period, who became known as 'Mrs Satan' because she preached the doctrine of 'free love'. Victoria Woodhull was, in her way, as remarkable a character as Beecher himself. She was the daughter of a riverboat gambler and maidservant, and as a child she discovered she was psychic. She became a clairvoyant and spirit medium. At fifteen she married an alcoholic doctor named Woodhull, to whom she bore a child. She divorced him when she met a spiritualist named Colonel Blood but allowed Woodhull to continue living in the household. Then she made her greatest conquest; she and her equally remarkable sister Tennessee Claflin persuaded one of America's richest men, old Commodore Vanderbilt, that they could heal his various ailments with 'magnetism'. Vanderbilt fell in love with Tennessee (or Tennie C, as Victoria's younger sister preferred to spell it). He set them up in a brokerage business and financed a magazine called *Woodhull and Claflin's Weekly*, in which Victoria preached her doctrines of free love, attacked the rich (though not, of course, Vanderbilt) and espoused Marxism.

On 22 May 1871, Victoria published in the *World* a letter in which she praised free love 'in its highest, purest sense as the only cure for immorality', and stated that people who attacked her were hypocrites. 'I know of one man, a public teacher of eminence, who lives in concubinage with the wife of another public teacher.' And she sent Theodore Tilton a message asking him to come and see her. Tilton had by now been sacked by Bowen, but with the help of Beecher, had started another magazine called *The Golden Age*. He was curious to see the notorious 'free lover' and hurried round to her office. He found her to be a highly attractive woman in her early thirties who seemed far less formidable than he expected – even when she showed him her letter in the newspaper. Soon he and Victoria became good friends – in fact, Victoria was later to declare that they became lovers. Tilton no doubt told himself that he was only trying to prevent a scandal by keeping Victoria friendly. Victoria Woodhull also met Beecher and admitted that she found him a magnetic and attractive personality. But when Beecher declined to introduce Victoria at a suffragette meeting (where he knew she was going to preach free love), Tilton stepped into the gap. It did his reputation no good at all to be publicly associated with 'Mrs Satan' and her scandalous doctrines. Unfortunately, Victoria was so carried away by her new popularity with the women's movement (which had formerly regarded her as a crank) that she allowed herself to denounce her former protector Commodore Vanderbilt as a capitalist; he promptly dropped her. In May 1872, Victoria announced that she was standing as the first woman president of the United States, with a Negro reform leader as her running mate. She was infuriated when Tilton declined to support her cause and instead declared his support for Horace Greeley. (Because of the bad reputation he was acquiring, Tilton's support did Greeley no good at all.) Victoria Woodhull became increasingly angry and embittered. And finally she did what Beecher had always feared she would do: she told the whole story of his affair with Libby Tilton and the subsequent 'cover-up', in her magazine. The result was as sensational as she had hoped. The magazine sold 100,000 copies and could have sold many times that number – copies began to change hands for as much as $40. A young man named Anthony Comstock, the vice warden for the Young Men's Christian Association, saw the story, was outraged at this smear on the saintly Henry Ward Beecher, and was responsible for the arrest of the Claflin sisters for sending indecent material through the United States mails. Victoria and Tennessee went to jail. But the damage was done. The whole country was now gossiping about the Beecher-Tilton scandal. Six months later, when Victoria and her sister were acquitted (on the grounds that their accusations did not constitute pornography), everyone in the country wanted to know whether Tilton was a cuckold and Beecher was a seducer.

Beecher's own congregation increased his problems by insisting on expelling Tilton from the church. If, as Beecher insisted, he was innocent of adultery, then Tilton was a wicked traducer. Tilton, who had so far been more or less on Beecher's side (at least in wanting to suppress the scandal) now began to smoulder with resentment. This was not assuaged when Beecher decided to air the scandal by holding a 'trial' in his own church and Libby was persuaded to leave her husband and take Beecher's side. The church committee, predictably, decided that Beecher was not guilty. Tilton was branded as a liar. On 24 August 1874, Tilton swore out a complaint against Beecher, charging him with having wilfully alienated his wife's affections.

The Beecher-Tilton trial began on 11 January 1875, and lasted until 12 July. The whole nation was agog. Beecher spent much of his time in court; so did his sour-faced wife Eunice (known locally as 'the Griffin'). Beecher took the line that he had never, at any time, sinned with Libby Tilton, but that he fully acknowledged his guilt in having allowed her to idolize him to the exclusion of her husband – this, he claimed, was the meaning of some of the letters he had written admitting his guilt.

During those six months, the American public had more than its fill of scandal. It learned that Beecher was accused of seducing Lucy Bowen as well as Lib Tilton. One newspaper cartoon showed a Brooklyn businessman locking his wife in a huge safe with a notice on the door Proof Against Fire And Clergymen, while another showed a hatter who sold the 'new style of Brooklyn hat' – with horns on it. The public also learned that the wronged husband was not entirely innocent. He was alleged to have seduced the seventeen-year-old daughter of a congressman named Lovejoy in Winsted, Connecticut, and to have made an unsuccessful attempt to seduce a young girl who formed part of his household; this girl, Elizabeth Turner, told how Tilton had laid on her bed, kissed her, and put his hand 'down her neck' (i.e. on her breast). On another occasion he had come into her bedroom when she was fast asleep and carried her out; if he had failed to seduce her, it was plainly not for want of trying. The story of Tilton's 'affair' with Victoria Woodhull was also raked up. On the other hand, various servants testified to having seen Beecher in situations of intimacy with Libby Tilton; even her own brother reluctantly admitted that he had walked into the room and seen Beecher and Libby separating with obvious embarrassment. Libby herself, like Beecher, denied any misconduct.

The jury was out for eight days; it was unable to reach a unanimous verdict but voted nine to three against Tilton. Beecher's supporters regarded this as a triumph and he left the court like a conquering hero. His trials were not quite over, however. Frank Moulton sued Beecher for malicious prosecution but the suit was dismissed. Then Henry Bowen demanded that the Plymouth Church Committee should try Beecher for adultery with Lucy Bowen. The Committee disbelieved him and Bowen, like the Moultons, was expelled from the church. Beecher made a lecture tour of the country and although he was booed in many places, he never failed to draw enormous crowds. When he died, thirteen years later (in 1887) his popularity with his own congregation was as great as ever.

Theodore Tilton also continued to lecture but his fortunes declined. He left the country in 1883, to settle finally in Paris, where he wrote novels and romantic poetry, and spent his days in a café playing chess. Libby, deserted by her husband and her lover, became a schoolteacher; she remains the most pathetic figure in the case. The Woodhull sisters both married rich men, and Victoria died in 1927, at the age of 89.

In retrospect, it is difficult not to agree with the reporter who wrote: 'Mankind fell in Adam and has been falling ever since, but never touched bottom until it got to Henry Ward Beecher.'

BYRON, LORD

'MAD, BAD AND DANGEROUS TO KNOW'

Not long after the death of Lord Byron in Greece in April 1824, two of his closest friends – Tom Moore and John Cam Hobhouse – met at the office of his publisher John Murray to decide what ought to be done with the poet's memoirs. The vote went against Moore, who wanted to preserve them, and they were consigned to the office fire.

What was in them that shocked Murray and Hobhouse so much? It may have been the admission that he had slept with at least two hundred whores, or that he had committed incest with his half-sister and fathered her child, or that he had sodomized his wife, or simply that he found boys as sexually enjoyable as girls. But although the memoirs are lost to us, the researches of biographers have uncovered most of Byron's scandalous secrets.

Byron's father, 'Mad Jack', was a notorious rake and gambler; he ran away with a married woman, the Marchioness of Carmarthen, who died six years later after presenting him with three children, two of whom died young. Then 'Mad Jack' married a plump and plain Scottish heiress, Catherine Gordon, who (like the Marchioness) was at first able to keep him in the style to which he was accustomed. But he soon spent her £23,000. On 28 January, 1788, the poet George Gordon, Lord Byron, was born. 'Mad Jack' deserted his wife soon after and died in France three years later, possibly by committing suicide.

The boy's childhood was miserable; he had a deformed right foot and his schoolfriends made fun of his limp. The attempts of various doctors to 'cure' it caused him a great deal of agony but made no difference whatever. Even his mother sometimes jeered at him as a 'lame brat' – she seems to have been subject to violent changes of mood, which laid the foundation of his lifelong mistrust of women. He took refuge from reality in books, preferring history and stories of the Mediterranean. When he was nine he had his first sexual experience with a young servant girl named Mary Gray. She seems to have been a nymphomaniac: when she was not introducing the shy boy to the delights of nakedness, she was giving herself to a succession of lovers, often with Byron looking on. It seems doubtful that he lost his virginity with her but she made him aware that he was attractive to women. Mary threatened him with hellfire if he told anyone their secret – as his biographer Frederic Raphael remarks: 'Cant and cunt revealed their proximity very early in Byron's life.'

Byron became next in line for the title when he was six and his cousin was killed in battle. He inherited on the death of his grandfather, when he was ten, and he and his mother moved to the decrepit and gloomy Newstead Abbey, near Nottingham, a picturesque ruin that was the ideal setting for a romantic poet. For the next four years he attended Harrow School and was probably introduced to homosexuality. He was in love with his cousin Mary Parker, and also with a neighbour, Mary Chaworth – but this feeling turned to hatred when he heard Mary Chaworth ask her maid, 'What, do you think I could feel anything for that lame boy?' His mother meanwhile had been forced to rent Newstead to a certain Lord Grey de Ruthyn, a 23-year-old rake who pursued Byron's mother and even made homosexual advances to Byron himself when he was home during the holidays. (Byron fled in terror – his own homosexual inclinations were always directed towards those younger than himself.)

Byron's real sexual initiation began when he went to Cambridge in 1805, where he began to frequent prostitutes with such vigour that even a French procuress had to advise him to season ardour with delicacy (i.e. be less rough). He had also renewed his acquaintance with his half-sister Augusta, who had married a Colonel George Leigh and had a fine house near Cambridge. Byron fell in love with a choirboy named Edleston, whom he saved from drowning, but he later insisted that his friendship was 'pure' – a clear hint that others of the same type were not. He began to put on weight; he had always been inclined to fleshiness, and soon weighed sixteen stones. For a man of his vanity this was intolerable and he starved himself and played cricket wearing half a dozen waistcoats to induce perspiration.

At this time he published his earliest poems but they were reviewed so unfavourably that he thought for a while of killing himself. However, instead he wrote a satire in the manner of Pope called *English Bards and Scotch Reviewers*, which gave him a certain reputation. Before leaving Cambridge, Byron had acquired his first mistress, a girl called Caroline, whom he liked to dress in boy's clothes and pass off as a male.

At the age of 21, he went off on his first tour of the Mediterranean with his friend Hobhouse, who was planning a book called *Sodomy Simplified, or Pederasty Proved to be Praiseworthy*. They visited Greece, Albania, Turkey and Spain, and when Hobhouse left him alone in Greece, Byron took the opportunity to enjoy a sentimental and impure friendship with a boy name Nicolo, who was fifteen. He also spent a great deal of money on prostitutes. One day his curiosity was aroused by a cart containing a sack that was wriggling; he bribed the driver to open it and found that it was a woman who had been condemned to be thrown into the sea for infidelity to her husband. Byron is said to have recognized her as one of the women he had slept with. He succeeded in smuggling her out of harm's way.

Back in England in 1812, Byron was deeply moved by the death of his mother. He later made his maiden speech in the House of Lords, supporting the Nottingham weavers who had smashed the mechanical frames that were putting them out of work. A few weeks later, John Murray published the poem that Byron had written during his period abroad: *Childe Harold's Pilgrimage*. This gloomy and romantic piece of work, about a young man who has tasted every forbidden pleasure in his early twenties and finds life an intolerable bore, made him famous overnight. Suddenly, Byron was the social success of the season. Young girls regarded him with adoration; young men imitated his brooding silence, his melancholy frowns, even his limp.

One of the women who learned *Childe Harold* by heart was a beautiful and wilful young married woman named Lady Caroline Lamb, the wife of the politician William Lamb (later Lord Melbourne). She declared in her journal that Byron was 'mad, bad and dangerous to know', and added: 'That beautiful pale face is my fate.' Soon, Byron was a regular visitor at Melbourne House and the two became lovers. But his attitude towards her remained detached and ironical, and he greatly preferred her mother-in-law, Lady Melbourne, who became a close friend. Byron's indifference drove Lady Caroline to desperation; on one occasion, she disguised herself as a page boy and hid in Byron's carriage. Such exploits amused him but he grew increasingly tired of her waywardness and of a certain lack of prudishness – on one occasion she sent him some of her pubic hairs as a keepsake. When – with the help of Lady Melbourne – he broke off the affair, she burned his image in effigy. Byron fled to Cambridge and his half-sister Augusta, whose husband was away hunting. No doubt seduced by the idea of incest as much as by Augusta's attractions, Byron began an affair with her. He had also allowed himself to be seduced by the promiscuous Lady Oxford, whose children were known as the Harleian Miscellany because of their doubtful paternity (her husband's family name was Harley). After an abortive affair with the wife of a friend – whom he decided to spare at the last moment – he and Augusta went to Newstead and she became pregnant. By way of flaunting his triumph, he inserted the incest theme into his latest novel in verse, *The Bride of Abydos*.

Byron, having been the darling of London Society, was now its chief source of malicious gossip. Caroline Lamb was still pursuing him and the affair with Augusta had become known largely through the lack of discretion of both parties. He decided that it was time to silence the gossip by marrying. Lady Melbourne's niece, an heiress named Annabella Milbanke, had already turned him down once, wounding his vanity; she was prim, serious-minded and demure. Rather to Byron's dismay, she accepted him the second time he proposed.

A character as spoiled and undisciplined as Byron was bound to be thrown into torments and ambivalence by marriage. In the carriage, on the way to their honeymoon (or 'treacle-moon', as Byron preferred to call it) he set out to make her miserable by assuring her that he was bound to hate anyone he married. But their first sexual experiment – on a settee before dinner – seems to have been successful. Anabella was totally inexperienced – it seems probable that she had never even been instructed in what lovers do in bed – and the evidence indicates that she came to accept sodomy as a perfectly normal variant of sexual intercourse. At first, Byron seems to have found marriage unexpectedly pleasant. But his natural gloom and self-pity, his determination to be unconventional, his obscure conviction that he was somehow 'accursed', made his temper uncertain. He flirted openly with his half-sister and was frequently drunk. And Annabella's demure virtue irritated him. Soon she was pregnant and that must have increased his feeling of being trapped. They moved to London although this was an extravagance they could not afford and the bailiffs became frequent visitors. His attempts to keep his weight within normal limits increased his irritability; sexual abstention may also have played its part – although later gossip stated that he continued to sodomize his wife until late into her pregnancy. The birth of a daughter was a disappointment; Byron had wanted an heir. Exhausted by a laborious birth and by quarrels with her husband, Annabella decided to go home to mother to recuperate. The separation was probably not intended to be permanent – certainly not as far as she was concerned. The deciding factor was probably her admission to her mother that Byron enjoyed anal intercourse. Sir Ralph and Lady Milbanke were undoubtedly what would now be called 'squares', and once Annabella had admitted to an act of 'criminal perversion' with a man who was reputed to be his sister's lover, nothing would have induced them to allow her to return to him. (In fact, Byron made some attempts at reconciliation.)

It is still not clear why the end of Byron's marriage caused him to become suddenly the most vilified man in London – Regency London was not the most virtuous place in the world. The answer is probably a combination of rumour – about incest, sodomy and so on – and envy. The desire to see idols hurled violently from their pedestals is strong in all human beings. Byron had been one of the most successful literary men of all times; poems like *The Corsair, The Bride of Abydos, The Giaour*, were the nineteenth-century equivalent of bestsellers. He had a reputation as a seducer of other men's wives. He was too successful. So London hostesses decided that it was time the wicked Lord was ostracized. If Byron had remained in England and ignored the disapproval, his next successful poem would probably have made society change its mind. But he was too moody and self-centred to endure the least suspicion of a snub. If society despised him, he would show that he despised society. He ordered an elaborate coach, costing £500, had one last fling with a young girl called Claire Clairmont, the stepdaughter of the social philosopher William Godwin (whose daughter Mary was about to run away with another poet, Shelley), and in April 1816 left England for the last time. The casual one-night stand with Claire eventually resulted in the birth of a daughter.

Claire reappeared in Switzerland, together with Shelley and Mary. When Shelley mildly reproached Byron for seducing Claire, Byron replied that no one had been more carried off than 'poor dear me' – he had been ravished more often than anyone since the Trojan War. He really believed this.

In Venice, Byron took lodgings in the house of a draper and quickly seduced his wife Marianna, whose appetite was so strong that Byron had to make love three times a day. Then he met a pretty 22-year-old peasant, Margarita Cogni, when he was out riding, and had soon persuaded her into his bed. In January 1818 he was asked to escort a young married woman – recently out of a convent – Teresa Guiccioli, to an art exhibition; she also became his mistress. The sale of Newstead (for £94,500) enabled him once more to live in the style he enjoyed and he rented a palazzo and moved Margarita in. Then, in the words of Frederic Raphael, 'he embarked on an orgy to challenge even the Venetian capacity to remain unshocked'. The Palazzo Mocigeno became virtually a brothel. When Margarita began to learn to read so that she could keep track of his amours through his letters, he decided to get rid of her. She threatened him with a knife and stabbed his hand, then threw herself into the canal. After that, Byron firmly put her out-of-doors and she returned to her husband.

Teresa, the girl he had taken to the art exhibition, was Byron's last great affair. Even in his early thirties, he was growing fat and his hair was receding fast; he began to feel the need for a more relaxed and domesticated existence. Teresa was nineteen, her husband, Count Alessandro Guiccioli, 58. The Count was reputed to be a dangerous man who had poisoned his first wife and murdered the novelist Manzoni. But it was tacitly understood that when a teenager from a convent marries a man nearly forty years her senior, he cannot expect permanent fidelity; in fact, one lover – or *cavaliere servente* – was thoroughly respectable. When, at one point, her husband protested about Byron, she replied indignantly: 'It is hard that I should be the only woman in Romagna who is not to have her *amico*.' The problem was that Teresa was nearly as indiscreet as Caroline Lamb and Byron was tactless enough to get mixed up in Italian politics. Eventually, the Count and Countessa separated; Byron found, to his disgust, that he was expected to be a substitute husband rather than an *amico*. She even ordered him to cease working on *Don Juan* which she detested. But he was getting older and no longer so disposed to revolt against anything that looked like conventionality. A flash of the old Byron appeared when he told Hobhouse apropos Teresa, 'Cain was right to kill Abel, that he might not have the bore of passing two hundred years with him.' The death of his daughter (with Claire Clairmont) Allegra – from fever – and the death of Shelley by drowning made Byron feel that he needed a change from Italy. And so, with the accompaniment of noisy tears from Teresa, he set off for Greece where, instead of fighting for freedom, as he had intended, he succumbed to a combination of boredom, non-stop rain and fever, and died in his 37th year.

CAMPBELL, MARGARET

THE DUCHESS OF ARGYLL AND THE HEADLESS MAN

Today divorce is rarely a subject for full-blown scandal – something that happens to 40 per cent of British marriages is no longer salacious, but merely painful and sad. This was not the case in Britain in the early 1960s. Although much more rare, divorce cases were a major source of stories for the lowbrow scandal sheets and the respectable press alike. Although nowhere near as intrusive (and arguably hypocritical) as the modern day press, newspapers in the 60s loved a good, messy celebrity divorce.

The break up of the marriage of the Duke and Duchess of Argyll in 1962, however, went beyond anything seen in Britain hitherto, and possibly marked the beginning of the steep decline of the British population's reverence and even respect for their hereditary aristocracy.

Margaret, the future Duchess of Argyll, was not a born aristocrat. Her father, George Hay Whigham, was a millionaire – largely through legally defrauding the Swiss inventors of Celanese (a precursor to nylon) of their rights to the invention – but the money could not, even in the early twentieth century, raise him to mix in the highest levels of British society. He was a civil engineer, and thus would have been seen as 'trade' – a term that covered anybody in the 'lower orders' and which implied that someone who worked for a living was both socially and morally inferior to those who lived on money inherited from their ancient, preferably titled, families.

Of course, such social bigotry did not extend to young Margaret, who was born in 1912. She *had* inherited her money (if only from one previous generation) and had no reason or intention of doing a day's work in her life. Moreover, how could the old aristocratic families stay rich if they banned their sons from marrying the daughters of the *nouveau riche*?

An only child, Margaret was both doted upon and starved of affection by her parents. Her mother, Helen, was a vain and selfish woman who found mothering a tiresome chore, and so left as much as she could to the servants. George Whigham, on the other hand, adored his daughter and treated her like a little princess. Unfortunately he was away from home much of the time, so his liberal affection only served to highlight how empty of love the rest of Margaret's life was.

Margaret grew up just as selfish and spoiled as her mother and, from her own admission, lost much of her ability to empathize with others – as often happens in cases of children who have been denied sufficient affection. She later commented that, aside from her father, the only things she truly cared about as a child were her numerous toys.

Fortunately, this bad start did not hold Margaret back socially. Despite having been thrown out of several of the better schools for young ladies and suffering from a nervous stutter that would be with her all her life, in 1930, at the age of eighteen, Margaret was hailed as 'débutante of the season' by several national British newspapers.

Now just another of the ceremonies of empire that faded away in the late twentieth century, the 'coming out balls' held for débutantes were once among the main events of the year for upper class British families. 'Debs', as they were often known, were aristocratic or very well-off girls of around eighteen who were formally introduced ('presented') to the reigning monarch. They were then presented to the rest of society at a coming-out ball – the 'coming out' being meant to imply that their families now regarded them of a suitable age to marry. The censorious often characterized such events as dolled-up cattle markets, where bachelors (and their mothers) eyed the girls like animals at an auction.

It was customary for the British press to treat each season's débutantes as budding film stars, since coming-out balls were the staple fare of the widely read 'society columns', but Margaret Whigham was treated to an unprecedented fanfare of publicity. This may have been because as well as being fashionably attractive – slim, dark haired and seductive being the in look for the early 1930s – Margaret's father threw a fantastically opulent coming-out ball for his beloved daughter. However, jealous voices were also heard to whisper that George Whigham had hired a publicity agent to get Margaret top billing – an unheard of act of bourgeois crassness that, if proved true, could have branded the whole family as underbred social climbers.

Fortunately Margaret had already developed the thick-skinned attitude to criticism that would serve her all her life. With her fine features and cut-glass accent, she was soon one of the most sought-after girls in London – both for parties and matrimony.

Sadly, her first marriage prospect ended tragically. Thirty-five-year-old Commander Glen Kidson was a famous sportsman and aviator. After meeting Margaret at several social gatherings in 1931, and showing no signs of being especially interested in her, he wrote to her from Africa, swearing passionate love and asking for her hand in marriage (as soon as he had divorced his present wife). He then, hours after breaking the record for flying solo from London to Cape Town, got himself killed on a sightseeing flight over Table Mountain.

Margaret then had a grim month in which daily letters from Kidson arrived via the painfully slow sea mail, outlining the dead man's rose-tinted plans for their marriage and future together.

The next proposal that Margaret considered seriously came from Max Aitken, son of the newspaper tycoon, Lord Beaverbrook. But she broke off this engagement a few months later to announce her engagement to Fulke Warwick, the Earl of Warwick.

Bizarrely, before the wedding could be planned, Lady Marjorie, Warwick's mother, called on Margaret's mother and told her: 'If you love your daughter, don't let her marry my son. He's a liar, he's ill-mannered, and he picks his nose.'

This startlingly un-motherly revelation moved Margaret's parents to pressure her until she called off the engagement. Fulke Warwick then went to America where he was paid a fortune to act in Hollywood movies.

After this run of bad luck, Margaret eventually married Charles Sweeny, a young American investment banker. Although he was hardly as romantic (or titled) a figure as her earlier matches, the press covered Margaret's wedding, in February 1933, as if she were a member of the royal family – she was still the darling of a public that, in the harsh Great Depression years, wanted to daydream about the rich and beautiful.

Margaret had to convert to Catholicism to marry Charlie Sweeny but, in her typically arbitrary style, she first argued terms with the Church. She later told her biographer, Charles Castle: 'I told [them] that I wouldn't recognize the infallibility of the Pope . . . and I wouldn't pray to a saint . . . If I'm ever going to say a prayer, it's going to be to the Head Man. They accepted me on those two conditions because they seemed anxious to get the publicity.'

It was at about this time that Ian Campbell – the future Duke of Argyll and the man she would one day divorce so acrimoniously – saw Margaret in the flesh for the first time. She was walking down the famous staircase of the Café de Paris, and her beauty struck him so forcefully that he leaned across to his dinner companion to say: 'That's the girl I'm going to marry some day.'

This would have been a rather romantic anecdote, if Campbell's companion had not been his wife, Janet. The Campbells, perhaps unsurprisingly, divorced shortly thereafter.

Margaret's marriage to Charlie Sweeny lasted rather longer and the couple continued to be the toast of high society on both sides of the Atlantic. Cole Porter even immortalized Margaret in his famous song 'You're the Tops':

You're the nimble tread of the Feet of Fred Astaire,
You're Mussolini,
You're Mrs Sweeny,
You're Camembert . . .

By the end of World War II, however, the Sweeny marriage was on the rocks. Perhaps surprisingly, considering her later track record, little of the blame for the marital break up seems to have come home to Margaret. There is no evidence that she was ever unfaithful to Charlie, and she had put herself through a heart-breaking time trying to provide him with children. She had a number of miscarriages before finally managing to produce a son and a daughter, Brian and Frances.

Charlie Sweeny, on the other hand, certainly did have affairs and showed little loyalty to his wife in times of trouble. When she contracted a liver infection and double pneumonia during one of her unsuccessful pregnancies, Charlie stayed by her bedside only as long as it looked likely that she was going to die. As soon as the doctors announced that she was over the worst of it and was likely to survive, Charlie immediately went out to his club for dinner and then popped in to visit her infrequently throughout the rest of her convalescence. He apparently regarded himself as still a bachelor in all but name.

When Charlie agreed to a divorce in 1946, Margaret not only felt freed of an unhappy marriage, but also felt herself to be a more worldly wise woman. From then onward she decided to do precisely what she pleased, especially when it came to making up for lost opportunities. Undoubtedly she felt she had been a fool for not indulging herself during her years of marriage, and this was a mistake she was not going to make a second time.

As an attractive and independently wealthy woman, there was little reason for Margaret to marry again. She could travel the world, live in luxury and take as many lovers as she liked, provided she was reasonably discreet. However, there was still one thing she wanted that all her father's money could not buy – something that could only be obtained by either a lifetime of public service (a route she had never been inclined to take) or by marriage: Margaret wanted a title.

She met Ian Campbell – the man who had declared his intention to marry Margaret in front of his wife – on the Paris–London boat train in 1947. Captured by the Germans in France in 1940, Campbell had spent five years in a prisoner-of-war camp, and his sex drive had been enhanced by abstinence. He had remarried after his first divorce and had two children from the marriage, but felt no hesitation in seducing Margeret – or allowing her to seduce him.

The affair might have gone no further than that, but Campbell fell head-over-heels in love with her and proposed marriage ... just as soon as he could get a divorce from Louise, his present wife. Any qualms Margaret might have felt were laid to rest by the fact that, although comparatively poor, Ian Campbell was the oldest male relative of the ageing Duke of Argyll.

The old duke died at the age of 77 in 1950, but it was not until a year later that Campbell, now the eleventh Duke of Argyll, managed to get a divorce from his wife Louise, and Margaret became a Duchess.

Unfortunately, as many have discovered, marriage can be a disastrous end to an illicit love affair. Margaret found that the man who had been such an energetic lover was now, by her standards, a very dull husband. Ian's years as a prisoner of war had developed a tendency to introversion and a desire for a quiet life. He preferred to spend most of his time on the Argyll Highland estate, living in the gloomy and mouldering Inveraray Castle.

Margaret, on the other hand, was a born townie, and felt starved of fun when she was in Scotland. It took only a year for the first signs of strain to show in the marriage.

On the day of the coronation of Queen Elizabeth II, the Argylls had duly attended the ceremony in Westminster Cathedral but, as divorcees, they were banned from the subsequent reception at Buckingham Palace. Instead they were invited to a party thrown by the wife of the French Ambassador. However, when the taxi in which they were travelling stopped at traffic lights near White's – the duke's London club – he suddenly clambered out of the vehicle and walked into the (males only) building, leaving his wife to attend the party unescorted.

During the first year of the marriage, the Argylls spent much of their time and energy – and a generous amount of Margaret's father's money – repairing and modernizing Inveraray Castle. After the coronation, however, the couple spent more and more time apart. The duke found little attraction in London – and when he was there he was generally found in White's – and Margaret reduced the number and length of her trips to the distant Argyll estate.

The former Margaret – the wife of Charlie Sweeny – would probably have found her estranged status upsetting; but the Duchess of Argyll was a changed woman, and saw no reason why she should be sex starved just because her stuffy husband chose to live in the middle of nowhere. Of course in the 1950s it was not unusual for an upper-class wife to be 'escorted' to functions and evenings out by a male friend, if her husband was away. Such arrangements were generally accepted, even if there was a suspicion that the escort was being overfriendly, provided everything was done with due discretion.

Margaret, however, was incapable of staying out of the limelight, both because of her continuing popularity in the society columns, and because she was as addicted to fame as any Hollywood starlet. Over the following years, her husband began to be thoroughly sick of reading about his wife and her 'escorts' in the newspapers and glossy magazines, but was not willing to solve the problem by moving to London and attending endless parties. So he kept his peace and got on with his own amusements.

The final straw came in 1954, three years into the marriage. Margaret had openly moved one of her young escorts into the mews cottage in the garden of her Upper Grosvenor Street home; short of having him living in the house with her, Margaret could not have advertised her infidelity more obviously.

The duke telephoned her and demanded that she get rid of the young man – she was not only humiliating him, he said, but she was dragging the Argyll family name through the dirt. Margaret replied – with her usual stammer: 'B-but surely I'm allowed to have . . . f-friends? How can you escort me when you're stuck up at that dreary hole in Scotland for most of the t-time?'

The duke probably wished he had kept silent when Margaret arrived at Inveraray with the Baron and Baroness von Braun in tow. The baron was the brother of the German rocket scientist, Werner von Braun, and was clearly one of Margaret's 'special' escorts. The duke had to stomach the humiliation of seeing the baron and the duchess disappear together for hours at a time, while he was forced to entertain the baroness with polite conversation.

It was probably at this time that the duke decided to divorce Margaret. The normal course of events would be for him to admit to adultery and allow Margaret to stake her claim as the injured party – it was unheard of for a man in the duke's position to publicly charge his wife with adultery, whatever the truth of the matter, since the Victorian notion of protecting women from public embarrassment was still alive and well among the British aristocracy. Ian, Duke of Argyll, however, had no intention of letting Margaret off scot-free – he kept his plans to himself and waited for her to give him the evidence he needed.

It was not until 1956, when the semi-estranged couple were on a tour of Campbell communities in Australia, that the duke accidentally came across Margaret's diary. It was a kind of desk diary – each page having sections for the same day over four consecutive years, thus allowing the owner to compare what they had been doing on the same date last year. Mixed in with harmless entries describing trains taken and cheques signed, the duke found the dates and times of meetings with over half a dozen men. Although not evidence of adultery in itself, the duke was certain that Margaret had been sleeping with at least two or three of these men.

The duchess walked in as her husband was reading the diary and demanded it back. Argyll handed it over and accused her of adultery. Margaret didn't deny the charge, insisting that she had every right to have affairs if her husband neglected her. From then on, the marriage was effectively over, and the duke was on a hunt to find conclusive proof of Margaret's infidelities.

This was made easier when Margaret decided to stay on in Australia after he returned to London, so he had the opportunity to let himself into her house and rummage through her belongings. In Margaret's bedroom he found more of her diaries, a number of private letters and, exactly what he wanted, a series of amateur pornographic photographs wrapped in a sheet of paper containing captions.

The first of the four pictures showed a naked man displaying a sizeable erection, but whose head and shoulders had been cut off by the edge of the picture. A naked woman – closely resembling Margaret, but with her face turned from the camera – appeared in the next picture, kneeling and holding the 'headless man's' penis in both hands while fellating him. In the third picture the man was lying on top of the woman, obscuring both faces from the camera, and clearly engaged in sexual intercourse. The last picture was much like the first, but with the man's erection obviously detumescing.

The captions, handwritten on the piece of wrapping paper, were: 'Before', 'During', 'Oh!' and 'Finished'.

Perhaps more sinister and certainly more disturbing, the duke also found a sheet of blank hotel writing paper on to which individual, handwritten words had been pasted to form a new letter. Even before he saw the cut out signature at the bottom, the duke recognized the handwriting – that of his ex-wife and mother of his two sons, Louise.

The words, he guessed, came from genuine letters from Louise. And he soon saw why Margaret had concocted the fake: it was a confession that the duke's sons were not his, but the result of adultery. If a poorly focused photograph of the letter was circulated, the allegation would certainly stick. Margaret was apparently faking evidence that might be used to disinherit the boys.

When she returned to London, Margaret found that her husband had taken the diaries, letters and photographs – along with all his own belongings that had been in her house; however, she was apparently unaware that he had taken the faked letter.

After a brief shopping trip to Paris, Margaret returned to London and showed the duke extracts that she claimed to have copied from letters she had been shown while in France. Again, these letters were supposed to have been written by Louise and, again, made damaging allegations about the paternity of the two boys; there were also disparaging comments about the duke himself.

Campbell decided to bide his time, and say nothing about the faked letter in his possession. Over the next few weeks, unaware that the duke knew exactly what she was up to, the duchess claimed that she had received several letters from an anonymous well-wisher, containing evidence that the heirs to the dukedom were the bastards of the previous duchess's lover. The duke decided that it was time to go to the police.

Why would Margaret choose to defame two innocent, teenage boys? The answer came out later when one of her friends, Diana Napier, admitted that Margaret had told her that she wanted her own son to inherit the dukedom.

Diana had asked incredulously what son Margaret was talking about. She had no children by Ian, Duke of Argyll – and certainly never would have. Margaret astounded her by replying: 'Darling, I want you to go to Venice at my expense. I would like you to use your Polish contacts to adopt a newborn child or get a newborn child over from Poland to Venice.'

According to Diana Napier, the duchess went on: 'I've padded my tummy with a cushion and put it about that I'm pregnant. I intend to go to Venice and bring back the Polish child as the duke's son.'

Apparently the Duchess of Argyll was unaware of the existence of blood tests to determine paternity – or maybe she had another madcap scheme to avoid such tests. With a 'son' who was heir to the dukedom, she might persuade the duke to change his mind. If not, she could maintain her place in the Argyll dynasty; if no longer a duchess, she wanted to be the 'mother' of the next duke.

Unsurprisingly, Diana Napier declined to be involved in the plot.

The previous duchess, Louise, was furious when she heard about the fake letters and, with the duke's co-operation, eventually forced Margaret to sign an agreement never to repeat the allegations; the duchess was also induced to pay £10,000 in damages, plus legal costs.

When the duke heard that Margaret had broken her part of the bargain by telling a friend, Air-Marshal William Thornton, that the boys were illegitimate, he sued and, in 1959, Margaret found herself on trial in a civil court. After hearing the evidence, the judge decided not to jail the Duchess of Argyll for contempt of court, but instead made a court order to the effect that if she repeated the offence, in private or public, she could be jailed without further ado.

While all this had been going on, Margaret's doting father, George Whigham, had been bankrolling his daughter's expensive lifestyle – to the extent of giving her 5 per cent of his capital every year. Then a new threat appeared. Margaret's mother had died in 1955. And in 1956, at the age of 76, George Whigham married a woman named Jane Brooke, 35 years his junior – in fact, a year younger than Margaret.

Whatever her feelings, the duchess had the sense not to show them. But her financial situation was becoming difficult. Following the expensive fiasco of the defamation case, Margaret found herself in increasing need of cash. Her father was no longer as wealthy as he had been and, in any case, Jane Whigham would inherit more than the duchess when the old man died.

George Whigham and Jane quarrelled in 1959 – possibly with the jealous Margaret acting as a catalyst – and the old man went to live with his daughter in London. The Whighams remained on fairly friendly terms, however, and apparently never thought of divorce.

In August 1959, Jane Whigham noticed that a pair of men were following her about. She took the number of their car and discovered that they were private detectives working for the Duchess of Argyll. Margaret of course denied everything and, when Jane asked Whigham to speak to his daughter, he refused to hear a word against her, becoming so irate that he blacked Jane's eye. The pair signed a legal separation a few months later, with Jane being given £20,000 and a house as alimony, with a promise of more to be paid each time George Whigham visited his ex-wife socially.

Of course, Margaret saw to it that this never happened (and certainly Whigham paid over none of the promised money). When the old man contracted throat cancer and died the following year, Margaret spitefully blocked Jane from seeing him in hospital. She even tried to stop her attending the funeral but, in spite of a lawyer's letter forbidding her to do so, Jane went anyway.

Thanks to the cleverly drawn up deed of separation, Jane Whigham received nothing in her husband's will, and all his money went to Margaret. But Whigham, aware of his daughter's spendthrift habits, had tied up the vast majority of his money in trust funds, leaving Margaret with what she considered a miserly allowance of £18,000 a year (a fortune by 1960s standards). But if Jane Whigham thought the duchess might now leave her alone, she was to be disappointed. Margaret filed for a divorce from the duke – pre-empting his own attempts to get her to a divorce hearing – citing adultery with Jane Whigham as the cause.

This seems to have been pure fantasy, without a shred of evidence to support it. But at some point, she is said to have offered £5,000 to Jane Whigham's brother Leslie to give false evidence to support the divorce claim – not surprisingly, he refused.

Margaret's lawyers pleaded with her to drop the case, but she refused, apparently obsessed by the notion that if the court found in her favour, the duke's attempts to publicly brand her as an adulteress would be blocked. But she lost her nerve – or saw sense – on the morning of the hearing, on 29 May 1962, and announced that she was dropping her claim. By that time, Jane Whigham was already suing Margaret for defamation of character.

In the meantime, Margaret had lost yet another case, this time to her husband's London secretary, Yvonne MacPherson. The latter claimed that the duchess had slandered and libelled her. To begin with, Margaret had been going around telling people that the confidential secretary was a blabbermouth who had gossiped about the problems in the Argylls' marriage. Rather more serious was the use of Mrs MacPherson's name on a telegram that had been sent to the duke at Inveraray Castle – purporting to come from Yvonne MacPherson, but actually sent by Margaret – saying, among other things: 'ALL IS READY TO TEAR STRIPS OFF MARGARET FINANCIALLY AND OTHERWISE.'

Yvonne claimed that these inventions would severely damage her career as a confidential secretary. The jury agreed and Mrs MacPherson was awarded £7,000, plus a rather larger amount in costs. More than the loss of the money, however, Margaret had lost yet another attempt to make her husband the villain of the piece in the forthcoming divorce proceedings.

The case of Ian, Duke of Argyll's claim for divorce, on the grounds of his wife's serial adultery, finally opened in the Edinburgh Court of Session on 26 February 1963. The duke had filed the claim four years earlier, and the record delay was mainly due to Margaret's various failed legal attempts to disallow the evidence that the duke had taken from her London house.

The duke named three co-respondents: Baron Sigismund von Braun (now the West German Ambassador to the UN), John Cohane (an American businessman) and Peter Combe (a former press officer for the London Savoy Hotel). All three denied the claims.

The hearing lasted three weeks and numerous witnesses and experts were called on both sides. The evidence – especially the pornographic photographs – were the subject of endless gossip.

Nowhere in the diaries and letters seized by the duke did the duchess actually say that she had sex with any of her male friends, but there was enough innuendo – especially in the letters – to allow any reader who knew Margaret's nature to read between the lines. Unfortunately for Margaret, the judge Mr Justice Plowman had also adjudicated on the Yvonne MacPherson libel case, so was already well informed of the lengths to which to which she was prepared to go to achieve her ends.

Of course, the photographs alone were conclusive proof of adultery, but Margaret fought anyway. First she insisted that she was not the woman in the pictures, since the face was not visible. That claim collapsed when it was pointed out that the pictures had clearly been taken in the en suite bathroom of her London house, and that the woman was wearing a pearl necklace with a distinctive diamond encrusted clasp that was known to belong to Margaret. Furthermore, in the oral sex picture, one of the hands that held the 'headless man's' penis wore a ring that could be proved to be an heirloom of the Argyll house and to which only Margaret had access.

The duchess then changed tack, admitting that she was the woman in the photographs, but insisting that the man in the picture was, in fact, Ian, her husband.

To overturn this claim the duke had himself examined by a doctor who then swore on oath that the duke's penis was not that which was shown in the photographs. The duke's genitals were notably smaller than those of the 'headless man'.

In his summing-up, Judge Plowman described the duchess as being 'wholly immoral', and her sexual activities as 'disgusting'. He concluded that she had indeed slept with all three of the co-respondents, as well as with the 'headless man' (if he was, indeed, not one of the three named men).

Argyll did not have it all his own way. The judge also concluded that the duke had been aware of his wife's affair with the Baron von Braun, and that his inaction at the time had been the equivalent of condoning her adultery. However, since the duke had not condoned her various other lovers, the judge ruled that the husband's petition for divorce be granted.

Both sides had lost heavily in the proceedings. To begin with, the legal costs alone were over £50,000. Then there was all the humiliating publicity. Although not allowed to report the evidence in detail during the trial, the press was free to publish its essence after the proceedings were over, and the duke and his ex-duchess – now plain Miss Margaret Campbell – became the subject of legend.

For Margaret had not only lost her title, but had been branded a nymphomaniac. Her own daughter, Frances (now Duchess of Rutland), decided that her mother was such a bad influence that she banned her from visiting, even to meet her grandchildren.

The duke was seen not only as a cuckold but as a weakling who had connived at his wife's adultery, then decided to dig in his heels for no discernable reason. The implication was that the size of his penis was too small to satisfy a woman with healthy appetites. To cap it all, White's, his beloved London club, blackballed him for publicly humiliating a lady. Whether or not he was the injured party, the committee felt that a gentleman does not blacken his wife's character in the courts, but shields her by admitting to adultery himself.

Worse still, the duke let down his class by selling his story to a newspaper (Margaret had already published hers before the divorce hearing). He thereupon retreated from the London scene to lick his wounds, remarried – this time the American widow of a Parisian professor – and took refuge in Inveraray Castle. He died in 1973, a tax exile in France.

Margaret's troubles were not yet over. With her usual idiotic bravado, she had been secretly staying with yet another lover throughout the divorce proceedings. In spite of this, she decided to fight her husband's newspaper revelations, and even succeeded in suppressing some of them, a pointless exercise since her reputation was by then beyond further damage. She lost the libel case brought against her by her stepmother, Jane Whigham, and had to pay her £25,000, plus costs. She then lost a further legal battle with Jane over George Whigham's property in Jamaica, losing another source of income.

As if to drive home her triumph, Jane Whigham later admitted to having an affair with her stepdaughter's husband, Ian, Duke of Argyll, but insisted that it had taken place *after* his divorce from the duchess.

Margaret Campbell never remarried, and managed to spend her father's entire fortune long before her death in 1993. However, her friends remained loyal, and she was never entirely reduced to penury.

The identity of the 'headless man' in the famous photographs has never been revealed. It has often been claimed it was government minister Duncan Sandys, but he had scar tissue on the back of his legs – the result of a war wound, and the picture of the 'headless man' on top of Margaret showed no such scarring.

Another candidate was the film star, Douglas Fairbanks Junior. He categorically denied he was ever Margaret's lover, but the fact that the pictures were taken with a Polaroid camera with a self-timer feature (a piece of equipment unavailable in Britain at the time, but just released for sale in America) might suggest an American.

Margaret's notoriety was soon eclipsed by that of Christine Keeler, but the Duchess of Argyll deserves to be remembered as a beautiful and distinguished practitioner of the long tradition of aristocratic impropriety.

CAROLINE, QUEEN

THE ONLY BRITISH QUEEN TO BE TRIED FOR ADULTERY

It is something of a mystery why the Prince of Wales, the son of King George III, agreed to marry the fat, ugly and tactless Caroline of Brunswick. It is true that he did it largely to persuade parliament to pay his enormous debts. But he could have married the queen's niece, the beautiful and talented Louise of Mecklenburg-Strelitz. His marriage to Caroline was a disaster for everyone.

George Augustus Frederick, the Prince of Wales, was born in August 1762. Determined that his son would grow up virtuous and serious-minded, George III had him brought up far from the court, according to a strict academic and physical regimen. It had the opposite effect: the prince became a rebel, a spendthrift and a waster. At the age of seventeen he embarked on an affair with an actress, Mary Robinson, and his letters to her had to be bought back eventually for £5,000. The prince became a member of a hard-drinking, hard-gambling set, which included the Whig politician Charles James Fox – one of his father's chief enemies – and the playwright Sheridan. He began to run up vast debts. He voted for Fox – and against his father – when Fox's India Bill came before Parliament but the Whig politician lost and was dismissed. When he was 23, the prince fell in love with the beautiful Catholic, Mrs Fitzherbert, and although she fled to France to escape his attentions, he finally persuaded her to go through a secret marriage. But constancy was not one of his strong points and he soon took another mistress, Lady Jersey.

By the time he was thirty, the prince was an embarrassment to his father and intensely unpopular with the British public. His debts now amounted to £630,000 – many millions in present-day terms – and Pitt's administration showed no eagerness to find the money. So when it was suggested by his father that he should marry and furnish an heir, he agreed on condition that Parliament paid his debts.

Caroline of Brunswick was short, plump and ugly, and she suffered from body odour – probably as a result of infrequent washing. Lady Jersey, the prince's current mistress, may have pushed him into marrying Caroline rather than the beautiful Louise of Mecklenburg-Strelitz as she would be less of a rival. On 5 April 1795, at St James's Palace, the prince was introduced to Caroline; he was shattered. He staggered to the far end of the room and called for a brandy. He went on drinking brandy for three days until the marriage ceremony. On the honeymoon – with Lady Jersey also in attendance – he seems to have done his duty as a husband for Caroline discovered she was pregnant soon thereafter. But the prince found her unbearable and stayed as far away from her as possible; in the following year he wrote her a letter saying that, 'our inclinations are not in our power', but that being polite to one another was. When she received the letter, Queen

Caroline was with the politician George Canning and asked him what he thought it meant; Canning replied that it seemed to give her permission to do as she liked. Whereupon Queen Caroline proceeded to do just that with Canning.

What no one realized at the time was that the royal line of Hanover suffered from the disease known as porphyria, the 'royal disease', a genetic disorder in which, due to an enzyme defect, the body accumulates large quantities of porphyrins (precursors of red blood pigment). The disease affects the digestive tract, the nervous system, the circulatory system and the skin; it causes psychotic disorders and epilepsy. George III had several attacks of it and died insane. The Prince of Wales was also subject to it and so was Caroline – two of her brothers were imbeciles, probably due to porphyria. It may explain Caroline's utter lack of self-control and her tendency to behave outrageously which led many to suspect she was insane.

Rejected by her husband she retired to a house in Blackheath and behaved in a manner that led Lady Hester Stanhope to call her 'a downright whore'. She had a Chinese clockwork figure in her room which, when wound up, performed gross sexual movements; she was also given to dancing around in a manner that exposed a great deal of her person.

In 1806, rumours that a four-year-old child in her entourage, William Austin, was her illegitimate son, led to what became known as 'the Delicate Investigation'. A Royal Commission repudiated the charge and found Lady Douglas, who had started the rumour, guilty of perjury. But years later, Caroline told her lawyer's brother that the child was the natural son of Prince Louis Ferdinand of Prussia, who had always been her love. Mrs Fitzherbert was to state later that Caroline had secretly married Prince Louis before she married the Prince of Wales.

Finally, in August 1814, Caroline decided to leave England. In Geneva, at a ball given in her honour, she shocked her hosts by dancing naked to the waist. In Naples she became the mistress of King Joachim, Napoleon's brother-in-law. When she left Naples – at the time Napoleon escaped from Elba – she had with her Napoleon's courier, a coarsely handsome Italian named Bartolomeo Bergami, a former quartermaster in a regiment of hussars. This swarthy, bearded, intensely masculine character looked like a brigand from a Drury Lane play. He travelled with her to Munich, Tunis, Athens, Constantinople and Jerusalem, and when they settled in her villa near Pesaro they behaved as man and wife.

James Brougham, her lawyer's brother, now wrote to England suggesting that the prince – he was now Prince Regent (his father having become insane) – should obtain a legal separation from Caroline so she could never become queen of England. But the prince wanted divorce or nothing. So nothing came of this suggestion.

George III finally died in January 1820 and his son became George IV.

Caroline of Brunswick was now Queen Caroline. The government quickly offered her £50,000 a year if she would agree not to return to England. In a fury, Caroline hurried across the Channel. Her husband was one of the most unpopular men in the country and on that count many people espoused her cause. To the intense embarrassment of the government, she settled at Brandenburg House, in Hammersmith. And on 17 August the government took the offensive by hauling her in front of the House of Lords. Its aim was to dissolve the marriage on the grounds that Caroline had engaged in 'a most unbecoming and degrading intimacy' with Bergami, 'a foreigner of low station'. But the government had bitten off more than it could chew. Noisy mobs demonstrated in favour of Caroline and the House of Lords had to be surrounded by two strong timber fences. The queen's coach was always surrounded by a cheering crowd. After 52 days the divorce clause was carried. But the oratory of Henry Brougham caused a turn in the tide and when the Bill was given its final reading, it had only a pathetic majority of nine. The Lords decided to drop it.

The coronation was scheduled for 29 April 1821. The queen wrote to the Prime Minister, Lord Liverpool, to ask what kind of a dress she ought to wear for the coronation. He replied that she could 'form no part of that ceremony'. But when George was crowned, Caroline arrived at the Abbey dressed in a muslin slip and demanded to be admitted. When she shouted, 'The queen – open!', pages opened the doors. She continued with 'I am the queen of England.' An official roared, 'Do your duty, shut the Hall door', and the door was slammed in her face. Undaunted, Caroline drove back to Brandenburg House and sent a note to the king asking for a coronation 'next Monday'.

She died two weeks later, on 7 August 1821 – so suddenly that it was widely rumoured that she had been poisoned. When her body was on its way to the ship that would take it back to Brunswick, there were riots at Kensington Church, bricks were thrown, and two men were shot by the Life Guards. Caroline was buried in Brunswick Cathedral, with an inscription on her coffin: The Injured Queen of England.

George IV remained intensely unpopular. He lived on for only nine years after the death of Caroline. The major issue of the time was Roman Catholic emancipation (England had been anti-Catholic since the time of Elizabeth I and George I had come to the throne of England from Hanover because of the Act that prevented a Catholic from becoming king of England.) As Prince of Wales, George had been in favour of Wellington who, as prime minister, carried the act of Parliament that finally achieved Catholic emancipation (although Wellington was himself basically opposed to it, believing it would finally destroy English rule in Ireland – as it did.) George IV became hysterical about the issue and threatened to use the royal veto. But the throne no longer held the political power it had under George III, and he was reluctantly forced to accept Catholic emancipation. After that, the king's health deteriorated swiftly and he died on 26 June 1830. He had a portrait of Mrs Fitzherbert round his neck on his death bed. But the two had been estranged for many years – ever since, at a dinner in honour of Louis XVIII in 1803, he had made sure there was no fixed place for her at table, so she must sit 'according to her rank'. After that insult, she had retired from the court.

CASTANEDA, CARLOS

THE DON JUAN HOAX

In 1968, the University of California Press published a book called *The Teachings of Don Juan: A Yacqui Way of Knowledge*, by Carlos Castaneda. Castaneda had entered the University of California – UCLA – as an undergraduate in 1959, and had received a BA in anthropology in 1962. The University of California Press accepted *The Teachings of Don Juan* as an authentic account of Castaneda's 'field work' in Mexico. The book told how, when he was an anthropology student, in 1960, Castaneda made several trips to the southwest to collect information on medicinal plants used by the Indians. At a Greyhound bus station, he was introduced to a white-haired old Indian who apparently knew all about peyote, the hallucinogenic plant. Although this first meeting was abortive – Castaneda tells with touching honesty how he 'talked nonsense' to Don Juan – Castaneda made a point of finding out where Don Juan lived and was finally accepted by the old *brujo* (medicine man or magician) as a pupil, a sorcerer's apprentice. The teaching begins with an episode in which Don Juan tells Castaneda to look for his 'spot', a place where he will feel more comfortable and at ease than anywhere else; he told Castaneda that there was such a spot within the confines of the porch. Castaneda describes how he spent all night trying different spots, lying in them, but felt no difference. Don Juan told him he ought to use his eyes. After this, he began to distinguish various colours in the darkness: purple, green and verdigris. When he finally chose one of these, he felt sick and had a sensation of panic. Exhausted, he lay by the wall and fell asleep. When he woke up, Don Juan told him that he had found his 'spot' – where he had fallen asleep. The other spot was bad for him, the 'enemy'.

This episode helps to explain the subsequent popularity of the book which was published in paperback by Ballantine Books and sold 300,000 copies. Don Juan is a teacher, a man of knowledge – the kind of person that every undergraduate dreams of finding – and he introduces Castaneda to the most astonishing experiences. When Castaneda first eats a peyote button, he experiences amazing sensations and plays with a mescalito dog whose mind he can read. On a later occasion he sees the mescalito god himself as a green man with a pointed head. When Don Juan teaches him how to make a paste from the *datura* plant – Jimson weed – he anoints himself with it and has a sensation of flying through the air at a great speed. (In their book *The Search for Abraxas*, Stephen Skinner and Neville Drury speculate that witches of the Middle Ages used a similar concoction and that this explains how they 'flew' to Witches' Sabbaths.) He wakes up to find himself half a mile from Don Juan's house.

During the period when the book was published every young American was smoking pot and experimenting with 'psychedelic drugs' like mescalin and LSD, and Timothy Leary was advising American youth to 'Turn on, tune in, drop out.' This apparently factual account of semi-magical experiences became as popular as Tolkien's *Lord of the Rings* and for much the same reason: it was escapist literature, but, more important, it claimed to be true.

Reviews were excellent. Anthropologists and scientists took the book seriously – the psychologist Carl Rogers called it 'one of the most vividly convincing documents I have read'. The philosopher Joseph Margolis said that either Castaneda was recording an encounter with a master or he was himself a master.

This was clearly a success that had to be followed up. *A Separate Reality* described how Castaneda had returned to Don Juan in 1968. A giant gnat, 100 feet high, circles round him; he rides on a bubble; he has a semi-mystical experience in which he hears extraordinary sounds and sees the sorcerer's 'ally', who shows him a 'spirit catcher'.

The demand for more about Don Juan remained strong but Castaneda had a problem. *A Separate Reality* came to an end in 1970 and was published in 1971; for the time being he had used up his Don Juan material. But not quite. He explained in his next book, *Journey to Ixtlan* (1973) that he had made the erroneous assumption that the glimpses of reality that Don Juan had give him could only be obtained through drugs. Now he realized he was mistaken. In fact, Don Juan had told him many things during his years as a sorcerer's apprentice, but although he had written these non-drug revelations in his 'field notes', he had failed to see their significance. Now, looking back over his notes, he realized that he had a vast amount of material that showed that drugs were not necessary for achieving unusual states of consciousness. So *Journey to Ixtlan* goes back to 1960 and recounts still more astonishing adventures: he has strange visions, mountains move, and Castaneda describes his encounter with a sinister but beautiful sorceress named Catalina.

In retrospect, it seems that Castaneda made his first major error in writing *Ixtlan* (although it was one that, according to his agent, made him $1 million). The 'lost' field notes sound just a little too convenient. Yet, oddly enough, scholars continued to take him seriously. Mary Douglas, a professor of social anthropology, wrote an article about the first three books called 'The Authenticity of Castaneda', which concluded: 'From these ideas we are likely to get advances in anthropology.' Moreover, UCLA granted Castaneda his Ph.D for *Ixtlan* and he lectured on anthropology on the Irvine campus.

If reviewers would swallow *Ixtlan* they would clearly swallow anything. Now that enough time had elapsed since his last visit to Sonora, Castaneda could renew his acquaintance with Don Juan and bring his revelations up to date. But *Tales of Power* (1974) seems to indicate that either Castaneda or his publisher felt that the game would soon be up. The dust jacket declares that this is the 'culmination of Castaneda's extraordinary initiation into the mysteries of sorcery'. At last, it declares, Castaneda completes his long journey into the world of magic and the book ends with a 'deeply moving farewell'. In many ways *Tales of Power* – covering a period of a few days in 1971 – is more rewarding than the earlier Don Juan books because it attempts to present a philosophical theory about reality, in terms of two concepts which Don Juan calls the *tonal* and the *nagual*. The *tonal* is 'everything we are', while the *nagual* is pure potentiality. The *tonal* is the pair of Kantian spectacles through which we see the world and impose meaning on it; it consists mainly of linguistic concepts and preconceptions. These conceptions are illustrated with the usual tales of magical experiences: Don Juan shows him a squirrel wearing spectacles which swells until it is enormous and then disappears; Carlos walks a few steps and finds he has travelled one and a half miles.

It was at this point, after publication of *Tales of Power*, that a teacher of psychology named Richard de Mille was persuaded by his niece to read all four Don Juan books one after the other. ('You have to take the whole trip.') *The Teachings* struck him as authentic and factual. *A Separate Reality* raised doubts; it was better written but somehow not so 'factual'. And the character of Don Juan had changed; he seemed more 'joky', while in the first book he had been grimly serious. Of course, Castaneda himself had already mentioned this. 'He clowned during the truly crucial moments of the second cycle.' But when he came to *Ixtlan*, de Mille was puzzled to find that the Don Juan of the notes made as early as 1960 was as much of a humorist and a clown as the later Don Juan. Made suspicious by this inconsistency, he began to study the books more closely and soon found contradictions that confirmed his feeling that he was dealing with fiction rather than fact. A friend pointed out one obvious inconsistency: in October 1968 Castaneda leaves his car and walks for two days to the shack of Don Juan's fellow sorcerer Don Genaro but when they walk out of the shack they climb straight into the car. De Mille discovered a similar contradiction. In *Ixtlan*, Castaneda goes looking for a certain bush on Don Juan's instructions and finds it has vanished; then Don Juan leads him to the far side of the hill, where he finds the bush he thought he had seen earlier on the other side. Later Don Juan tells him, 'This morning you *saw*', giving the word special emphasis. Yet six years later, in 1968, Castaneda is represented (in *A Separate Reality*) as asking Don Juan what is *seeing* and Don Juan tells him that in order to find out, Castaneda must *see* for himself. He seems to have forgotten that Castaneda had an experience of *seeing* six years earlier. And while it is understandable that Don Juan should forget, it is quite incomprehensible that Castaneda should.

These and many similar inconsistencies convinced de Mille that one of the two books had to be fiction, or that, more probably, they both were. He published his results in a book called *Castaneda's Journey* in 1976 and it led many anthropologists who had taken Don Juan seriously to change their views. Joseph K. Long felt 'betrayed by Castaneda'. Marcello Truzzi, on the other hand, admitted that he had felt aghast at the initial reactions of the scientific community to Castaneda's books and that he was equally outraged by the lack of serious reaction now de Mille had exposed them as frauds.

Castaneda's admirers were mostly infuriated. Their feeling was that even if Castaneda had invented Don Juan, the books were full of genuine knowledge and wisdom, and should be gratefully accepted as works of genius. One lady wrote to de Mille saying she was convinced he didn't exist and asking him to prove it. de Mille had, in fact, accepted that the Don Juan books had a certain merit, both as literature and as 'occult teaching'. But when, in 1980, he edited a large volume of essays on the 'Castaneda hoax' called *The Don Juan Papers* his admiration had visibly dwindled. Some of the essays present an even more devastating exposure of Castaneda than de Mille's original volume: for example, Hans Sebald, an anthropologist who had spent a great deal of time in the southwestern desert, pointed out that it was so hot from June to September that no one with any sense ventures into it; dehydration and exhaustion follow within hours. Yet acording to Castaneda, he and Don Juan wandered around the desert for days, engaged in conversation and ignoring the heat. Sebald goes on to demolish Castaneda's animal lore: 'Where . . . are the nine-inch centipedes, the tarantulas big as saucers? Where are the king snakes, scarlet racers, chuckawallas, horned toads, gila monsters . . .' A lengthy appendix to *The Don Juan Papers* cites hundreds of parallel passages from the Castaneda books and from other works on anthropology and mysticism that bear a close resemblance. The book establishes, beyond all possible doubt, that the Castaneda books are a fraud.

Richard de Mille's own researches revealed that Carlos Arana was born in 1925 (not 1935, as he had told an interviewer) in Cajamarca, Peru, and came to San Francisco in 1951, leaving behind a Chinese-Peruvian wife who was pregnant. In 1955 he met Damon Runyon's distant cousin Margaret and married her; they separated after six months. In 1959 he became an undergraduate at UCLA and the Don Juan story begins . . .

Castaneda himself has proved to be an extremely elusive individual, as *Time* discovered when it sent a reporter to interview him in 1973. In the light of de Mille's discoveries this is easy to understand. Castaneda's career can be compared to that of the Shakespeare forger, William Ireland (*see* page 170) who began by forging a few Shakespeare signatures to gain his father's attention and found himself forced to continue until he had concocted a whole new Shakespeare play, which brought about his discovery and downfall. Castaneda presumably produced the original *Teachings of Don Juan* as a mild form of hoax. The publication by Ballantine launched him, whether he liked it or not, on the career of a trickster and confidence man. It would, perhaps, have been wiser to stop after *Ixtlan*, or possibly *Tales of Power*. But the demand for more Don Juan books presumably overcame his caution. In fact, the fifth, *The Second Ring of Power*, reads so obviously as fiction that it raises the suspicion that Castaneda wanted to explode his own legend. But he shows caution in offering no dates, no doubt to escape de Mille's vigilant eye. Castaneda tells how he went back to Mexico looking for Don Juan and instead encountered one of his disciples, a sorceress named Madame Solitude. Last time he saw her she was fat and ugly and in her fifties; now she is young, slim and vital, and within a few pages, she has torn off her skirt and invited him to make love to her – an invitation he wisely resists. Then Castaneda somehow invokes his own double out of his head – not a mild-mannered scholar but a super-male authority figure who hits Madame Solitude on the head and almost kills her. Then four lady disciples arrive and make more assaults on Castaneda, which he overcomes, and after which they all encounter other-worldly beings . . .

In his sixth book, *The Eagle's Nest*, Castaneda returns to Mexico as 'a sorcerous leader and figure in his own right' (as the blurb says) and enters into a closer relationship with one of the female sorcerers of the previous book, La Gorda. The two of them develop the ability to dream in unison. It is clear that, since writing the earlier book, Castaneda has come across split-brain physiology and now we hear a great deal about the right and left sides of a human being, the left being the *nagual* and the right the *tonal*. De Mille had pointed out that the Don Juan books seem to chart Castaneda's literary and philosophical discoveries over the years and this book confirms it. For those who read it with the certainty that the previous books were a hoax, it seems an insult to the intelligence. But it appears to demonstrate that Castaneda can continue indefinitely spinning fantasies for those who regard him as the greatest of modern gurus.

CLEVELAND STREET SCANDAL

THE 'SEX-FOR-SALE' TELEGRAPH BOYS

In early July 1886, there was a theft of money from a room in the General Post Office in St Martin's-Le-Grand, in the City of London. A telegraph messenger boy named Charles Thomas Swinscow came under suspicion and when he was searched, he proved to have eighteen shillings on him – a far larger sum than he was likely to save up from his wages. On 4 July 1886, a police constable named Hanks questioned the boy, who told him that he had obtained the money for doing some 'private work' for a gentleman named Hammond, who lived at 19 Cleveland Street, just north of Soho. Finally, he admitted that he had been taken to the house by a post office clerk named Henry Newlove – who, like Swinscow, was fifteen. Newlove, it seemed, had earlier persuaded Swinscow to go with him to a lavatory in the basement of the Post Office where he had 'behaved indecently'. Then Newlove had suggested that Swinscow might like to earn a little money by doing the same thing with a gentleman. At the house in Cleveland Street, Swinscow had got into bed with a gentleman who, in the language of the police report, 'put his person between my legs and an emission took place'. The gentleman then gave him half a sovereign, which Swinscow handed to the landlord of the house, Hammond. Hammond had given him back four shillings. The same thing had apparently happened on a subsequent occasion.

Swinscow mentioned two other telegraph boys who had gone to Cleveland Street: seventeen-year-olds George Wright and Charles Thickbroom. Wright admitted that he and Newlove had gone to the basement lavatory and 'Newlove put his person into me . . . and something came away from him.' Wright went with Newlove to the Cleveland Street house where he went to a bedroom with a 'foreign looking chap'. They undressed and got into bed. 'He told me to suck him. I did so. He then had a go between my legs and that was all.' Wright also received four shillings. Thickbroom told how Newlove had persuaded him to go to Cleveland Street, where he went to bed with a gentleman and they 'played with one another. He did not put his person into me.' He also received four shillings.

Newlove admitted the truth of the statements. The next morning he hastened to 19 Cleveland Street and warned Hammond. Charles Hammond, a 32-year-old male prostitute, married to a French prostitute known as 'Madame Caroline' – on whom he had fathered two sons – lost no time in fleeing. So did another homosexual, George Veck, who liked to pose as a clergyman. Veck moved to lodgings nearby under a false name, while Hammond fled to France.

Chief Inspector Frederick Abberline of the CID applied for warrants for the arrest of Hammond and Newlove on a charge of criminal conspiracy. But when the police arrived at Cleveland Street the next day the house was shut up.

On his way to the police station, Newlove commented that it was hard that he should be arrested when men in high positions should be allowed to walk free. Asked what he meant, he replied, 'Lord Arthur Somerset goes regularly to the house in Cleveland Street. So does the Earl of Euston and Colonel Jervois.'

Lord Arthur Somerset, the son of the Duke of Beaufort, was a major in the Royal Horse Guards, and superintendent of the stables of the Prince of Wales, Queen Victoria's son, whose name was to be associated with many scandals (including the Tranby Croft card scandal: see page 44). When Lord Arthur – known as 'Podge' – was identified by the two telegraph boys Swinscow and Thickbroom as the man who had climbed into bed with them, 'Podge' hastily obtained four months leave of absence and vanished to the Continent. His elder brother Henry had been deserted by his wife because of his homosexual inclinations.

Veck was also arrested and he and Newlove were committed for trial at the Old Bailey. But by that time, the press had got hold of the story. The *Pall Mall Gazette* published a paragraph deploring the 'disgraceful nature' of the charge against Veck and Newlove and asking whether the 'two noble lords and other notable persons in society' were going to be allowed to get away with it. It obviously had the makings of a first-class scandal. It may have been at this point that Arthur Newton, 'Podge's' solicitor, breathed another name that made the Director of Public Prosecutions raise his eyebrows: that of 'Eddy', the Duke of Clarence, son of the Prince of Wales. Eddy, according to rumour, had also visited the Cleveland Street brothel. Meanwhile, 'Podge' was in more trouble; another teenager, Algernon Allies, had been interviewed by the police and admitted that he had been intimately involved with Lord Arthur Somerset, whom he called 'Mr Brown'. 'The prosecution wishes to avoid putting any witness in the box who refers to "Mr Brown",' wrote the Director of Public Prosecutions, Sir Augustus Stephenson to the Attorney-General.

It was no surprise to anyone when the case came up at Bow Street on 18 September 1876 and lasted a mere half hour. Veck and Newlove both pleaded guilty and were both given light sentences: Veck nine months' hard labour and Newlove four months'. That, it seemed, was the end of the case.

But the press was not willing to allow it to rest there. There were many crusading editors in London, like W.T. Stead of the *Pall Mall Gazette*, Henry Labouchere of *Truth*, and Ernest Parke of the *North London Press*. It was Parke who put the cat among the pigeons. On 16 November 1889 – three years after the case – Parke identified the aristocrats whose names had been so carefully suppressed at the time of the trial: Lord Arthur Somerset and the Earl of Euston. (These names, we may recall, had been mentioned to Abberline by Newlove when he was arrested.) Parke also commented that 'a far more distinguished and more highly placed personage . . . was inculpated in these disgusting crimes.'

The Earl of Euston, Henry James Fitzroy, was 38 years old at the time of the Cleveland Street trial. He immediately instructed his solicitor to sue for libel. Parke's trial opened at the Old Bailey on 15 January 1890. One of the most serious points against Parke was his allegation that the Earl of Euston had fled to Peru; Euston had done nothing of the sort. (It had been unnecessary, for his name had never entered the case after Newlove mentioned it to Abberline.)

Euston admitted that he had been to 19 Cleveland Street. But, he said, it had been a misunderstanding. He had, he said, been in Piccadilly in May or June 1886, when someone had put an advertising card into his hand. It said 'Poses plastiques', and gave the address of 19 Cleveland Street. Poses plastiques meant naked girls posing in Grecian attitudes. So, according to Lord Euston, he hurried to 19 Cleveland Street. He was admitted by a man who told him there were no women there but left no doubt about what the house had to offer. 'You infernal scoundrel, if you don't let me out I'll knock you down,' said Lord Euston and rushed out.

The defence called several witnesses who said they had seen Lord Euston going in or out of Cleveland Street. The final defence witness was a male prostitute named John Saul. He claimed to have been picked up by Lord Euston and took him back to Cleveland Street where they went to bed. The Times declined to report what Saul claimed then took place but we can reconstruct what he said from a comment Saul had made to Ernest Parke about Euston: 'He is not an actual sodomite. He likes to play with you and then "spend" on your belly.'

The judge emphasized the contradictions in the statements of witnesses, and described Saul as a 'loathesome object'. The strongest point against Parke was his statement that Euston had fled to Peru. The jury found Parke guilty of libel without justification. He was sentenced to a year in prison without hard labour. The sentence was not regarded as severe by the press.

The case was still not quite over. In December 1889, 'Podge's' solicitor, Arthur Newton, was accused of conspiring to defeat the course of justice. The charges said that he had tried to get an interview with Algernon Allies – the youth who had admitted being 'Podge's' lover – and had collected three of the accused telegraph boys after they had left police custody and sent them to a lodging house while he arranged for them to leave the country. Newton's defence was that his clerk Frederick Taylorson, who was charged with him, had met Allies by accident and exchanged a few words with him. And so to the second charge, it was true that he had sent the boys to a lodging house overnight, telling them that they ought to go abroad, but that this was because 'Podge's' father, the Duke of Beaufort, wanted to interview them to see if they had been bullied by the police. The Duke had subsequently changed his mind. Newton was, he admitted, therefore technically guilty of conspiracy. The judge took a light view of it and sentenced him to six weeeks in prison. Taylorson, who pleaded not guilty, was acquitted.

Hammond, the man who ran the brothel, had fled from France to America and was never tried. 'Podge' spent the rest of his life living abroad, under an assumed name, and died in Hyères, on the French Riviera, in 1926. The scandal undoubtedly ruined his life. In his book *The Cleveland Street Scandal*, H. Montgomery Hyde suggests that he would have been wise to return and 'face the music'; a good solicitor could almost certainly have secured his acquittal, as in the case of Lord Euston. (The evidence suggests that Euston was a regular visitor at Cleveland Street.) Euston's trial certainly did him no harm; at the time of the Cleveland Street case he was a prominent Freemason, the Provincial Grand Master of Northamptonshire and Huntingdonshire, and subsequently became Grand Master of the Mark Masons. He was also appointed an aide de camp by King Edward VII in the coronation year, 1901. He died of dropsy in 1912.

Ernest Parke became a Justice of the Peace after he retired as a newspaper editor. But the subsequent career of Arthur Newton, who went to prison for conspiracy, was less fortunate. In 1910 he defended the murderer Crippen and received much favourable publicity. But he then conceived the idea of forging a Crippen 'confession' and selling it to a newspaper: *The Evening Times* bought it for £500, the writer Edgar Wallace acting as a go-between. Although Newton got cold feet at the last moment, the newspaper forced him to deliver the promised confession and sold a million copies as a result. Newton was suspended from practice by the Law Society for unprofessional conduct. In 1913 he was charged with being involved in a Canadian timber fraud, sentenced to three years in jail, and struck off the rolls as a solicitor.

CLINTON, BILL

THE MONICA LEWINSKY AFFAIR

History will probably rate William Jefferson Clinton – 42nd President of the United States – as one of the most successful American leaders of the twentieth century. Serving the maximum two terms as president, Bill Clinton (whose birth name was actually W J Blythe IV) was elected and re-elected on a strong mandate and was often favourably compared with fellow Democrat and chief icon of the Democratic Party, Jack Kennedy.

As president, Clinton oversaw a prolonged period of economic expansion and prosperity in the US, did much to undermine the international tariffs that were strangling free trade, passed rigorous laws to protect the environment, helped bring peace to Haiti, the Balkans and (for a brief few years) the Middle East, and repeatedly faced down and defeated an almost unprecedented Republican majority in both the Senate *and* the House of Representatives. Yet, for the present generation at least, President Clinton is mainly seen as the man who was exposed as having an affair with a young White House intern called Monica Lewinsky.

The Clinton administration was saddled with controversy and scandal from the beginning. One of the president's first acts after his election victory over George Bush Sr, in 1993, was to try to outlaw the automatic bar against gays and lesbians serving in the US military. His policy of 'don't mention it, and we won't ask' was condemned by the religious right as going too far, and jeered by the liberal left as not going far enough.

He then promised to reform the rapidly deteriorating US medical service by bringing in a universal health insurance system for all citizens, rich and poor alike. Unfortunately, he made the mistake of putting his wife Hillary at the head of the commission dealing with the matter – an unprecedentedly powerful post for an (obviously unelected) First Lady. Hillary Clinton's forthright pro-feminist stance, coupled with the unworkably complex health insurance system produced by her commission, only gave more ammunition to the extremely vocal Republican opposition.

At this point Bill Clinton was probably tempted to think that the road to political hell must be paved with good intentions. However, he continued to act in a relatively enlightened, non-partisan fashion, and thus made the biggest mistake of his political career: he failed to veto the appointment of lawyer Kenneth Starr – an avowed Republican – to the post of Special Prosecutor in charge of the powerful Office of the Independent Council.

The OIC's role is to police the corridors of power and investigate governmental and/or individual corruption. As its name suggests, it is free of any political constraint, and can even investigate the president if the Special Prosecutor deems it necessary. The OIC was instrumental in the investigations into both the Watergate and the Iran-Contra affairs and, in

1994, the OIC began investigating President Clinton's possible involvement in a banking fraud over a small area of real estate in Arkansas called Whitewater.

As governor of Arkansas in the late 1970s, Bill Clinton had invested in the Whitewater housing development through a small bank, called the Madison Guaranty Savings and Loan. The MGS&L eventually went bust during the great 1980s savings-and-loan scandal that saw almost all such small (and often corruptly managed) local banks going bankrupt, leaving the American taxpayer saddled with the bill. In the case of the MGS&L, the cost to the state was a cool $45 million.

James McDougal, the owner of the MGS&L and partner with Bill and Hillary Clinton in the Whitewater housing development (that, of course, was never built), was initially acquitted of the charge of bank fraud – only to be convicted of fraud years later, at the instigation of the OIC. Clinton himself claimed to have lost $69,000 in the MGS&L collapse, but his Republican enemies felt sure that there was still a 'smoking gun' to be found – that is, evidence that as Governor of Arkansas, Bill Clinton had used his power to somehow defraud the taxpayer and his fellow Whitewater investors.

However, the Whitewater accusations remained largely out of the public eye until July 1993, when Vincent Foster – a former member of Hillary Clinton's law firm and later lawyer to the Clinton family – was found dead, apparently a suicide. Obviously Foster, as the Clinton family lawyer, would have dealt with matters pertaining to Whitewater, and the discovery that, within hours of his death, White House aides had removed numbers of files from his office, led many to suspect that a scandal was being covered up. It was even suggested, by the more radical of the president's enemies, that Foster had been murdered to prevent him revealing Clinton's Whitewater misdemeanours.

In a congressional investigation into the behaviour of the White House aides, many of the staffers who were called to give evidence suffered unexplained lapses of memory while under oath, which suggested to many that there was indeed something being covered up. However – apart from the resignation of the Deputy Secretary of the Treasury over accusations of misleading Congress – the scandal hunters came up with nothing substantial, and President Clinton, although undoubtedly embarrassed by the whole affair, remained above the political mêlée.

The OIC, under Special Prosecutor Kenneth Starr, began its investigation into the Whitewater affair in August 1994. However, apart from securing the conviction of the then sitting Arkansas State Governor (a Democrat) on unrelated fraud charges in 1995, the OIC failed in what to many seemed to be Ken Starr's main aim – to find enough evidence to impeach President Clinton.

This was not to say that Clinton was in the clear as far as scandal went. In

1996 – the year James McDougal was finally jailed along with ten others for fraud connected to the MGS&L collapse and Whitewater – the novel *Primary Colors* was published and went straight into the bestseller list. Its anonymous author describes the rise of Jack Stanton, an unscrupulous and philandering state governor, to the White House, as seen through the eyes of an (initially) innocent party worker.

Although the names were different, the physical description of the fictional governor and of his lifestyle – for example, habitually eating enormous meals, but still remaining surprisingly fit – and that of his scheming, but still partly idealistic wife, left few in doubt who the book was really about. Events in the book also closely mimicked real events that had taken place during the 1993 presidential election. At the time, *Primary Colors* was generally believed to be the partly fictionalized diary of a senior Clinton aide, so the scandalous behaviour of the principal character read like an indictment of the sitting president.

In fact it later emerged that the novel was actually written by *Newsweek* columnist Joe Klein, who admitted the whole plot was based on rumours about the Clintons rather than on solid facts, but the damage had already been done. The public had read and half-believed the descriptions of Jack Stanton/Bill Clinton habitually cheating on his wife and generally behaving with a mixture of the charismatic rascal and the cynical politician.

The sexual rumours about Bill Clinton, satirized in *Primary Colors*, had first come to the public eye in 1992 – just before his run for the presidency – when a woman called Gennifer Flowers suddenly claimed that she and Clinton had conducted an affair for over twelve years. The timing of the revelation, added to the fact that Flowers offered no conclusive proof to back her claim, made it fairly easy for Clinton to flatly deny any such relationship had ever happened. In fact, the Flowers assertion probably did Clinton more good than harm in the short run, as commentators and the public took Clinton's side in what seemed to be a case of particularly low political mudslinging by either Flowers or her (presumed) Republican backers. Certainly the scandal did not stop Bill Clinton comfortably winning the 1993 presidential election.

In the long run, however, Bill Clinton's denial of ever having had a sexual relationship with Gennifer Flowers was going to cost him. Forced on to the witness stand and placed under oath in 1998, he admitted that he had indeed slept with her – just once, he insisted – in 1977. Of course, the difference between the two stories – an affair of twelve years against a single one-night stand – meant that the public had to decide whether Flowers or Clinton were lying. The fact that the president had already had to confess to his earlier lie meant that it was easy for his enemies to condemn him, and public opinion started to swing against him.

The Flowers scandal had been resurrected during the court proceedings of another, much more serious allegation against Clinton. In 1994 an article in the *American Spectator* magazine had suggested that Bill Clinton had once had an affair with a woman called 'Paula'. This had incensed Paula Jones, a former Arkansas state clerk, who was convinced that the article was referring to her. She immediately contacted the media to insist that, far from being a sexual conquest, she had totally rebuffed the then governor Clinton in 1991.

She said that she had been working behind the reception desk of the Arkansas Excelsior Hotel on 9 May 1991, when the governor checked in with his entourage. A state trooper had later asked her to go to Clinton's suite, escorted her there and left her alone with the governor. She and Clinton, Jones said, had chatted amiably on a sofa for a few minutes. Then, without a word of warning, he had suddenly pulled down his trousers and underpants to reveal his erect penis. The governor had then indicated that she should perform oral sex. Jones told the press that she had flatly refused and had tried to leave but, after hauling up his trousers again, Clinton had briefly blocked her from leaving so that he could ask her not to tell anyone what had happened. He had also mentioned that he was a friend of her boss's boss, and that if she ever wanted anything she just had to ask. She added that the state trooper, who had stood guard outside the door of the suite, had smirked at her knowingly as she hurried out.

Clinton's last words to Paula Jones were phrased to sound like a friendly offer, but she later said that she had detected the possibility of a threat to her future employment in them, so had told no one what had happened until she saw the article in the *American Spectator*. Clinton immediately denied the incident had ever taken place.

Having made such a damaging allegation in public, Jones was now open to being sued for slander by the president, so she decided to take the initiative and sue *him* for abusing her civil rights by 'creating a hostile work environment'. The case dragged on for four years – mainly because Clinton tried to use his presidential immunity to avoid having to give testimony. In 1997, however, the Supreme Court ruled that his immunity was invalid in civil cases and he was forced onto the stand. There the prosecution took the opportunity to question him about Gennifer Flowers – hoping to show a general laxity of moral character in the president – and he confessed to his earlier lie.

The judge threw the Paula Jones case out on 1 April 1998, stating that the evidence presented by the prosecution simply wasn't enough to allow for a conviction. She also said that Jones had not been able to show any real evidence that the incident in the Excelsior Hotel had significantly damaged her financially, mentally or emotionally – so, even if the case had continued to a conclusion of guilty, the judge would have been unable to award significant damages against the president. On the other hand, lest anyone think this ruling was an unconditional victory for Clinton, the judge suggested that Clinton and Paula Jones should come to a financial settlement out of court – effectively saying that she, the judge, thought Clinton *had* done something unseemly, but there wasn't enough evidence to support a judicial conviction.

Clinton eventually paid Paula Jones $850,000, but refused to admit wrongdoing or make a public apology. Jones had to pay $700,000 of the money to her lawyers, but later managed to make some extra cash from her notoriety by posing nude for *Playboy* magazine – much to the horror of the feminist groups who had unquestioningly backed her during the trial.

Another person who had been subpoenaed to give a statement in the Jones vs Clinton case was a young former White House intern called Monica Lewinsky. The prosecution had asked her to give a written statement as to whether she had ever had an affair with the president – thus rather tenuously proving that Clinton might be the sort of immoral person who would expose himself to a total stranger – but, legally under oath, she had flatly denied that she and the President of the United States had been lovers. This, as it later turned out, was a lie, and several people watching the trial suspected or knew that it was.

Monica Lewinsky was a pretty, if slightly chubby, Jewish girl from California. She was 21 when she arrived at the White House in 1995 to act as an unpaid intern – usually a short-term post that involved being a cross between a secretary and a general gofer, but one that carried a lot of weight on a person's future CV. Initially attached to the office of the Chief of Staff, Leon Panetta, Monica Lewinsky rarely saw, let alone spoke to, the president.

However, the White House is run as a social venue as well as the home of the Head of State, with regular leaving parties for departing members of staff. Although, thanks to the tight presidential schedule, Bill Clinton could not often attend these gatherings, he attended enough to notice and become attracted to Monica – who later admitted deliberately flirting with him by maintaining strong eye contact while they chatted. Their affair began on 15 November 1995.

By December, Monica had been moved to a posting in the Office of Legislative Affairs. She was now in a paid position and, not co-incidentally, had to make regular trips to the Oval Office (the president's place of daily work) to deliver documents. The pair would sometimes spend long periods of time alone in the Oval Office, with security guards at the door being ordered to allow nobody in. Monica later said that Clinton would also telephone her at home in the small hours – he was in the habit of working until one or two in the morning – and they would indulge in phone sex, graphically describing sexual acts to each other.

However, despite the lurid and salacious slant later put on the relationship by the media and the president's enemies, Bill Clinton and Monica Lewinsky's affair seems to have been largely affectionate and light hearted in nature. Monica later stressed that she and the president chatted and gossiped together at least as much as they fooled around. It is also worth noting that, despite Monica's willingness, Clinton refused ever to have vaginal sex with her, telling her apologetically that he considered that as going too far.

By May 1997, the president had decided that the affair itself was also a step too far, and broke with Monica as gently as he could. By this time she had been moved from her post in the Office of Legislative Affairs to the office of Pentagon spokesman Ken Bacon – where, possibly co-incidentally, she would have no formal reason to meet with the president. Clinton seems to have had nothing directly to do with this effective demotion of Monica, and the White House Chief of Staff later said she had been moved because of her inattention to work and her generally 'inappropriate and immature behaviour'. Certainly, during the affair, it must have been hard for Monica to maintain a proper degree of professional decorum when the President of the United States was keeping her up at night with raunchy telephone calls.

The end of the affair left Monica unhappy and lonely. Being from California, she had few friends in Washington DC and sorely missed her night-time chats with her lover. However she had already made a very good friend at work, a 46-year-old veteran Pentagon worker called Linda Tripp. By the summer of 1996, Monica had come to look on Linda as a bosom friend and confidante: she told her candidly about her relationship with Bill Clinton and they would often spend hours on the phone to each other, discussing every detail of the affair. Monica even showed Linda a blue dress with a little staining to the upper body caused, she said, by the president accidentally ejaculating over her during a bout of oral sex.

(Monica later stressed that she had *not* kept the dress as a slightly lurid keepsake, as some in the media had suggested. The fact was, she said, that she had put on weight after the affair had ended and the dress had ceased to fit. She had meant to have the dress dry-cleaned but, while it was hanging unused in her wardrobe, she had simply forgotten to send it to the cleaners.)

If Linda Tripp was tempted to believe that Monica was telling her a long and complex lie about her affair with the president, she claims to have seen evidence, in mid 1997, that convinced her the president was quite capable of 'fooling around' during office hours. She told *Newsweek* reporter Michael Isikoff – who happened to be the magazine's expert on the Paula Jones case – that as she, Linda, was passing the entrance to the Oval Office she had seen Kathleen Willey, another White House volunteer intern, leaving the room looking 'dishevelled. Her face red and her lipstick off.' Clear evidence, Tripp thought, that the president might have dropped Monica, but he was still chasing pretty girls.

With the Paula Jones trial so much in the news, Linda Tripp became convinced that the national media would be very interested in further presidential sex revelations, whatever the consequences for her friend

Monica. So, at the beginning of October 1997, she started taping her telephone conversations with Lewinsky while, at the same time, deliberately inciting her to reminisce about her affair with Bill Clinton. It should also be added that Linda believed that she was at risk of being sacked for mentioning the Kathleen Willey incident to *Newsweek* – so she also saw the tapes as a method of protecting her job, if push came to shove.

In the meantime, Monica was looking for a new job, having tired of the Pentagon. Betty Currie, Bill Clinton's personal secretary, contacted an old friend of the president, a well-connected Washington DC lawyer called Vernon Jordan, to see if he could find Monica a decent job. Lewinsky and Jordan met on 11 December 1997, and he was able to make several helpful suggestions as to where she might find high-flying jobs.

However, the rumours about Monica and the president were out by this time, if not actually in the public eye. Linda Tripp had played a selection of her Lewinsky tapes to a small group of journalists from *Newsweek* magazine, and Paula Jones's lawyers had somehow come to hear of the alleged relationship between the president and the pretty intern. On 17 December, Monica Lewinsky was subpoenaed to give evidence in the Paula Jones trial.

On 28 December, Monica Lewinsky made her final visit to the White House, apparently to meet with the president. It has been alleged that he encouraged her to be 'evasive' in her deposition to the Jones trial. On 7 January 1998, Monica filed an affidavit in the Jones vs Clinton case, denying any sexual relationship had ever existed between her and Bill Clinton. She could now be found guilty of perjury if evidence of her affair with the president ever came out. Linda Tripp delivered her collection of 'Monica tapes' into the keeping of her lawyer, Jim Moody, two days later.

All this time, OIC Special Prosecutor Ken Starr had been following the Paula Jones case with interest. His Whitewater fraud investigation into the involvement of the Clintons had borne no fruit, despite costing the taxpayer tens of millions of dollars. But the Whitewater investigation remained open, and Starr now made a momentous decision – against all previous OIC practice, he decided to *expand* his present investigation to encompass a totally unconnected matter – the sexual scandal currently engulfing the White House.

On 13 January, Linda Tripp met with FBI agents who were working with Starr and the OIC, and allowed them to place hidden microphones in her clothes. Thus 'wired' she met with Monica Lewinsky in the Virginia Ritz-Carlton Hotel for lunch. Their subsequent three hour conversation – mostly about Linda's fears over being called to give evidence to the Paula Jones trial – was recorded by the FBI. All this was necessary because Tripp's phone tapes of Monica's revelations had been made in the State of Maryland, whose law forbids secret phone taping and thus, arguably, made them inadmissible as evidence in a federal case.

The following day Tripp and Lewinsky met again, and this time Monica handed Linda a document titled: 'Points to make in an affidavit.' It was not in fact anything to do with her affair with the president, but coached Linda in what to say about what she knew about Kathleen Willey. The latter had recently given evidence – following the *Newsweek* article about her – that Bill Clinton had made unsolicited sexual advances to her.

On 16 January, Ken Starr made an official request to Attorney General Janet Reno to extend the OIC Whitewater investigation to cover 'possible subornation of perjury and obstruction of justice in the Paula Jones case'. A panel of three Federal Court judges agreed the request and, within hours, FBI agents were interrupting another meeting between Monica Lewinsky and Linda Tripp at the Ritz-Carlton Hotel.

The federal agents took Monica to a suite in the hotel and questioned her for several hours. At Monica's insistence, Tripp came as well, to witness the results of what Monica considered Linda's base betrayal of her. The FBI agents told Monica that they believed that she had been offered a job by the president, via Vernon Jordan, in return for giving a false affidavit in the Jones trial. Monica was then offered the stark choice of at least several years in jail for perjury, or to give evidence as to who had influenced her to give the false testimony, in which case the OIC would grant her full immunity from prosecution. She was not arrested, and was eventually allowed to leave, but Monica must have felt the sword of Damocles was hanging over her head.

Matters then began to move quickly. The next day, 17 January, Monica's lawyer, an old family friend called William Ginsburg, advised her not to sign the immunity agreement until he had negotiated a better deal with Ken Starr and the OIC. On the same day Bill Clinton gave a written (and therefore non-public) deposition to the Jones trial, denying sexual misconduct with Monica Lewinsky. If he had known that the OIC had evidence against Monica, he probably would have not committed the perjury. But Monica did not contact him – doubtless fearful any communication would be detected by the FBI/OIC who might withdraw their immunity offer.

Also on 17 January, the editorial desk of *Newsweek* decided not to run their story – provided by Linda Tripp – about the Monica tapes. They no doubt regretted this decision three days later when an internet gossip column, the *Drudge Report*, mentioned rumours of a relationship between Clinton and Lewinsky – the first public revelation of the rumour. The following day, 21 January, the story made headlines across the world.

In the following week, Bill Clinton made several denials, both private and public, to ever having sex with Monica Lewinsky, and also denied trying to influence her evidence to the Jones trial. Famously, he even went on television to state unequivocally: 'I did not have sexual relations with that woman, Miss Lewinsky.'

Vernon Jordan, the friend of Clinton's who had offered Monica several job opportunities, also denied any and all allegations of wrong-doing and went on to state that Monica had, during their conversation, specifically denied ever having an affair with the president.

Starr reacted by convening a federal grand jury to hear evidence, and immediately subpoenaing several White House staffers to give testimony, including Clinton's secretary, Betty Currie. He also demanded access to the White House Logbooks – which, of course, would have shown just how often and for how long Monica had visited and had been closeted alone with the president in the Oval Office. At the same time, talks between Starr and Monica's lawyer failed to come to any agreement over her possible immunity from prosecution.

Hillary Clinton, with characteristic tenacity, refused to believe the rumours of her husband's adultery and even suggested that a 'vast right-wing conspiracy' was trying to blacken the president's name. Even Bill Clinton publicly distanced himself from this radical theory, but may have agreed with Hillary in private. Hillary later said that she believed the allegations would 'slowly dissipate over time under the weight of [their] own insubstantiality'.

On 29 January, to the relief of all in the Clinton camp, the trial judge sitting on the Jones case ruled any evidence relating to Monica Lewinsky was 'not essential to the core issues' being investigated, and therefore could not be pursued by the prosecution. But by now, Starr's federal grand jury was an even greater threat to the presidency than the Jones trial. By early February, it was already being publicly mooted that Clinton might resign over the Lewinsky affair. He reacted by giving a press conference in which he told reporters and the world: 'I would never walk away from the people of this country and the trust they've placed in me.'

In the meantime, in the absence of an agreement to testify between Monica Lewinsky and Ken Starr, Marcia Lewis – Monica's mother – was called to give evidence before the grand jury. She was extensively questioned as to any knowledge she might have as to the alleged affair between the president and her daughter, but denied any such knowledge.

On 11 March, it is alleged by some that the grand jury spent the day listening to the Linda Tripp telephone tapes, despite their possible inadmissibility as evidence, thanks to the Maryland anti-bugging law.

At the same time Kathleen Willey – the 'other intern' – had not yet left the public stage, and gave an interview to the popular TV show, *Sixty Minutes,* accusing Clinton of sexually harassing her. The White House reacted by denying her claims and suggesting she was a publicity seeker, trying to sell the book rights to her (false) story for $30,000. Willey's lawyers, in turn, denied this claim.

On 20 March, Bill Clinton formally invoked his right to presidential immunity from having to give evidence to the federal grand jury. Many saw this as a dubious strategy, as it made it look as if he had something to hide. Clinton clearly did not want to be put under oath, as he already had been earlier that year in the damaging and humiliating Paula Jones case. More damaging revelations on the witness stand, like those that had come out about Gennifer Flowers, could terminally damage the president's standing. As noted above, the Jones case was thrown out by the judge on 1 April, but with a summing-up that further damaged Clinton's credibility.

Shortly thereafter Ken Starr filed for the right to call the White House Secret Service staff to give evidence – a controversial request, as the men and women of the security staff were considered legally the deaf-mutes of government circles, before whom anything could be said with safety. Even former president George Bush Senior, the man who had lost the White House to Clinton, came out to publicly attack Starr's request, and some wondered if he had political skeletons of his own he was anxious to conceal.

The White House counteroffensive against Starr was, by now, well under way. His open support of the Republican party was heavily stressed and Clinton went so far as to suggest that Starr was the cutting edge of a 'hard, well-financed, vigorous effort' to undercut the Democrat presidency – an echo of Hilary Clinton's 'vast right-wing conspiracy' statement.

However, on 5 May, a federal judgement denied Clinton's claim to presidential immunity to subpoena by the grand jury. It was clear that he would have to take the stand and give a statement under oath for a second time that year. Then, on 22 May, the Clinton camp (and presumably ex-president George Bush) received another blow when a federal judge ruled that Starr could indeed call White House Secret Service personnel to the grand jury witness stand.

Matters were not all going Ken Starr's way, however. Public feeling against what many believed was an overforceful, prurient and partisan hunt for evidence of sex in the Oval Office was growing. It was neatly expressed by William Ginsburg, Monica's lawyer, in an open letter to *California Lawyer* magazine: 'Congratulations, Mr. Starr! As a result of your callous disregard for cherished constitutional rights, you *may* have succeeded in unmasking a sexual relationship between two consenting adults.'

Meanwhile, in an odd side issue, Starr was trying to obtain the purchasing records of Kramer's bookstore, seeking to prove that Lewinsky had purchased a book called *Vox* – a novel about a couple that indulge in phone sex. Some commentators believed that in doing this he was showing both the weakness of his basic case and his cavalier disregard for rights privacy granted by the First Amendment of the US Constitution.

By late June, however, Starr's case against the president was gaining momentum. Dale Young, a friend of Monica's, testified that Monica had confided intimate details of her affair with Clinton to her as early as 1996. Shortly thereafter, Linda Tripp took the stand for the first time, accompanied by her children, to make much the same claim. She also stressed that she did not consider secretly taping Monica's telephone revelations as a betrayal of friendship. The public did not agree; Linda Tripp rapidly became an object of national revulsion and even received death threats. The Maryland State's Attorney also opened an investigation into her apparently illegal taping of telephone conversations without the agreement or knowledge of her interlocutor; Monica Lewinsky, unsurprisingly, offered unconditional help in the state attorney's investigation.

The White House Secret Service personnel gave their evidence in late July but, despite the previous legal fuss about their giving testimony, added little to the OIC's case. A secret serviceman's concentrated effort is aimed at preventing the president coming into contact with potential assassins, not pretty interns, after all. So, on 25 July, Ken Starr decided to go for the jugular, and subpoenaed William Jefferson Clinton – 42nd President of the United States. He was scheduled to give his testimony the following week.

Of course, if Clinton decided to flatly deny having an affair with Monica Lewinsky (and thus to committing perjury in his written statement to the Paula Jones trial) he might still have gotten away. For Starr and the OIC, it became imperative that Monica herself admit to the affair and her own subsequent perjury.

On 28 July, Monica's lawyers finally came to an agreement with the OIC: in return for total immunity, she would admit to the sexual affair and her perjury to the Jones trial. She would not, however, allow that any pressure had been put on her, by the president or others, to lie on her affidavit. In the face of this major defeat, President Clinton decided to be as graceful as possible, so offered to give his testimony voluntarily, without the need of an enforcing subpoena. His date to give evidence was set for 17 August, in the White House itself.

On 6 August, Monica Lewinsky appeared before the federal grand jury. She made a generally good impression on the stand – an apparently pleasant-natured young woman, surprisingly free of bitterness, despite her trapped situation. Naturally she was asked about sex:

Jury Member: With respect to physical intimacy, other than oral sex [to which Lewinsky had already admitted] was there other physical intimacy performed?

Monica Lewinsky: Yes. Everything up until oral sex.

Jury Member: OK. And just for the grand jury . . . I'll just read it . . . It states 'Definition of Sexual Relations.' For the purpose of the grand jury session, a person engages in 'sexual relations' when the person knowingly engages or causes contact with the genitalia, anus, groin, breast, inner thigh, or buttocks of any person with an intent to arouse or gratify the sexual desire of any person. Contact means intentional touching, either directly or through clothing. Ms Lewinsky, do you understand that definition?

Monica Lewinsky: Yes, I do.

Then there was the matter of the (soon to be) infamous blue dress:

Jury Member: Now directing your attention back to February 28th, 1997, the day that you wore the blue cocktail dress. You mentioned that you believe that there could be semen on it. Could you describe what you did with the president that led you to believe that?

Monica Lewinsky: We were in the bathroom and I was performing oral sex. I'm sorry, this is so embarrassing. And usually he doesn't want to . . . he didn't want to . . .

Jury Member: Ejaculate?

Monica Lewinsky: Yes. And this has sort of been a subject that we had talked about many times before and he was always saying it had issues to do with trust and not knowing me well enough at first, and then not feeling right about things and – not that he said this – but I took away from that to sort of mean that maybe in his mind if he didn't [ejaculate] then maybe he didn't need to feel guilty about that. That maybe that was easier for him to rationalize. And it was on this occasion that after we had engaged in oral sex for a while and he stopped me as he normally did and I said to him: 'You know . . .' This is so embarrassing. I'm sorry. I said to him: 'You know, I really . . . I want to make you [ejaculate].'

The president acquiesced on this occasion, allowing Monica to bring him to orgasm. As they embraced afterwards, Monica said, some of the president's semen spotted her dress. Of course, by this time the blue dress was already in the hands of the OIC and had been sent for DNA testing.

    The other, later famous event that came out during Monica's testimony was the so-called 'cigar incident'. On one occasion, in a deserted hallway leading to the Oval Office, the president had been fondling Monica's breasts and genitals. He then inserted the end of a cigar into Monica's vagina, put it in his own mouth and said, grinning: 'It tastes good.'

    Monica's testimony, although videotaped, was given in a non-public session – as was the president's sitting before the grand jury on 17 August. He made a very poor impression – equivocating and self-evidently trying to avoid telling the truth without actually lying. He repeatedly used vague wordplay and overstretched definitions to avoid the central issue as to whether he had had a sexual relationship with Monica Lewinsky. At one point he even replied to a straight question with the sentence: 'It depends on what the meaning of the word "is" is.'

    Two days later, one of the many press leaks that apparently originated from the OIC told the public that Clinton had handed over DNA material to allow cross-matching with the semen on the blue dress. Proof positive if there ever could be.

On 11 September, the Republican-controlled House of Representatives received all eighteen boxes of evidence collected by the OIC, and promptly published 445 pages of the less damaging material. A week later, ignoring furious Democrat Party and White House objections, the House Judiciary Committee released all 3,183 pages of the Starr Report to the public, plus the incredibly embarrassing videotaped testimony of the president.

At the cost of making the leader of the USA look like a slippery fool before the entire world, the Republican Party believed that they had won a major victory. The following December, the House of Representatives voted to impeach the president on charges of perjury and obstruction of justice. However, a slim Democrat majority in the Senate overturned the decision and, after a year of damaging allegation and scandal, President Clinton was free to continue as if nothing had happened.

In retrospect, the Lewinsky investigation most hurt those who had been behind it. Linda Tripp remains a national hate figure and is rumoured to have been forced to live under an assumed identity. Kenneth Starr's reputation as a biased inquisitor spoiled any hopes he may have had for further public office, forcing him to resign from the OIC and return to his legal practice. Even the Republican Party – who must, at one point, have thought they were in a win-win situation with the Lewinsky affair – did badly in the polls thereafter, winning the 2000 presidential election only by what many believe to have been gross vote rigging.

Former President Clinton, on the other hand, is generally respected as a statesman, is tipped for the Nobel Peace Prize for his presidential efforts to bring peace to the Middle East, and is said to be making a fortune on the international lecture circuit. As a guest speaker at the 2002 British Labour Party Conference, for example, he got a bigger ovation than Labour prime minister, Tony Blair.

The long-suffering Hillary Clinton – still firmly married to Bill – has arguably done even better. She won the election to be Senator to New York, and is thought by many to be on the road to being the first female president of the United States.

The generally ill-used Monica Lewinsky, after publishing her biography, has retired into private life.

DAVIDSON, THE REVEREND HAROLD

'THE PROSTITUTE'S PADRE'

The curious affair of the rector of Stiffkey sounds like high comedy – the vicar who spent his life pursuing ladies of easy virtue and ended by being caten by a lion. Even the name of the village has an air of double entendre. But for the central character and his family, it was a bleak tragedy.

Harold Francis Davidson, born in 1875, was the son of the vicar of Sholing, a suburb of Southampton. His father decided from the beginning that Harold should enter holy orders, so he was brought up with Victorian strictness, as befitted a future clergyman, and not allowed to play with rough boys. At the age of fourteen, he was placed in the charge of two maiden aunts who lived in Croydon. There, at the Whitgift School, he became friendly with a boy named Leon Quartermaine, who wanted to become an actor; Harold was also bitten by the theatre bug. In a school entertainment Harold recited comic monologues of George Grossmith and decided that he preferred the stage to the pulpit. When he was nineteen he made his debut as a comedian at Steinway Hall in London and was successful enough to decide to defy his father and make the stage a career. He became a 'drawing-room entertainer', a kind of stand-up comedian of the sort who plays modern clubs – except that his repertoire was strictly proper. He was a hit in a touring production of *Charley's Aunt*, in the title role.

However, the church was in his blood and when on tour he made a habit of calling on vicars and finding out if any of their ageing parishioners would like to hear the Bible read aloud. On one occasion he was just in time to save a sixteen-year-old girl from jumping into the Thames one foggy night; he gave her the money to return to her home and seems to have acquired a lifelong taste for helping young ladies who had fallen or were about to fall.

By the time he was 22 he had decided he preferred the church to the stage after all and with the help of the Reverend Basil Wilberforce, chaplain of the House of Commons, he was able to secure a scholarship to Exeter College, Oxford, to study for holy orders. Although he was always late for exams and took five years instead of the usual three to obtain his degree, he finally gained his first curacy at Holy Trinity, Windsor. In 1905 he was transferred to St-Martin's-in-the-Fields in London. Through the patronage of the Marquis of Townshend, whom he joined in wedlock to a company promoter's daughter, he was finally awarded the living of the little Norfolk village of Stiffkey – worth over £500 per annum and later increased to £800, an excellent salary in 1906. (His own father had only been paid £120 a year.) He was able to marry a pretty Irish actress whom he had met at Oxford and to whom he had been engaged for six years. During the next eight years she presented him with four children. But she seems to have possessed a violent temper and to have disliked being a vicar's wife for she never called on the parishioners. Soon her husband took to spending most of the week in London, returning only at weekends (he was usually so late for the service that most of the congregation had gone home by the time he arrived). He was working with underprivileged boys in the East End and helped to found the London Dockland Settlement. His zeal was tremendous and attracted the attention of Queen Mary. Then he became chaplain to the Actor's Church Union and began to frequent the dressing rooms of actresses. Bert Ross, a theatrical historian who knew him, records that he would ogle the girls as they stripped for a quick change and was finally barred from some theatres.

During World War I he became a chaplain in the Royal Navy and soon acquired himself a name as an utter nuisance for holding church parades at inconvenient times. It seems clear that he greatly enjoyed his authority and when captains objected, he appealed over their heads to Vice-Admiral Tupper, known as 'Holy Reggie'. During the war, he was arrested in a police raid on a Cairo brothel – he explained he was tracking down a diseased whore who was infecting his men.

When he came back from the war, he was shocked to find his wife about to give birth to a child – he later told someone it was the child of a colonel, for at the time one of his old friends, a colonel, was living in the vicarage. It was the end of the marriage; Davidson applied to go to India as a chaplain and even hired a locum tenens to take over in Stiffkey. The India appointment failed to materialize and Davidson returned to his habit of spending most of his time in London.

One late night in September 1920, Davidson was standing in Leicester Square when he saw a slim, poorly clad girl who looked as if she needed a good meal. He asked her what she was doing in that notorious area and she said she had no money and nowhere to sleep. Davidson gave her fifteen shillings for a room and arranged to meet her in a Lyons tea shop a few days later. Meanwhile he went home to take the services in two local churches. The girl's name was Rose Ellis and she was twenty years old, she had just become a prostitute but was not particularly successful. She became one of Davidson's protégées; he found lodgings for her and tried to find her jobs. Rose Ellis was one of the first of a long string of young ladies that Davidson attempted to 'help' during the next ten years – he himself later admitted that he picked up between one hundred and fifty and two hundred girls a year.

The rector's usual method was to approach a waitress in a tea shop – they were known as 'nippies' – and to tell her that she looked like a film star and ought not to be working in such a place. He became a great nuisance and was forbidden entry to certain tea shops. His greatest asset was undoubtedly that he looked so inoffensive. He was a tiny man with a high-pitched voice, and a chirpy manner and a great deal of charm. He seemed to be a father figure. The girls usually felt there could be no possible harm in taking tea with him; after all, he might, as he promised, be able to get them on to the stage. (In fact, he did succeed, at one point, in getting Rose Ellis a job with a touring company.)

Typical of these relationships was the one that developed with an attractive girl named Barbara Harris. In August 1930, Barbara, who was sixteen, was walking out of Marble Arch tube station when Davidson approached her with the words. 'Excuse me, miss, but has anyone told you how much you look like Mary Brian, the movie actress?' Barbara was a shop girl who spent her days reading movie magazines. Without hesitation, she agreed to accompany the bright-eyed little man to the nearest Lyons Corner House, where she listened, fascinated, as he flattered her and told her she ought to be on the stage.

Barbara Harris had no father and her mother was in an asylum for the insane. She had been seduced at fifteen by an Indian who had infected her with gonorrhoea – the seducer had been sent to jail – then been taken in charge by the church army. She had been in Holloway prison for stealing and had already taken up prostitution when Davidson met her. He gave her small sums of money, tried to help her find jobs – although she preferred to lie in bed all day reading fan magazines – and tried hard to persuade her to yield to him. Like many of Davidson's 'protégées', Barbara was invited down to Stiffkey – she went with Rose Ellis – but when she discovered that Mrs Davidson expected her to work in the kitchen, she left.

According to Barbara, Davidson kissed her at every opportunity and put his hands 'all over her'. The judge in the later court case asked 'Where?', and she repeated: 'All over.' At one point when she was penniless and out of work, Davidson told her she could move into his lodgings while he stayed with his sister in Ealing. But after a week, he sneaked into her room, saying he had missed his train. That night he slept in a chair. Then he moved on to the bed sleeping on top of the bedclothes until he eventually got into the bed wearing only a pyjama top. But Barbara firmly declined to allow him to make love to her. On another occasion he came in and found her in her pyjamas; he pushed her back on to the bed. A few days later, he sat beside her on the bed and again tried to possess her: this time he undid his trousers and as a result of his excitement, 'made a mess' of his trousers. According to Barbara, he 'made a mess two or three times'.

By the mid-1920s, Davidson's habits were getting him into trouble. To begin with, he became acquainted with a Canadian confidence man called Arthur John Gordon, who claimed to have vast sums of money tied up in Australian mining interests. Davidson invested £5,000 in Gordon's dubious schemes and predictably lost it. But instead of breaking with Gordon, he introduced him to other potential clients and did his best to persuade them to invest money. Some of these lost thousands of pounds. Davidson began to borrow from moneylenders at 250 per cent interest and in 1925 had to declare himself bankrupt, with debts of £3,000. Half his living was earmarked to satisfy his creditors – £400 a year – so his family and his various 'lame dogs' (his wife called them 'lame cats') had to live on the remaining £400 a year. In 1925 that was still an adequate income and the rector of Stiffkey continued to part with ten-shilling notes to fallen women and to promising-looking shopgirls.

Nemesis was approaching in the form of a magistrate called Major Philip Hammond who lived in the village of Morston – also included in the rector's parish. Most Sunday mornings, Davidson arrived late for the service at Morston. Hammond felt this was deplorably 'slack'. When he heard that various young ladies were staying in the vicarage at Stiffkey and that, as a result, villagers were likely to stumble over couples closely intertwined in ditches, he became indignant. A clerical cousin told him that he could make a formal complaint about Davidson to his bishop, Dr Pollock, the Lord Bishop of Norwich, under Article 2 of the Clergy Discipline Act. This Act stated that a clergyman could be brought to trial before a consistory court if charged with moral offences.

Now it so happened that the bishop knew all about the vicar of Stiffkey. Davidson was a born nuisance who often plagued the bishop with his problems. But although Dr Pollock knew about Davidson's interest in fallen women, he had never had the slightest doubt that it was solely an interest in their spiritual welfare. So when he received the complaint, his first reaction was to defend Davidson. Then he gave it more thought and decided that there would be no harm hiring a private-detective agency to look into the rector's activities. In June 1931, Charles Arrow, a retired CID officer began to follow Davidson around London. Davidson seemed to scurry like a rabbit from appointment to appointment. He spent much time in the company of various young ladies – although these did include his own daughter. He certainly seemed to make no secret of his 'charitable' activities. In December 1931, Davidson was finally summoned before the bishop to account for himself. Under the impression that the bishop was interested in his financial dealings, he took his friend Arthur Gordon along. But Gordon was sent away and Bishop Pollock explained that Davidson was under investigation. Davidson already knew this for in the previous November, Rose Ellis had come to him in a state of tearful remorse and told him that a detective had taken her out for a drink, given her a great many ports (Rose had a drink problem) encouraging her to speak at length about her relationship with Davidson. She had subsequently signed a long statement and had been given forty shillings. Davidson apparently treated this betrayal as a joke and told her that she had done better than Judas, who only got thirty pieces of silver.

The bishop's proposal was that Davidson should resign his living to avoid a scandal; in exchange, the bishop would promise that he should not be defrocked. They discussed it again at a meeting at the Athenaeum Club the following January. The bishop was anxious to avoid a public scandal and

Davidson saw this as his strongest card. His wife Molly, not unnaturally, also had the strongest objection to his being deprived of his living – it would leave her destitute. She advised her husband to defy the bishop and to threaten to give full details of the whole unsavoury affair to the press if he persisted in trying to make Davidson resign.

The bishop persisted. The result was that on 1 February 1932, when the bishop arrived in London intending to make Davidson a new offer of substituting a lesser charge of 'indiscipline', he was shocked to see newspaper placards announcing: Rector To His Accusers: I Will Fight To The Bitter End.

From that moment onward, Davidson was front-page news. The notion of an amorous vicar, endlessly pursuing tea shop waitresses, tickled the humour of the British public. For the first time since he had been ordained, Davidson preached to a packed church. He was extremely popular in Stiffkey; although his parishioners only saw him at weekends, they liked him and found him charitable, good-humoured and hardworking. They simply declined to believe any evil of him – they still felt the same nearly half a century later when the writer, Tom Cullen, went to Stiffkey to collect material for his book *The Prostitute's Padre*.

The trial – an ecclesiastical affair – opened on 29 March 1932, at Church House. On his arrival Davidson was cheered by admirers, including some parishioners, as he climbed out of a taxi. Roland Oliver was counsel for the prosecution; Davidson was defended by Richard F. Levy. The judge was F. Keppel North, chancellor of the diocese of Norwich. The prosecution opened the proceedings by explaining that this case was about sex and that for years Davidson had been systematically misbehaving with young women.

The first witness for the prosecution was Barbara Harris. She had written voluntarily to the Bishop of Norwich to tell him about the Reverend Harold Davidson. Barbara told the court how Davidson had picked her up outside Marble Arch tube station, telling her she looked like a film star. She went on to reveal how Davidson had tried to persuade her to give herself to him and had 'relieved himself' in the process of trying to rape her. It emerged that Barbara had had many lovers and that it would not have been inaccurate to describe her as a prostitute. However, her evidence made it clear that she was sexually frigid. After Barbara Harris, a number of waitresses testified that Davidson had 'pestered' them. He seems to have invited most of them down to the rectory at Stiffkey for the weekend and many had accepted.

The trial dragged on through April and into May. On 20 May 1932, Davidson himself went into the witness box. He was not a good witness. He was inclined to talk too much, and his occasional facetiousness or impertinence was detrimental to his case. Asked if he had put his arm round a certain young lady in a car, he replied that it would have been uncomfortable. The judge pointed out that he seemed to be saying that if it had been more comfortable, he might well have put his arm round her. He failed to take advantage of the hint and insisted that, in spite of his landlady's evidence to the contrary, he 'couldn't have' had his arm round the girl's waist. There were times when he seemed to be trying to irritate the judge: at one point, he claimed to be ignorant of the meaning of the word 'buttock'. Evidence about his finances revealed that he was a habitual begging-letter writer; he tried to borrow £500 from the Duchess of Devonshire, telling her that his wife and children were starving, when he was taking actresses out to dinner and the theatre. His openness often damaged his own case – such as when he admitted that he had not realized that Barbara Harris's gonorrhoea was catching. His own counsel had earlier established a point in his favour when he induced Barbara to admit that she was suffering from VD while Davidson was doing his best to make love to her and that Davidson knew this: now Davidson had undone all the good work.

Yet the most incredible example of Davidson's capacity to do himself harm came towards the end of his cross examination. It seemed that an actress named Mae Douglas had a great liking for Davidson and in an interview with the *Daily Herald* she had declared that she had often left her fifteen-year-old daughter in his charge when she was working at the theatre. Mae Douglas had also asked Davidson to arrange a photographic session for her daughter, Estelle. On Palm Sunday 1932, Estelle and three other girls went down to the vicarage, where a freelance photographer took photographs of them in pyjamas on the lawn. The photographer ran out of plates and some photographs of Estelle in a bathing costume had to be postponed until Easter Monday. On the evening of Easter Monday, Davidson escaped from his son Nugent and his fiancée, hurried to Mae Douglas's flat and posed for some photographs with Estelle. When the prosecution asked Davidson whether the photographer had taken a picture of Estelle in the nude, he said no. Then, with a flourish, Oliver produced a photograph. It showed Estelle with her back to the camera, naked except for a shawl draped only on her right shoulder and across the front of her body. Davidson faced her with one hand on her right shoulder.

Davidson looked shocked and incredulous, and suggested that the photograph was faked or touched up. Then he explained that the shawl had slipped out of his hand 'accidentally without my knowledge'. He went on to tell the court that someone was conspiring against him. Only a few weeks earlier he had been warned not to go to a certain house because a lady of title would slip off her dress and reveal herself to be wearing nothing underneath and two detectives would step out of hiding. Presumably he was hinting that the Bishop of Norwich was trying to entrap him in this way. As to the photograph of Estelle, he said later that she had originally been wearing a bathing costume under the shawl, but that the strap had been showing so she went up to the bedroom to adjust it. He had not known that when she reappeared she was naked underneath the shawl. He was asking the judge to believe that, confronted by a girl who was obviously not wearing a bathing costume, he had not even noticed that she had removed it.

The newspaper headlines proclaimed: Nude Photo Bombshell. Anyone who thought about it for a moment must have seen that Davidson could hardly have been engaged in seduction in a room with two photographers. (As it happened, his son Nugent and his fiancée had charged into the room a moment after the photograph was taken and the session ended.) But as far as the public was concerned, the photograph was the final proof of Davidson's guilt.

After a nine-week trial, the case was adjourned for a month to give the chancellor time to consider his verdict. On 8 July 1932, he gave it: Davidson was guilty on all five counts of immoral conduct. Davidson's testimony, said the judge, had been a tissue of falsehoods; he preferred to believe Barbara Harris. The judge ended by ordering Davidson to pay costs. But why had Davidson refused to call three vital witnesses: Rose Ellis, his wife, and his crooked friend Gordon?

Davidson continued to protest his innocence, pointing out that Christ had consorted with sinners.

Ten days after his trial he appeared in a variety act in Wimbledon. Leave to appeal was refused at the end of July. On 9 August he was ejected from a nudist camp at Harrogate and told reporters that he was thinking of establishing something of the sort at Stiffkey. Finally, on 21 October 1932, he arrived late for his defrocking ceremony at Norwich Cathedral and interrupted the proceedings with the assertion that it was the church that was on trial, not himself.

Deprived of his living, Davidson decided to accept an offer from Luke Gannon, the 'Showman King of Blackpool', to exhibit himself in a sideshow in a barrel. He and Gannon came into conflict because Davidson wanted to harangue his audiences about the wickedness of the church authorities, while Gannon wanted the crowds to move on as fast as possible. Davidson spent five years at Blackpool during the summer season and it is estimated he earned between £5,000 and £20,000.

He tried hard to get his case reopened. When his right to appeal was turned down, he wrote a pamphlet called *I Accuse* and distributed it to anyone who would take it. He jumped up in the Church Assembly in Westminster Hall in 1936 and tried to interrupt the proceedings – he was chased out by stewards. He continued to get into trouble and appeared in front of Blackpool magistrates on several occasions for obstruction of the public footpath. He went to prison for nine days for rent arrears owing to his London landlady. And in November 1936 he demonstrated that his problems with the law had not blunted his taste for young girls: on Victoria station he accosted two sixteen-year-old girls and told them he was looking for an actress to play a leading role in a West End play and offered them £5 to audition for the part. They made an appointment with him for the next day but when he arrived, the railway police arrested him. He was fined forty shillings.

His appeal as a sideshow was diminishing as the public forgot the scandal. He had undertaken a 35-day fast in 1935 and when arrested and charged with unlawfully trying to commit suicide by starvation, had successfully sued Blackpool Corporation and won £382 in damages. But a rumour spread that food and drink were smuggled into his cabinet at night and the suggestion that he was an old fake as well as a hypocrite made the public cynical. When his Blackpool contract was not renewed, he signed an agreement with a menagerie owner in Skegness to appear in a cage with two lions, billed as 'A Modern Daniel in the Lion's Den'. It was a courageous decision since he was terrified of animals.

The act consisted of a talk by Davidson about his case after which he would enter the cage for a few minutes. The lions were apparently very tame but in case of trouble a lion tamer stood outside the cage with a pole. On 28 July 1937, Davidson was a little too self-confident, snapping his whip at the lions and ordering them to 'get a move on'. Suddenly, the male lion, Freddy, reared up and struck Davidson with his fore paws, knocking him down. The audience roared with laughter. Then Freddy picked up Davidson by the neck, like a mouse, and began to carry him round the cage. While one man tried to poke the lion with a stick, a sixteen-year-old girl named Irene Somner rushed into the cage and grabbed Freddy by the mane, trying to make him let go. Freddy dropped the rector and the lioness immediately tried to jump on him. Irene dragged him out of the cage and slammed the door.

Davidson was taken to the Skegness Cottage Hospital. It is reported that he opened his eyes as he was pulled out of the cage and gasped, 'Telephone the London newspapers – we still have time to make the first editions.' In fact, he was more or less in a coma when admitted to hospital – he was found to have a broken bone in the neck and he died two days later.

The most baffling part of the story is why Davidson behaved as he did. Was he, as many suggested, slightly insane? Or just an incorrigible publicity seeker? Or a dirty old man?

In *The Prostitute's Padre* (1975) Tom Cullen quotes Davidson's lifelong friend J. Rowland Sales, who was convinced that Davidson was a classic case of 'multiple personality'. Cullen cites the look of total incredulity that appeared on the rector's face when he was shown the picture of the naked Estelle Douglas in court as evidence that, up until that moment, he had no memory whatever of the photograph being taken. Sales believes that Davidson was at least three totally distinct persons: 'Uncle Harold', the respectable clergyman, 'Little Jimmy', a mischievous child who loved getting

Uncle Harold into trouble, and 'the Bunco Kid', an incorrigible confidence swindler. Cullen cites the famous case of 'Sally Beauchamp', recorded by Dr Morton Prince, to show that in many ways Davidson conforms to the medical picture of a multiple personality. The objection to this view is that nearly all cases of multiple personality are people who have had horrifying or traumatic experiences in childhood. Davidson's childhood, while rather Victorian and depressing, was quite unremarkable.

The clue to the real explanation probably lies in a remark made by Molly, Davidson's wife. She commented about his conviction that he was always right. 'It is useless to tell a lunatic who says he is a poached egg that he is not one, for he will exhaust your logic and outstrip your reasoning powers.' The clue to Davidson is his refusal to admit, under any circumstances, that he was ever in the wrong. The writer A. E. Van Vogt has called such types 'Right Men'. The Right Man's ego is as hard as a rock and is based on the conviction that he cannot be wrong. Van Vogt makes another interesting observation when he explains that the Right Man will have affairs with other women, but if his wife so much as looks at another man, he becomes almost insane with jealousy. This is borne out by Davidson's reaction to discovering that Molly was pregnant by another man. This shock seems to have started him on his career of 'pestering' young girls.

Davidson's conduct during World War I shows a man of immense self-importance and conceit. His own counsel in court admitted that he was a 'troublesome busybody'. For such men, eccentricity is a way of asserting their uniqueness. His son described an occasion when Davidson spent the afternoon with himself and his wife: when it was time to catch the last train, he rushed out to the Rayner's Lane tube station but a few minutes later they heard him rushing back up five flights of stairs. He burst into the room, gasped, 'Your clock is three minutes fast by the station clock', and rushed out again. Nugent Davidson's comment was, 'Mad, utterly mad, that was father.' But one may be forgiven for suspecting that Davidson loved being thought 'mad' and that the effect of rushing back – when he was already late – to shout that his son's clock was fast was intended to be dramatic and memorable – the kind of story his son would tell again and again.

Oddly enough, Davidson still has his warm defenders – Ray Gosling proved to be among their number when he presented a programme about the rector of Stiffkey on the BBC. They believe that Davidson was, as he insisted, only interested in helping fallen women and that he was telling the truth in court when he insisted that any suggestion of sex would have shocked him. Davidson's supporters believe that Barbara Harris was lying when she claimed Davidson wanted to seduce her – Davidson's own version of the story was that she tried to seduce him, thrusting her tongue into his mouth and wrapping her legs round him and he claimed he threw her onto the bed. Cullen even quotes a senior Health Officer who treated Barbara

Harris and Rose Ellis for syphilis as saying that Davidson was impotent but this hardly seems to be borne out, either by the size of his family, or by Barbara Harris's story that he 'relieved' himself against her.

The truth is probably that, like most 'Right Men', Davidson was an incurable self-deceiver and an obsessive seducer – some of the thousand or so women must have been more obliging than Barbara Harris. He lived in a dream and firmly refused to wake up. It is his family that deserves our pity.

DIANA, PRINCESS OF WALES

THE SCANDALOUS PRINCESS

On 30 August 1997, Princess Diana was on a cruise along the coast of Sardinia, in the yacht *Jonikal*, owned by businessman Mohammed al Fayed, together with the new man in her life, al Fayed's son, Dodi. As usual, they were being observed by hordes of *paparazzi*, including two who were following the yacht in a rubber dinghy with a powerful engine. Sick of being pursued, Dodi decided to fly to Paris. They left by a Harrods Gulfstream jet at 1:45 pm, and when they arrived at Le Bourget an hour and a half later, they were driven to a villa that had been owned by the Duke of Windsor, now the property of Mohammed al Fayed.

Although they had been followed there by *paparazzi* on motorcycles, the ever-restless Diana decided that they would leave the security of the villa and go on to the Ritz Hotel in Paris, also owned by al Fayed, so she could go shopping for birthday presents for her son, Harry. Once in the Imperial Suite, Diana went to have her hair done. She also rang a friendly reporter on the *Daily Mail* to say she intended to quit public life for good. He would mention in his story a rumour that she and Dodi Fayed intended to announce their engagement.

Dodi now decided to go to his apartment in the Champs Elysées to change for dinner – once more followed by photographers, and by two bodyguards in a Range Rover. Later, finding that a bistro where they had intended to eat was surrounded by photographers, they returned to the Ritz, and started to eat a meal there. But, nervous about having their privacy invaded by photographers, they left it unfinished and returned to their suite, where they finally ate dinner.

For some reason, Dodi then decided he wanted to return to his apartment. And he decided that his regular chauffeur, Philippe Dourneau, should drive off in a Range Rover to mislead the *paparazzi*, while Henri Paul, who had met them off the plane, should take them to the Champs Elysées apartment, leaving the Ritz by the back way. Paul had been off duty, expecting a quiet evening. He had undoubtedly been drinking.

The *paparazzi* were at the back door too, and lost no time in revving their engines. Henri Paul decided to outrun them, and was soon driving at sixty miles an hour. As they plunged into the steep Alma tunnel, a 142-metre underpass, the car went out of control and smashed into a concrete pillar. Dodi al Fayed and Henri Paul were killed outright, and Diana was so badly injured that she died later in hospital. Only the bodyguard employed by al Fayed, Trevor Rees-Jones, survived, his life saved by an air bag.

The sense of shock was tremendous. Since the announcement of the engagement to Prince Charles in February 1981, Diana had been the British public's favourite member of the royal family, her beauty and shy demeanour turning her into a media goddess. Crowds would wait all day outside her home, Kensington Palace, to catch a glimpse of her. Rumours of her marital problems created widespread anger. The marriage broke up in 1992, and public sympathy soon swung in Diana's favour when Andrew Morton's book, *Diana: Her True Story*, revealed that the cause of the split had been the long-standing love affair between Prince Charles and Camilla Parker-Bowles.

The lack of public grief displayed by the royal family following Diana's death undermined even the Queen's popularity, and it may have been in response to the rising tide of criticism that the royal family took the unusual step of arranging for the funeral to be televised internationally.

Sixteen years earlier, on 29 July 1981, 750 million people had watched the marriage of Prince Charles, the Prince of Wales, to Lady Diana Spencer, and a frenzy of media attention had preceded the ceremony. The diffident bride-to-be had been pursued everywhere by gangs of reporters, and the curiosity of the British public was fed to bursting by daily stories in competing tabloid newspapers. In the battle for circulation each one was desperate to outdo the others with pictures of the couple taken in private, or stories of their courtship wheedled from close friends. Diana's face smiled from the cover of nearly every magazine on the news-stands.

The British public's delight at the prospect of a royal wedding had been mingled with relief. During the late 70s, Charles's name had been linked with many eligible socialites – Davina Sheffield, Princess Marie-Astrid of Luxembourg, Susan George, Sabrina Guinness, Amanda Knatchbull, Anna Wallace, Jane Ward – the latter the manageress at the Guards Polo Club where the Prince regularly played – but every time the gossip column writers predicted that a royal wedding was in the offing, their hopes had been frustrated. 'Sources' close to the prince would report that the relationship was over, or had never even happened. The general opinion among royal observers was that Charles, at 31, was taking rather longer than necessary to sow his wild oats.

So when his engagement to Diana was announced on 24 February 1981, the same royal observers agreed that his choice showed excellent taste. The bride-to-be was attractive, charmingly shy in front of the cameras and, most importantly, from the right background; Diana was the third daughter of Earl Spencer. In the tradition of the British royal family, she was not formidably intellectual – she had left school with only two O levels, and had then taken a course in cookery and worked as a child minder. Clearly Diana was not intended to take up a professional career. She had 'wife of the gentry' written all over her.

What no one realized until later was that Prince Charles himself was not entirely happy about the idea of marrying Diana Spencer. He had finally given way to family pressure to settle down and provide an heir – pressure from his mother and father, his Uncle Dickie (Lord Louis Mountbatten), and from the Queen Mother, who virtually chose Diana herself – a demure, compassionate girl with the right social background.

In fact, Diana had not had the happy, sheltered life everyone assumed. When she was three, her mother had fallen in love with another man, and the Spencers were divorced three years later. She had been brought up by her father. The divorce disturbed her deeply, and it may have been in reaction that she began to devote much attention to sick animals. It also seems to have been responsible for a tendency to overeat that made her plump and – in her own eyes – unattractive. As a teenager she had worked at a kindergarten in Pimlico, and shared a flat with three friends. But although she had boyfriends, she remained – according to her flatmates – sexually inexperienced; one commentator says this was because she saw sex as the cause of the breakup of her parents' marriage, and was afraid of it.

Charles, on the other hand, had had three serious sexual relationships in the year before the engagement was announced. Since the mid 1970s, many women had been to dinner in his flat in Buckingham Palace and stayed the night. The prince's valet, Stephen Barry, later told a gossip columnist how he had frequently retrieved items of ladies' underwear from under the bed or behind the cushions of the settee. If the owner was known, these were laundered and returned to her in an Asprey gift box; if not, they might be presented to members of the Palace staff – occasionally gentlemen. (The same gossip columnist remarks that many of the male staff at Buckingham Palace are homosexual, since homosexuals have no wives to divide their loyalties, and tend to enjoy the protocol of Palace life.) Prince Andrew is reported to have told a girlfriend that his brother was trying to emulate actor Warren Beatty, who had the reputation of having slept with every attractive starlet in Hollywood. According to gossip columnist Nigel Dempster, there was even a 'slush fund' that had been set up to pay off the women who objected to being one-night stands, a few of whom received a dollar cheque running to six figures. Unlike the Prince Regent, described in an earlier chapter, Charles seems to have had no problem financing his high turnover of mistresses.

Charles had also had a brief romance with Diana's sister Sarah (who later insisted it had remained platonic), and so the general assumption was that Diana had begun to feel an interest in Charles at this time – many girls develop a crush on their elder sister's boyfriends. (Sarah had apparently been finally rejected by Charles's vetters because she suffered from anorexia and was a chain smoker – her sister called her 'fag-ash Lil.') The only slight problem seemed to be the difference in the ages of Charles and Diana. At twenty, Lady Di was more than ten years younger than her royal husband-to-be.

On 29 July 1981, St Paul's Cathedral was the focus of the world's attention. In the surrounding streets, many were unashamed to weep with joy at the sight of their future king and queen. When the couple kissed on the balcony of Buckingham Palace after the ceremony, the crowds that jammed the Mall screamed their approval. Despite the economic recession and Britain's declining importance in the league of world powers, the nation was proud; there had been nothing so romantic since Prince Rainier married Grace Kelly in Monaco.

Perhaps it was the feeling of anti-climax that followed the wedding that started the reaction. Newspapers that had whipped their readership into a frenzy of nationalism with massive souvenir pullouts and photo specials found it difficult simply to drop the story and return to more mundane and depressing news. Even if the newspapers' editors had wanted to, competition would not allow it. A paper with a new picture of Diana outsold its Diana-less rival. The publicity was unrelenting: every minor occasion at which the Prince and Princess of Wales appeared in public received blanket attention. In the fever of interest in the future queen, Charles was sometimes forgotten. At public appearances, it was clear who the crowds had turned out to see; Charles seemed to take the implied affront in good part, apologizing to crowds in Wales that he only had one wife.

Soon the purely descriptive news items, praising Diana's dress-sense and cooing about the happy couple, began to sound a little repetitive. Clearly, while the public's appetite for royal gossip was undiminished, every tabloid editor sensed that they were beginning to get bored with positive stories. To vary the diet, feature writers began turning out pieces expressing concern about Diana's well-being. They pointed out that in February, when the engagement was announced, Diana had been a rosy-cheeked, healthy-looking girl who looked as if she played hockey every morning before breakfast. By the time of the wedding, she had shed considerable weight, and her cheeks were no longer so rosy. No doubt she had been dieting for her wedding day – but could it be that she was overdoing it?

When, in the months following the wedding, the princess seemed to go on losing weight, the newspapers clucked and worried like maiden aunts. Their anxiety communicated itself to the public, who responded by buying the newspapers that sounded most concerned. So when, on 21 November 1981, the palace announced that Diana was pregnant, everyone heaved a sigh of relief – not least the newspaper editors, who now had an excuse for beginning the party all over again.

In February 1982, five months into Diana's pregnancy, the Waleses holidayed on Windermere Island in the Bahamas. For many years there had been an unspoken agreement between Fleet Street and the Palace that royal holidays were no-go areas. This tradition soon fell victim to the circulation war, and newspaper photographers secretly photographed Diana in her bikini. These pictures revealed that, although pregnant, she was still obviously underweight.

The publication of these pictures brought a strong rebuke from the Palace. It was, said the spokesman, 'one of the blackest days in British journalism'. Such a criticism from the royal family was unheard of, mainly because long-established guidelines of good taste had previously governed what could be printed. But in Fleet Street times were changing. The struggle for circulation meant that such tacit agreements were luxuries that could no longer be afforded.

All this prying and intrusion involved a slow change in the attitude of reporters towards Prince Charles. The tacit agreement that had operated since the time of Queen Victoria meant that reporters addressed the Prince of Wales as 'Sir' and treated him with respect. They still continued to address him as 'Sir', but the respect was eroding. Charles's admission that he talked to his plants in order to encourage them to grow resulted in acres of ridicule in the tabloids. Taken in combination with his avowed liking for the mystical writings of Sir Laurens van der Post, Charles was made to appear to be a kind of blue-blooded hippy. Yet he had many sympathizers when, in 1983, he attacked plans for an addition to the National Gallery in Trafalgar Square, describing it as a 'carbuncle on the face of a much-loved and elegant friend'. (The plans for the extension were then dropped.)

The couple certainly had to endure trial-by-camera. Every time they appeared together, the expressions on their faces were analysed and discussed in the captions, and they sometimes had to endure intrusion by long telephoto lens. (Charles had been sensitive about such matters ever since he had been photographed, in May 1960, lying on a blanket by the river at Balmoral with a girlfriend named Anna Wallace.) Moreover, the smallest physical contact between Charles and any other woman who happened to be in the entourage was subjected to the same minute analysis.

There was also an attempt to 'humanize' the royal couple with 'chatty' (i.e. disrespectful) and 'homely' (impertinent) stories – for example, after the Waleses' second son, Harry was born, the newspapers revealed that William and Harry were known by their parents as the 'heir and spare'.

Now in their fourth year of marriage, Charles and Diana were granted a respite. Finally starved of new material for gossip, the tabloids had turned their attention to Prince Andrew, Charles's younger brother. Andrew's relationships with women provided more substantial fare than the diet of innuendo and rumour in the stories about Diana. Andrew was portrayed as libidinous and cheeky. A convenient contrast to the intellectual and contemplative Charles, Andrew played up to the 'Randy Andy' tag. He attempted to get TV presenter Selina Scott's phone number while being interviewed by her for Terry Wogan, and was often photographed 'out on the town' with one-time soft-porn actress Katherine 'Koo' Stark.

But by 1985, Andrew was 25, the age when royal tradition dictated that he should be thinking of marriage. Then, during the Royal Ascot week party at Windsor Castle, the invited guests were surprised to see Andrew hand-feeding profiteroles to the freckled and bouncy redhead who was seated next to him. The woman was Sarah Ferguson, daughter of Major Ronald Ferguson, Prince Charles's polo manager. Such open friskiness tied in well with Andrew's playboy image, and the papers immediately began to cover the couple's meetings extensively.

And meet they did, often and publicly. At the time of the Ascot party, Sarah had been the girlfriend of racing driver Paddy McNally. It was rumoured that, after giving MacNally the ultimatum 'Marry me or else . . .', Sarah had decisively dropped him. The Palace plainly approved of Fergie (as Sarah was known). It was, after all, the seating arrangements at a royal party that had brought them together. Such things are not random or accidental.

Andrew and Fergie's engagement was announced in February 1986, to no one's great surprise. Their wedding took place in Westminster Abbey in July of that year. Although not as grand an affair as the wedding of his elder brother, Andrew's wedding excited the same public enthusiasm. Fergie, of course, could hardly be less like Diana; where Diana's image was shy and demure, Fergie's was effervescent and mischievous. Everyone liked her – she looked as if she would enjoy a game of darts in the local pub. When newspapers reported that Diana and Fergie had dressed up as policewomen in order to gatecrash Andrew's stag night, no one had any doubt who had thought up the idea.

On his marriage, Andrew inherited the title of the Duke of York. The Queen's present to the couple was a lease on the Sunninghill estate, as well as the money to build a family house there.

The tone of the articles about the two royal couples became less and less positive as the decade wore on. The Duchess of York seemed to be permanently on holiday: she beamed from the ski-slopes or golden beaches at least once a week. Rightly or wrongly the British public suspected that it was their tax revenues that were enabling her to live this enviable life. The 'respectable' newspapers began to voice a certain irritation with the British obsession with the younger members of the royal family, and the *Independent* newspaper, which had just been established, expressed the broadsheets' boredom with royal stories by covering Beatrice's birth with a single line in the Births, Marriages and Deaths column in the back pages. Again there was criticism when, after the birth of Princess Beatrice, the Duchess of York went off to join her husband in Australia without her daughter, and yet again when she took her daughter skiing in Switzerland while she still had a chickenpox rash. Her plans for her new home in Berkshire were derided as vulgar and ostentatious.

What was worse, from the point of view of the royal family, was that it was very obvious that all was not well between Charles and Diana. She was blamed because members of Charles's household were said to have resigned because they found her too demanding. Even in the mid-1980s it was noted that the couple seemed to spend little time together, and that they seemed to barely tolerate each other in public. The days of sunny smiles for the cameras seemed to be past.

By the late 1980s the tabloids were busy spreading doubts about the strength of both marriages. Prince Charles, they hinted regularly, was having an affair with Camilla Parker-Bowles, an old girlfriend now married. Fergie was also suspected of infidelity with Texan millionaire Steve Wyatt, her financial advisor. Yet no real evidence, apart from whispered confidences from sources 'close to Charles' or 'a Palace insider', were offered. But it seemed clear that the newspapers knew more than they were prepared to print; they regularly hinted that they could not tell the full truth.

Things began to fall apart for the Yorks in January 1992. Maurice Marple, a window cleaner, had been hired by an estate agent to clean a flat in Cadogan Square. While throwing out the unwanted property left by the previous tenant, Marple happened upon a thick stack of photos perched on top of a wardrobe. Idly flicking through them before consigning them to the black plastic sack, Marple suddenly recognized the face of the Duchess of York, Sarah Ferguson. Some of the photos showed the duchess and a handsome tanned man in swimsuits, laughing and having a good time. Others showed the unidentified man playing with Princess Beatrice, and riding a horse beside Fergie. What the other photos showed is not known.

Marple decided that the newspapers would be interested in his discovery. He took them to the *Daily Mail* who advised him to give them to the police. Whether he did this is not clear; all that *is* known is that some of the photographs were published in *Paris-Match*.

During the next few days the British tabloids made much of their restraint in not publishing the pictures. But they dropped very broad hints that the photos showed the duchess in inappropriate positions with a man identified as the Texan millionaire Steve Wyatt.

In fact, the affair had been known to all Fergie's friends for a long time. Wyatt was undoubtedly handsome, in a lean, Texan way, with very white teeth. He and Fergie had met in 1990, when Prince Andrew was away from home – in the navy – for all but 42 nights of the year. She was pregnant when she visited Wyatt's ranch in Texas, but the affair progressed nevertheless. In a French Riviera restaurant with Fergie and Saddam Hussein's oil marketing chief (this was soon after Saddam's invasion of Kuwait), Wyatt embarrassed Lord McAlpine and his guests by pulling Fergie into his lap with the comment: 'Mah woman and I sit together.' Eventually, Fergie was persuaded by the Queen and her own mother to drop the indiscreet Wyatt. By January 1992, when the photograph scandal was the talk of London, the affair with Wyatt was already over.

For Prince Andrew, this seems to have been the last straw. On 19 March 1992, two months after the Wyatt photos story, the Yorks announced that they had decided to separate. To a stunned public, this seemed to be a full acknowledgement of the duchess' adultery. Before this new information had had time to sink in, the public was hit with a bigger revelation.

DIANA DRIVEN TO FIVE SUICIDE BIDS BY 'UNCARING CHARLES' shrieked the headline of the *Sunday Times* on 7 June 1992. The story beneath contained some of the most startling revelations from a new book by Andrew Morton, a royal journalist, entitled *Diana: Her True Story*. What made this book different from other similar works – like Lady Colin Campbell's *Diana in Private* – was that it was plainly written with some co-operation from the Princess of Wales. Morton had quite a story to tell. The book revealed that Diana had been doubtful about marrying Charles from the start. Since 1972, Charles had been friendly with Camilla Parker-Bowles; they were so close that they addressed one another as Fred and Gladys. Camilla was married to Andrew Parker-Bowles, a member of the Queen's household, and Diana had known her since 1980. At first, Diana was unsuspicious, even when she learned that Camilla was reputed to 'vet' all Charles's girlfriends. She remained unsuspicious when Camilla asked her if she meant to hunt when she was at Highgrove (Prince Charles's new house), and looked relieved when Diana said no. But a few weeks before their wedding, she learned that Charles and Camilla used nicknames when Charles had sent Camilla a get-well bouquet inscribed 'from Fred to Gladys.' And when, on the eve of her wedding, she learned that Charles intended to give Camilla a bracelet inscribed *GF* (which, according to an alternative source, stood for 'Girl Friday', another of Charles's pet nicknames for Camilla), it dawned on her with an awful sense of certainty that Camilla was her future husband's mistress, and that he had no intention of breaking off the relationship when he married. She came close to calling the wedding off the night before the ceremony.

When, on their honeymoon, photographs of Camilla fell out of Charles's diary, and when she noticed that he wore cufflinks with two 'Cs' intertwined – which he admitted had been given to him by a woman he had loved and lost – her worst suspicions were confirmed.

Understandably, she was shattered. Ever since her parents' divorce she had been afraid of love, but was willing to suspend her distrust and learn to become a caring wife and mother. Now it was obvious that she was simply the third in a triangle and that, like so many women who had married princes of the British royal family, she was going to be expected to close her eyes to her husband's infidelities.

On the eve of the wedding, Charles allayed her fears when he sent her a signet ring and an affectionate note. But all the tension made her eat more than she intended to, then vomit it all up.

They spent the honeymoon on the royal yacht *Britannia*, and here again, she began to feel excluded. She wanted to spend time getting to know her husband – with whom she was by now deeply in love. Charles took along his fishing tackle and a pile of books by his mentor, Laurens van der Post, who had written of the bushmen of South Africa, and had been a friend of the psychologist Carl Jung. They hardly ever seemed to be alone. Again, Diana's response to stress was to creep into the kitchen and eat bowl after bowl of ice cream.

What no one realized was that Diana was suffering from the nervous disorder called bulimia nervosa, which involves overeating, usually followed by vomiting. Its sufferers tend to experience extreme mood-swings, and may become suicidal.

Clearly, both Charles and Diana had problems. He had thought he was marrying an uncomplicated girl who would enjoy being Princess of Wales and then queen; to learn – as he soon did – that she had nervous problems must have been a shock. For her part, she thought she was marrying a kind of protective father-figure who would help her to adjust to her new life. But he seemed to live on another plane, and although he took her for long walks and read her page after page by Jung and van der Post, she felt she was being talked down to.

But the major problem, of course, was her suspicion that her husband was still in love with Camilla Parker-Bowles, and meant to renew their relationship at the first opportunity. They began to have violent rows about Camilla. And once a newly married couple start having violent rows, the marriage has lost its chance of the kind of slow and idyllic growth that can form the basis of a lifelong partnership; the golden bowl had developed a crack.

What she now needed was some close support from her husband, a reassurance that all would be well. But Charles seemed unable or unwilling to offer such reassurance. He seemed to feel that she was suffering from neurotic schoolgirl tantrums, and that what was really needed was that she should pull herself together. Most of the royal family seemed to feel much the same. On New Year's Day 1982, when she was three months pregnant with Prince William, she threatened suicide, and Charles accused her of being hysterical. When he went off riding on the Sandringham estate, she hurled herself down a long wooden staircase.

It was the Queen Mother, the major architect of the marriage, who found her lying dazed at the bottom, trembling with shock, and who sent for help. A hastily summoned gynaecologist was able to assure everyone that both Diana and the foetus were unharmed.

Far from winning sympathy from her husband, it infuriated him as a piece of melodramatic hysteria. In a sense, the marriage ended then, less than a year after it had begun.

According to Lady Colin Campbell in *Diana in Private*, Diana also felt that she was an outsider in the royal family. The Queen, says Lady Colin, had absolutely nothing in common with Diana, and 'the gulf between them grew worse and worse'. Princess Anne simply regarded Diana as 'an airhead and a lightweight' and could not understand why Charles had married her. But one day, at the dinner table, when Diana dropped into the conversation a question about how they saw the role of the royal family in a united Europe, they regarded her with puzzlement for a few moments, then went back to discussing hunting. Diana's increasing frustration is understandable. Morton describes how Diana one day threw herself against a glass display cabinet, and how, during one argument with Prince Charles, she seized a penknife and cut herself on the chest and thighs. Charles's reaction was to ignore her.

For Charles it must have seemed that the fairytale marriage had turned into a kind of hell. The sweet, shy twenty-year-old, who was supposed to adore him and be delighted that he had introduced her to a new and wonderful life had turned out to be a vengeful neurotic who spent half her time in tears and was always complaining. He must have wished that he had taken his courage into his hands all those years before, and married Camilla, who thoroughly understood him.

The arrival of Prince William improved things for a while; Charles loved being a father, and was well suited to the role. Then there was a reaction, and Diana plunged back into depression. She began to see a psychiatrist (Jungian, naturally), but continued to lose weight. Diana and Charles moved between their two homes, Kensington Palace and Highgrove, but they had so little social life that their butler described working for them as boring.

On the other hand, Charles continued to hunt with the Parker-Bowleses, and saw Camilla regularly. And Diana 'found a shoulder to lean and cry on' in her personal bodyguard, Sergeant Barry Manakee. Morton notes that 'the affectionate bond that built up between them did not go unnoticed either by Prince Charles or Manakee's colleagues'. Manakee was later transferred to other duties, and was killed in a motorcycle accident. No impropriety has ever been alleged, but it seems clear that, lacking emotional support from her husband and the royal family, she felt a need to look for it elsewhere.

The romance between Prince Andrew and Fergie provided a welcome diversion. Diana and Fergie became close friends, and Diana, now more confident, guided Fergie through the routine of being a 'royal'. In public, she was self-possessed and as charming as ever. But she still felt that she was a kind of royal cipher. There was the occasion when she prepared a surprise for the royal family when they were due to spend an evening watching ballet at Covent Garden. She and leading dancer Wayne Sleep had rehearsed a routine in secret at Kensington Palace. The audience gasped when Diana stepped out onto the stage in a silver silk dress, and danced a specially choreographed routine to the song 'Uptown Girl', revealing that she had the makings of a first-class dancer. The audience applauded wildly, and she took eight curtain calls, even curtseying to the royal box. But Charles later told her he thought that it had all been undignified and 'showy'.

Even by 1987, it was becoming obvious to the press that the royal marriage was under some strain. Diana and Fergie came in for criticism for 'frivolity' when both were photographed at a race meeting poking a friend in the backside with their umbrellas. When Diana and a group of friends had a weekend party at the stately home of the parents of a young man named Philip Dunne, a gossip columnist reported that Diana had spent the weekend alone with him. When she was ambushed by a photographer as she emerged from a cinema with a group of friends that included a young man called David Waterhouse, Waterhouse leaped a pedestrian barrier and fled into the night, causing more gossip than if he had stayed put.

In 1987, her confidence fortified by a new doctor who seemed to be helping her to conquer her bulimia, Diana cornered Camilla Parker-Bowles at a birthday party and accused her of sleeping with her husband. Whether Camilla admitted it or not Morton does not record, but he tells us that the explosion 'helped Diana to come to terms with her jealousy and anger'.

At about this time – in 1988 – a polo player named Captain James Hewitt came into Diana's life when he began to teach Princes William and Harry horsemanship. She visited his home in Devon, and they were soon the subject of suspicion on the part of the royal family. A colour-sergeant later told the *News of the World* that he had been part of a surveillance team whose job was to spy on the couple and photograph them making love in the garden. Hewitt's friend, Anna Pasternak, later wrote a book – with his co-operation – in which she admitted that they had been lovers.

The reason for this oddly brash piece of behaviour on Diana's part seems to lie in Morton's comment that the royal couple drifted apart to the extent of marshalling rival battalions of friends in their support. In a book called *Closely Guarded Secret,* Inspector Ken Wharfe, who became Diana's official 'minder' in 1987, states that Hewitt was deeply in love with Diana, and wanted her to marry him; Diana, unattracted by the idea of becoming nothing more exciting than an officer's wife, decided to drop him.

Morton also commented that Prince Charles 'counted on' Andrew and Camilla Parker-Bowles for social support. Their home, Middlewich House, was only twelve miles from Highgrove House. A Sunday newspaper spoke about the unmarked Ford estate car in which Charles frequently drove to Middlewich House.

When, in January 1992, Prince Andrew and Fergie visited the Queen at Sandringham to confess that their marriage was on the rocks – partly due to the latest press uproar about her relationship with Steve Wyatt – the Queen asked them for a two-month 'cooling off' period before they announced their separation. This completed, the press was informed that their marriage was over. Yet Charles and Diana were still officially together, even though they lived apart.

When Andrew Morton's *Diana, Her True Story* was published in 1992, after serialization in the *Sunday Times*, it combined all these scandalous revelations with a glowingly positive assessment of the princess, in which her work for charity and her love for her children featured prominently. In this respect it read like one of the countless glossy coffee table books that portrayed the royal family as practitioners of all the old-fashioned virtues, but Morton, with the help of Diana's friends, had taken this genre and cross-bred it with kiss-and-tell Hollywood scandal sheets. It sold massively, making Morton a wealthy man.

In the postscript to the paperback edition, Morton begins: 'The days of pretending were over forever.' The book, apparently, had led the couple to face up to the collapse of their marriage. From now on, they were to live separate lives.

That summer of 1992, Fergie was back in the news. 'Fergie's Stolen Kisses' shouted the *Daily Mail* headline. An Italian long-lens paparazzo, Daniel Angeli, had snapped the duchess with her financial advisor John Bryan, a tall, prematurely balding Texan who had been a schoolfriend of Steve Wyatt. They were holidaying together, with the duchess' children, in a villa in the woods outside St Tropez. In one photo, Bryan kisses the duchess' toes. The duchess is topless in the shots. Fergie was already virtually unmentionable within the royal family, and the photographs seemed to make any reconciliation out of the question.

Then, just at the point when Fergie was squirming uncomfortably in the spotlight, it was switched back to Diana again. On 24 August 1992, the *Sun* published an account of a taped conversation between Princess Diana and a second-hand car dealer, James Gilbey. 'My Life Is Torture: Dianagate tape of love call reveals marriage misery' declared the headline. The conversation opens arrestingly:

GILBEY: And so, darling, what are the other lows today?
DIANA: So that was it . . . I was very bad at lunch. And I nearly started blubbing. I just felt really sad and empty, and I thought: 'Bloody hell, after all I've done for this fucking family.'

On the 23 minute tape, Gilbey addresses her as 'Squidgey' (fourteen times) and 'darling' (53 times), and at one point they blow kisses to one another down the phone. He tells her that he hasn't played with himself for 48 hours, and that something was 'very strange and very lovely too.' Diana replies: 'I don't want to get pregnant.' 'Darling, that's not going to happen. All right? . . . You won't get pregnant.' After more general conversation, Gilbey tells her: 'Just have to wait till Tuesday.'

In fact, the tape had been recorded two years earlier, in December 1989, by an eavesdropper on the princess' mobile phone, using a device called a 'scanner'. It appeared to reveal that Diana had been on intimate terms with Gilbey while she and Charles were still living together. Yet the real interest of the tape lies in the enormous weariness Diana expresses regarding her in-laws. Here was further proof of the misery of the princess and the lack of communication at the heart of the monarchy. A debate about whether Diana and Gilbey did or did not have sex raged in the papers for weeks.

Oddly enough, the tape did Diana no harm with the British public. The suggestion that she had a lover added a dimension to her personality; the comment: 'I don't want to get pregnant' substituted the image of a woman capable of sexual passion for the demure schoolgirl persona that had made her seem a permanent virgin.

Prince Charles was reported to have been disgusted by the publicity, while Diana is on record as saying that it was a catharsis.

On 9 December 1992, Buckingham Palace announced 'with regret' that the Prince and Princess of Wales had decided to separate.

Five weeks later, on Sunday 17 January 1993, the *Sunday Mirror* and the *People* published in full a tape of another recorded telephone conversation, this time between Prince Charles and Camilla Parker-Bowles; like the Gilbey-Diana tape, it had been recorded by an eavesdropper. This conversation had, in fact, taken place on 17 December 1989, two weeks before the Gilbey-Diana tape. It was considerably more explicit. When Camilla says: 'You're awfully good at feeling your way along,' Charles replies: 'O, stop! I want to feel my way all along you, all over you, and up and down you and in and out . . . particularly in and out.' Camilla replies: 'O, that's just what I need at the moment.' Charles suggests: 'I'll just live inside your trousers or something. It would be much easier.' 'What, are you going to turn into a pair of knickers? You're going to come back as a pair of knickers.' 'Or,' says Charles, 'God forbid, a Tampax. Just my luck! . . . to be chucked down a lavatory and go forever swirling around the top, never going down . . .'

In *Behind Palace Doors,* an even more revelatory book than Morton's, gossip columnist Nigel Dempster reports that when Charles heard about the tape, four days before it was published, he kept repeating: 'How can it all have gone wrong so quickly?' He may have been cheered when, after newspaper publication of the tape, a crowd of well-wishers at Sandringham shouted: 'Good old Charlie', but a close friend commented:

> It was the worst moment of his life. He wanted to be taken seriously, to be given respect as a man. He sincerely believed that he had important things to say. He wanted to be thought profound. And in six minutes of private conversation, a conversation that was nobody's business but his and the woman to whom he was speaking, his reputation was ruined. Maybe it was a delusion that he was something of a sage and a philosopher, but it was a fairly harmless delusion. The downfall of a prince holds a terrible fascination, but he really didn't deserve to be destroyed so publicly.

A passage from the *Encyclopedia Yearbook* for 1992 summarizes succinctly the various problems encountered by the royal family in 1992:

During 1992 the media chronicled the breakdown of the marriage of the Prince and Princess of Wales. Andrew Morton's *Diana; Her True Story* revealed that their marital problems had provoked several suicide attempts by the princess. Although Morton had not interviewed Diana, it quickly became clear that he had spoken to several of her closest friends, and that she had, tacitly at least, authorized their disclosures. The stories about the couple, amplified by aggressive reporting by tabloid newspapers, added to the pressure on the royal family, which had seen the divorce of the Princess Royal (the Prince of Wales's sister) and the separation of the Duke and Duchess of York earlier in 1992. Finally, on 9 December, Buckingham Palace announced that the Prince and Princess of Wales would separate. This announcement completed what the Queen described as an 'annus horribilis' in a rare public comment on her troubles during a speech on the occasion of her 40th anniversary on the throne. Not only had every one of the first marriages of her children ended in separation, but she also had to contend with a fire that destroyed much of the interior of Windsor Castle on 20 November. The government agreed to finance the castle's restoration, in line with established policy towards the royal castles, leaving the Queen to pay only for the furnishings that had been destroyed within her private apartments. Controversy over whether the Queen should make a greater contribution was only softened by an announcement six days later that she had volunteered to give up her tax-free status. The one undoubted source of joy to the royal family in the final weeks of a difficult year was the Princess Royal's wedding on 12 December to Commander Timothy Laurence, a former equerry (aide) to the Queen.

The story is, of course, ongoing. The prince's 'downfall' was not as catastrophic as his friend seemed to suspect, and time has blurred the memory of the 'Camillagate' tape, although it was revived in 1995 by the divorce of Andrew and Camilla Parker-Bowles. And although a *Daily Mirror* poll indicated that 63 per cent of readers believed that Charles was not fit to be king, and that the crown should pass direct to Prince William, there seems to be little doubt that, when the time comes, Prince Charles will become King Charles III.

Princess Di continued to be controversial up to her death. After announcing that she was giving up public appearances and returning to private life, she continued to appear at many public events. And scandals continued to be associated with her name. Her friend, Oliver Hoare, complained to the police that a caller was ringing his home in the early hours of the morning, then hanging up without speaking; when the police investigated, they found that the calls were coming from Kensington Palace. And the year-old marriage of England's rugby captain, Will Carling, came to an end after reports that he was seeing a great deal of Diana.

The *Daily Mirror* poll also found that 42 per cent of readers thought that Britain would be no worse off without a royal family, and that one in six felt that the monarchy would not survive beyond the end of the twentieth century.

Diana's endless capacity to generate scandal was demonstrated again in October 2002, with the trial of her butler, 43-year-old Paul Burrell – whom she had called her 'rock' – on a charge of stealing hundreds of items belonging to Diana and Prince William. Paul Burrell, a lorry driver's son, had been a member of the Queen's household before he became Princess Diana's butler.

On 31 August 1997, Burrell had flown to Paris, and been handed the clothes in which Diana had died. He had dressed her body in clean clothes for its return to England. That November he was appointed a member of the committee to choose a memorial to Diana. But a month later he was sacked because of disagreements with fellow members.

In January 2000, Burrell was arrested at his Cheshire home, accused of stealing over 300 items belonging to Princess Diana. He was granted bail, and later charged at Bow Street Magistrate's Court on 16 August 2001. The trial itself did not begin until 14 October 2002, but was stopped two days later for legal reasons, and started again on the 17th.

Then, on 1 November 2002, the trial collapsed dramatically when the Queen corroborated Burrell's story that he had told her two years earlier that he had taken certain of Diana's possessions into 'safe keeping'. But the Queen's intervention was received with widespread scepticism. Was it coincidence that Burrell was about to appear in the witness box on the day the trial was stopped?

Burrell's acquittal was soon followed by rumours that he had been offered immense sums of money by tabloid newspapers for his story.

No one believed that he would be tempted. At a butler's convention in Denver in 2001, Burrell had made the keynote speech, underlining the importance of discretion, and been received with a standing ovation.

So there was general astonishment when it was revealed that he had accepted £300,000 from the Labourite tabloid the *Daily Mirror,* turning down a million from another tabloid – he had chosen the *Mirror* because it had agreed to his insistence that he should not 'tell all', but only what he wanted to tell.

A foretaste of the revelations appeared in the *Daily Mail*, in an article by Richard Kay, a journalist Diana had treated as a friend. Kay explained that what had worried the butler was what was happening to Diana's possessions. Her letters were being shredded, and the Spencer family were taking many of her possessions to their home, Althorp, the Spencer family seat in Northamptonshire. Just before Christmas 1998, Burrell asked if he could see the Queen, and spent three hours pouring out his heart. Diana had not even spoken to her mother, Frances Shand Kydd, for the last six months before the car accident, because her mother had criticized her taste in lovers, with special reference to Muslims: heart surgeon Hasnat Khan, and businessman Gulu Lalvani. Yet now the Spencers were setting themselves up as sole guardians of her memory. Butler felt particularly bitter because when he was sacked from the fund, a 'senior figure' (Kay is too discreet to name names) sneered at his working class origin: 'Remember where you're from.' Burrell ended that long session with the Queen by telling her that he was taking some of Diana's possessions back home with him 'for safe keeping'.

When the Serious Crimes Squad arrived at Burrell's home in January 2001, they were searching specifically for the contents of a large mahogany box in which Diana kept intimate papers and possessions – what some tabloids came to refer to as 'the crown jewels'. The box itself was now at Althorp, empty. The police were armed with a list supplied by Diana's elder sister, Lady Sarah McCorquodale, of certain things – such as cufflinks and ties – that Burrell was entitled to keep. Anything else, it was implied, was stolen. And so it was that in June that year, Burrell was charged with theft.

Why did he not do the obvious thing, and direct the Serious Crimes Squad to Buckingham Palace, where the Queen would back up his story that he was trying to keep Diana's private possessions out of the hands of the Spencers? The answer seems to lie in Burrell's well-known discretion. The butler felt he had a pact of confidentiality with the royal family. Was he to drag the Queen's name into this sordid squabble about love letters?

The royals were infuriated at the way Burrell was being treated. Prince Charles even had a row with his police bodyguard, Stuart Osborne, about Burrell, whom he wanted to help, while Osborne was on the side of the police investigators. Charles felt Burrell was being persecuted because of his loyalty to Diana, and he got so angry with Osborne that he ordered the driver to stop the car and told the bodyguard to get out.

Burrell had had a bad time of it while he was awaiting his trial, and money had dried up, so he was on the verge of bankruptcy. So that last-minute rescue by the Queen must have come as an immense relief. Without it, Burrell would fairly certainly have faced prison and ruin. The *Daily Mail* had no doubt who was responsible for this; its headline declared: THE BITTER SPENCERS, JEALOUS OF HIS INTIMACY WITH DIANA, INSISTED ON PROSECUTION.

Inevitably, the Serious Crimes Squad was also blamed – it was felt that they had plunged into this prosecution, hoping it would bring them as much kudos as the Jeffrey Archer investigation, and allowing themselves to be convinced of Burrell's guilt by the Spencer family. (In fact, Earl Spencer declared after Burrell's acquittal that he was furious with the police for bringing the prosecution on such slender evidence.)

The picture of Diana that emerged in Burrell's *Daily Mirror* revelations showed her as tense, emotionally insecure and thoroughly neurotic. She had been emotionally fixated on a Pakistani heart surgeon, Hasnat Khan, whom she had met at the Royal Brompton Hospital in August 1996, where he was working under the famous heart surgeon Sir Magdi Yacoub. Khan, six feet tall and good looking, was sitting by a patient's bed when Diana came to visit the husband of her acupuncturist Oonagh Toffolo. They soon became lovers, and Burrell used to smuggle Khan into Kensington Palace in the boot of his car. On one occasion Diana dressed up in sapphire and diamond earrings before going into her bedroom and removing all her clothes. Then she came out to go and meet Khan in only a long fur coat. She was on her way to his flat near the Brompton's sister hospital, Harefield, in Middlesex, where she would often gain access by climbing through the window.

Khan was a quiet, good-natured man, modest, unassuming, and totally obsessed by his work. He had been twice engaged to marry Muslim girls who had been chosen by his family, but both engagements had fallen through. And it seems clear that he was soon feeling under pressure from Diana's highly emotional nature. After they had spent the night together, she would often telephone him as soon as he arrived at work, once even insisting on speaking to him when he was in the operating theatre. When he was unable to take her calls, she assumed that he was avoiding her, and rang friends in floods of tears. 'She was besotted with him', said one friend. This was obviously a recurring pattern – it had happened with Major James Hewitt and Oliver Hoare.

The mild, studious Khan, whose ambition was to become a professor, was soon wishing he had not been drawn into the relationship. Diana was determined to marry him, and to this end she insisted on meeting his family in the small town of Jhelum, in Pakistan, where she made a close friend of his grandmother, Nanny Appa; she also became a regular visitor at the home of his uncle Omar and wife Jane at Stratford-upon-Avon, and enjoyed feeling a part of the family, insisting on doing the washing up.

She confided in one friend that she was thinking of getting pregnant to make sure Khan married her.

Khan found the emotional pressure-cooker atmosphere unbearable, and disliked it even more when rumours of their relationship began to circulate, and he became an object of curiosity. He realized that marrying her would simply have the effect of turning him into 'Mr Diana' and making him a media celebrity. When Paul Burrell delivered letters from Diana into his hands, sitting in the hospital waiting room, the surgeon began to feel persecuted. The less responsive he became, the more obsessive became his frantic lover; finally, he was in full flight, with Diana in pursuit. When he saw her car waiting near his flat, he would hurry away.

When they finally parted in May 1997, they did so on friendly terms; but even then, Diana failed to keep her side of the bargain and stayed in touch.

It was after this that she had an affair with an electronics tycoon, Gulu Lalvani. It has been reported that he now accepts that she was simply using him in an attempt to make Khan jealous. She did not succeed. Neither did her affair with Dodi al Fayed have that effect; besides, they were basically unsuited, for Dodi was too much under his father's shadow to offer her the kind of qualities she was looking for in a husband. Burrell dismisses the idea that the two became engaged just before her death.

The butler's acquittal lit the touch paper of another scandal. Among the 'stolen' articles belonging to Diana, the police were hoping to find a cassette of an interview with a former palace footman, George Smith, who claimed he had been the victim of a homosexual rape by one of Prince Charles's servants; this, he alleged, had taken place in a kitchen in 1989. (David Davies, a retired chief superintendent who had been in charge of the royal protection squad, would later complain about the problems caused by 'promiscuous' gay staff who sometimes brought male prostitutes into the palace.) Smith reported the rape in 1996, and there was a seven-month internal enquiry, which ended by deciding that there was not enough evidence to prosecute the accused man, one of Prince Charles's closest aides. But it seems that Diana decided to pursue her own enquiry, and made a tape-recording of Smith's story, which subsequently vanished. Diana was clearly out to embarrass her former husband when the opportunity arose. A friend of Smith reports him as saying that the rapist then stole the tape from Diana's apartment.

Another item that had now vanished, according to Burrell, was seven videotapes made by the princess, staring straight into the camera, laying bare 'her innermost feelings about her loneliness and isolation, making stunning new disclosures about how Prince Charles betrayed her with Camilla Parker-Bowles.' The tapes were found when the Serious Crimes Squad made its raid on Burrell's home, but were deemed 'too sensitive' to be mentioned at the trial.

When the trial of Paul Burrell was abruptly terminated, there was inevitably speculation that there was a cover-up involving the Smith 'rape tape', and there were demands for an enquiry into whether there had been an attempt to pervert the course of justice.

Prince Charles called in a prestigious law firm, Kingsley Napley, to represent his 'trusted aide', at an initial cost of £100,000; he also approached a top barrister for advice on what to do if the aide should be named in the press.

When the Palace then announced that there would be another 'internal enquiry' into the rape allegations, there were groans of disapproval from the press, and more allegations of a cover-up. Why, they wanted to know, an internal enquiry, rather than calling in the police?

One of Prince Charles's top aides, Michael Fawcett, also found himself spotlighted in this storm of allegations and counter-allegations. He was accused of 'fencing' Prince Charles's cast-offs, as well as official gifts (of which heads of state inevitably receive a vast quantity), and taking a cut of between 10 and 20 per cent on the sales, the prince receiving the remainder. The Labour MP Ian Davidson, a member of the Commons Public Accounts Committee, said that if the allegations were true, 'we would certainly want to look into that. All the money they receive should be used to offset the huge sums that the public purse provides for them.' Mr Fawcett, it was later announced, was to go on indefinite leave.

All of which made it clear that, even five years after her death, Princess Diana's ability to cause embarrassment to the royal family remains undiminished.

At the close of 2002, the media revealed that James Hewitt was offering Diana's letters to him for sale on the open market for ten million pounds. Princes William and Harry, it was reported, were considering buying them. Prince Charles showed no reaction.

THE DREYFUS AFFAIR

THE POLITICAL SCANDAL THAT SHOOK FRANCE

The Dreyfus scandal, usually known simply as 'the affair', is probably the most famous *cause célèbre* of all time. It divided France, caused unprecedented bitterness, and finally became an international scandal that tarnished the reputation of France.

On the morning of 26 September 1894, Major Hubert-Joseph Henry, a French intelligence officer, summoned a number of War Office colleagues and showed them a handwritten document written on onion-skin paper. It was unsigned, but its last sentence: 'I am just going on manoeuvres', made it clear that it had been written by an officer. The writer said that he was sending five documents and then listed them: a note on an army field gun, on artillery formations, and similar items. It had been recovered from the waste-paper basket of Colonel Max von Schwartzkoppen, the German military attaché in Paris and it indicated unmistakably that a French officer was betraying his country by spying for Germany. After the Franco-Prussian war of 1870–1, the French general staff suffered an understandable phobia about Germany and no one doubted that the two countries would soon be at war again. This is why the unsigned letter – the *bordereau* (list) as it came to be known – caused so much fury and dismay. Colonel Jean-Conrad Sandherr, Henry's immediate superior, had the letter photographed and copies circulated to all departments of the War Office, asking if anyone recognized the handwriting. A certain Captain Alfred Dreyfus soon came under suspicion. He was not much liked, partly because he was a Jew – there was much anti-Semitism in the French army – and partly because he was inclined to be critical of his superiors. A sample of Dreyfus's handwriting was compared with the *bordereau* and there was a general agreement that they were identical.

There were obvious reasons for doubting that Dreyfus could be a spy. To begin with, he was rich – his family owned a cotton-spinning mill in Mulhouse – and secondly, he came of an intensely patriotic family who, when the Germans had seized Alsace, had preferred to emigrate rather than adopt German citizenship. But the evidence of the handwriting struck Sandherr as conclusive. Dreyfus was summoned to the War Office and asked to write down words that would be dictated by a certain Major Du Paty de Clam. The major dictated the words of the *bordereau*, then suddenly grabbed Dreyfus by the shoulder and shouted, 'Captain Dreyfus, in the name of the law I arrest you . . .' The bewildered Dreyfus retorted, 'I'm going mad!'

Long before his trial, the French Press – known as the most irresponsible and corrupt in Europe – had convicted him. France was in political turmoil with mass unemployment, falling prices, widespread hunger, and the wine industry ruined by a curse known as phylloxera; the Dreyfus scandal was exactly what was needed to distract the public from these miseries. One newspaper reported that Dreyfus was a gambler who had been losing thousands of francs a night; another declared that he had confessed to his treachery. Major Henry kept the press fed with rumours. And when the trial opened, on 19 December 1894, no one had the slightest doubt that Alfred Dreyfus was a traitor. The defence protested at the decision to hold the trial *in camera*, arguing that it would surround Dreyfus with a wall of secrecy. The protest was overruled. Major Henry declared on oath that an 'honourable person' had told him that there was a traitor in the war ministry, then pointed at Dreyfus and declared, 'There is the traitor.' When Dreyfus demanded the name of his accuser, Henry replied, 'There are secrets in an officer's head which must not even be revealed to his *képi* [his cap].' Asked to swear on his honour that an 'honourable person' had named Dreyfus as a traitor, Henry declared in his stentorian voice, 'I swear it!' The famous criminologist Bertillon testified that the handwriting of the *bordereau* bore a strong resemblance to that of Dreyfus. The members of the court were also shown a letter – intercepted by the French Secret Service – from the Italian to the German attaché, referring contemptuously to *ce canaille de D–* (that scum D) who had passed on certain secret plans to him. Still, the evidence was thin and Dreyfus had no doubt he would be acquitted. He was stunned when, on the third day of the trial, he was found guilty and sentenced to deportation. On 5 January 1895, Dreyfus was publicly stripped of his rank and his sword was broken. Then he was shipped off to Devil's Island, off French Guiana, a former leper colony, where he was incarcerated in a tiny hut; at night, his ankles were chained to his bed. There he was to remain in solitary confinement for more than four years.

Dreyfus's problem was that he was a victim of France's political conflicts. The economic problems were spawning revolutionaries. In 1891, troops had fired on a crowd of demonstrating workers, killing women and children – it became known as the massacre of Fourmies. Anarchist bombs exploded in public places – in December 1893, an anarchist named Auguste Vaillant detonated a bomb in the Chamber of Deputies. Only three months before Dreyfus's arrest, President Carnot was stabbed to death in Lyons. The Trade Union Congress at Nantes adopted the principle of the general strike. The middle classes expected bloody revolution any day. The Church, the monarchists and the army stood shoulder to shoulder to hold back the tide of destruction. As a Jew, Dreyfus was hated by the right; his natural allies and supporters were the left. It was the right-wing press that clamoured for his conviction and celebrated his downfall with howls of triumph. Dreyfus became a kind of political football; whether he was really guilty was almost an irrelevance. It was liberalism that was on trial, not Dreyfus.

For the prisoner on Devil's Island – who was now prematurely aged – help was to come from an unexpected quarter. In 1895, Sandherr – head of the

Statistical Section which had been responsible for Dreyfus's arrest – became paralysed and his place was taken by Major Marie-Georges Picquart. Picquart was asked to continue to find conclusive evidence of Dreyfus's guilt and accordingly had all letters to and from Devil's Island intercepted. Another source of information was a cleaning woman called Bastian who worked for the German attaché Schwartzkoppen and regularly sifted the contents of his waste-paper basket – she was probably the source of the original *bordereau*. On 15 March 1896, Madame Bastian handed over the latest consignment of discarded scraps of paper, among which was a postcard known as a *petit bleu*. It had been torn into fragments but was painstakingly reconstructed by one of Picquart's subordinates. It was addressed to a certain Major Marie-Charles-Ferdinand Walsin-Esterhazy and the message was cryptic and incomprehensible. But it was obvious that it meant something sinister – which in turn meant that Esterhazy was probably a spy for the Germans.

Esterhazy was a ne'er-do-well who spent as little time as possible with his regiment; he preferred women and gambling. As a result, he was always heavily in debt. Picquart instituted cautious enquiries; he soon discovered that a number of Esterhazy's brother officers were fully aware that the major had a curious thirst for classified information about gunnery. Then Picquart received two letters from Esterhazy himself requesting a transfer to the War Office. He recognized the handwriting immediately; it was that of the infamous *bordereau*. Picquart was a man of courage and honesty; he went to his superior, General Boisdeffre, and told him that he was convinced Dreyfus was innocent and that the real culprit was Esterhazy. Boisdeffre pulled a face and told Picquart to go and see General Gonse, who had been intimately involved in the Dreyfus investigation. Gonse said, 'So it looks as though a mistake has been made?' Then, after further reflection, he added, 'Keep the two cases separate.' In other words, forget Dreyfus, and concentrate on investigating Esterhazy. To Picquart, this was preposterous; if Esterhazy was the real spy, then the two cases could not be separated. 'But Dreyfus is innocent!' Gonse shook his head. 'If you keep silent, no one need know.' Picquart was outraged. 'What you say is abominable! I shall not carry this secret to my grave.'

Even darker depths were being revealed. It turned out that Major Henry, who had first announced the existence of the *bordereau*, had been a friend of Esterhazy's for years – although he claimed he had not seen him for a long time. It began to look as if Henry might have recognized his friend's handwriting on the *bordereau* from the beginning. He might well have decided to destroy it had not another subordinate seen it first.

Picquart's inconvenient streak of honesty pained his superiors. In November 1896, Picquart was summoned before three generals, rebuked for 'lack of discretion', and told that he was being removed from his job and posted to the frontier of Tunisia, where the Arabs were giving trouble.

If Picquart had died in Tunisia, as Boisdeffre obviously hoped he would, the Dreyfus affair would have been over. But Picquart was not killed and he continued to brood about Dreyfus. He even wrote a long letter to the President of the Republic, stating his belief in Dreyfus's innocence and stating his reasons but he did not mail it. Instead, he handed it over to a lawyer friend, agreeing that its details could be secretly 'leaked' to certain sympathetic members of Parliament. The lawyer, Louis Leblois, began cautiously to circulate the truth about Dreyfus and Esterhazy.

Dreyfus's brother Mathieu had never ceased his efforts to have the case reopened. Now he began to find powerful allies, among them Georges Clemenceau, a radical Republican and editor of L'Aurore. Clemenceau opened his columns to the 'Dreyfusards' – as they were now called – and the conservative government began to realize that it had a scandal of immense proportions on its hands. Mathieu Dreyfus provoked the next major development by publicly denouncing Esterhazy as the author of the bordereau. Esterhazy had already been retired on half pay, after quarrelling with his former ally Henry. (Oddly enough, neither he nor Schwartzkoppen had realized they were the cause of Dreyfus's downfall as the trial had been held in camera – Esterhazy only found out when the bordereau was finally leaked to a newspaper.) Now Esterhazy was forced to try to clear himself by demanding to be court-martialled. It was granted and on 11 January 1898, it took the judges only three minutes to acquit him. Crowds cheered him in the streets, shouting 'Long live Esterhazy!' and 'Death to the Jews.' But anyone who believed that was the end of the affair was being naive. Two days later, L'Aurore exploded a bombshell – a long open letter to the President of the Republic by the novelist Emile Zola. In a flash of inspiration, Clemenceau called it 'J'accuse'. It denounced the trial as a frame-up and named various officers, including Paty de Clam, of having ordered the acquittal of Esterhazy. He ended by daring the government to prosecute him for libel.

The government had no alternative. Zola's trial, in February, lasted two weeks. The charge was simply that Zola had accused the army of ordering Esterhazy's acquittal; the government was still trying hard not to reopen the Dreyfus case. After a fortnight of tumult, Zola was found guilty; he was fined the maximum 3,000 francs and sentenced to a year in jail. The mob screamed, 'Death to Zola', and tried to lynch him. The Chamber of Deputies passed a resolution ordering the 'energetic repression' of people who wanted to rehabilitate the traitor Dreyfus. Picquart was dismissed from the army and his friend Leblois was suspended from the bar for six months for his part in circulating the story of Esterhazy's guilt.

Now came the dramatic climax of the astonishing affair. The new war minister, Godefroy Cavaignac, announced in the Chamber that the army now had irrefutable proof of Dreyfus's guilt, in the form of three letters that had passed between the Italian attaché Panizzardi, and the German attaché,

Schwartzkoppen. One referred to *ce canaille de D–*, while another named Dreyfus as a traitor. The whole Chamber cheered wildly and voted to have the speech posted on official billboards all over France. This, certainly, looked like the final end of the *affaire Dreyfus*.

Then Picquart dropped his own bombshell. In a letter to *L'Aurore*, he declared that he was in a position to establish before a court that one of the letters was a forgery and the other two did not refer to Dreyfus at all. The war minister reacted with fury and ordered Picquart's arrest. Esterhazy was also arrested for 'conduct unbecoming to an officer'.

A young officer on the general staff, Captain Louis Cuignet, was appointed to re-examine the Dreyfus file with a view to refuting Picquart's charge. To everyone's dismay, Cuignet quickly realized that the three letters revealed that Picquart was telling the truth. The one that named Dreyfus was an obvious forgery. The likeliest culprit was Henry – now a colonel – and in the presence of the war minister he confessed to the forgery.

What had happened, it seemed, was that French Intelligence had intercepted a letter from the Italian attaché asking the German attaché to dine. A letter implicating Dreyfus was then forged on a blank sheet of paper by a petty crook named Lemercier-Picard; this was carefully glued on to the invitation that contained the Italian attaché's signature. On closer examination, Cuignet could see at once that the letter had been fabricated. (His motive was not a desire for justice – he spent the rest of his life denouncing Dreyfus as a traitor and trying to atone for causing his superiors so much embarrassment.)

Colonel Henry was arrested and General Boisdeffre resigned. The next morning, Henry was found dead in his prison cell; he had cut his throat with a razor. His accomplice Lemercier-Picard hanged himself. The war minister Cavaignac also resigned. The government was further embarrassed when more of Henry's forgeries were later published – seven letters from Dreyfus to the German kaiser and a reply from the kaiser. The affair was now thoroughly out of hand. France was now virtually in a state of civil war with mobs of Dreyfusards and anti-Dreyfusards clashing in the streets. The Dreyfusards were still very much a minority, regarded as dangerous left-wingers and hated by most 'decent' Frenchmen. When the High Court of Appeals agreed to review the case, one right-wing journalist suggested that the judges should have their eyes put out – the only way to handle traitors. In spite of its defeats, the right still seemed so much in charge that the pretender to the throne, the Duc D'Orleans, held himself in readiness at the Belgian border to take over the throne. (The last French king had abdicated as a result of the 1848 revolution.)

On 16 February 1899, the president, Felix Faure, died of a stroke – probably in the act of making love to the pretty young wife of a painter, who was hastily spirited away. Faure had been the chief obstacle to the reopening of the Dreyfus case, a die-hard Conservative. The new president, Emile Loubet, was a moderate and he agreed to a retrial. There was an almost successful *coup d'état* by right wingers but when it failed, the judges summoned their courage and, on 3 June 1899, annulled Dreyfus's conviction and ordered a retrial before a military court. Picquart was released after almost a year in prison, Zola returned from exile in England, and Dreyfus was finally brought back from Devil's Island. (Ironically, most of his supporters found him a disappointing little man – dull, prosaic and rather irritating.)

It might seem that now was the time to right the injustice and put an end to the affair; after all, Henry had confessed to forgery and Paty de Clam was in prison on a charge of forging documents in the case. But France was still full of hysteria. Anti-Dreyfusards were demanding that Dreyfus should now be sentenced to death. In August 1899, Dreyfus's court martial took place in Rennes. Dreyfus, who was only 39 years old, had a white beard and looked like an old man. The trial lasted four weeks and the generals who entered the witness box rehashed all the old evidence, including the forgeries, and insisted on Dreyfus's guilt. Incredibly, the court ended by finding Dreyfus guilty of treason and sentencing him to ten years in prison.

There was talk of pardoning Dreyfus; the Dreyfusards objected strenuously, saying that this would be an admission of guilt. Dreyfus himself had a nervous breakdown – he had been absolutely certain that he would be vindicated. Finally, worn out by suffering, he agreed to accept the pardon, and on 19 September 1899, became a free man again.

The left, naturally, had no intention of allowing matters to rest there. They could see that they had the enemy on the run. The army was now thoroughly discredited. As a result of the affair, socialism had gained enormous ground in France. The Church was also on the run. In France, the Catholic Church had always held enormous power – much as it still does in Spain or Ireland. In 1801, Napoleon had concluded a Concordat with the Pope; the French clergy were to be paid by the government. The Dreyfus affair led to such powerful anti-clerical feeling that it finally brought about the separation of the Church and the State in 1904, and the takeover of Church property by private corporations. In effect, Catholicism ceased to be the official state religion of France. One writer on the affair (Guy Chapman) has called this the 'Dreyfusian revolution'.

Meanwhile, the Dreyfusards continued their attempt to clear Dreyfus's name. The Socialist leader Jean Jaurés lent his support. In 1903, Dreyfus himself requested a new enquiry. A search of War Office records revealed new evidence supporting his innocence and Esterhazy's guilt. The Minister of Justice agreed to allow the Rennes verdict to go to the Court of Criminal Appeal. Baudouin, the Proceureur-Général, studied all the documents, expecting to find at least some reasonable ground for the Rennes verdict and was shocked to realize that there were none whatever. Finally, on 12 July

1906, a court decided that not a fragment of the original evidence against Dreyfus was valid. The verdict of the Rennes court martial was finally annulled. Dreyfus was reinstated in the army with the rank of major; Picquart was made a Brigadier-General. Dreyfus was also decorated with the Legion of Honour. Picquart later became war minister and eventually died in January 1914 after a fall from a horse. He seems to have shown a certain small-minded resentment of anti-Dreyfusards among army colleagues and obstructed certain promotions. Dreyfus himself served honourably in World War I, commanding an ammunition column. He died at the age of 76, in 1935. An amusing story is told of these final years. A companion of Dreyfus's at bridge remarked that a certain person had been arrested for espionage, then, realizing that this sounded tactless, added hastily 'I daresay there's nothing in it.' 'Oh, I don't know,' said Dreyfus placidly, 'there's no smoke without fire.'

Esterhazy had been forced to flee the country and moved to London. Accused by his cousin of embezzlement, he was sentenced to three years in prison in his absence and so decided never to return to France. He later changed his name to Fitzgerald and became a journalist, writing anti-British articles for a French newspaper. Later still, he called himself the Comte Jean-Marie de Voilemont, moved to Harpenden and lived by selling tinned foods. He died in May 1923.

On Sunday, 28 September 1902, Emile Zola and his wife Alexandrine returned to their house in Paris and told the servant to light a fire in the bedroom stove. The next morning, both were found lying in their bedroom: Zola was dead and his wife was only just breathing. The cause of death was carbon monoxide poisoning, due to a blocked chimney. Yet when the fire was lit in the bedroom by two investigators and guinea pigs were locked in for the night, the animals were unharmed. It has been plausibly argued that the chimney was stopped up deliberately by anti-Dreyfusards and the blockage removed the next day.

L'Affaire has been written about extensively, both in fiction and non-fiction. It figures prominently in Proust's novel *A la recherche du temps perdu* – Proust (who was half-Jewish) was understandably a Dreyfusard. Zola fictionalized the affair in his novel *Truth* and Roger Martin du Gard wrote about it in his novel *Jean Barois*. Perhaps the most amusing account is to be found in Anatole France's *Penguin Island*, where Dreyfus figures as Peyrot, accused of stealing 80,000 trusses of hay intended for the cavalry. France's satire on the case occupies many pages and tends to strike the modern reader as long-winded and heavy-handed; yet anyone who reads it after studying the affair itself will realize that, far from being heavy-handed, it understates the realities of the Dreyfus affair. The facts of the case, and the emotions to which it gave rise, are so extreme that they defy all attempts to fictionalize them.

GESUALDO, CARLO

COMPOSER OF GENIUS AND MURDERER

The Prince of Venosa, who died virtually insane, was known to his contemporaries as the man who murdered his wife when he caught her in bed with her lover. For posterity, he is one of the greatest of all composers of madrigals.

Gesualdo's grandfather was made a prince in 1560 when his son married a niece of the pope. His grandson Carlo was born a year later. Gesualdo's father, Fabrizio, kept his own band of musicians. His son became a close friend of the paranoid poet Tasso, who wrote several poems about the tragic events which ended in murder.

In 1586, Fabrizio arranged a betrothal for his son, Carlo, with his cousin, a beautiful young girl named Maria d'Avalos. At the age of 25, she had already been widowed twice. The wedding in Naples was followed by magnificent celebrations that lasted for days. In due course a son, Don Emmanuelle, was born. For four years, they lived 'more like lovers than man and wife' says a *chronique scandaleuse* of the period. But it seems that the lady became bored with her intellectual husband, whose greatest enthusiasm was for music. One of the visitors to their palazzo in Naples was a handsome young cavalier named Don Fabrizio Carafa, the Duke of Andria, described as 'perhaps the most handsome and graceful cavaliere in the city [of Naples], vigorous and flourishing and not yet thirty years of age.' The Duke was already married to a lady of religious inclinations, on whom he had fathered five children.

Donna Maria – who is depicted in a painting as a typically plump Italian beauty – seems to have been a woman of irresistible charm, so much so that Gesualdo's uncle, Don Giulio, fell in love with her and, 'not heeding the fact that she was the wife of his nephew', left no stone unturned to persuade her into his bed. She turned him down with sharp words, threatening to tell her husband if he did not stop pestering her.

Don Giulio was thrown into a passion of jealousy when he observed that his niece-in-law was obviously fascinated by the handsome Duke of Andria, Fabrizio. 'The first messages of their desires were their glances which, with the tongue of the heart, betrayed the fire that burnt in each other's breast. From glances of love they proceeded to written messages . . .' When husband and wife were on a visit to the house of a friend, Don Garzia of Toledo, in the town of Chiaia, the Duke hid in a pavilion in the garden, and bribed the wife of the gardener to help him. Donna Maria walked in the garden with her maid and some gentlemen, which must have struck her husband as safe enough, then she pretended she had a pain and persuaded the others to go on. The gardener's wife led her to the pavilion, where the Duke took her in his arms 'and kissed her a thousand times, as she did him, and with the greatest ardour they were moved to enjoy together the ultimate amorous delight.' After this, they used the house of Don Garzia for secret rendezvous and sometimes even in Donna Maria's own bedroom, with the maid acting as sentinel.

When Gesualdo's lecherous uncle heard the news he rushed to tell the Prince, who was 'more dead than alive' after receiving this unpleasant piece of information. Being an artist and an intellectual, he was not the type to challenge the Duke to a duel (besides which, the Duke had a reputation as a formidable swordsman). But the Duke soon divined – probably from his scowls – that the secret was out and told Donna Maria that it would be safer to end the affair, or at least suspend it until Gesualdo had ceased to be suspicious. Donna Maria's response was to pour scorn on him and tell him that if he loved her as much as she loved him, he would not be afraid of anyone. The Duke's pride was stung and he told her that if she felt like that, then he was willing to die with her.

According to one chronicler, Gesualdo announced that he intended to go hunting and would not be back until the following day. This does not accord with the testimony of Gesualdo's valet, who states that Gesualdo had supper in his room at his usual time, 'three hours of the night' (probably about nine o'clock). Donna Maria had supper at 'four hours of the night' – evidence that they led separate lives. Then she went to bed and was undressed by her two maidservants, Silvia Albana and Laura Scala. The maids seem to have slept in an ante-room between the bedroom and the corridor – and from which a flight of stairs led down to the mezzanine where Don Carlo had his bedroom. An hour later, Donna Maria called Silvia and asked her to bring some clothes; she had heard the Duke whistling in the street below and wanted to go out on to the balcony. Silvia brought her a skirt and shawl and Maria opened the window. Presumably her lover then climbed up onto the balcony and joined her. Not long after, Donna Maria called Silvia again and asked to be undressed and also asked for another nightdress, claiming that hers was damp with perspiration. It is not clear where the Duke was hiding during these proceedings. Silvia brought her a nightdress with ruffs of black silk and fringes at the bottom, then went back to her own room where she sat dressed on the bed and read a book until she dozed off to sleep.

She was awakened by the sound of her door opening. Opposite the door was the spiral staircase leading down to Gesualdo's room. Three men came into the room, one carrying a halberd. They went straight into the bedroom of Donna Maria. Silvia heard two shots. A moment later, Gesualdo came into the room, followed by his valet, who was carrying two torches. Gesualdo snarled at Silvia, 'Traitress, I shall kill you', and ordered his manservant not to let her escape. Gesualdo strode into his wife's bedroom, whereupon Silvia escaped into the bedroom of Donna Maria's small son and hid under the bed. Meanwhile, Gesualdo was heard to shout, 'Kill that scoundrel, along with this harlot. Shall a Gesualdo be made a cuckold?' There were sounds of a struggle. Then the three men came out, followed by Gesualdo, whose hands were covered with blood. Gesualdo said, 'I don't believe they are dead', and went back into the bedroom. His valet looked into the room and saw a man, wearing a bloodstained woman's nightdress, lying near the door. Gesualdo went back to the bed, where his wife was lying, and stabbed her several times more – according to one chronicle 'especially in those parts which most ought to be kept honest'. Gesualdo then ordered the two bodies to be dragged out onto the spiral staircase, and the same chronicler alleges that 'while the said cadavers were lying on the said staircase, a monk of San Domenico used the said Donna Maria even though she was dead.' But this chronicler is suspect; he is the one who tells the story of Gesualdo pretending to go hunting, which seems to be embroidery; he also states that when the Duke entered Donna Maria's bedroom, they 'gave each other solace several times', when it is obvious that there were no witnesses, so he could not possibly have known.

Gesualdo knew that his life was now in danger from Donna Maria's kinsmen and fled from Naples to his castle, destroying the surrounding woodland so that enemies could not take him by surprise. The Duke's wife, Donna Maria Carafa, retreated to a convent; there was a widespread rumour that she had suddenly experienced the conviction that her husband was about to die as she knelt in prayer a few hours before his death.

In the retirement of his castle, Gesualdo began to suffer from melancholia. He also began to write madrigals; his first two books were published in 1594 and made him a reputation as a fine composer. Until then he had been regarded as an aristocratic amateur. In 1594 he also married again, this time Leonora d'Este, a member of a rich and artistic family. But his second marriage was no happier than the first. Leonora was bored with her composer husband and with the castle at Gesualdo; she preferred to spend much of her time at Modena with her brother. Between Gesualdo's marriage and his death in 1613, there was a steady deterioration in his mental state. A son by Leonora died in 1600, and his eldest son by Donna Maria died only a few weeks before Gesualdo himself.

The first two books of madrigals are relatively conventional in style. Thereafter, Gesualdo's work became increasingly difficult and complex, full of dissonances and chromaticism. Most of his contemporaries regarded these peculiarities as a sign of his madness. It is only in the twentieth century that his genius has been appreciated.

HOLLYWOOD

SCANDAL IN THE 'DREAM FACTORY'

The history of Hollywood begins in 1886, when Mrs Deida Wilcox, the wife of a Kansas City estate agent, gave that name to a huge ranch not far from the small city of Los Angeles (population around 12,000), where they had decided to retire. But if by Hollywood we mean the motion-picture industry, then it is arguable that the history of Hollywood – and of Hollywood scandal – began twelve years earlier, on 17 October 1874, when the photographer Eadweard Muybridge murdered his wife's lover. On the afternoon of that day, Muybridge was at work on his photographic plates in San Francisco when he was interrupted by a lawyer who wished to discuss a debt of $100 that Muybridge owed to a midwife named Susan Smith. By way of inducing Muybridge to settle the debt, the lawyer hinted that Mrs Smith knew of a scandal concerning Mrs Muybridge and that she might spread the word unless she received her money. Muybridge rushed off to interview Mrs Smith. He had reason to be jealous, for his wife Flora was a pretty girl of 23 while Muybridge was an introverted and bad-tempered man of 47. What Mrs Smith told him threw him into a frenzy. A certain Major Harry Larkin had brought Flora Muybridge to her house for the delivery of a baby and from the tender love scene that took place between them, it was to be inferred that Larkin was the baby's father. Mrs Muybridge was in Dalles, Oregon, far from her husband's rage, but the handsome and debonaire Major Larkin, a San Francisco reporter, was closer at hand at the health resort Calistoga. Muybridge took a boat there, went to the house where Larkin was living and called out for him. Larkin came to the door. 'Here is a message from my wife', said Muybridge, and shot him in the heart.

In California in those days, shootings were commonplace and a man who had murdered from an outraged sense of honour aroused public sympathy. The defence pleaded temporary insanity, pointing out that Muybridge had received serious head injuries in 1860 in a runaway stage-coach accident. The Napa Court found him not guilty.

Mrs Muybridge had vanished after the trial, and Muybridge himself disappeared into obscurity. The drama had interrupted Muybridge's work on an interesting scientific enterprise – an attempt to photograph a horse in motion. In 1872, Governor Leland Stanford had bet a friend that when a horse is galloping at full speed, all its feet leave the ground for a brief moment. Stanford was a rich man – he owned a racing stable – and he was willing to spend money to back his assertion. Muybridge had been trying, without much success, to photograph a horse in motion; his plates showed little more than a blur. But when he emerged from his five years obscurity in 1880, photographic emulsion had improved so much that a mere fraction of a second was enough for a successful exposure. Stanford spent $40,000 equipping Muybridge with a whole row of cameras. Then a machine with a metal cylinder and projecting pins (like a music box) closed a series of electrical contacts, setting off the cameras one after the other, as the horse galloped past. Governor Stanford won his bet and Muybridge achieved a certain celebrity.

A friend of Muybridge, Wallace Levison, took the next major step when he evolved a method for moving photographic plates on a wheel behind a lens. And by 1888, Thomas Alva Edison had discovered how to take a series of pictures on a moving strip of film. From there, it was a short and very obvious step to projecting them on to a screen like slides. In 1889, his workmen had solved the problem of synchronizing a moving picture with sound. The first 'film' showed his engineer William Dickson stepping on to the screen, raising his hat, and saying 'Good morning, Mr Edison. I hope you are satisfied with the kinetophonograph.'

The Kinetoscope was basically a peep-show machine for use in fairgrounds. It showed such subjects as a man sneezing or girls dancing. But when the first dramatic motion picture, The Passion Play, was presented at the Eden Musee on 30 January 1898, its producer Rich Hollaman knew he had taken an important step. He commented, 'I knew I had them when I saw the tears in the eyes of those Broadway sports.' This was, in fact, the most incredible thing about the film as a medium: its emotional impact. Today we take it for granted because we are familiar with television and cinema since childhood. It is difficult for us to grasp the overwhelming effect of the first films: the way they transported the audience into 'another world'. Edison was the first to make full use of this potential in a film of 1902 called The Life of an American Fireman. It showed a house on fire and a man being rescued from an upstairs window followed by a woman and child, coughing and staggering as they were overcome by smoke. The firemen dashed through the streets on their horse-drawn wagons. As the mother and child collapsed, unconscious, a fireman burst in through the door. He carried the unconscious mother to a ladder; she awoke and begged him to save her baby. He took her down, then went back for the child. Mother and child were united as the house blazed. At the first showing there was not a dry eye in the place; the film had lasted only a few minutes but people felt as if they had been through a crisis together – they smiled through their tears at their next-door neighbour.

It was this emotional impact that turned the film star into something far more renowned and illustrious than the great actors of the past. David Garrick, Edmund Kean, Henry Irving, all had 'set the town on fire' in their time. But their admirers were separated from them by the footlights. In the cinema, you were there, in the blazing bedroom, clinging to the upturned boat about to be swept over the waterfall, or clambering over the rooftops of the runaway train in an effort to reach the engine. It was ten times as real as the theatre. Furthermore, every woman in the audience was in the arms of the romantic hero as he swept her onto his horse and galloped away from the murderous ruffians hired by the villain; every male in the audience gazed into her adoring eyes. Of course, there had been plenty of romantic heroes in literature, from Byron's Childe Harold to Owen Wister's' Virginian but they were for the literate. The screen brought romance, excitement and laughter to people who never read a newspaper. The result was that film stars achieved a degree of celebrity that had been unknown in the nineteenth century, even to popular idols like Dickens and Jenny Lind. Charlie Chaplin came to Hollywood in 1912 to make pictures for Mack Sennett at Keystone. He knew his films were popular because they made money. But when he took a trip to New York in 1915, he was staggered to be met by enormous crowds at every station; the telegraph operators, who had relayed a telegram announcing his arrival, had passed on the news to the press. When he came to England in 1920 there was even greater excitement; telegrams began to arrive by the dozen when he was halfway across the Atlantic. Every time he stepped off a train he was met by the local mayor and a brass band.

It was because the film star was regarded as a kind of god that the slightest breath of scandal could be magnified into a tempest of opprobrium. The first great Hollywood scandal broke in 1920, when news arrived that the lovely and popular Olive Thomas had committed suicide with poison capsules in Paris. Hers had been the classic success story. As a teenager she had escaped from a Pennsylvania slum and an unhappy marriage to become a shopgirl in New York. Then she entered a competition for the 'perfect artist's model' and won it. After that she became a Ziegfeld girl, then a Hollywood film star. She was married to another screen idol, Jack Pickford – Mary Pickford's brother, a clean-cut young man who was regarded as the all-American boy. But investigations into Olive Thomas's death revealed that she was not quite the charming innocent she played on the screen. Olive had arrived in Paris ahead of her husband and her perambulations included sleazy night clubs where she drank with members of the French underworld. Newspapers began to publish reports that she had been in these places trying to buy heroin for her husband who was an addict. Later still, an American government investigation revealed that she herself had been purchasing heroin and cocaine before her marriage to Pickford. The headlines declared: Olive Thomas, Dope Fiend. The American public had been prepared to believe that its idols were not angels – after all, Mary Pickford and Douglas Fairbanks had just divorced their respective mates in order to marry – but this was beyond belief. Olive Thomas's husband survived the scandal but made only a few more films.

The next scandal was greater still. In 1921, the comedian Fatty Arbuckle was charged with criminal responsibility in the death of Virginia Rappe (see page 23), who died of a ruptured bladder after being raped by him. Again, it seemed incredible, as if Santa Claus had turned out to be Jack the Ripper. The inference seemed to be that the inhabitants of the 'dream factory' were dope fiends or sex fiends.

Chaplin himself was lucky to escape the same fate as Arbuckle. When he came to Hollywood in 1912 (at the age of 23), his love life had been minimal and he suffered from shyness and loneliness. His natural penchant was for very young women – in fact, for underage girls. When he met Mildred Harris at a beach party in 1917 she was fifteen and looked younger. In the following year her announcement that she was pregnant led to her marriage to Chaplin but followed two years later by divorce. (Chaplin confided to Fairbanks that his wife was 'no mental heavyweight'.) He charged infidelity and she charged cruelty – a concept his admirers found hard to associate with the sentimental little tramp. It seemed to confirm the notion that Hollywood was the opposite of what it seemed and that the great film moguls – Adolph Zukor, Samuel Goldwyn, Jesse Lasky, Louis B. Mayer – were trying to deceive the public.

Chaplin's next major involvement was with a girl named Lillita McMurray – she preferred to spell it Lolita – whom he had met for the first time in April 1914 – her sixth birthday. When she was twelve, she appeared as a child angel in *The Kid.* Her mother was distinctly suspicious of Chaplin's intentions and kept a beady eye on him. Two years later, Lita was invited to play in *The Gold Rush,* which was filmed in Trukee, California. In her autobiography, *My Life With Chaplin,* Lita admits: 'I wanted to be his little girl – and yet I wanted him to put his tongue in my mouth. I knew I was playing with fire . . .' Chaplin's response to this teasing attitude was to leap on her in his red silk pyjamas. Lita was duly horrified at his 'animal movements' and fled. The next time, he tried the softly, softly approach. 'He was softer; even before he touched me I sensed I wouldn't have to struggle . . . With deft, still unhurried movements he peeled the bathing suit off me and sat back on his knees to look at me nude. Instinctively I began to cover with my hands the parts of me that no man had seen until this moment, but looking at him again, I saw the absence of lewdness in his eyes, and abruptly there was no shame. My hands fell to my sides.' At the last minute she changed her mind. ' "No", I whimpered, shaking my head wildly, taking my arms from around him, trying to close my legs. "Oh, I can't, I can't!" ' The next time he tried was in the back of a limousine. 'Wordlessly he found his way to the top of the elastic-banded underpants, and wordlessly he yanked them down; I murmured for him to stop, though without much force, for he was kissing me again. Then he was struggling with his own clothing and pulling me over on top of him.' Their position made it impossible, and again Chaplin gave up. Finally, he took her to his home in Beverly Hills and the long-awaited deflowering took place in the bathroom. 'The foglike mist billowed, grew thicker and thicker, finally filled every inch of the room. I couldn't see anything. . . . What happened next was Charlie, lying beside me and teasing my neck with swift darting kisses. . . . Then there was a sharp, piercing pain inside me and I cried out, but I did not release my grip. The pain blinded me far more than the encircling steam, but I writhed wildly, as though in ecstasy, to let him know I belonged to him – and then I received all of him.'

Chaplin disliked contraceptives and the result was that his child-mistress became pregnant. He had to marry in haste or face a charge of statutory rape. Chaplin and his fifteen-year-old bride tried to marry quietly in Mexico but were pursued by hordes of reporters. Chaplin is quoted as saying to his friends of the wedding party, 'Well, boys, this is better than the penitentiary, but it won't last.' Mrs McMurray moved in with the newly weds. Chaplin began to spend most of his time with old cronies while Lita and her clan took over the household. After two years, Chaplin fled to New York and Lita filed for divorce. While Chaplin was fighting off a nervous breakdown, the McMurray clan swooped on his home and studio. A pamphlet entitled *Complaint by Lita Grey* passed from hand to hand; it contained details of her allegations against Chaplin, including the accusation that he had tried to persuade her to perform the 'abnormal, against nature, perverted degenerate and indecent act' called fellatio and that when she declined he had said, 'Relax, dear – all married people do it.' It went on to state that after their original lovemaking scene, they never had normal sex together. The newspapers made the most of the revelations and H.L. Mencken commented in the Baltimore *Sun:* 'The very morons who worshipped Charlie Chaplin six weeks ago now prepare to dance around the stake while he is burned.' When Lita's lawyers threatened to reveal in court the name of five prominent actresses with whom he had slept since his marriage, Chaplin capitulated and Lita was paid $625,000. Chaplin could afford it; his total estate was reckoned to be worth $16 million. He was so embittered about the episode that he does not even mention Lita Grey in his autobiography. But the divorce case did no permanent damage to his popularity and when his next film *The Circus* was released in 1928 it was as popular as ever.

The experience with Lita Grey made Chaplin secretive and when he married the twenty-year-old Paulette Goddard (at sea) in 1933, he kept it a secret for three years; Chaplin was 44 at the time of the marriage. Before this marriage ended in divorce in 1942, Chaplin was the defendant in a paternity suit brought against him by a young actress named Joan Barry and he was also charged under the Mann Act – transporting a minor across state lines for immoral purposes. He was found not guilty of this charge but ruled to be the father of the child. A year later, in 1943, Chaplin married the eighteen-year-old daughter of playwright Eugene O'Neill, Oona; he was then 54. They lived together happily until his death in 1977. The final scandal in which he was involved was not sexual but political. During the McCarthy era he was accused of being a communist and his film *Monsieur Verdoux* was widely boycotted in America. In 1952, he was in mid-Atlantic when he was told that the Attorney-General had decided to deny him re-entry into the United States unless he submitted to an enquiry into his 'moral worth'. He preferred to move to Vevey in Switzerland. He was knighted in 1975. A few months after his death two years later his body was 'kidnapped' from the graveyard in Vevey and demands for ransom were received – probably the only occasion on which the victim of a kidnapping has already been dead; his body was later recovered.

Chaplin's career epitomizes the basic problem of Hollywood. The famous always attract members of the opposite sex and since most famous people are naturally dominant they are also, in most cases, highly sexed. Where sex is offered casually, it will inevitably be accepted casually. Chaplin tells of a typical episode in his autobiography. In a hotel room in Los Angeles, he was undressing and humming a popular tune when a feminine voice from the next room took it up. He whistled it and again the girl hummed it. When he laughed the girl said, 'I beg your pardon.' Chaplin persuaded her to open her door and saw 'the most ravishing young blonde' dressed in a negligée. He introduced himself but it was unnecessary for the girl already knew who he was. They slept together that night, taking care not to acknowledge one another in public the next day. The next night, she tapped on his door and again they slept together. On the third night he was beginning to feel tired and his work was suffering. On the fourth night, he tiptoed into bed and ignored her when she tapped on the door. The next day, she passed him icily in the hotel lobby. But that night, the handle of his door turned – the door was locked – and she knocked impatiently. He decided it was time to check out of the hotel.

If this episode had been told in court or in the newspapers, it would have ruined his popularity as surely as the Virginia Rappe case ruined Arbuckle's. Everyone who watched the little tramp flirting awkwardly with some pretty maiden would have found themselves thinking about Chaplin's 'sex orgies' with a beautiful stranger in a negligée and the illusion would have been destroyed. Yet Hollywood was no more a Sodom and Gomorrah than Broadway or Shaftesbury Avenue in London were. And Chaplin's methods of seduction were endearingly innocent compared to the 'casting couch' method inaugurated by Lewis J. Seltznick about 1914, in which the corridor to his office was guarded by men whose job was to ensure his privacy, and any young actress who wanted a part was expected to remove her clothes and lie down. (The method was later imitated by Harry Cohn of Columbia – the film star Louise Brooks described how her refusal to lie on the couch led to the end of her career in films.)

The next major Hollywood scandal occurred before Fatty Arbuckle had been acquitted of killing Virginia Rappe. William Desmond Taylor, an Irish actor and film director, was head of one of the most successful of the early

Hollywood film companies, Famous Players-Lasky. (The trio of Jesse Lasky, Cecil B. De Mille and Samuel Goldfish – who later changed his name to Goldwyn – had virtually founded Hollywood as a film colony in 1914, when De Mille rented an old barn and made *The Squaw Man* there.) In 1922, Taylor was 45 years old; he had the kind of thin, keen face that would have made him ideal for the part of Sherlock Holmes. He looked and spoke like a typical English aristocrat. On 2 February 1922, his valet entered the living room at 7:30 in the morning to find his master lying dead on the floor, with two bullet holes in his back. Investigations revealed that the film star Mabel Normand, Chaplin's first leading lady in Keystone, had been with him for an hour the previous evening. Another Chaplin leading lady – and girlfriend – Edna Purviance, had rung his doorbell about an hour later but received no reply. It looked as if a killer had been waiting for Mabel Normand to leave. When the police began investigating Taylor's love life, they found that he seemed to have had affairs with half the beauties in Hollywood. Mabel Normand had written him passionate love letters; as had twenty-year-old Mary Miles Minter – and, in fact, her mother. Silken undergarments belonging to many different women were found in his bedroom – apparently left as mementoes by his mistresses. Mary Miles Minter played the same kind of 'little girl' parts as Mary Pickford and Olive Thomas, and was another symbol of girlhood innocence. When handkerchiefs with the monogram MMM were found in Taylor's bedroom and newspaper reporters revealed that she was not twenty but thirty, her career came to a sudden end. Taylor's murderer was never found but it seems likely that it was a woman. Many clues were destroyed when Zukor and other Famous Players executives descended on Taylor's home and incinerated love letters and other telling evidence. The police found pornographic photographs showing Taylor in the act of lovemaking with a number of female stars.

At the funeral, Mary Miles Minter kissed the corpse on the lips, then announced that the corpse had whispered, 'I shall always love you, Mary.'

A new dimension was added to the scandal by the discovery that Taylor's previous valet had been a homosexual (like his present one, Peavy), who had forged cheques in his name, smashed up his car, and burgled his home twice. Was Taylor a bisexual who was being blackmailed? This mystery was cleared up when it was discovered that the previous valet was Taylor's brother, an actor who had fallen on hard times.

Further shock was caused when it became evident that Taylor had been a drug addict. He also seems to have spent much of his time at parties where men dressed as women – the collection of underwear seemed to hint at transvestite tendencies.

The final blow to Mabel Normand's career came a year later, when her chauffeur shot one of her admirers, Cortland Dines, at the home of Edna Purviance. It was clear that she was having affairs with both men. An article in *Good Housekeeping* suggested that she was too 'adulterated' (perhaps intending a pun) for domestic consumption and her career foundered.

The newspapers of the millionaire tycoon William Randolph Hearst took every opportunity to thunder about the immorality of Hollywood; they continued to make the most of Fatty Arbuckle's problems even after he had been acquitted. Hollywood moguls felt that they had to do something quickly to improve the image of the film capital. An organization called the Motion Picture Producers and Distributors of America was formed and Will H. Hays, who was Postmaster General in Harding's administration, was appointed head of the organization and censor-in-chief at a salary of $100,000 a year. It was only later that it emerged that Hays himself was a man of dubious moral standards – he had accepted gifts and 'loans' of a quarter of a million dollars in exchange for his part in getting the unsuitable Harding into the White House. But at least his appointment averted censorship by the federal government. After Hays became Hollywood's conscience, a 'morality clause' was inserted into most contracts, stating that any action likely to result in public scandal would be a sufficient reason for rescinding the contract. But the double standard continued to prevail. Cecil B. De Mille insisted that his stars should regulate their personal life so that 'any degrading or besmirching' behaviour should be avoided. However, he himself was known to make full use of his position to sleep with his female stars, while his religious films always included a sinful orgy and an undressing scene in the bath-house.

In the month Hays was appointed – March 1922 – Famous Players suffered another major blow when their popular leading man Wallace Reid was consigned by his wife to a private nursing home. The studio told the press he was suffering from overwork, but Reid's wife Florence preferred honesty and admitted that her husband was a morphine addict. In 1919 Reid had suffered head injuries in a rail crash and had been given morphine to ease the pain; he became an addict and accelerated his breakdown with heavy drinking. He was in a padded cell for much of the time until his painful death in 1923.

Juanita Hansen, one of the original Mack Sennett comediennes, was a victim of the Reid scandal. Her name was discovered in a letter from a doctor from whom she had sought treatment, and she was arrested and held in jail for three days to determine whether she was still on drugs. In fact, she had been cured but her arrest destroyed her career. She later launched a foundation to help narcotics addicts.

Other drug scandals followed. In 1926, Barbara La Marr, the actress who had played the beautiful but villainous Lady de Winter opposite Douglas Fairbanks in *The Three Musketeers,* died of a drug overdose. The studio tried to blame her death on dieting but the truth soon came out. Alma Rubens, star of *East Lynne* and *Show Boat,* suffered a 'brainstorm' when her doctor tried to incarcerate her in a private sanatorium in 1929, and stabbed a gas station attendant. Released from an asylum for the insane, she announced her intention of making a comeback but was arrested for being in possession of forty cubes of morphine. She died two weeks later in January 1931.

Hollywood was treading a tightrope. America was enjoying the age of jazz and bootleg liquor, and the film audiences wanted to know all about it. The Hays office wanted 'virtue' but the public wanted sin. In 1921, a young unknown called Rudolph Valentino created a sensation by the manner in which he danced with Helen Domingues in *Four Horsemen of the Apocalypse* – he made it look as though they were having sex or were about to vanish to the nearest bedroom. In his next film *The Sheik*, the lustful gleam in his eye as he lifted Agnes Ayres clear of the ground left no doubt whatever that she was about to be subjected to a long-drawn-out rape. But Valentino's private life was unhappy; both his wives proved to be lesbians – the first deserted him on their wedding night. A newspaper article calling him a 'pink powder puff' plunged him into gloom and he died from discouragement as much as from a perforated ulcer. Thousands of women mourned his death on 23 August 1926; some even committed suicide.

The female equivalent of Valentino was Clara Bow, who became a symbol of the jazz age in 1927 when she starred in Elinor Glyn's film *It*. Elinor Glyn was herself a symbol of liberated womanhood; her novel *Three Weeks* is about a young Englishman who has a three-week orgy with a princess before she marries a decrepit old king. The book sold five million copies in 1907. A popular rhyme of the time ran:

Would you like to sin
With Elinor Glyn
On a tiger skin?
Or would you prefer
With her to err
On some other fur?

No doubt this was a reference to the famous seduction scene on a tigerskin rug. After *It*, Clara Bow became the 'It girl' – 'it' being some indefinable quality that made a woman irresistible. She became the archetypal 'flapper' – the zany young lady who rushed from party to party gulping cocktails and shrieking with laughter. ('Flapper' at first referred to any innocent teenager whose pigtail, tied with a bow, flapped as she ran about; by the 1920s it simply meant any unconventional young lady.) For the studio, the problem was that Clara's private life was a little too much like the roles she played on screen. She was the co-respondent in a divorce case, when the wife of her physician alleged that he found it necessary to remove all his own clothes before examining Clara. Clara was forced to pay $30,000 for alienating the doctor's affections. She was also the mistress of B.P. Schulberg, the man who launched her into stardom. He came to refer to her as 'crisis-a-day Clara'. There was the occasion when she wandered into a gaming casino at Lake Tahoe and played blackjack, then roulette. She was convinced that her chips were worth 50 cents each when they were, in fact, worth $100. She ended by signing a cheque for $24,000. The next day, on the advice of Schulberg, she stopped the cheque. Menacing bruisers called on her, then on Schulberg; but behind the curtains in Schulberg's office were two concealed policemen, who overheard a threat to throw sulphuric acid in Clara's face. The bruisers were placed in handcuffs. Schulberg and Clara needed police protection for some months after this incident. The newspaper stories portraying Clara as a bad loser tarnished her image as a 'bright young thing'.

Then came the Wall Street crash and bright young things ceased to be admired by families on the breadline. The advent of talkies further damaged Clara's image: the fans had imagined her as the kind of girl whose father owned a mansion on Long Island and the sound of a flat Brooklyn accent issuing from that inviting cupid's bow of a mouth was a disillusionment.

The final crisis came in the form of a lady named Daisy De Voe, who became a secretary-companion for three years standing between Clara and the world. A young actor named Rex Bell fell in love with Clara and became increasingly suspicious of Miss De Voe. After inducing Clara to fire her, he obtained a warrant to open Daisy's bank vault; it was found to be stuffed with Clara Bow's jewellery and records of endless transfers from Clara's special bank account into Miss De Voe's – Daisy had the power to sign cheques on Clara's account.

Threatened with the law, Miss De Voe tried to blackmail the studio for $125,000 in exchange for Clara's love letters from the numerous stars with whom she had had affairs – these included Gary Cooper, Eddie Cantor and Bela Lugosi. Since Clara's career had taken a downward turn, the studio felt she was not worth that much money. Miss De Voe was told to publish and be damned. The court case was a sensation; with so many irrelevant revelations about Clara's bedroom behaviour that the judge had to remind Daisy that it was she who was on trial, not Clara. She was found guilty and sentenced to eighteen months in jail. When she emerged, she took her revenge by selling a lengthy series on Clara's love life to a Hearst scandal sheet. It included such revelations as a description of the time Clara had given herself to a whole football team, including a young man called Marion Morrison (who became John Wayne). By mutual agreement, the 'It' girl and her studio tore up her contract. As a result Clara had a nervous breakdown – the first of many. She married her admirer Rex Bell and moved to a ranch in Nevada, where a combination of alcohol and sleeping pills induced a weight problem and more nervous breakdowns. She spent much of the rest of her life (she died in 1965) in sanatoriums. Her career had ended when she was 26.

The star who replaced Clara Bow as Paramount's major attraction was twenty years Clara's senior and her sex life was just as uninhibited, if more private. Born about 1886, Mae West was billed as 'the Baby Vamp' before she was a teenager. In 1926, starring on Broadway in her own play *Sex,* she was jailed for ten days on obscenity charges. She followed it up with a play called *Drag* about homosexuals, which she decided not to risk on Broadway. She then scored an enormous success in her play *Diamond Lil.* In her first film, *Night After Night* (a typical Mae West title) she uttered one of her classic lines – when a hat check girl says 'Goodness, what beautiful diamonds!' she replies (in her sexy drawl), 'Goodness had nothing to do with it.' She had the gift of making sex funny. Middle-aged men and women chuckled when she sang, 'I like a man who takes his time'. After *She Done Him Wrong* (1933) she became identified with the line (addressed to Cary Grant), 'Come up and see me sometime.' (In fact, it was 'Come up sometime, see me.') Her films were a tremendous success and she saved Paramount (Zukor's company) from bankruptcy. But the innuendos scandalized the Hays Office and caused a tightening up of regulations. They refused to permit dialogue like:

MAE: I like sophisticated men to take me out.
MAN: I'm not really sophisticated.
MAE: You're not really out yet either.

When her film *It Ain't No Sin* was advertised on Broadway, a squad of priests marched up and down with a poster: Yes It Is. The title had to be changed to *Belle of the Nineties.* For her next film, Will Hays appointed a censor to stay on the set; despite this, she managed to get away with lines like, 'A man in the house is worth two in the street,' and 'It's better to be looked over than overlooked.' But in a later film, *Every Day's a Holiday,* she lost at least two of her best lines: 'I wouldn't even lift my veil for that guy,' and 'I wouldn't let him touch me, even with a ten-foot pole.' Even so, lines like: 'Beulah, peel me a grape' and 'It's not the men in my life that count; it's the life in my men', entered the public domain. Finally driven to bowdlerize her material by a combination of the Hays Office and the Hearst Press, she returned to the theatre. At the age of 68, a cabaret act, in which she was surrounded by musclemen, ran for three years.

The scandal caused by Mae West was all on the screen. She was known to love hulking, muscular males but she was discreet about them. Hollywood's other sex image, Jean Harlow, had indiscretion thrust upon her by the suicide of her husband, Paul Bern, production assistant of 'wonder boy' Irving Thalberg at MGM. Bern was a soft-spoken intellectual who treated women as if they were ladies in King Arthur's court. He had been wildly and romantically in love with Barbara La Marr and was rumoured to have attempted suicide when she died of a drugs overdose. In 1932, after the highly successful premiere of *Grand Hotel,* Bern drove Jean Harlow to see his home and as they drank sherry by his swimming pool he talked at length about wine. Harlow later told her director why she liked Bern, 'He explains things and lets me know I've got a brain. He's different and doesn't talk fuck, fuck, fuck, all the time.' Two months later Bern and Harlow were married.

Jean Harlow was Hollywood's latest sex symbol, the 'blonde bombshell'. She attracted attention in a Laurel and Hardy film in which she lost her skirt when it caught in a door; she became famous in 1930 in Howard Hughes's *Hell's Angels*. Her conversation was laced with obscenities and she looked and sounded like a gangster's moll. In fact, she was intelligent (she wrote a more-than-passable novel), sensitive and a delightful comedienne.

Three months after the marriage, on 5 September 1932, Bern shot himself in the garden of his house in Benedict Canyon. He left a note saying:

Unfortunately this is the only way to make good the frightful wrong I have done you and to wipe out my frightful humiliation.
Paul

PS. You understand last night was only a comedy.

On the previous evening, apparently, he had gone into their bedroom wearing an enormous artificial phallus. Harlow had burst into shrieks of laughter. Bern had laughed too and together they slashed the phallus to pieces with scissors and flushed it down the lavatory. Was this what Bern was referring to? If so, the implication was obviously that he was impotent and that he had intended to improve his wife's sex life with the dildo. But Harlow denied that Bern was impotent. Bern's brother Henry, however, was able to provide a more plausible explanation. For five years, Bern had lived in the Algonquin Hotel in New York with another attractive blonde, Dorothy Millette, who was known as Mrs Paul Bern. She had had a nervous breakdown and suffered amnesia; she was confined in a Connecticut sanatorium and doctors agreed her condition was incurable. But it was not. When Dorothy Millette came out of hospital, she learned that her 'husband' was now married to Jean Harlow. She wrote to him and told him she was coming to California.

On the evening before Bern's suicide, neighbours heard sounds of a quarrel near the swimming pool. A chauffeur-driven limousine with a veiled woman had been seen in the area. It seems probable that Dorothy Millette arrived at the house late at night and there was a quarrel. The 'wrong' Bern was referring to in his suicide note was probably the scandal that would be unleashed by Dorothy's public denunciations. (In America, a couple need to live together for five years to achieve a common-law marriage so Dorothy would have been able to bring a charge of bigamy.)

On the day after Bern blew his brains out, Dorothy Millette boarded the steamer that left San Francisco for Sacramento and threw herself overboard.

In her hotel room were found a number of letters from Bern, typed by his secretary, all courteous but formal.

Oddly enough, what frightened the studio was not that Harlow's reputation would be ruined by the scandal, but that people might feel sorry for her, which would destroy her image as the hard-boiled blonde-on-the-make. But nothing of the sort happened, for Louis B. Mayer stopped the scandal before it began. Her love life continued to be unhappy; a marriage to cameraman Harold Rosson – sixteen years her senior – lasted only eight months. After that, she fell in love with her co-star William Powell – twenty years her senior. But their relationship was stormy, punctuated by quarrels, and he declined to marry her on the grounds that he had already been married to one blonde bombshell – Carole Lombard – and was too old to start again. On Saturday, 29 May 1937, she began feeling ill on the set of *Saratoga* and returned home. Her mother, who was a Christian Scientist, declined to call a doctor; she died a week later of uremic poisoning, at the age of 26.

In 1960, the screen writer Ben Hecht provided an interesting footnote to the Bern case when he stated in *Playboy* that Bern had been murdered – almost certainly by Dorothy Millette – and that the studio had forged the suicide note.

Hollywood's most publicized scandal of the 1930s was the divorce of Mary Astor from her husband, Dr Franklyn Thorpe. Mary Astor had a sad, dark-eyed prettiness that made her look vulnerable. Appearances were deceptive: her diary revealed that she was a highly dominant lady who thoroughly enjoyed sex. The diary was found in her underwear drawer and when Dr Thorpe opened it, his eye fell on the words: '. . . remarkable staying power; I don't know how he does it.' The man referred to was the playwright George S. Kaufman, co-author of the Marx Brothers' film *A Night at the Opera* and (later) of *The Man Who Came to Dinner.* Mary's diary recorded how she 'fell like a ton of bricks' when she first met Kaufman. He kissed her for the first time in a taxi on the way to the theatre and during the third act 'my hand wasn't in my own lap . . . It's been years since I felt up a man in public but I just got carried away.' The couple had then hastened back to George's flat and settled down to an all-night lovemaking session. 'Once George lays down his glasses he is *quite* a different man. His powers of recuperation are amazing, and we made love all night long . . . It all worked perfectly, and we shared the fourth climax at dawn.' She described how 'we went frequently to 73rd Street [Kaufman's flat] where he fucked the living daylights out of me.' When Kaufman came to Hollywood, Mary hastened to his hotel. 'He greeted me in pajamas and we flew into each other's arms. He was rampant in an instant, and in a few moments it was just like old times . . . he tore out of his pajamas and I never was undressed by anyone so fast in all my life. . . . It was wonderful to fuck the entire sweet afternoon away.' And when they went to

Palm Springs together, she recorded: 'Ah, desert night – with George's body plunging into mine, naked under the stars.'

Dr Thorpe's reaction was to beg his wife to break off the affair; with tears in his eyes he pleaded that he needed her. Mary's reaction was impatience; she was determined to continue to test George's staying power for the remainder of his stay in Hollywood. She moved out of her Beverly Hills mansion and Dr Thorpe proceeded to file for divorce. At the trial, in July 1936, the judge declined to allow the diary to be read aloud in court – he later ordered it to be burned – but the doctor's lawyers leaked extracts to the press, including the desert-night quotation, which were printed with asterisks in the appropriate places.

For a while, it looked as if Mary Astor's career was finished. It would have been if she had been identified with the kind of parts played by Mary Pickford but her screen image already had a touch of sin in it – she had played Dreiser's *Jenny Gerhardt* – and her fans found these revelations piquant rather than disgusting. Mary went on to play a number of ladies of doubtful morals, like Brigid O'Shaughnessy in *The Maltese Falcon*.

The effect of the divorce case on Kaufman is not known but Miss Astor's recommendations can scarcely have done his love life any harm.

In the last weeks of 1935, Hollywood had another murder mystery to rival the death of William Desmond Taylor. The lovely Thelma Todd had become Miss Massachusetts in 1921. She threw up a job as a schoolteacher to make her way to Hollywood and in due course showed her talents as a comedienne opposite the Marx Brothers – in *Monkey Business* and *Horse Feathers* – and Laurel and Hardy – in *Fra Diavolo*. In 1932, she married an agent named Di Cicco but divorced him two years later. In 1935, she had decided to give up films and go into the restaurant business and she and a director named Roland West co-managed Thelma Todd's Roadside Rest, on the Coast Highway. Thelma was living with West although he was already married. On Saturday, 14 December 1935, Stanley Lupino and his daughter Ida gave a party for Thelma at the Trocadero; Thelma's former husband Di Cicco turned up and there was a quarrel. In the early hours of Sunday morning, Thelma was driven back to her home in Santa Monica. More than 24 hours later, at 10:30 on Monday morning, she was found dead in her car in the garage above her beach restaurant. There was blood on her face but she had died of carbon-monoxide poisoning. Yet her evening slippers showed no sign of having climbed 270 rough concrete stairs to the garage. West finally admitted that he and Thelma had quarrelled violently after she returned home that Sunday morning and that he had pushed her out of the front door; neighbours had heard her kicking the door and shouting obscenities. The inference was that she had gone to the garage and switched on the ignition. But why, in that case, were her clothes so rumpled, as if in a struggle? And what of the witnesses, including West's wife, who claimed to have seen her alive on Sunday, driving a Packard with a dark, handsome man beside her?

The Grand Jury brought in a verdict of 'death due to carbon-monoxide poisoning'. Her lawyer insisted that she had been murdered on the orders of Lucky Luciano, who had tried to take over the upper storey of Thelma's Roadside Rest to set up a crooked gambling establishment; she had turned down his offer. But at the mention of Luciano's name, Thelma's director Hal Roach insisted he was perfectly satisfied with the suicide verdict. The police received a telegram from Ogden, Utah, stating that Thelma's killer was in a hotel there but they did nothing about it.

One theory of her death, noted by Kenneth Anger, in his delightful but inaccurate *Hollywood Babylon,* is that she was murdered by Roland West, who was getting tired of the relationship and of the financial problems associated with their restaurant. According to this theory, West persuaded a girlfriend to knock on the door and scream, while he knocked out Thelma inside before she was carried to the garage and left to die. West himself never made another film after Thelma's death, and died, forgotten, in 1952.

Whether she was killed by West or by a Luciano henchman, or by some unknown man who drove her into the garage and left the ignition running, there seems little doubt that Thelma Todd was murdered. Her death remains a mystery.

For the remainder of the 1930s, Hollywood managed to keep out of serious trouble. The moguls found it very hard to get used to the idea that scandal did not necessarily mean public outrage and the banning of films. It came to them as a pleasant surprise after Errol Flynn was found not guilty of rape in 1943. Flynn had become famous playing the swashbuckling lead in *Captain Blood* in 1935, and by 1942 he was one of Hollywood's most successful male actors. That he was sexually insatiable he admits himself in *My Wicked, Wicked Ways.* Director, Vincent Sherman felt that Flynn had a basic urge to debase women and tells how Flynn brought two prostitutes on to the set. When he asked how he could find the energy after a hard day's work, Flynn explained, 'I just lie there reading the trade papers while they work on me.'

In *Bring on the Empty Horses,* David Niven tells an amusing story that indicates the swiftness of Flynn's technique. After suffering from one of Flynn's practical jokes, Niven planned revenge. A writer friend mentioned that his aunt and niece were coming from Ohio, and suggested bringing them to the establishment shared by Flynn and Niven for drinks. In fact, the 'aunt' was a 35-year-old prostitute, while the niece was a beautiful whore of seventeen. Aunt and niece were introduced to Flynn, then the telephone rang, and the writer announced that he had to return to the hotel to collect the girl's mother. Niven, together with the writer and the 'aunt', watched outside the window as Flynn grabbed the girl without further ado, pushed her on to the settee and raised her skirts above her head. The girl had been instructed to hold on to her panties for a few minutes but Flynn overcame this obstacle within seconds. Shortly afterwards, the 'aunt' strode into the room and shrieked: 'Eunice, what are you doing?', and the girl peeped out from under Flynn and replied: 'I don't know, mom. Ask Mr Flynn.' The 'aunt' retorted: 'Mr Flynn, get off my daughter immediately and explain yourself ...' Eunice was sent out of the room suitably discomfited, whereupon the 'aunt' made a grab for Flynn's flies, explaining: 'I sent Eunice out because I want a bit of that myself.'

On 27 September 1942, Flynn drove to a party in Bel Air. Towards dusk, a car with half a dozen teenagers arrived. Among these was a studio messenger boy named Armand Knapp and his seventeen-year-old girlfriend named Betty Hansen. Betty drank too much and at one point, flopped on to Flynn's lap, while he continued the conversation over her head. At dinner, she had to rush out of the room to be sick. Afterwards, Flynn suggested she should come up to the bathroom attached to his bedroom; there he told her he thought she should have a sleep. According to Betty, she lay on a bed and Flynn began to undress her, removing everything but her shoes. She explained that she thought he intended to tuck her up in bed. Then Flynn removed all his own clothes, except his shoes, and proceeded to make love to her for half an hour. One of the girls who had brought Betty to the party came upstairs to look for her; by this time Betty had douched herself in the bathroom and was back in bed while Flynn was taking a shower. The next day, Betty told her sister that Flynn had seduced her and was taken into protective custody in Juvenile Hall.

The District Attorney recalled that fourteen months earlier, another seventeen-year-old named Peggy Satterlee had claimed that she had been raped by Flynn on his yacht. Flynn later insisted that the DA was inspired by a determination to 'clean up' Hollywood and felt that this was his opportunity. On 11 January 1943, Flynn appeared in court. He was defended by the brilliant lawyer Jerry Giesler. Betty described how she had allowed Flynn to remove her tight jeans in the belief that he was putting her to bed. Giesler asked her whether she still believed this as Flynn removed her panties and she said yes. 'When did you first think about sexual intercourse?' asked Giesler. The court roared with laughter when she replied, 'When I had sexual intercourse with him.' Without much effort, Giesler induced her to contradict herself. She had told the juvenile officers that she had undressed herself; now she said Flynn had undressed her. She flatly denied that she had helped him, then admitted that she had given him some assistance in removing her shirt. Asked if she had helped remove her panties she said, 'I might have.' Finally, Giesler obliged her to admit that when she had been 'raped' by Flynn, she was already in trouble with the juvenile officers for twice committing an act of oral sex on Armand Knapp.

After this, Peggy Satterlee gave her evidence: how she had been on a trip on Flynn's yacht; how she had climbed into bed in her underskirt and panties and how Flynn had come into her cabin, got into bed with her and had intercourse with her. Flynn seems to have used the same technique as with 'Eunice', pushing her underskirt over her head, her panties down, then making love to her for half an hour. After this they went up on deck and he brought her a glass of milk. The following day she swam with him and they had pictures taken together for *Life*. That evening, he invited her to his state-room to look at the moon through a porthole. Still in some pain from the previous night – she had been a virgin – she tried to resist but Flynn insisted that, since he had possessed her once, he could see no reason why he shouldn't do so again. When he tried to remove her slacks, she fought so hard that the bed curtains were pulled down. Even when Flynn was inside her, she struggled so hard that his penis came out. This was damaging evidence. So was the testimony of a police doctor that Peggy's genitals were bruised and swollen and that the hymen was newly torn. But Giesler scored a point when he pointed out that Peggy could have seen the moon just as well from the deck and that in any case, she could not have looked at the moon through the porthole since it was on the other side of the yacht. He also managed to bring out in evidence the fact that, in the following year, Peggy Satterlee had had an abortion – then an illegal operation – and that the charge still hung over her. The implication was clear: that both girls were hoping for leniency from the police in exchange for their testimony against Flynn.

In the witness box, Flynn denied everything. If the girls had been older, he might have argued that the intercourse occurred with their consent but since they were both underage at the time of the offence, he could still have been convicted of statutory rape. So he perjured himself in the witness box. And in due course, the jury found him not guilty. A hysterical woman rushed over to him and kissed him on the lips. And to the unspeakable relief of Warner Brothers, the scandal actually seemed to increase his popularity: his films *Desperate Journey* and *Gentleman Jim* played to crowded cinemas.

Most writers on the case take the view that Flynn had been 'set up' by a couple of 'tramps'; but no one who studies the transcript of the case can take this simplistic attitude. Betty Hansen had just been violently sick, so she was probably telling the truth when she said that she objected to Flynn's lovemaking. Peggy Satterlee had been a virgin; she may or may not have been willing to surrender her virginity to Flynn in due course, but it seems clear that he did not give her the choice. And her story of her struggle to avoid a second bout of lovemaking when she was still sore from the first has a ring of truth.

In his autobiography *My Wicked, Wicked Ways*, Flynn admits having sex with Peggy Satterlee, insisting that he had no idea she was under eighteen.

On the delicate question of Betty Hansen, he avoids difficult questions by simply omitting to mention her appearance on the witness stand.

This close brush with the law seems to have taught Flynn nothing about the dangers of having intercourse without first asking the girl's permission. During the trial he noticed a pretty girl serving behind the tobacco stand in the Hall of Justice. Her name was Nora Eddington. Flynn persuaded her to go out with him and discovered that she was an innocent virgin who regarded herself as engaged to a marine. He bided his time, took her out, and tried repeatedly and unsuccessfully to steer her towards the bedroom. One night, after drinking heavily (and, according to one biographer, taking cocaine) he took her back to his house, pushed her into the bedroom and tore off her clothes. Then he undressed and raped her. She testified, 'I didn't know what was happening. I was terrified. Suddenly he was thrusting into me. It was like a knife. . . . There was blood everywhere.' Afterwards, Flynn wept and begged forgiveness; Nora married him but then, when she discovered he was incapable of staying faithful, divorced him.

Flynn's career went downhill in the 50s, largely as the result of heavy drinking that caused the once-handsome face to become fleshy and coarse. He died in 1959 of a heart attack at the age of fifty. In 1980, in a book called *Errol Flynn, The Untold Story*, a writer named Charles Higham accused Flynn of being a bisexual and a German spy. It is impossible to tell whether there is any truth in the bisexuality charge – Higham alleges that Flynn's frequent trips to Mexico were spent in pursuit of teenage boys – but the spy charge certainly remains unproven. Flynn was apparently a close friend of a certain Dr Hermann Friedrich Erben, whom Higham describes as 'one of the most important and ingenious Nazi agents'. Flynn apparently met him on the island of New Britain, in the Pacific, after Flynn had been shipwrecked in 1933. Subsequently, Erben seems to have turned up frequently in Hollywood. But even if, as Higham insists, Flynn had Nazi sympathies, it is impossible to see how, as a film star, he had any opportunity to do espionage work for Erben. Higham tells a story of how Flynn and Erben went to Spain during the civil war, their intention being to interview Germans fighting for the loyalists, and to report their names to Berlin, so their families could be persecuted. But it hardly seems necessary to send a famous film star from America for this purpose as an ordinary German infiltrator would have served just as well. Higham's account of Erben makes it clear that, for an 'important and ingenious Nazi agent' he was unbelievably incompetent and regrettably accident-prone. The reaction of most reviewers to Higham's 'untold story' was one of understandable scepticism; they found it difficult to credit the hard-drinking, sexually insatiable Hollywood playboy with the firmness of purpose necessary for a spy. It is true that there have been such spies, but none of them made highly successful films in their spare time. Whatever the final judgment on his life and personality, Errol Flynn will continue to live on in folk memory for the satisfyingly descriptive catch-phrase 'In like Flynn'.

At the time Flynn was deflowering Peggy Satterlee on the *Sirocco,* Hollywood was contemplating another evolving scandal with a mixture of eagerness and alarm. Hollywood's two leading gossip columnists were Louella Parsons and Hedda Hopper; the former worked for the multi-millionaire newspaper magnate William Randolph Hearst, the inventor of 'yellow journalism' (i.e. stories of doubtful authenticity but high scandal value). Early in 1940, the young theatrical director Orson Welles had arrived in Hollywood and before the year was out, the town was full of rumours that he was making a film based on the life of a well-known newspaper publisher. The obvious candidate was Hearst, although no one was sure (since there was only one script and Welles slept with that under his pillow). Hearst was one of the most powerful men in Hollywood – in fact, in America – so there were expectations of an explosion. To Louella Parsons, Welles solemnly denied that his film was about her boss. But when he invited her rival Hedda Hopper to a private screening of *Citizen Kane,* she watched it with increasing dismay. It was not a matter of 'accidental resemblance' to Hearst; this was a carefully considered, deliberately unfair attack on the arch-capitalist tycoon. Hearst was an old friend of Hedda Hopper's. 'You won't get away with it', said Hedda. 'You want to bet?' said Welles.

In making *Citizen Kane* Welles had every intention of creating a scandal. He had, in a sense, built his career on scandal, and so far it had done him no harm. His acting career began at the age of sixteen with a touch of deceit. He had presented himself at the stage door of the Gate Theatre in Dublin and announced himself as a star of the New York Theatre Guild. The theatre's director, Hilton Edwards, was not entirely deceived but liked the young man's cheek, and offered him a part in *Jew Süss.* Three years later he made his Broadway debut in Shakespeare. In 1937, he and John Houseman set up the Mercury Theatre project in New York; it was an attempt to transplant the left-wing theatre of Brecht and Weill to America. In July 1937, Welles had an opportunity to demonstrate his genius for improvisation and also for making the headlines. The theatre project had scheduled the production of Marc Blitzstein's satirical operetta *The Cradle Will Rock,* a violent attack on capitalism and glorification of trade unionism. At the last minute, the government cancelled the production. It happened so late that a queue had already formed outside the theatre. Welles told some of his actors to entertain them, while he tried to find a theatre. Finally a little man who had been trying to see Welles all day – and whom Welles had been avoiding because he looked like a process-server – managed to explain that he owned a theatre nearby which they could use. The whole audience of two thousand was led up Broadway to the Venice Theatre. A piano on a truck followed them. An Equity (union) ban prevented actors from appearing on stage but there was nothing to stop the actors from standing up in the audience and playing their parts, while Blitzstein himself played the piano on stage. A spotlight picked out each actor as he stood up. The evening was a sensation. The next morning, Welles was deluged with offers from other theatrical managers to present *The Cradle Will Rock* in exactly the same manner.

In the following year, Welles began presenting Mercury Theatre projects on the radio; for the fourth show he chose H.G. Wells's *War of the Worlds*. On hearing the recording, Welles decided it was dull and that the only way to improve it was to make it more 'newsy' by presenting it as a series of newsflashes. After the introduction (read by Welles), an announcer explained that the programme would be continued from the dance floor of a hotel. Then the music was interrupted by a newsflash about explosions on the planet Mars. A second newsflash announced a meteorite in New Jersey that had killed many people. After that, more news bulletins and on-the-spot reports described the arrival of the Martians, horrible leathery slugs with murderous ray guns.

Many people who switched on after the beginning were thrown into a panic. Families rushed out of their houses and took to the roads; others went and camped in the open. Meanwhile, on the radio, the voice of President Roosevelt – in reality an actor – begged the nation not to panic. Before the end of the broadcast, the mayor of a mid-Western town had rung up to say that there were terrified mobs in the streets. The New York police department received 2,000 calls in fifteen minutes. The CBS network had to make broadcasts every ten minutes for the next 24 hours, reassuring America that the Martians had not really landed. Welles had achieved overnight fame – or at least, notoriety.

It was inevitable that he should be invited to Hollywood and equally inevitable that he should think of his first film there in terms of scandal or sensationalism. His leftist affiliations suggested capitalism as a target and a super-capitalist as its subject. He chose one whose income was $15 million a year.

William Randolph Hearst, born 1863, was the son of a multimillionaire owner of silver mines. He used his inherited fortune to become a press baron. In 1917, at the age of 54, he had fallen in love with a Ziegfeld Follies girl, Marion Davies, a delightful blonde with a stutter and a sense of humour. He had set out to turn her into another Mary Pickford. He spent millions on her films. (When a friend told him there was money in the movie business Hearst replied drily, 'Yes, mine.')

Inevitably, the Hearst newspapers – he owned about forty – hailed every new Marion Davies film as a triumph. Unfortunately, Marion was no Mary Pickford; her real talent lay in light comedy, not drama. All her films lost money and Hearst's aggressive publicity campaigns alienated the public. Hearst was discreet about his affair but it became public knowledge in 1923 when a crooked attorney named Fallon, charged with corruption, stated in court that Marion Davies was the mother of twins and Hearst was the father. (The whole story was an invention.)

Three months after the Fallon trial, in November 1924, Hearst and Marion Davies were the subject of even more scandalous gossip. On 15 November a group of Hollywood celebrities was invited on to Hearst's yacht *Oneida* for the birthday party of the pioneer Western director Thomas Ince. Ince became ill, apparently with acute indigestion, and was put on a train for his home in Los Angeles. He died two days later of a heart attack. His body was cremated. But there were persistent rumours that Ince had been shot by Hearst, who had caught him making love to Miss Davies. The rumours were so persistent that the District Attorney felt obliged to investigate them. He concluded that they had no foundation. But inevitably, this only led to rumours that Hearst had paid out thousands of dollars to suppress the truth. In *Hollywood Babylon*, Kenneth Anger describes how Charlie Chaplin and Marion Davies had slipped off together to the lower deck and that when Hearst went looking for them, he found them *in flagrante delicto*. Marion screamed, 'M-m-m-murder!', which brought other guests rushing to the spot as Hearst ran for his diamond-studded revolver; when Hearst fired, it was Ince who dropped dead with a bullet in his brain.

In his autobiography, Chaplin insists that he was not even present on Hearst's yacht and explains that the rumours about Ince's death were absurd because he and Hearst went to see Ince two weeks before his death: 'He was very happy to see . . . us and believed he would soon be well.' Since Ince died only four days after being taken off Hearst's yacht, this story hardly disproves the 'ugly rumours'. Even a standard reference work like Ephraim Katz's *International Film Encyclopedia* states that 'Thomas Harper Ince was mysteriously and fatally injured aboard William Randolph Hearst's yacht. . . . He died before regaining consciousness.' So it is just conceivable that the death of Ince occurred under suspicious circumstances.

All this explains why there was alarm and fury in the Hearst encampment when Hedda Hopper telephoned to say that *Citizen Kane* was a thinly disguised portrait of Hearst, complete with scandal. Hearst's film columnist Louella Parsons was asked to arrange a private screening and to take some lawyers along. Welles was delighted to oblige – his fellow actor George Coulouris believes that he had been hoping to create a scandal. Louella Parsons left the screening looking shattered and rushed to tell Hearst that he was being portrayed as a ruthless capitalist exploiter. Hearst immediately sent a telegram to the film's producer at RKO demanding that the film should be withheld pending legal action. The producer, George Schaefer, defiantly refused. There was panic in Hollywood; it was generally felt that if Hearst was offended, then his newspapers would boycott Hollywood films which might lead to the bankruptcy of some studios. Louis B. Mayer offered to pay

RKO $800,000 – the cost of the film – to destroy it; Schaefer refused. Louella Parsons proceeded to attack Welles in her column, which was syndicated all over America. Her rival Hedda Hopper thereupon announced that she would devote six of her radio programmes to a biography of the young genius Orson Welles. The nationwide furore was a publicity godsend. When *Citizen Kane* was finally shown in April 1941, it was an immense critical success, one critic declaring it to be 'the finest film of all time'. (The truth is that *Citizen Kane* is rather a silly film, with its presupposition that the wicked newspaper magnate – the man who never loved anybody – has a sentimental yearning for childhood innocence, symbolized by his sledge 'Rosebud'. In fact – as Welles knew – 'Rosebud' was Hearst's pet name for Miss Davies' private parts.)

The scandal that Welles envisaged in *Citizen Kane* ('Newspaper Boss Caught In Singer's Love Nest') had no foundation in fact; apart from their one brush with scandal in the Fallon case, Marion and Hearst lived together as placidly as an elderly married couple until Hearst's death, at the age of 88, in 1951. It is an ironical footnote to the story that *Citizen Kane* was a box-office failure.

The year 1943 saw the downfall of the actress Frances Farmer, a determined individualist who frequently confessed that the only thing she liked about Hollywood was the money. She had won a trip to the Soviet Union in an essay competition when she was a student; when she came to New York in the late 30s, she acted in the Group Theatre, which (like Welles's Mercury) had strong leftist tendencies; she also acted in Clifford Odets's *Golden Boy*. A few decades later, she would have fitted perfectly comfortably into the anti-Vietnam war movement but in Hollywood in the 40s, she was a misfit. Her increasing exasperation with the triviality of her Hollywood films led her to alienate 'old timers' like Zukor and she began drinking too much. In October 1942 she was arrested for drunken driving on the Pacific Highway and screamed abuse at the cop who arrested her. She was put on probation. Arrested again for failing to report to her parole officer, she hid in a bathroom and was carried off naked by the police. At police headquarters she signed her occupation as 'cocksucker'. In court, the judge asked her about her drinking and she screamed: 'Listen, I put liquor in my milk, liquor in my coffee and liquor in my orange juice. What do you want me to do – starve to death?' The judge stood up and shouted out a sentence of 180 days. She screamed back, 'Have you ever had a broken heart?' (alluding to her stormy affair with Clifford Odets). Then she hurled an ink pot at the judge's head and was carried out kicking.

Her mother told the press that this was only a publicity stunt but nevertheless declared her a mental incompetent and signed committal papers. In hospital, she was subjected to insulin shock treatment. For the most part, Hollywood was delighted with her downfall. Director, William

Wyler commented, 'The nicest thing I can say about Frances Farmer is that she is unbearable.' She spent much of the remainder of the 40s in mental homes and although she made one film, *The Party Crashers* in 1958, never succeeded in making a 'comeback'. She died of cancer at the age of 57 in 1970.

Chaplin's paternity case, already mentioned, occupied the headlines through much of 1943. He had suddenly lost his popularity when he appeared at a rally in New York demanding that the Allies open a second front to help the Russians. He records in his autobiography that after this, he suddenly ceased to be invited to the houseparties of the rich. The final verdict in the paternity case was paradoxical in that he was adjudged the father of Joan Barry's daughter although a blood test proved conclusively that it was impossible. Since he had admitted that he had been 'intimate' with Miss Barry, the court no doubt felt that he deserved to be the father.

In 1944, Chaplin was acquitted of transporting Miss Barry over state lines for immoral purposes and that year saw the suicide of one of Hollywood's most tempestuous actresses, Lupe Velez, at the age of 36. Born in Mexico and educated in a Texas convent, she made her name starring opposite Douglas Fairbanks in *The Gaucho* in 1926. In 1929, she played in *Wolf Song* opposite Gary Cooper and had an affair with him. (Cooper's sex life seems to have been very nearly as eventful as Errol Flynn's – he made a habit of sleeping with his leading ladies; but since he was discreet about it and everyone liked him he managed to stay out of the gossip columns.) Cooper found her fiery temper too much for him and she transferred her affections to Johnny Weismuller, the Olympic swimmer who played Tarzan. Their married life was stormy – according to Kenneth Anger, 'She couldn't understand why Johnny would get mad when she'd flash her charms at Hollywood parties by flinging her dress over her head – she was always innocent of lingerie.' After her divorce from Weismuller, her love affairs became legendary – Anger calls her a 'man-addict'. Finally, heavily in debt, pregnant by her latest boyfriend (and barred from abortion by her Catholic upbringing), she swallowed 75 Seconal tablets and was found lying on her bed with her hands crossed on her breasts in the position of a sleeping madonna.

The news sensation of the summer of 1947 was the murder of the gangster Bugsy Siegel in the home of his mistress Virginia Hill, at 810 Linden Drive, Beverly Hills. Siegel was one of the major figures of Murder Incorporated, the Mafia organization headed by Luciano, and had the dubious distinction of turning Las Vegas into the gambling capital of the United States. Benjamin Siegel – known as 'Bugsy' because he appeared to become insane when he lost his temper – had been involved in many murders since he had shot Lucky Luciano's boss Joe Masseria – one of the old-fashioned style of gangster – to oblige Luciano. By the time he was 25 he had his own suite in the Waldorf-Astoria in New York – Luciano lived two floors above him. He was sent out to California as an emissary of Murder Inc., chosen, perhaps, because he was a friend of actor George Raft, whom he had known since childhood in Brooklyn. Soon the handsome, charming Siegel had forced his way into the drugs racket in California and had gained control of the movie extras and bit-part players. His sex life was also rumoured to be extremely active among the starlets – he had a reputation as a rapist in New York. His wife and family had moved west with him but Siegel always behaved like a bachelor. In November 1939, Siegel and two more gangsters – Frankie Carbo and Whitey Krakower – were ordered to kill Harry ('Big Greenie') Greenberg, a New York mobster who had fled to California and was threatening to 'sing' to the DA. Greenberg was found dead outside his Los Angeles home late at night. In the following August, another member of Murder Inc., Allie Tannenbaum, had reason to believe that he was also on the death list and began to 'sing' to the DA of King County, New York, and implicated Siegel in the murder of 'Greenie'. In January 1942, Siegel and Carbo finally went on trial for the murder of Greenberg. They were defended by that Hollywood veteran Jerry Giesler, who was able to discredit Tannenbaum's testimony so effectively that Siegel was 'sprung'.

Siegel had been driving through the quiet little town of Las Vegas in 1945 when it struck him that this would be the ideal place for a gambling casino. He raised $6 million from the 'Syndicate', and built the Flamingo Hotel – his girlfriend, Virginia Hill's nickname.

Luciano was deported from America in 1946. One year later, he called a meeting of members of the Syndicate in Havana, Cuba, whose crime was controlled by the Syndicate's 'accountant', Meyer Lansky. When Siegel was asked about repayment of $3 million, he lost his temper and stormed out of the room. Lansky was asked to talk sense into him but Siegel still refused to talk about repayment, no doubt pointing to the vast sums of money he had syphoned into Murder Inc. from the drugs racket in California.

At about 10 o'clock in the evening of 20 June 1947, Siegel and some friends drove back from a Santa Monica seafood restaurant to Virginia Hill's home – she was away in Europe at the time. (She was a Syndicate courier.) As Siegel sat reading the *Los Angeles Times* on the settee, there was a sound of breaking glass and then the deafening roar of gunfire. Siegel had his nose shot off, his eyes blown out, and his vertebrae smashed; one eye was found on the other side of the room. At almost the same moment, a Syndicate member named Little Moey Sedway walked into the Flamingo Hotel in Las Vegas and shouted, 'We're taking over.' Few people attended Siegel's funeral and Jerry Giesler reflected that if he had not 'sprung' Siegel five years earlier, the gangster would probably have still been alive.

In 1947, Hollywood had more serious problems than the occasional gang murder. The cold war had brought a wave of anti-communism. Senator

Joseph McCarthy had not yet arrived on the scene – that would take another three years – but what would later become known as McCarthyism was already causing deep divisions in Hollywood.

In retrospect, it is easy to blame the Americans for overreacting. But in the cold war climate of 1946, it seemed obvious that the Russians were hoping to take advantage of the chaos in Europe to implant communism from France to the Balkans. In due course, America would combat the growing threat with Marshall aid, which revitalized the economies of Europe. In the meantime, it struck many Americans that an enormous number of the refugees who had fled from the Nazis were members of the communist party, and that they had implanted a communist 'fifth column' in their own country. The House Un-American Activities Committee, founded in 1938, was given a new lease of life in 1946. In Hollywood, the Motion Picture Alliance for the Preservation of American Ideals came into existence under the presidency of John Wayne. (He was followed by Hedda Hopper.) This was a direct result of a 'Reds under the bed' scare campaign initiated by New Hampshire congressman J. Parnell Thomas, who set out to prove that the communists had infiltrated the film industry.

Hollywood's problem had always been a certain tendency to view things simplistically, in terms of goodies and baddies. Its domination by a few powerful cliques also bred the conspiratorial mentality. In fact, very few actors or directors were deeply interested in politics. The problem was that those who were interested were usually the more intelligent ones and since many of them had been involved in the anti-fascist movement of the 1930s, it followed that their views were distinctly towards the left.

Thomas and his committee subpoenaed many actors and writers. Ten of the writers refused to tell the committee whether they had ever been communists and were sent to jail – they became known as 'The Hollywood Ten'. (Ironically, one of the ten, Dalton Trumbo, was to meet J. Parnell Thomas in jail – he had been sentenced for sharp practice concerning the payroll.) The thriller writer Dashiel Hammett was later sentenced to six months in jail for refusing to reveal names and all his books were allowed to go out of print. Charlie Chaplin was excused from appearing before the committee when he explained that he was simply a 'peace monger', but attacks on him in the Press led to the widespread banning of his latest film, *Monsieur Verdoux*. Many careers were ruined: John Garfield, Gale Sondergaard, Larry Parks (who had played the title role in *The Jolsen Story*); many others – like Joseph Losey and Jules Dassin – found themselves unemployable in Hollywood and had to move abroad.

Humphrey Bogart, who was an individualist and a libertarian without having the slightest communist tendency, organized a protest group called The Committee for the First Amendment, which included Lionel Barrymore, John Ford, Gregory Peck, John Huston, Billy Wilder, Ira Gershwin, Gene

Kelly, June Havoc and Danny Kaye. On 24 October 1947, a planeload of stars and directors, led by Bogart (accompanied by Lauren Bacall), flew to Washington, with press conferences *en route* at St Louis, Kansas City and Chicago. It was not a good idea. 'We went in there green and they beat our brains out', said Bogart later. 'In the shuffle we became adopted by the communists, and I ended up with my picture on the front page of the *Daily Worker* ... That the trip was ill-advised and even foolish I am ready to admit ...' Bogart was fortunate; he was the studio's biggest star. But many other of the three hundred members of his protest committee found themselves on a permanent blacklist that ended their careers in Hollywood.

The irony was that there were no real villains in this particular drama. The names who supported the Un-American Activities Committee – Ronald Reagan, John Wayne, Gary Cooper, Robert Taylor, Charles Coburn, Adoiphe Menjou, George Murphy, Walt Disney, Howard Hughes – were equally sincere and well-meaning; they also regarded themselves as libertarians. It was basically a problem in communication – an art, paradoxically, in which Hollywood has never been skilled. The political scandal of 1947 was really a storm in a teacup, yet it came closer to destroying Hollywood than 25 years of sexual scandal.

In 1948, 29-year-old Carole Landis, star of the original version of *A Star is Born,* and described as having 'the best legs in town', told *Photoplay,* 'Every girl in the world wants to find the right man, someone who is sympathetic and understanding and helpful and strong, someone she can love madly. Actresses are no exception.' For Carole, the man who fitted these specifications was the English actor Rex Harrison, who was already married to Lilli Palmer. On 4 July 1948, in a fit of depression, Carole Landis took an overdose of sleeping tablets. One of the underlying causes of her depression may have been the fact that, although talented, she had never succeeded in starring in anything but second-rate B pictures.

A few weeks later, the studios had their biggest publicity headache since the Errol Flynn rape case. Late on the evening of 31 August 1948, Robert Mitchum, the idol of the 'bobby soxers', arrived at a party at the house of his friend Lila Leeds in Laurel Canyon, where everyone was smoking pot. Mitchum had only just lit up when the door burst open and two policemen rushed in. Mitchum was the major catch. RKO executives bit their nails at the thought of the moral outrage of American parents at the revelation that the hero of the teenagers was a 'dope fiend'. Mitchum declined to worry. As a teenager he had been a convict in a Georgia chain gang, on a vagrancy charge, and had escaped; later he worked as a drop-hammer operator. He got into films by accident, as a result of wandering on to a 'Hopalong Cassidy' set, and the sleepy-eyed, menacing expression – the look of a born rebel – soon made him, together with Frank Sinatra, the dream-man of every underage girl. He had frequently remarked that acting was not a suitable job for a grown man; the thought of losing his public was, therefore, not entirely alarming.

He hired Jerry Giesler – it cost him $50,000 that he didn't possess – whose advice was not to enter a plea, either of guilty or not guilty. If he pleaded not guilty, it meant a lengthy trial and many revelations about pot-smoking in Hollywood that would be bad for the film industry in general. The minor disadvantage was that Mitchum would almost certainly draw a prison sentence. He decided to take the risk and the press ground its collective teeth when Giesler announced in court that he would waive a jury trial. There was one bad moment for Mitchum when the judge announced that the sentence would be two years, followed by considerable relief when this was reduced to sixty days, with the rest on probation. Mitchum served his two months without complaint and had it shortened by a day for good behaviour. It emerged later that the whole thing had been set up by the police. The friend who had taken Mitchum to the party had been trying to persuade him to go all day. The police had hidden a microphone in the room and informed the press in advance that they expected to arrest a major film star; they waited for Mitchum's arrival before bursting in.

The main question was how the fans would take it. In fact, it made no obvious difference to Mitchum's popularity – and neither did a great deal of bad publicity during the next decade about public brawls and a tendency to rip telephones off walls. It underlined the point that the public has no objection to stars behaving in private as they behave on the screen; the baddie who behaves like a baddie upsets no one. It is when the goodie behaves like a baddie that the fans ask for their money back.

As this recognition sank in, the whole concept of scandal became increasingly blurred in Hollywood. If 'bad behaviour' can, under the right circumstances, improve a star's image, then clearly it may be a waste of time to be good. In any case, the notion of what constituted a film star was changing. From 1920 onward, the women were expected to be glamorous and the men handsome and sophisticated. When 23-year-old Marlon Brando created a sensation as the brutish working-class lout in *A Streetcar Named Desire* in 1947, the male image began to change. Brando talked in a mumble – a technique known as 'the Method' (which meant acting natural) – and slouched around with no attempt at athletic grace. In Hollywood he dressed in a rumpled T-shirt and jeans and ate cherries out of a bag. His admirer James Dean improved on this image to the extent of taking out his penis on the set to urinate.

The public now seemed to expect its stars to behave scandalously and in 1952 a publisher named Robert Harrison decided to satisfy their expectations by launching a magazine called *Confidential,* whose first issue sold a quarter of a million copies. Its aim, quite simply, was to dig out the dirt on the stars – who was a nympho, who was a drug addict, who was sharing her boyfriend with her daughter, who was a homosexual or a lesbian. The financial success of the magazine was so enormous that Harrison could afford to pay spies considerable sums of money for a gossip-column item. The concealed tape recorder and the mini-camera took the place of the prying reporter whose manner invited a snub. What Harrison soon realized was that most stars prefer to minimize the damage by ignoring the attack – the principle utilized by Jerry Giesler in the case of Mitchum's arrest for pot-smoking. But finally, one of the victims decided the risk was worth it; after an article alleging nudist romps in a forest, Dorothy Dandridge sued *Confidential* for $2 million. Other stars followed suit. The movie chiefs realized that this could end as an unprecedented series of revelations about the private life of the stars and some of the more vulnerable – including Clark Gable – were hastily despatched on vacations to distant parts. All attempts by the Hollywood moguls to hush-up the scandal failed and the case came to court in August 1957. Dorothy Dandridge had dropped her charge, in exchange for a substantial out-of-court settlement. Maureen O'Hara moved into the front line. She sued *Confidential* because they had accused her of various indecent intimacies with a handsome South American in Grauman's Chinese Theatre. Her defence was that she had been in Spain on the date of the alleged indecencies and she was awarded $5,000. Liberace received an out-of-court settlement of $40,000. (Two years later, in England, he sued the *Daily Mirror* for implying he was a homosexual and received £8,000.) So many other stars received settlements that Harrison decided to call it quits and sold *Confidential* soon afterwards. Polly Gould, a member of his editorial staff, committed suicide the day before she was due to give evidence and it emerged later that she was virtually a 'double agent' selling the magazine's secrets to the DA and passing on the DA's secrets to the magazine.

After *Confidential*, the age of Hollywood scandal was virtually over. Stars realized that nothing short of murder was likely to cause adverse public reaction. Errol Flynn was one of the first to cash in with his autobiography *My Wicked, Wicked Ways,* and other stars followed suit. The next major Hollywood scandal did involve a murder. On 4 April, Good Friday, 1958. Jerry Giesler was summoned to the home of Lana Turner at 730 North Bedford Drive, where a corpse was lying on the floor, the stomach stained with blood. It was her gangster boyfriend, Johnny Stompanato. He had been fatally stabbed by Lana Turner's daughter, fourteen-year-old Cheryl, after hearing Stompanato threaten to painfully disfigure her mother.

Lana Turner's career had started at about the same age when she was playing truant from school, and sipping a milkshake in a drugstore on Sunset Boulevard, wearing a tight sweater. A journalist approached her and asked if she had ever thought of getting into the movies. Through an agent friend of the journalist, Lana (real name Mildred) achieved a bit-part in a film called *They Won't Forget* in which she was raped and murdered at an early stage. As 'the sweater girl' she achieved fame during World War II and became a favourite pin-up of American servicemen. Her first marriage to bandleader, Artie Shaw, lasted two months and caused her to have a nervous breakdown. The second husband, a young executive named Stephen Crane, asked her to dance for a bet, and married her nine days later; he was the father of Cheryl. Her third marriage was to a millionaire, Bob Topping; the fourth to the screen Tarzan, Lex Barker. There were also a number of well-publicized romances, with Frank Sinatra, Howard Hughes, Tyrone Power and Fernando Lamas, the Argentinian star. By the mid-1950s, her sweater-girl image had been outgrown and her career was foundering. It was after the breakup of the marriage to Lex Barker that Johnny Stompanato, former bodyguard of gangster Mickey Cohen, telephoned her out of the blue – for a bet – and invited her out on a blind date. Stompanato was a muscular, hairy-chested specimen who was nicknamed Oscar, apparently because a vital part of his anatomy was about the height of a Hollywood Oscar when upright. Like most dominating females, Lana apparently liked her men athletic and rough. On one occasion Stompanato told her, 'When I say hop, you'll hop; when I say jump, you'll jump.' Lana was not averse to obeying orders but when her own latent dominance surfaced, there were explosions.

It seems clear that there was a mutual obsession. When she came to England to star with Sean Connery, Stompanato followed her, and attempts to strangle her and threats to slash her with a razor led the police to have him deported. Back in America, she and Stompanato went on holiday to Acapulco, and then she returned in time to receive her academy award for her part in *Peyton Place*, a welcome upswing in her career.

On Good Friday 1958, Stompanato and Lana went to her home in Beverly Hills in a state of violent disagreement. The quarrel was so noisy that Cheryl was afraid he was about to attack her mother; she removed a carving knife from the kitchen drawer. The quarrel continued in Lana's bedroom and Cheryl looked in to see what was happening; her mother asked her to go away. But when her mother began to scream, Cheryl again looked in and saw Stompanato swinging at her mother with a coat on a coathanger. This time Cheryl rushed at him and, apparently, hit him in the stomach. Stompanato groaned, clutched at his stomach and collapsed. At this point, Lana Turner saw the carving knife in her daughter's hand.

A doctor was sent for and administered adrenalin, while Lana tried the kiss of life. It was useless. Shortly afterwards, Stompanato's heart stopped.

The case made all the front pages and fuel was added to the flames when Stompanato's former boss Mickey Cohen handed over a dozen of Lana Turner's love letters to the press. The scandal sheets hastened to print them in facsimile. They certainly revealed that she was hopelessly infatuated with Stompanato. In court, Lana and Cheryl had all the sympathy of the jury, which arrived at a verdict of justifiable homicide.

The dead man's brother filed a suit for $800,000 damages against Cheryl's parents, alleging parental negligence. It was settled for $20,000.

This time the studios had no doubt that their star would not survive; murder was surely going too far? But to everyone's astonishment, the scandal had the opposite effect; Lana Turner's declining career revived triumphantly. During the showing of *Another Time, Another Place* – the film she had made with Sean Connery – members of the audience shouted: 'We're with you, Lana.' And her career once more prospered as it had in the early 1940s. The scandal had proved to be the best kind of publicity.

The Stompanato scandal could be regarded as a watershed in the history of Hollywood. For it meant, in effect, that the age of scandal was over. A scandal is not a scandal unless people are shocked – or at least, pleasantly titillated. When, in 1958, the press discovered that Marlon Brando's latest wife, formerly Anna Kashfi, was not (as she claimed) an Indian actress but the daughter of a Welsh factory worker named Pat O'Callaghan, the news was splashed in the tabloids because it aroused malicious amusement. Brando, the great tamer of women, had been fooled by a scheming Welshwoman. But this was not true scandal, only gossip laced with spite. Real scandal, the kind that had destroyed Fatty Arbuckle in 1921 and almost destroyed Ingrid Bergman when she deserted her husband for the director Roberto Rossellini in 1947, was a thing of the past. In retrospect, it seems symbolic that the decade of the 60s opened with the publication of *Lady Chatterley's Lover* in England and America, followed shortly by Henry Miller's *Tropic of Cancer.* It meant that adultery and fornication had ceased to be shocking and had become only mildly reprehensible. And as far as Hollywood stars were concerned, it was taken for granted as part of their lifestyle. When Frank Sinatra came to Hollywood in the early 1940s, legend has it that he pinned on his dressing-room door a list of the actresses he wanted to sleep with and crossed them off one by one as he achieved his object. A current joke had it that among Hollywood's hat-check girls, the definition of a square was someone who hadn't slept with Frank Sinatra. But the studio's publicity men were at pains not to allow this image to reach all those fans who adored Sinatra for the warm sincerity of his voice and the boyishly innocent smile. By the 1960s, a rock star was expected to prove his virility as a stud. Elvis Presley had been shocking the middle classes since the mid-1950s with his unashamedly sexual gyrations on stage. When he came out of the army in 1960, he brought a fourteen-year-old girl back with him from Germany and began to sleep with her immediately. Although he married Priscilla Beaulieu, he left her behind when he went to Hollywood in the early 60s, when his name was linked with a series of actresses. After his death from a drugs overdose in 1977, a cinema cashier described how Presley had made her his mistress fourteen years earlier. Before he married Priscilla, Presley had told his stepmother that he had slept with about a thousand girls. A biography published after his death described how one of his lieutenants would go out to the gate of his Memphis mansion, select one of the mob of girls waiting outside and bring her in for Elvis. Even during his lifetime, no one was shocked by rumours like this; it was expected of a rock star.

Jimi Hendrix, the black 'rock demigod' of the 60s, deliberately tried to outdo Presley in open sexual movements so there were times when he looked as if he was sodomizing his guitar (which, typically, he called 'Electric Lady'). Often he ended his performance by smashing his guitar to pieces and on one occasion he set it on fire with lighter fluid. Surrounded permanently by 'groupies', Hendrix was able to 'use girls like some people smoke cigarettes', as one of his more permanent girlfriends put it. His virility was apparently extraordinary. Two groupies started an interesting project of taking plaster casts of the erect members of rock stars and other celebrities; one of them would induce the erection by fellatio. Hendrix was one of the few who could not only sustain his erection until the plaster dried but who made it impossible to remove the plaster because his penis refused to go limp. In 1970, at the age of twenty-seven, Hendrix took too many sleeping pills one night and drowned inhaling his own vomit. He was mourned as wildly and intensely as Rudolph Valentino had been in the 20s.

Even the Beatles, whose public image was more seemly, made no real attempt to conceal active sex lives, aware that such revelations would do them no harm. Biographers Peter Brown and Steven Gaines in *The Love You Make* (1983) describe how, on the set of *A Hard Day's Night,* the Beatles hired a movie projector to watch porno movies, and, 'boys being boys, the young girls on the set being used as extras were discreetly lured into the trailers for quickies between takes.' Their two road managers had the task of keeping them supplied with sex when on tour. 'Mal wasn't above the "If you fuck me first I'll introduce you to *them*"' routine. The girls were screwed, blewed and tattooed, before Mal and Neil swept them out of the Beatles' suite at dawn. The girls left with an autographed picture, forged by Neil and Mal, and were told to keep their mouths shut. Miraculously, for no reason anyone can explain, the girls kept their mouths shut. In America, at least, there were no 'My Night with Paul' stories in the tabloids, nor were there paternity suits. It was no small wonder, either, since it was not uncommon to find fifteen girls waiting in line in Neil's and Mal's rooms, passing the time by ironing the Beatles' stage costumes.

All this, then, helps to explain why there have been so few Hollywood scandals since 1960. The nearest thing to the old 'shock headlines' of the 20s and 30s were the headlines announcing the killing of Sharon Tate and her three guests on 8 August 1969, an altogether different and more tragic affair, covered in a later chapter on Roman Polanski.

IRELAND, WILLIAM

THE GREAT SHAKESPEARE FORGERY

In the summer of 1793, a prosperous gentleman named Samuel Ireland went from London to Stratford-upon-Avon with his eighteen-year-old son William. Ireland, an architect and painter, the author of a number of popular illustrated travel books, was in search of relics of his idol Shakespeare; the Stratford tradesmen were delighted to oblige. They sold him a goblet carved from a mulberry tree planted by Shakespeare's own hand, a purse presented by Anne Hathaway to Shakespeare, and the oak chair on which the Bard sat in his courting days.

Samuel William Henry Ireland was his father's youngest child; he had two elder sisters. All three were bastards, for Samuel Ireland's 'wife' (he called her his housekeeper) was a cast-off mistress of the Earl of Sandwich, a notorious rake. The father was not particularly fond of his son; he considered him dull and lazy. As a child, William had been sent home from school with a note saying that it was a waste of money trying to instruct him. William craved affection but he received none. It is just conceivable that Samuel Ireland was not his real father.

William had been apprenticed to a conveyancer named Bingley, at New Inn. The Ireland family lived nearby, in Norfolk Street, off the Strand. In the evenings, Ireland senior often read aloud to his family from the works of Shakespeare. One evening, the conversation turned to the 'marvellous boy' Thomas Chatterton, who had forged the poems of a fifteenth-century priest called Thomas Rowley. William was fascinated by the story. He read a novel called Love and Madness by Herbert Croft, in which a long passage is devoted to Chatterton's tragic life. William decided that he would try his own hand at forgery. Like Chatterton, he was an unappreciated poet; he would see whether he could not put his own literary talent to good account.

He began cautiously. He had picked up cheaply a small quarto volume that had belonged to the library of Queen Elizabeth I; it had her arms on the cover. He wrote a 'dedicatory letter' from its author to the Queen and inserted it in the end of the book. He took a bookseller friend into his confidence and asked if it looked convincing. A journeyman who overheard the conversation showed William how to mix an ink that looked ancient. William rewrote the 'dedicatory epistle', and took the book home to his father. Samuel Ireland received it with gratitude and William basked in his approval. He decided to try a more ambitious forgery. He found a terracotta relief head of Oliver Cromwell and wrote on old parchment a letter saying that it had been presented to John Bradshaw, president of the court that condemned Charles I to death, by Cromwell himself. Once again, his father was taken in. So were some of his knowledgeable friends; like young William, none of them was aware that a strong dislike existed between Cromwell and Bradshaw.

Now William was prepared for greater things. He told his father that he had met an aristocratic gentleman in a coffee house and had been invited to the man's chambers to look through a chest of old documents. The gentleman himself had no interest in antiquities and told William he could have anything he fancied. When Ireland finally availed himself of this invitation, he discovered a document signed by Shakespeare in the chest. The gentleman declared that he would keep his promise and that William could take the document away if he would first make a copy of it.

Samuel Ireland naturally wanted to know more about this generous aristocrat. That, William explained, was impossible. The man had made him swear a solemn oath not to reveal his identity. Samuel Ireland apparently found this perfectly acceptable for aristocrats were eccentric. All he now wanted to see was the document. Two weeks later, William brought it home – a deed of mortgage made between Michael Fraser and his wife, and John Heminge and William Shakespeare. When William presented this to his father, Samuel Ireland impulsively handed him his library keys and told him to take any book he wanted. William refused but his father presented him with a three-guinea volume anyway. For William, with his impulsive, sentimental nature, his craving for affection, it must have been a moment of triumph.

All Ireland's literary and artistic friends gathered to examine the acquisition and were duly impressed. The forgery was convincing – on parchment of the right period, with the Shakespeare signature carefully traced from one of the few extant genuine ones. Even the seal seemed authentic – taken from some old document. Ireland's friend, Sir Frederick Eden unhesitatingly pronounced the document genuine.

Delighted with the attention he was receiving, William forged a short note, in which Shakespeare promised to pay his friend Heminge five guineas for some unspecified service, together with a receipt from Heminge dated a month later, to prove that Shakespeare had kept his word.

Samuel Ireland grew greedy; he wanted to know what else there was in the gentleman's chest. William's next forgery was of a letter by Shakespeare to his patron the Earl of Southampton and a reply from Southampton (written with the left hand in case the handwriting was too like the Bard's). William was deeply gratified when all his father's friends agreed that the style of Shakespeare's letter revealed that its author was a man of genius. The inference was obvious.

William had often heard his father raise the question of whether Shakespeare had been a Roman Catholic – a question that had been discussed by many scholars. William determined to scotch that rumour by producing nothing less than a profession of faith in Shakespeare's own hand. It was a document full of conventional piety, with a few echoes of Shakespeare's plays: 'O Manne whatte arte thou whye considereste thou thyselfe thus greatlye where are thye great thye boasted attrybutes buryed loste forre everre inne colde Deathe . . . 'It is hard to understand why, for all his intelligence, William felt that the way to sound Elizabethan was to avoid punctuation and put an 'e' on the end of every word. Yet two eminent Shakespeare scholars, Joseph Warton and Samuel Parr, both declared the Profession of Faith genuine.

William's trouble was that he was as greedy for his father's praise and approval as his father was for Shakespeare relics. He told his father he had seen a full-length portrait of Shakespeare and that the gentleman – now called 'Mr H' – had promised he could have it sooner or later. His father nagged him endlessly to produce it. He claimed he had seen Shakespeare's own edition of Holinshed's *Chronicles* – from which Shakespeare had taken much of his historical information; again, his father badgered him night and day to produce it. He managed to get hold of a number of Elizabethan books, which he annotated in Shakespeare's handwriting, and presented to his father as items from Shakespeare's library. But Samuel Ireland remained insatiable. He was like a spoiled child – nothing is more surprising than that William's admiration for his father remained undiminished.

Soon after this, William was caught at work. Fortunately, it was only by a fellow clerk, Montague Talbot – who had suspected all along that William was a forger. Talbot was so amused by the game that he was delighted to join in, supporting William's tales about the mysterious Mr H.

Driven by his father's greed, William now returned home almost every day with some new item: a drawing of Shakespeare's head executed by the Bard himself, a watercolour of Shakespeare in the role of Bassanio, a love letter from Shakespeare to Anne Hathaway, even a poem that began:

Is there inne heavenne aught more rare
Thanne thou sweete nymphe of Avon fayre
Is there onne Earthe a Manne more trewe
Thanne Willy Shakspeare is to you.

As usual, William dispensed with punctuation, which had never been his strong point.

His next major discovery was a letter from Queen Elizabeth to Shakespeare, thanking him for some of his 'prettye Verses' and revealing that they had been on terms of easy intimacy. Here, once again, William came close to giving himself away; he made the Queen refer to the Earl of Leicester, who died in 1588, when Shakespeare was only 24. The letter was also addressed to the Globe Theatre which was not in existence in 1588. But no one noticed.

Understandably, Samuel Ireland longed to possess fragments of the plays in Shakespeare's own hand. William decided to go one better; he proceeded to copy out the whole text of *King Lear,* making his own alterations and expurgations as he went along. He had often heard his father say that he suspected the bawdy lines in Shakespeare had been inserted by hacks later; he now proved it by producing the original manuscript of *Lear* without a single word that might make a maiden blush.

The extraordinary spelling in the manuscript caused some hilarity in the press; the *Telegraph* parodied it in an invitation sent by Shakespeare to Ben Jonson which began: 'Tooo Missteeree Beenjaammiinnee Joohnnssonn, Deeree Sirree, Wille youe doee meee theee favvourree too dinnee Wythee mee onnn Fridaye nextte . . .'

Unabashed, William followed up the complete *Lear* with some selected pages of *Hamlet* – which he spelled *Hamblette* – in which Hamlet's bawdy pleasantries to Ophelia are expurgated and various other improvements made. When James Boswell came to examine the Shakespeare manuscripts, he fell on his knees and kissed them. Fortunately for Ireland, Dr Johnson had been dead ten years; the man who had unmasked 'Ossian' would have been a more formidable critic.

When one of his father's visitors raised the interesting legal question of whether these new Shakespeare papers should not belong to descendants of Shakespeare, William promptly produced a Deed of Gift from Shakespeare to a person called William Henry Ireland, who had saved him from drowning. That took care of that.

Now, finally, William took the step that led to his downfall. Convinced that his own talents were equal to Shakespeare's, he began to produce an 'original' Shakespeare play called *Vortigern and Rowena*. His father was now clamouring day and night for new Shakespeare material and William lacked the time to write out the whole play in Shakespeare's handwriting; instead, he wrote it in his own hand, explaining to his father that he was copying it piecemeal. Theatrical managers immediately made offers to produce it; Richard Brinsley Sheridan, the manager of the Drury Lane Theatre succeeded. Sheridan decided that the play was genuine but that it belonged to Shakespeare's earliest period, before his style had developed its later subtlety. Delighted at the prospect of having his work presented on the stage, William dashed off another play, *Henry II* and began *William the Conqueror*. The following is an extract in which Earl Edwyn meditates outside the Abbey:

O my good Lord how lingering passed the time
Whilse in yon porch I did wait your coming
Yet as this Cloistral Arch, this bright heaven
Doth shone upon the Emerald tipt wave
And paints upon the deep each passing cloud
E'eene so the smallest and most gentle Plant
That waves fore the breath of thee sweet heaven
To man gives food for contemplation.

It can be seen that Ireland's passion for terminal e's had been curbed but his grasp of meter still inadequate. *Henry II* and *William the Conqueror* were to be part of a whole series of Shakespeare histories, covering all those periods that Shakespeare had missed.

Sheridan had originally agreed to present *Vortigern* at Drury Lane on 15 December 1795. (All the forgeries had been produced in an incredibly short space of time, beginning in December the previous year.) But the more he read the play, the less happy he felt about it. Moreover, when Samuel Ireland published the *Miscellaneous Papers of William Shakespeare*, including the new version of *Lear* (but not *Vortigern,* which had been found too late), the murmurs of critical dissent became a chorus of mockery and ridicule. On the very day when Samuel Ireland was invited to meet the Prince of Wales, William came dangerously close to discovery. A neighbour of his father's unearthed an authentic deed signed by John Heminge and pointed out that the signature bore no resemblance to that on Ireland's deed. When William saw the authentic signature, he had to agree. He excused himself and said he had to call on Mr H to find out what had happened. In fact, he went to his employer's office, imitated the signature he had seen on a piece of old parchment, then wrote above it a receipt for some theatrical disbursement. He ran back to Mr Wallis's – the neighbour who had detected the fake – and showed him the new document; Mr Wallis had to agree that the signature was incredibly like the one on his own deed. William said Mr H had immediately produced the new document from his desk, explaining that there were two John Heminge's, one at the Globe and one at the Curtain Theatre, and that Shakespeare had had dealings with both. Mr Wallis was convinced.

The actor manager, John Kemble, had agreed to play Vortigern. His own view of the play may be guessed from the fact that he tried to put on the first performance on April Fools' Day but this was frustrated and the first night was announced for 2 April 1796. An immense queue formed. Ireland distributed copies of a handbill, defending the play against the 'malevolent and impotent attack' of the eminent Shakespeare critic, Edmond Malone; it was only one of many such attacks. Samuel Ireland was convinced that the play would silence these mockers once and for all.

The first act passed off well enough. In fact, actors like David Garrick had so often rewritten Shakespeare that Drury Lane audiences were used to a certain effect of absurdity. William had used various Shakespeare plays as his model, particularly *Macbeth,* so the situations had a certain pleasant familiarity. The second act rattled along at a good pace and was warmly applauded. It began to look as if William had got away with it. But, the third act began disastrously. An actor with a high tenor voice had to declaim:

Nay, stop not there, but let them bellow on
Till with their clamourous noise they shame the thunder...

He had the wrong voice for the lines and the house rocked with laughter. From then on, it found everything funny. A Member of Parliament who was present had to roar, 'Give the thing a fair trial.' Kemble had cast a comedian with an enormous nose to play a touching death scene; the curtain came down on his neck and as he struggled to free himself, the audience howled. Finally, Vortigern had to apostrophize death:

O! then thou dost ope wide thy honey jaws
And with rude laughter and fantastic tricks,
Thou clapp'st thy rattling fingers to thy sides:
And when this solemn mockery is ended . . .

That was as far as he got; the audience set up 'a most discordant howl', which continued for ten minutes. When they were quiet again, Kemble again delivered the same line with a lugubrious expression and continued:

With icy hand thou tak'st him by the feet,
And upward so, till thou dost reach his heart,
And wrap him in the cloak of lasting night.

The actors managed to finish the play, in spite of laughter and catcalls, and the popular actress Mrs Jordan was even accorded an ovation when she took a curtain call. But when an actor announced that the play would be repeated the following night, his voice was drowned with yells of protest and fights broke out. It was undoubtedly the end of *Vortigern*.

The newspapers were derisive. But what hurt Samuel Ireland more than the jeers were the suggestions that he himself was the forger of the play. A committee of Ireland's friends was set up to investigate the matter but William was a thoroughly unsatisfactory witness, refusing to reveal Mr H's identity. His father became very angry, insisting that William had to divulge the identity – otherwise, he, Samuel Ireland, would remain under suspicion. William finally nerved himself to take the step he had always dreaded. He lacked the courage to confess to his father; instead, he told the full story to his sisters. They immediately passed it on to Samuel Ireland. Incredibly, Ireland refused to believe a word of it; he dismissed it outright as 'arrogance and vanity'. So William went to Mr Wallis, the man who had almost tripped him up on the subject of John Heminge, and confessed to him. Meanwhile, since his father declined to allow him to broach the subject of the plays, William soared into more absurd flights of fancy. He was about to marry a beautiful, rich girl who had fallen in love with him; Mr H had sent magnificent presents to all the actors involved in the fiasco; moreover, he had agreed to give William an allowance of £300 a year. The manager of Covent Garden had read *Henry II* and was anxious to present it next season. Samuel Ireland rushed to Covent Garden where the manager listened to him with a look of blank astonishment.

William drew up an advertisement, with Mr Wallis's help, which was placed in various newspapers. It stated that his father was innocent of all deception but stopped short of the admission that he, William Ireland, had forged the papers.

Finally, Samuel Ireland wrote his son a long, affecting letter, begging him to tell him the truth about the papers – making it quite clear that he was absolutely certain of their authenticity – and left for the country to give William time to reflect. William, deciding that this tangled web could be unravelled neither by honesty nor by new flights of fancy, fled from the house in Norfolk Street, never to return.

At Mr Wallis's instigation, he wrote his father a long, circumstantial letter describing his own part in the forgeries. It was no good; Samuel Ireland was too determined upon self-deception to take it seriously. He sent his son a furious reply, condemning his 'gross and deliberate impositions'. He was supported in this view by his wife-mistress, who was also totally convinced that her son was too dull to have written *Vortigern.*

So, at the age of twenty, William Ireland, the most gifted and audacious literary forger since Chatterton, found himself thrown out upon the world and obliged to support himself. The first thing he did was to marry a certain Miss Alice Crudge, a short, ugly girl about whom nothing else is known. He lived off small loans from friends of his father and on hopes of the production of *Henry II* but they came to nothing. Finally, he issued a pamphlet, an *Authentic Account of the Shakspearian Manuscripts;* this was so badly written that it only confirmed Samuel Ireland's view that his son was lying. Worse still, it confirmed the opinion of the newspapers that Samuel Ireland must have had a hand in the forgeries.

The scandal rumbled on for years. Samuel Ireland wrote a pamphlet defending himself and published *Vortigern* and *Henry II* to a new chorus of derision. For what was abundantly obvious was that Samuel Ireland was too unintelligent to see the difference between Shakespeare's confident precision of language and William's spirited but mediocre imitation. Samuel Ireland died in 1800, shaking his fist at the world.

William, who lived on for another 35 years, at least made some kind of career out of literature. In 1799 he published a three-volume novel called *The Abbess,* then went on to produce more than sixty titles, including a three-volume life of Napoleon. A full-length book describing the forgeries, the *Confessions* (1805), aroused rather less interest than it deserved because by then everyone had forgotten the affair. One of his more successful works was a long poem called *The Neglected Genius,* which contained an account of his hero, and model, Thomas Chatterton.

Ireland was undoubtedly a 'mythomaniac', for he lied for the sheer pleasure it gave him. What gives the case its psychological interest is that he would almost certainly never have written a word if it had not been for this

'Billy Liar' aspect of his personality. His father and mother cannot have been entirely mistaken to regard him as a dullard. Yet when he was driven by the need to invent convincing lies, he became a more-than-competent Shakespeare scholar and a writer of considerable talent. It is an interesting example of what can be accomplished by putting one's mind to it.

JOAD, 'PROFESSOR' C. E. M.

THE RAIL-TICKET SCANDAL

When 'Professor' Joad was caught out trying to dodge paying his rail fare in January 1948, he was a famous public figure, a writer and broadcaster whose favourite expression 'It depends what you mean by . . .' had become a popular catch-phrase. The incident of the rail ticket brought his career to a premature close.

Cyril Edward Mitchinson Joad was born in Durham on 12 August 1891, the son of a school inspector. He was educated at Blundell's, the famous public school, and at Balliol College, Oxford. At 23 he was awarded the John Locke scholarship in mental philosophy and on coming down from Oxford, he became a civil servant in the Board of Trade. He later declared that he used his sixteen years as a civil servant mainly to write his books. By 1924, his *Introduction to Modern Philosophy* had underneath his name: 'Author of *Essays in Common Sense Philosophy, Common Sense Ethics, Common Sense Theology,* etc.' In his book on Shaw, Joad tells how he came to Oxford in 1910 and read simultaneously Wells's *Tono Bungay* and Shaw's *Candida,* and of the 'heady exhilaration' of this 'intoxicating intellectual brew'. A meeting with Shaw soon after that turned him into a 'Shawworshipper'. Joad himself had something in common both with Shaw and Wells: like Shaw, he was an incorrigible 'performer' who loved to propagate the myth of himself – even his titles reveal his obsessive self-preoccupation: *The Book of Joad, The Testament of Joad, The Pleasure of Being Oneself;* like Wells, he was an incurable philanderer. He once said that at the age of eleven he thought all women were solid from the waist down; his discovery that they were, so to speak, accessible seems to have resulted in a lifelong desire to prove that there were no exceptions to the rule. He also said once that he had no interest in speaking with a woman unless she was willing to sleep with him. He called all his mistresses Maureen, in case he made a slip of the tongue in addressing them. His wife, whom he married in 1915, seemed to accept his affairs.

Joad was one of the great popularizers; his *Guide to Philosophy* (1936) was as influential, in its way, as Wells's *Outline of History* or Hogben's *Mathematics for the Million.* But Joad was by no means an intellectual lightweight; his *Matter, Life and Value* (1929) is a brilliant and original exposition of the philosophy of 'vitalism'. He believed firmly in the reality of objective values and had no sympathy with the tendency of the logical positivists to dismiss metaphysics. He was, in his way, a religious man. But he was inclined to model himself on Shaw and to waste a great deal of his time in controversy to the detriment of his serious work. From the age of 39, he became head of the department of philosophy at Birkbeck College, London; but he was never, strictly speaking, a 'professor'.

In 1941, the British Broadcasting Corporation started a programme called 'The Brains Trust', broadcast on its 'Forces' wavelength. It was so popular that it was soon repeated on the Home Service. Soon it had become – together with Tommy Handley's comedy show ITMA – one of the most successful programmes of the war years. Joad had a rather precise, high-pitched voice, and sounded exactly like the popular idea of a university professor. *Punch* carried a cartoon of him saying to a waiter: 'It all depends on what you mean by (a) thick, and (b) clear.' He became so popular that police had to escort him through the crowds at public meetings, and the Ministry of Food launched a dish called 'Joad in-the-Hole'. He loved his notoriety. 'He was an immensely vain individual', his BBC producer told Fenton Bresler, who devoted a chapter to Joad in his book *Scales of Justice*. The least suggestion of a snub could throw him into a towering rage but a soft answer – particularly if it was mixed with a judicious dose of flattery – had him cooing like a dove. He was not much liked at the BBC, partly because of a pathological meanness that made him dodge paying for his round of drinks whenever possible.

At 10:50 on the morning of 5 January 1948, Joad boarded the Atlantic Coast Express at Paddington, bound for Exeter in Devon; his secretary was with him. Both booked for the second sitting at lunch. When the ticket collector came to their table at lunch, his secretary held out her ticket but Joad explained: 'I haven't got one. I was late and the collector let me through. I got on at Salisbury.' The ticket collector gave him a return from Exeter to Salisbury. But the dining car attendant, who overheard the exchange, told the collector that there was something odd going on; Joad and his secretary had booked for lunch before the train reached Salisbury. The inspector went back to question Joad, who persisted in saying that he had boarded at Salisbury. It was only when the train stopped at Exeter that Joad admitted: 'I made a mistake. I did come from Paddington. . .' He had indeed made a mistake to admit his guilt. If Joad had kept silent, he would undoubtedly have heard the last of it. He made a further mistake by writing to the railway authorities and explaining that the problem had been a 'misunderstanding'.

What decided the authorities to take Joad to court was undoubtedly their discovery that this was not the first time and that he had made a habit of travelling without a ticket for years. On 12 April 1948, counsel on his behalf pleaded guilty at the Tower Bridge magistrates' court to 'unlawfully travelling on the railway without having previously paid his fare and with intent to avoid payment.' Joad was fined £2, with 25 guineas costs. That evening a newspaper carried the headline: Joad Fined For Common Ticket Fraud. Joad had tried to save himself 17s. 1d. On the same evening, Joad was on 'The Brains Trust' and seemed as jaunty and confident as ever. But in Parliament the following Friday, a Tory MP said, 'In the last week a public figure was convicted for telling lies and defrauding the public and he was hired the same evening by the BBC to entertain people.' On the evening of Joad's next scheduled appearance, he was dropped in favour of Commander King-Hall. He never again appeared on 'The Brains Trust'.

Joad continued to write books but he knew that, as a moral philosopher, his authority was gone. He became a practising Christian and wrote books about his new religious belief. In 1953, at the age of 62, he died of cancer.

Why did Joad do it? When he was asked this question by the 'Brains Trust' question master, Donald McCullough, he replied: '*Hubris*' – the Greek word for pride or conceit. Another motive was clearly his meanness. But his friend Hugh Schonfield, the Biblical scholar, has a different explanation. He told the present writer (CW) that Joad always had a need to 'kick over the traces'. Rebellion was a basic necessity of his nature – thumbing his nose at authority. So although he was 'Britain's foremost philosopher' (as he claimed at the head of his newspaper column) and a famous public figure, there was a need to reassure himself that he was still a rebel at heart by small acts of antisocial defiance.

KENNEDY, JACK

ALL THE PRESIDENT'S WOMEN

During his political career – spanning the late 1940s, the prudish 50s and the pre-hippy years of the 1960s – John F Kennedy pursued a sex life that would make most of us dizzy to contemplate.

Protected and covered up for by friends and colleagues, tactfully ignored by a more gentlemanly (not to say timorous) media, and almost unassailably popular with his supporters, he indulged himself with almost every attractive woman who showed willing – and there were plenty of those for the glamorous Jack Kennedy. Nobody has ever tried to put a figure to his conquests, but these must have been well into the upper hundreds.

In his book, *Kennedy and His Women*, Tony Sciacca records numerous accounts of Kennedy's philandering from those close to him throughout his political career. Reading the anecdotes one soon forms an impression that Jack Kennedy must have viewed attractive women in the same light that a voracious reader might consider paperbacks. He clearly needed a continuous and ever-changing supply of lovers, yet he seems to have viewed sex more as a relaxing and necessary pastime than the driving force of his life.

However, this did not stop him from allowing his sex drive occasionally to impinge on his political life. He often spent pleasant afternoons (when his wife Jackie was away) bathing naked in the White House swimming pool with whatever young lady or ladies he presently had attached to his entourage. Hassled presidential aides had a lively time stopping uninitiated ministers and diplomats wandering round to the pool to have a quick word with Mr President.

Richard Nixon, a US president with a very different set of vices, later had the pool filled in and turned into the White House pressroom. Televised presidential statements are now given in exactly the same space where President Kennedy once enjoyed aquatic philanderings.

During the 1962 Nassau conference Kennedy shocked the British Prime Minister, Harold Macmillan, by offhandedly saying: 'You know, I get very severe headaches if I go too long without a woman.' He then excused himself and left with two attractive members of his personal staff, who up to then had seemed to fulfil no specific purpose. An hour later he returned alone, looking much refreshed. Smiling, he told the mildly indignant Prime Minister: 'My headache's gone.'

Life as a Kennedy White House staffer could be both hectic and demanding. The secret service men seconded to protect the president were given the additional duty of unobtrusively sneaking in his girlfriends on demand. Presidential aides often had to rush about tidying up the evidence of the president's visitors when Mrs Kennedy's arrival was unexpectedly announced. Hairpins were searched for in thick carpets, beds were rapidly remade and the odd female garment swiftly relocated.

On one occasion they were a bit lax in their efforts and Jackie Kennedy found a pair of panties stuffed into a pillowcase. She calmly handed them to her husband saying, 'Would you please shop around and see who these belong to? They're not my size.'

It seems clear that Jackie knew about at least some of the other women, but aside from creating a slight distancing from her husband, she did not let it spoil their marriage. One has to respect her fortitude; she not only had to put up with the arduous life of the first lady, but also had to contend with the fact that her husband was totally incapable of being faithful to her.

In contrast to contemporary American politicians, Kennedy seems to have been totally unconcerned that his enemies might use his private life to wreck his career. In 1952, during his first campaign to enter the Senate, a photograph of Kennedy and a young lady lying naked on a sun-drenched beach came into the hands of his Republican opponent, Henry Cabot Lodge. Instead of handing it straight to the media, Lodge had a copy of the photograph sent to Kennedy's campaign headquarters, where it caused quite a stir.

Kennedy's campaign strategists examined the photograph and despaired; it looked like the end of his electoral chances and possibly his entire political career. It was decided that Kennedy must be informed of the situation and several unhappy aides took the photograph to his office. One later said that Kennedy 'just looked at the picture a long time and then told us about all the great times he had had with the girl and how fond he'd been of her. He put it in his desk and told us not to worry about it.' Lodge didn't publish the photograph, perhaps merely hoping to shake his opponent's confidence, and Kennedy won the election easily.

A fellow congressman who attended an informal dinner party thrown by Jack Kennedy at his Washington house in 1948, relates another example of Kennedy's predatory attitude to women. Also present were several of Kennedy's Navy friends from his war service days and an attractive redhead from an airline ticket office that Kennedy had casually asked along.

She noticed that he was not eating and asked him why. Kennedy replied: 'How can I eat when all I'm thinking about is taking you upstairs?' She replied that she wasn't hungry either and they excused themselves and went upstairs.

Later they all went to the movies after which Kennedy packed his date off in a cab. As soon as she was gone he called another young lady. He said he had met her a few weeks before at Palm Beach, and had offered to show her the sights of Washington. They picked her up at her hotel and drove back to Kennedy's house. After a brandy nightcap, the congressman and his date tactfully left.

The next day the congressman met Kennedy on Capitol Hill and asked how things had gone. Kennedy said he had had a terrible time. His new date seemed to have thought that 'after one screw with Jack Kennedy she was going to marry him.' She had finally stormed out at about two in the morning. 'Then he turned and waved toward some real luscious woman sitting up in the House gallery. And he stage-whispered to me: "She's the one I spent the night with." Jack wasn't bragging. To him, it was all very casual, something that a bachelor had coming to him ... I tell you, I was awfully jealous of that man. The women seemed to be coming out of the woodwork ...'

This detachment seems to have characterized Kennedy's dealings with women. Yet, despite the modern view of Don Juanism, his womanizing almost certainly did not spring from a contempt for the female sex. Even his detractors admit that he invariably behaved with courtesy and tact in his love affairs and, as can be seen above, he was at pains to avoid giving the impression that he took people for granted.

Although most of Kennedy's affairs were short term – as little as a couple of hours in some cases – he also maintained a few longer-lasting relationships – the most notorious perhaps being with the two iconic goddesses Marilyn Monroe and Jayne Mansfield. His basic good nature was again illustrated by his conduct in these affairs. He would go to elaborate lengths to ensure that the lady was protected from press difficulties while being almost cavalier with his own reputation.

At the beginning of World War II, Kennedy was stationed in Washington, working in the Office of Navy Intelligence. Captain Alan Kirk, director of the ONI, was an old family friend, and Jack's father, Joe Kennedy – then Ambassador to Great Britain – had pulled strings to get his boy a plum job. Yet by January 1942, Jack had been kicked out of Naval Intelligence and sent to a minor desk job in South Carolina. The reason was Inga Arvad, a gorgeous Danish journalist whom Adolf Hitler had once described as 'a perfect Nordic beauty'.

Inga had come from Europe with her pro-Nazi husband, had left him for a suspected pro-Nazi and had eventually ended up working on the *Washington Times-Herald* on a society column, through which she met Jack. The FBI already saw her as a potential Mata Hari and her involvement with a young intelligence officer in a key position decided them. They bugged her telephone and had her kept under surveillance.

Meanwhile, great pressure was placed on Jack – by the Navy and his father – to break with Inga, but he remained intransigent. His lover was not, he insisted, a Nazi spy – she had told him so herself. Indeed, rather than meekly surrender, Kennedy then went on the offensive to save his girlfriend's reputation.

He eventually pulled enough strings to receive an interview with FBI director J. Edgar Hoover himself. Hoover was forced to admit that there was absolutely no evidence against Inga and apologized on behalf of the Bureau.

Jack Kennedy, at the age of 25, with the mere rank of Navy Ensign, had faced down one of the most powerful men in the country to protect the reputation of his lover.

Hoover must have recalled the Inga Arvad incident with some irony when he was handed a report, late in 1961, on Judith Campbell. It seemed that Judy, as she was known to her friends, had been ringing the White House to speak with the president. Hoover was, of course, well aware of Jack Kennedy's affairs. The prudish bureau chief – himself a secret homosexual and transvestite – was obsessed by the need to gather information about the sex lives of the famous and powerful. He can have had little doubt about the nature of the attractive Miss Campbell's connection with the president. The trouble was that the FBI also had information that she was a lover of Sam Giancana, one of the most powerful Mafia bosses in the United States.

Kennedy had met Judy in February 1960, at a party thrown by his friend and supporter Frank Sinatra. She was one of Hollywood's many aspiring actresses and was also known as something of a 'party girl' – a facet that endeared her to the hard-playing Sinatra and his circle.

Jack and Judy soon became lovers and saw each other fairly frequently over the next two years. Judy later claimed that he rang her often and that she had visited him at the White House at least twenty times for intimate lunches. She called him quite often as well. The White House telephone logs recorded seventy calls from Judy Campbell during a 54-week period in 1961 and early 1962. Some of those calls were made from a house in Oak Park, Illinois: the home of mobster Sam Giancana.

Whether Giancana was using Judy to get a blackmail angle on Kennedy has never been made clear, but he certainly must have known that he was sharing his girlfriend with the president. Once, when Judy was staying with Giancana in the luxurious Miami Beach Hotel, Kennedy got word to her that he was vacationing alone at Palm Springs and would appreciate a little female company. Apparently with Giancana's blessings she left to join the president immediately.

J Edgar Hoover contacted Bobby Kennedy, Jack's younger brother, then serving as Attorney General. Bobby Kennedy had a particular hatred for organized crime and had personally insisted on the multi-level FBI surveillance on Sam Giancana. (Ironically this operation took place against the wishes of Hoover, who insisted – against all available evidence – that there was no organized crime in America.) First Bobby, then J Edgar Hoover remonstrated with the president and he was finally persuaded to stop Judy ringing him at the White House. Even so, he continued to see her until the summer of 1962.

It may seem insanely foolish of Kennedy to have continued such a dangerous affair once he had been appraised of the facts, but on closer inspection one realizes that it was yet another illustration of his cool political insight. He had no intention of breaking off an enjoyable relationship and he knew that Giancana could not harm him; in fact, quite the opposite. One of his former aides later commented on the affair: 'Back in those days no reporter in the country would have touched the Judy Campbell story, no one would have believed Jack was screwing around and certainly not with a mobster's woman. If it got out in any way, we would have just said that it's a vicious tale spread by a murderer from Chicago named Giancana because the Kennedy Administration is seriously damaging the mob. We could have easily turned it into a plus for Jack. And Jack knew it.'

Various psychological explanations for Jack Kennedy's womanizing have been offered over the years, one of the most frequent being that he was trying to live up to his father. Old Joe Kennedy Senior was one of the great American entrepreneurs in every sense of the word. He made a huge fortune from the stock market, from the movie business and, it is alleged, the bootlegging trade during prohibition. Joe Kennedy nursed a lifelong chip on his shoulder over his family's exclusion from the East Coast 'Brahmin' upper-class circles, due to their Irish background. As a result he was as aggressive in his sexual affairs and home life as he was in the business and political worlds, and encouraged his boys to behave in the same way. Jack Kennedy, frequently ill during his early years, is known to have felt inadequate compared to his father's demands and spent much of his youth fighting with his father's favourite, Jack's elder brother, Joe.

During World War II, two events seem to have deeply marked Jack. The first was his own near death when a Japanese destroyer rammed his small 'PT' patrol boat. Jack's backbone was badly damaged when the enemy destroyer ploughed over and sank the little patrol boat, but he managed to assemble his crew in the water and swam with them to a nearby island. Despite his agonizing back injury, he then swam out into the strait every night until he managed to flag down another US patrol boat to rescue them.

Kennedy was cited for conspicuous bravery, but was virtually crippled. Shortly after the war his doctors informed him that there was a revolutionary new operation that might help him, but that his survival chances during the procedure were at best 50–50. He immediately insisted on going through with it and, of course, survived. However, he was forced to wear a support corset for the rest of his life and, despite his Herculean taste for women, had to make love with considerable caution.

The second event to deeply affect the generally carefree Jack, was the death of his older brother Joe, on a volunteer-only bomber mission against a German V-1 missile base in northern France in 1944. Afterwards, Joe Senior's ruthless determination to put at least one of his sons in the White House settled on Jack – who up to then had shown little intention of a political career.

Moreover, both these events seem to have caused Kennedy to be driven by the certainty of his own death and a determination to live life to its full. Indeed, his very poor state of health throughout his life actually seems to have reinforced this drive. He once admitted to a colleague, 'The doctors say I've got a sort of slow-motion leukaemia, but they tell me I'll probably last until I'm 45.'

In this light one can see that Kennedy's hyperactive sex life was only part of the picture. Everything he did, including his successful run for the presidency, was part of his need to enjoy and excel in life. In his eulogy after the Dallas assassination, Bobby Kennedy pointed out that at least half of Jack's days had been spent in agony due to his poor health, yet he was one of the most fulfilled people that he had ever known.

Jack Kennedy was 46 years old when he was assassinated in Dallas, in 1963.

LAW, JOHN

THE LOUISIANA SCANDAL

John Law was a Scots adventurer whose brilliant but over-ambitious financial schemes brought France to ruin. He was born in Edinburgh in April 1671, the son of a goldsmith who made a fortune from moneylending. As a child, Law developed into a remarkable linguist and mathematician. He was tall, handsome and had enormous charm. His father died in 1685, leaving him two country estates. But Law's temperament was unsuited to country life; he wanted excitement and adventure. Besides, he was a born gambler. In London, he had a love affair with a certain Mrs Lawrence and fought a duel with another of her admirers, a man called Beau Wilson whom he killed in Bloomsbury Square. He was convicted of murder but managed to secure a royal pardon. But then Wilson's brother filed a suit against him and he was imprisoned; he escaped and fled to the Continent. He was 26 years old.

John Law was a gambler but he was fascinated by high finance, believing that it could be turned into a science. He studied banking in Amsterdam – then the financial centre of the world – and later in Venice. In 1700, he returned to Scotland and approached the government with a proposal which, he said, would relieve the poverty of the Scots. He proposed that a national bank should be founded and it should issue paper money instead of gold. This money was always to be instantly redeemable against gold in order to create confidence. Once confidence had been created, the government could then increase its wealth simply by printing more money. Nowadays, we are aware that this procedure creates an inflationary spiral but to Law, it seemed foolproof. The Scots declined to try the scheme. And since a union with England was imminent, Law had to return to the Continent to avoid arrest. There he continued to live by gambling – being periodically moved on by the police as dejected losers reported their suspicion that he was cheating. He was also staggeringly successful in love in spite of the fact that he was married to the Earl of Banbury's daughter Catherine.

He continued to try to interest influential politicians in his scheme for a national bank without success. King Victor Amadeus of Sardinia told him, 'I am not wealthy enough to survive bankruptcy.'

In Paris in 1708, he was received into the innermost circles of the aristocracy and his skill – and luck – as a gambler became legendary. He ran a faro bank in the house of a famous actress, Madame Duclos, and had private counters made, each worth eighteen louis. There he met a man who took an immediate liking to him: the Duc D'Orleans. The duke was soon convinced that Law was a financial genius; he introduced Law to the Minister of Finance, Desmarets. Just as it seemed that the long-awaited turn in his fortunes had arrived, the Chief of Police, D'Argenson, ordered Law out of the country. Presumably D'Argenson must have had some evidence of illegal dealings otherwise Law could have appealed to his influential friends to countermand the order. As it was, he left France and spent the next five years travelling from capital to capital around Europe and amassing a fortune of £80,000 by gambling.

When he heard that Louis XIV had died in 1715 and that the Duc d'Orleans had become regent (Louis XV being only five years old at the time), Law hastened back to Paris. He found that France was on the verge of bankruptcy, largely due to the extravagance of the 'Sun King'. Money, Law told the Duke, was the lifeblood of a country and credit is to business what the brain is to the human body. If a sound system of credit could be established, a merchant could embark on schemes that would normally be far too ambitious for his pocket. In this way, business would be stimulated and wealth increased.

The Regent was impressed but the Council of Finance was not and rejected the idea of a national bank. They agreed, however, to allow Law to set up a private bank. This he did, using his capital to start a bank in the Place Vendôme in Paris. His aim was to establish confidence. He sold shares in the bank at a price that attracted everyone who knew anything about finance: a quarter in gold and the rest in government bonds which were worth only one-fifth of their face value. At first, he lost money heavily but he created confidence. The government was impressed when he devised a dubious scheme which enabled it to make a 50 per cent profit on all bonds.

Law's problem was that he had issued sixty million's worth of francs in notes and he only had 6 million francs in gold. If confidence ebbed, he would be bankrupt. He needed to find ways of increasing his capital until he could withstand any 'run' on the bank – some business that would expand and yield rich profits. He decided that the answer lay across the Atlantic, in Louisiana, which had been 'discovered' by the French. A businessman named Crozat had been granted a monopoly, but was finding that he lacked the capital to take advantage of it. Law persuaded the Duc to transfer the monopoly to him; Crozat seems to have been glad to get rid of it. From August 1717 Law's company became known as the Mississippi Company. It owned a piece of land 3,000 miles long and the company could plant colonies and develop it as it liked.

Law's first step was to organize 'propaganda'. He sent his agents all over the country, telling tales of the immense riches of the Mississippi basin, including whole rocks made of emeralds. He imported six dusky maidens from Louisiana and showed them off in Paris; one of them, who was described as the 'Daughter of the Sun', was married to a French sergeant with enormous publicity and the man sailed off to America with his royal bride. (Unfortunately, she exercised her royal prerogative of executing any husband who failed to please her and the marriage lasted only a few months.) The foundations of New Orleans were laid; Law himself started a German reservation in Arkansas. But there were still not enough colonists to provide the quick returns he wanted. Law took advantage of his privilege to raise his own troops –they were dressed in blue and silver and known as Law's Archers – and sent them round Paris collecting vagrants, ex-convicts and women of the streets, and packing them off to Louisiana. When his troops began seizing ordinary men and women in the streets, there were riots; twenty Archers were killed, and the government hastily decided that powers of recruitment should be confined to criminals.

In spite of these setbacks, things looked promising. Law had been granted a monopoly of the Canadian fur trade and his profits were immense. He began to absorb other French colonial companies in the East Indies, China, Senegal and other regions. He even acquired a tobacco monopoly in Virginia.

For years, Law had been plotting to get his own back on the police chief D'Argenson for ordering him out of the country. In fact, he had made D'Argenson one of his chief lieutenants, to keep him out of mischief. In 1719, Law struck. D'Argenson and some business associates had made enormous profits by purchasing the right to collect taxes – the French government preferred ready cash. D'Argenson's group paid 48 million francs for this privilege. In 1719, Law stepped in and offered 52 million – one of D'Argenson's chief sources of income suddenly dried up.

Law now launched his biggest gamble of all. He offered to pay the national debt (the money the government borrows from various sources). The idea was that he would pay the government the sum of 1,500 million livres to enable it to repay all its creditors. The government in turn would pay Law a 3 per cent interest on his money instead of the usual 4 per cent. And what would the creditors do with the money that had been returned to them? They could re-invest it in Law's company. And Law guaranteed that he would repurchase at their original value in six months if the investors wanted to 'unload'.

Law's office in the Rue Qincampoix suddenly became the centre of a permanent scramble. In less than a year – between June 1719 and February 1720 – his shares increased eighteen times in value. Crowds packed the street and tried to push their way to the desk where Law sat with a huge pile of shares in front of him. Anyone who could buy a few shares could walk outside and immediately sell them for several times what he had paid. Every house or shop in the dingy street rented rooms at thousands of francs a week to people who wanted to be outside the door the moment Law opened up in the morning. A poor cobbler made a fortune overnight; Law's own coachman became a rich man, and came to his master with two more coachmen, saying, 'Choose which one you want and I'll take the other.'

No one quite understood how money could be created so quickly, but it was obvious that Law had some secret. The result was a kind of frenzy. All over the country, the crime rate soared as people scrambled to lay their hands on the gold that could be doubled or trebled overnight. A young nobleman, the Comte de Horn, related to the Regent, lured a speculator to a house, and beat him to death to lay his hands on 150,000 francs the man had just made. He was broken on the wheel as an example but this example made no difference to the crime wave.

Shrewd speculators realized that the bubble was bound to burst and began smuggling their profits out of the country. One Dutch financier converted a million francs into gold and silver and smuggled it out in farm carts covered with hay; he himself dressed as a farm labourer. The word 'millionaire' was coined to describe a phenomenon that was becoming increasingly common.

It was the people without wealth enough even to buy one share who suffered. Prices rose because most people had more money to spend while the poor could not afford the new prices. Law was causing mass starvation as well as crime.

His greatest problem was that speculators were bound to decide to take their profit while the going was good and every time this happened, it drained the bank's capital. Law persuaded the Regent to make it illegal for anyone to possess more than 500 livres in gold and silver. Goldsmiths were ordered not to make any gold articles that weighed more than one ounce. But this only increased the general anxiety to turn their paper money into gold. The Prince de Conti brought carts to carry away his gold. Law was forced to issue a statement saying that he would not change more than a 100-livre note per person. He issued an edict threatening shopkeepers who refused to accept his notes; they ignored it. There were still crowds outside Law's bank but they no longer had the same purpose; they wanted their money back. On 17 July 1720, a huge crowd waited all night – 15,000 of them. By morning, it was discovered that sixteen people had died of suffocation. A mob marched to the Palais Royal, carrying four of the dead on stretchers, to show the Regent what his policies had led to; they were finally persuaded to disperse. But revolution had been very close.

Law hid in the Palais Royal for ten days then escaped to one of his country houses. His family was taken under the protection of the Duc de Bourbon at his house at St Maur. Law was in a state of shock; he found it incomprehensible that the tremendous edifice had collapsed and seemed unable to understand what had gone wrong. He was still hoping that the Regent could save his bank with a huge loan but the French parliament flatly refused a loan. On 21 December 1720, Law finally left for Brussels in a post chaise. He had a shock at Valenciennes when he was arrested by the son of his old enemy D'Argenson, for if, as he suspected, the Regent had been deposed, then he would probably never escape from France alive. But within a few days, an order arrived from the Regent allowing him to proceed on his way.

In Brussels, he was approached by an agent of the Tsar of Russia, Peter the

Great, who wanted him to take over the financial reorganization of the Russian empire. Law politely declined on the grounds that he needed a rest from his labours – in fact, his nerve was shattered.

In the following year, 1771, he journeyed to London and was received by King George I (who finally granted him his pardon). The news that he had been virtually the Prime Minister of France made the British decide that he deserved treating with respect. No one held it against him that it was his example that had led to England's greatest social disaster of the century, the South Sea Bubble, which had left thousands bankrupt.

Law continued to be on good terms with the Regent – in fact, he received a pension from him. When he asked in a letter: 'What did you do about the bankruptcy?' the Regent replied: 'I disposed of it by simply making a bonfire of all the documents.' Law hoped to be recalled to France to take charge of its finances but the death of the Regent in 1723 dashed his hopes. He was separated from his wife but her relatives gave him a small allowance. And he made a small fortune by offering to bet anyone £1,000 to a shilling that they could not throw six double sixes in succession with dice; the number who tried was incredible. Law moved to Venice where he died on 21 March 1729, aged 58.

Napoleon later sold Louisiana to the Americans for $15 million.

MCKINNEY, JOYCE

THE CASE OF THE MANACLED MORMON

From a British tabloid journalist's point of view, the 1977 case of the kidnapped Mormon missionary had everything: religion, obsession, conspiracy, sex, bondage, true love and a beautiful (and apparently maidenly) young woman who was supposedly the perpetrator, not the victim, of an abduction and a sexual assault. Short of the involvement of the Loch Ness Monster, the story could not have been better front-page material.

The first official suggestion of scandal came on 15 September, when Scotland Yard officers announced that a visiting Mormon minister – 21-year-old Kirk Anderson from the town of Provo in Utah – had apparently been abducted the previous day from outside his church in East Ewell, near Epsom (south of London). The Yard's news bureau told pressmen that Anderson had been lured into a car, then, out of the sight of witnesses, had apparently been overpowered and abducted. Although there was no known motive and no ransom demand, the police viewed the matter very seriously.

The investigators' only lead was that a moustachioed young man calling himself Bob Bosler seemed to be at least part-responsible. This Bosler was evidently a stranger to Kirk Anderson, but had telephoned him several days before, asking to be schooled in, and hopefully accepted into, the Church of Jesus Christ of the Latter-Day Saints (a.k.a. The Mormons).

Anderson's fellow missionary and roommate, 21-year-old Kimball Smith, had gone with him on the morning of Wednesday 14 September to meet with Bosler; Mormon missionaries always travel in pairs to provide spiritual support to each other (and also to help each other avoid sinful temptations). Bob Bosler had pulled up at the front of the East Ewell Mormon Church in his car, got out and had chatted pleasantly with both the young missionaries. He had then asked Anderson to get into the car with him to point out the way to the local Mormon headquarters on a road map he had there.

Had this request come from a woman, Anderson would have undoubtedly refused. However – perhaps lulled by the fact that Bosler, judging from his accent, was also an American – Anderson willingly accompanied his would-be convert to the parking area.

Moments after both had got into the vehicle (and were out of Kimball Smith's view) it suddenly sped away, leaving Smith wondering what was going on. Eventually, when they did not return, he realized that his fellow missionary had been snatched away and reported the matter to his superiors. They called the police.

The investigating officers did not say so directly to the press, but the spate of political kidnappings in recent years by terrorist groups like the IRA, the communist Baader-Meinhof gang and the Palestine Liberation Organisation must have meant that the unexplained abduction of an American citizen on British soil was automatically a cause of concern in high places. All ports and airports were being monitored, in case there was an attempt to smuggle Anderson out of the country, and officers were also looking into the possibility that somebody with a grudge against the Mormon Church might be responsible.

Nevertheless, most British newspapers paid the case little or no heed – at most giving it a paragraph or two on an inner page. The whole thing sounded too much like either a student prank or some sort of petty internal dispute in the odd-sounding foreign religion.

The Church of the Latter Day Saints originated on a small farm outside Palmyra, New York State, in the 1820s. A farmer's son, Joseph Smith Jr, claimed to have been visited by visions of both Jesus and God the Father, and that it had been revealed to him that all the present human religions were false. Later, in 1827, Joseph was further visited by an angel called Moroni – actually the spirit of the last member of the Lost Tribes of Israel – who commanded him to dig into a local hillside. There Joseph found a number of inscribed golden tablets and two magical stones set into a silver frame like a pair of opaque eyeglasses.

Angel Moroni told Smith that on no account was anybody else to see these holy items, but that he could borrow them to transcribe the story written on the golden tablets. Fortunately the magic stones allowed Smith to translate the archaic writing on the plates (said to be 'Reformed Egyptian') but he needed someone to take down what he read, so he enlisted the help of a literate neighbour called Martin Harris. To hide the gold plates and the magic glasses from the sight of Harris, Joseph is said to have sat under a blanket and shouted the translation out to his friend who, in turn, transcribed every word.

The result was the Book of Mormon (titled in honour of the rather unfortunately named angel, Moroni). It tells of how a lost tribe of Israel crossed the Atlantic and settled in America several thousand years ago. Due to God's curse, this people split into three skin colours – white, red and black. The evil reds (later to be called Native Americans) eventually wiped out the equally evil blacks and the saintly whites, but not before Jesus of Nazareth had paid the white tribe a proselytizing visit. The Christian faith of the extinct white tribe was the only true religion in the world, and it now fell upon Joseph Smith to revive it.

Modern, non-Mormon readers might think that this sounds like a racist science fiction story, and they would not be alone: when the Book of Mormon was first published in 1830, most critics reviled it as a particularly feeble piece of fantasy fiction masquerading as the Holy Writ. Some even suggested that Smith had stolen the entire plot from a recently deceased New York clergyman, Solomon Spaulding, who had written a similar story as fiction, but had not bothered to get it published.

However, despite the almost universally negative reception the Book of Mormon received in East Coast intellectual circles, a good number of poorer New Yorkers were drawn to the new religion. 1830s America was undergoing what was later called the Religious Fever, and many new (usually neo-Christian and Apocalyptic) religions sprang up in that decade – although few have survived to the present day.

Finding that he had a talent for outdoor preaching and mass conversions, Smith and his followers headed for the western states (then reaching no further than Illinois in the Midwest): converts were much easier to find on the wild frontier where life was brutal and usually short, and thoughts of the hereafter were consequently on most people's minds. Unfortunately, Smith's abrasive style and – later on – his insistence that he and the twelve members of the Mormon ruling council had a special dispensation from God to take as many wives as they liked, shocked and infuriated whole communities of non-Mormons as the self-styled 'Saints' travelled westward.

The Prophet Smith, as his followers called him, was shot dead by an Illinois lynch mob in 1844 – leaving 27 widows. He was replaced as Mormon leader by the equally forceful Brigham Young.

Aside from winning new converts, the Saints, now numbered in thousands, sought a place to settle and start a religious community. Young decided that, in the face of local hostility, it was a time for the sword rather than the ploughshare, and waged what amounted to a religious guerrilla war on the unbelievers of Illinois. However, he and his people were eventually driven west, into the wilderness.

They crossed the Rocky Mountains and, after appalling hardships, arrived on the desert-like Utah plateau. Most people would have given up and died in the face of such a brutal existence and such hostile geography but, with Herculean efforts, the Mormons irrigated the region around the great central salt lake and built a municipality there: the pragmatically named Salt Lake City.

Brigham Young rewarded his followers by consenting – with God's permission – to the spread of multiple spouse-taking (polygamy) to all male Mormons. In fact, this was arguably something of a necessity, as the Saints then had rather more women than men in their surviving population.

Utah was blocked from joining the United States for many years, because the Mormon practice of polygamy was illegal under US law. Fortunately in 1890 – just as the US Congress was about to pass a law that would impose a crushing economic blockade on Utah – President Wilfred Woodruff (Smith's third successor to the Mormon leadership) was granted a vision from the Lord.

Henceforth, Woodruff announced, polygamy was an abomination in the eyes of the Lord, and any Mormon who had more than one wife was to be ejected from the Mormon fellowship. The only exception to this rule was to be himself and his own harem of wives. Utah was thus allowed to join the United States, but the unbelievers in the federal government eventually prosecuted Woodruff, forcing him to give up all but one of his wives.

From this controversial start, Mormonism soon settled into being one of the most respectable religious communities in the world. Mormon towns are generally pictures of order and neighbourliness, where habits of respectable dress, general abstinence and moral rectitude are expected of all citizens, old or young. Polygamy does still take place here and there, but almost always in secret and usually in the more out-of-the-way parts of America's vast outback.

Mormons live under a strict religious infrastructure: sin is dealt with harshly by more senior Mormons (Smith refused to initiate a priest caste) and tithes of 10 per cent of a believer's income (before tax) are demanded on a yearly basis. This may seem a rather austere lifestyle in modern, hedonistic America but, on the other hand, any Mormon in trouble – spiritual or financial – can always turn to fellow Mormons and the hierarchy of the Church of the Latter Day Saints for help and support.

Male Mormons in their early twenties are encouraged to go abroad as missionaries – struggling to convert heathens to Mormonism and living as respectably as they would at home. They are forbidden alcohol and drinks containing caffeine, wear respectable suits (whatever the weather) and – as noted above – are strictly prohibited any but the most blameless contact with women. Any white person is a potential convert but, up until recently, non-whites (especially Native Americans and blacks) were not welcome in the Church of the Latter Day Saints. A missionary's only rewards for this often fruitless and frustrating work are a swifter advancement in the church hierarchy in later life and a better chance of achieving eternal reward after death.

Male Mormons believe that they do not simply go to Heaven when they die – they become gods themselves and go on to create life in a new star system (Adam is the same as God the Father in the Mormon creed). Female Mormons, however, do not become goddesses unless they are married to a worthy Mormon; this allows them to be spiritually piggy-backed to a lesser form of deity as the 'celestial partner' of the husband.

Faithful Mormons look upon sex before marriage, homosexuality and adultery with particular repugnance. These 'ungodly acts' specifically undermine heterosexual marriage – one of the principal elements of what a Mormon believes leads to a happy life after death. As we will see, the taboo on premarital sex was to prove an important factor in the events that led to the kidnapping of Kirk Anderson in 1977.

Kirk reappeared on Saturday, 17 September, just over three days after his disappearance from East Ewell. He was physically unhurt and had apparently been freed and returned to his lodgings in Epsom without a ransom being paid or even demanded. Nevertheless, he insisted that he had been kidnapped.

A news story that breaks on a Saturday is a godsend to the Sunday newspapers – who generally find themselves picking over the old news of the previous week and rarely getting good scoops – so the return of the Mormon missionary kidnapee was now enthusiastically followed up by the press, even though the public remained largely unaware that he had even been missing. All the Sunday papers sent reporters to Epsom Police Station to get an official statement and were there met by Richard Eyre, director of the southern region of the Mormon Church in Great Britain.

Kirk Anderson's abduction, the soberly suited Eyre announced from the steps of Epsom Police Station, was the result of 'a personal problem' stemming from his connection with a woman called Joyce McKinney. That was all he, or his church, were willing to say publicly at that time.

The official police spokesman would only add that Kirk Anderson and several other persons were helping them with their inquiries and that the mysterious Joyce McKinney remained at large. Investigators were anxious to speak to her. She was described as an American in her mid-twenties, average height with shoulder-length blonde hair and a distinct Southern accent. She had a small triangular scar on her jaw and wore glasses with notably thick lenses. She was believed to be in the company of another American – the sandy-haired, moustachioed young man who had called himself Bob Bosler during the abduction of Anderson. Police now believed Bosler's real name to be Keith Joseph May.

Of course, the pressmen wanted one question answered above all others, and Detective Chief Superintendent Bill Hucklesby – in charge of the case – was politic enough to answer it: yes, Joyce McKinney was said to be a very attractive young woman.

Unofficially, of course, police officers are often willing to give details 'off the record' to the press, provided they don't risk prejudicing their case and, perhaps, if there is an off-duty pint of beer in it for them. Quiet journalistic persistence soon revealed that Kirk Anderson had claimed to have been manacled to a bed for at least part of his three-day abduction. This was more than enough for news editors to work up some highly speculative, but eye-catching headlines.

The police were also pleased when, the following day, Monday, Joyce McKinney and her accomplice, Keith May, were picked up in a police roadblock on the A30 in Devon. Anderson's description of his enforced journey and his place of incarceration had sounded as if he had been taken to the West Country, so Kent police had enlisted the help of the Devon and

Cornwall Constabulary. These soon found the cottage McKinney and May had rented – an isolated place on the edge of Dartmoor, near Okehampton. Inside there was evidence of recent habitation, including a pair of handcuffs, a set of foot manacles and a length of heavy chain attached to a double bed. Anderson's claim to have been held against his will seemed to have been confirmed.

Now that the daily newspapers were also front-paging the story, foreign correspondents in the States soon turned up new details about the people involved. Joyce McKinney was from a small village called Minneapolis in North Carolina (not to be confused with the city of Minneapolis in Minnesota). To the delight of the tabloids, she was found to be 27 years old, sported a '38-inch, C-cup bosom' and had been a successful beauty queen – Miss Wyoming 1974.

Joyce had converted to the Mormon church after leaving Tennessee University – which had caused something of a rift with her parents – and had moved to the town of Provo in Utah to immerse herself in her new faith. Joyce's mother told reporters that her daughter was 'an introvert and a terribly lonely person'. However, her conversion had taken place a year *before* her success as Miss Wyoming, so Joyce had evidently not taken the Mormon teachings on maidenly self-effacement too much to heart.

Joyce's mother also told pressmen that her daughter had met Kirk Anderson in Provo in 1975, and soon after had announced that they were engaged. However Kirk had apparently broken it off immediately thereafter – for which Joyce had blamed her parents' objections to the Mormon Church – and had subsequently gone away without telling Joyce where he was headed. Joyce had been making frantic efforts to find him ever since, according to her mother.

Kirk Anderson's mother, on the other hand, simply told the press: 'We didn't know anything about this girl. We do know that [Kirk has] had very little to do with girls – only to teach them about the church. I personally think that he has been living very close to the Lord.'

Investigators found this all rather inconsistent. Joyce's choice of such a strait-laced religion and her mother's description of her as an 'introvert' seemed rather at odds with her winning of the Miss Wyoming beauty contest – not to mention her involvement in an alleged kinky kidnapping.

Further investigation then turned up another odd fact about her: during her time in Utah, she was believed to have attempted suicide after a romantic involvement with Wayne Osmond – a member of the world-famous Mormon pop group, The Osmonds.

Mrs Olive Osmond (mother and manager for the wholesome boy-band) flatly denied that any such relationship had ever taken place, claiming that Joyce had been just one of the many adoring fans who constantly pestered her sons. However, Joyce's apparent obsession with the Osmonds – then the most famous Mormons in the world – highlighted an aspect of her personality that almost every acquaintance mentioned sooner or later – that Joyce McKinney was sure that she was going to be famous one day.

Although she was unavailable to give even restricted interviews until (and if) she was granted bail, Joyce McKinney sent an open letter from Holloway Prison to the local newspaper in her home village of Minneapolis, North Carolina. Certain that journalists would interview those she had grown up with, she wrote: 'I urge you to tell them the truth. That my nickname in high school was "Iceberg", that I was boy-shy, and seldom dated. (I was the more studious type.) And I didn't even play kissing games at parties. Also that I was never known to smoke, drink or use any types of drugs or profanity and that I came from a very good family. Also that I represented Avery County in the Miss North Carolina High School contest as "North Carolina's ideal high school girl", as well as being a North Carolina Junior Miss and later Miss Wyoming in the "Miss USA" Pageant.'

This odd mix of respectability and downright egotism only further whetted British newspaper interest in Miss McKinney, but little more of her personal charms were expected to be revealed until she and Keith May were sent to their first preliminary hearing on 12 October 1977.

Preliminary hearings are primarily to help the presiding magistrates to decide if there is a criminal case to be heard and, if they deem it so, the entire process of evidence presentation needs to be begun again before a judge and jury. British reporting restrictions for preliminary hearings limit journalists to revealing only the name, age, address, physical appearance and plea of any defendant. Nevertheless, Joyce McKinney was determined to have her say in public as soon as possible . . .

Held for eighteen days in Holloway Women's Prison, Joyce had requested a bible – which she consulted constantly during her stay there. However, as well as presumably taking strength from its teachings, she also wrote in the 'good book' herself.

Joyce was placed in a windowed police van, to be taken to the preliminary magistrate's hearing on 12 October. Strictly speaking, she should have either travelled in an enclosed vehicle or should have had the traditional blanket over her head as the vehicle arrived at Epsom courthouse (this covering of a suspect is to prevent the risk of press photographs contaminating the evidence of witnesses at any later identity parades). However, as the police van pulled through a gaggle of pressmen, Joyce was under no such constraint. Turning to the window closest to the eager journalists she pressed her open bible to the glass. Written over the pages of Book of Job were the words: 'PLEASE TELL THE TRUTH. MY REPUTATION IS AT STAKE.'

Joyce's escort of female officers struggled with her, but she managed to open her bible to another page, on which was written: 'HE HAD SEX WITH ME FOR FOUR DAYS.' And on yet another page she had written: 'PLEASE GET THE

TRUTH TO THE PUBLIC. HE MADE IT LOOK LIKE A KIDNAPPING.'
Finally, as she was about to be dragged into the court building, she held up a
last message: 'ASK CHRISTIANS TO PRAY FOR ME.'

Potentially solid gold as these messages were for the newspapers, news
editors could not print anything but Joyce's pleas for truth and prayer. The
statements about sex and faked kidnapping came directly under the British
sub judice rule, which bans the public revelation of any fact that could be
considered prejudicial in a future trial.

The first preliminary hearing itself was rather dull compared to the scene
that had taken place outside the court. Joyce's profession was described as
'model' and Keith May as 'trainee architect'. Both plead 'not guilty' on charges
of kidnapping, but admitted to entering the country on false papers (Keith
had been arrested carrying documents with nine different identities, Joyce
with four). Bail was denied May on the grounds that he was a trained pilot
(and thus was a greater escape risk). Joyce was denied bail for her own
protection as she had an admitted history of attempted suicide.

Joyce herself asked that non-*sub judice* reporting restrictions be lifted, so
her council could later make a statement to the press concerning her false
passports: Joyce McKinney lived in fear of the Church of the Latter Day
Saints, he stated, and carried false papers to hide herself from them. She
believed, he went on, that the Mormons sought retribution on her as a
convert who had later renounced the faith. Her pursuit of Kirk Anderson
following his becoming a missionary – and was thus supposed to have
nothing to do with non-believing women – had only increased her fear that
the Mormon hierarchy would seek to harm her in some way.

Joyce also made her own direct statement to the press when again being
transported in a police van. She pressed a piece of card to the window,
revealing the hand-printed message: 'KIRK LEFT WITH ME WILLINGLY!
HE FEARS EXCOMMUNICATION FOR LEAVING HIS MISSION AND
MADE UP THIS KIDNAP-RAPE STORY.'

Again, the message could not be printed due to the *sub judice* law, but
Joyce had made plain to the press what her defence would be.

At a preliminary hearing, Queen's Council Neil Denison stated the case for
the prosecution. Joyce McKinney was obsessed with Kirk Anderson, he said.
She had driven him from his native Utah, but even his taking-up of
missionary work abroad had not put her off her relentless pursuit. Tracking
him down, with the aid of her associate, Keith May, she had kidnapped Kirk
at gunpoint, had taken him to an isolated Devon cottage, had chained him
to a bed and had then forced him to indulge in sexual acts with her before
he was released. She and her associate were guilty of kidnapping and Joyce
herself was guilty of sexually abusing Kirk Anderson, Denison insisted.

Here the reader should note that under British law, it is deemed
impossible for a woman to rape a man. The law takes the view that if the man

is genuinely unwilling to have sex, he will naturally fail to achieve an erection. If, on the other hand, he achieves enough to sustain intercourse, then it is deemed that he must have been willing in the first place. A charge of sexual abuse is, on the other hand, possible even if the man in question achieves an erection, provided his partner is proved to have used excessive threats, force or physical restraint on him.

The obvious witness to support the prosecution's case was Kirk Anderson himself – the man whose charms had drawn a beauty queen across the Atlantic was a person the public and press were keen to see, but he had, with laudable Mormon self-effacement, stayed away from the public eye up to that point. As he now made his way to the witness stand, all eyes were on him.

In fact, Kirk Anderson was a remarkably unstriking figure. His bespectacled, fairly average-looking face topped a big body – at least seventeen or eighteen stone. Although he appeared more big-boned than actually fat, Kirk moved in a gawky way and walked with a flat-footed shamble. He was arguably a fine example of a milk-fed young Mormon missionary, but he hardly looked the catalyst of so much trouble in two countries.

Under questioning by the prosecution, Kirk described meeting Joyce at a Provo drive-in ice cream parlour. Joyce had a maroon, open-top Chevrolet Corvette – a very flashy sports car for a female Mormon convert to own – and Kirk had wandered over to ask her about it. They became friendly and started to date. Joyce had liked Kirk so much that she had suggested marriage on their third meeting.

Kirk had doubts, not only because he hardly knew Joyce, but because he was signed up to do his tour of missionary work. He was also worried because he and Joyce had already broken the rules of premarital chastity, so Kirk consulted his Bishop (a more informal title in Mormonism than in other branches of Christianity, but still a religious director with the power to hand out spiritual judgements and church punishments). Kirk was firmly told to break off his relationship with Joyce McKinney and to prepare himself spiritually for his missionary tour.

Joyce, Kirk told the court, 'did not accept that position'. She had made several embarrassing scenes in public and, at one point while he was riding a motorcycle, had forced him off the road by driving dangerously close in her Corvette. Eventually, to avoid further such problems, Kirk had been sent to California to begin his missionary work early. He indicated that Joyce's persistent hounding of him had then driven him to relocate from California to Oregon, and eventually to Epsom in England. It was there that she had finally caught up with him, and had abducted him.

Kirk went on to describe the actual kidnapping. He had met with the young American who called himself Bob Bosler (Keith May) and had agreed to point out the location of the Mormon Southern England Headquarters on a map in 'Bosler's' car. As they moved out of view of Kimball Smith (Kirk's missionary partner) Kirk had felt something hard poked into his ribs:

'I was startled,' Kirk told the court, 'and as I looked down I saw it was a gun. I was quite scared.

'He took me over to the car, that was parked fifty yards away, and I got into the rear seat. Joyce was in the front seat wearing a dark wig and she had another gun.

'She said something like how did I think eight thousand miles of ocean was going to keep us apart, or something to that effect.'

Keith May had got into the driver's seat and drove away from the church. Joyce then climbed into the back seat with Kirk, still threatening him with the gun and, on May's suggestion, made Kirk lie down so she could cover him with a blanket.

There followed a long and, for the bulky Anderson a presumably uncomfortable journey. At one point he managed to peek out of the car window long enough to see a sign reading 'Yeovil', but he had no idea where he was when the car eventually pulled up outside the isolated Dartmoor cottage McKinney had rented.

'I was taken to the bedroom and allowed to sit while Joy cooked dinner,' Kirk continued. 'They explained they had brought me to the cottage so we could sort out the things that had happened since I had known her.

'She told me she still loved me and wanted to marry me.'

While Keith May had politely slept in another room, Joyce and Kirk had shared a bed. Nothing sexual happened that night, Kirk insisted, and he had spent a lot of the hours of darkness listening to the affectionate chattering of his kidnapper.

The next day 'Bob' had attached a leather strap to Kirk's ankle and ran a long chain from the strap to the heavy bed frame – 'for Joyce's protection' Anderson was told.

'I had thought of escape,' Kirk explained to the court, 'but I didn't really know where I was. I decided if I tried to co-operate and gain their confidence I would be able to sort out a release.'

Joyce emphatically told him that the price of his freedom – short of full matrimony – was to 'give her another baby'.

'That night (15 September) she spent the night with me in bed. I kissed her and held her in my arms. But there was nothing else. I was trying to co-operate.'

The metaphorical gloves came off, he said, on the third night of his incarceration.

'When she came into the room there was a fire in the fireplace and she put some music on. I recognized it because she played it in the apartment two years earlier when we first had intercourse.

'She was wearing a negligee. She came to me as I lay on the bed. I said I would like my back rubbed. She proceeded to do that, but I could tell she wanted to have intercourse again. I said I did not and she tried to convince me. She then left the room and returned a few minutes later with May. May was carrying chains, ropes and padlocks.'

The pair then tied and chained Kirk, spread-eagled on his back, to the four bedposts. Keith May left and Joyce ripped off Kirk's pyjamas and his sacred undergarment, then forced him to have full, penetrative sex.

Prosecution Council Neil Denison asked Kirk: 'You mentally didn't want it to happen, so how could it physically have occurred?'

Anderson replied that first 'she had oral sex.'

As Stuart Elgrod, council for the defence, cross-examined Kirk, he was probably quite unaware that he was, at one point, making religious history. He asked Kirk what he meant by the 'garment' he said he had worn beneath his pyjamas. Kirk, clearly uncomfortable with the question, replied that all faithful Mormons wear a sacred garment beneath their normal clothing – resembling a woman's one-piece swimsuit. This item is embroidered with sacred symbols – usually by the Mormon's mother – and is supposed to protect their chastity, both physically and spiritually.

This was the first time that this inner secret of the Church of the Latter Day Saints had ever been revealed in public. Some people jeered at such an odd precaution – especially as it had failed so singularly in Kirk's case – but Mormons pointed out that it was no sillier than the traditional accoutrements sported by those in other religions. It has been reported, however, that certain unscrupulous non-Mormon lawyers in the United States have since deliberately worn fake 'chastity garments' during trials with Mormons sitting on the jury. The idea being that a Mormon will note the tell-tale rumpling of the lawyer's clothes and might be more sympathetic towards their case.

On matters of more import to the immediate case, Elgrod asked Kirk how many times he and Joyce had made love on the night before he was released.

'Three times,' Kirk replied. The two times following the first he had been just as unwilling, he stressed, but allowed himself to be coaxed by Joyce because she had threatened to get Keith May to chain him to the bedposts again.

'I am suggesting,' Elgrod continued, 'that a no stage were you ever tied up in that cottage except for the purpose of sex games.' Kirk flatly denied this.

Elgrod's questioning later turned up the fact that Keith May had politely left Kirk and Joyce alone in the cottage for around 24 hours, but Kirk had made no attempt to escape, even though he must have guessed that Joyce would never shoot him (in fact, the guns turned out to be harmless replicas).

'I was bolted in,' Kirk replied, referring to his ankle chain.

Lord and Lady Archer arrive at the Central Criminal Court, London, 19 July 2001.
The Court had returned a verdict of guilty on charges of perverting the course of
justice, and perjury. Summing up at Archer's original libel action in 1987, Mr Justice
Caulfield had mused that a man married to the 'fragrant' Mary Archer would be
unlikely to pay for 'cold, unloving, rubber-insulated' sex with a prostitute.
(Popperfoto)

Above Fiction Factory: Jeffrey Archer poses with his set of Andy Warhol Marilyn Monroe pictures prior to their going on sale in October 1998. *(Popperfoto)*

Top right Stand by me: President Clinton and First Lady Hillary hold hands as they arrive at a Washington Methodist church on 16 August 1998, the day before his Grand Jury testimony. *(Popperfoto)*

Bottom right The eyes have it: Monica Lewinsky smiles at President Clinton at a ceremony gathering the White House interns, 6 November 1996. *(Popperfoto)*

Looking drawn during an event announcing new childcare proposals on 26 January 1998, Clinton denies that he had a sexual affair with Monica Lewinsky.
(Popperfoto)

The cat who got the cream: President Clinton poses with Monica Lewinsky in a 17 November 1995 photo that was released to the press by Independent Counsel Kenneth Starr. According to Lewinsky's deposition, she and Clinton had a sexual encounter in the White House that day. *(Popperfoto)*

Left Writ large: Robert Maxwell promoting a biography in 1988. He remains a man of whom it is still impossible to tell fact from fiction. *(Popperfoto)*

Top right Bitter Moon: police outside the home of Roman Polanski on 10 August 1969 after five bodies, including that of his pregnant wife, Sharon Tate, had been found. *(Popperfoto)*

Bottom right The beautiful people: Polanski (*right*, with John Finch and Francesca Annis) in Cannes, 1972. *(Popperfoto)*

Above The last known photo of the man known to *Private Eye* as 'Cap'n Bob', taken midday aboard the *Lady Ghislaine* in Funchal harbour, before she departed for the open sea. *(Popperfoto)*

Above Sure to go to Heaven? Beaming for the press, Joyce McKinney arrives at court in November 1977 for her pre-trial hearing on charges of abducting Mormon missionary Kirk Anderson. *(Popperfoto)*

Top right Kinky Californian? Joseph May *(centre)*, charged with kidnapping along with Joyce McKinney, arrives in court in June 1977. *(Popperfoto)*

Bottom right Payne and Pleasure: Cynthia Payne, former brothel madam in the sex-for-luncheon-vouchers scandal, launches her bid to enter politics on 25 March 1992. Her career was immortalised in the film *Personal Services*. *(Popperfoto)*

Liberal Party leader Jeremy Thorpe and his wife arrive at the Old Bailey for the first day of his trial on charges of conspiracy to murder Norman Scott, May 1979.
(Popperfoto)

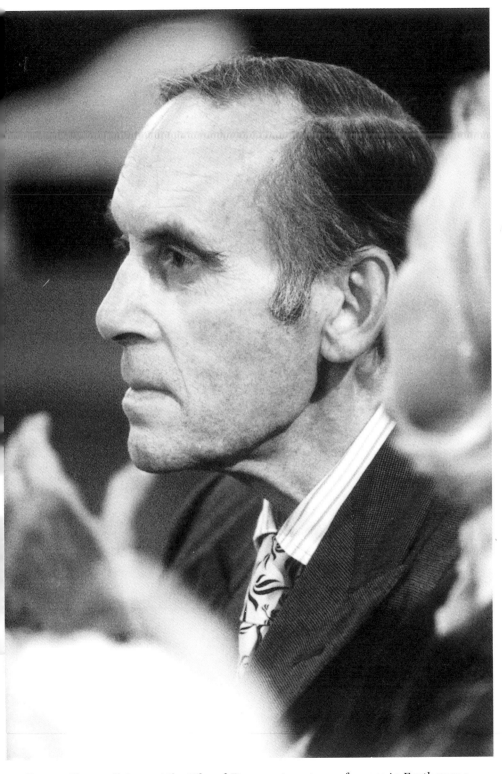

Jeremy Thorpe listens at the Liberal Democrat party conference in Eastbourne, September 1997. Thorpe, suffering from Parkinson's disease, was making what was believed to have been his first conference appearance for twenty years. *(Popperfoto)*

Above A brave face: Richard Nixon (*right*) makes his resignation speech, 1974. *(Popperfoto)*

Left Campaign smile firmly in place, a poker-faced Richard Nixon makes a double victory sign as he leaves office after his resignation, 1974. From 'Squidgygate' to 'Camillagate' and 'Cheriegate', the scandal opened the gates to a much-abused form of journalistic shorthand. *(Popperfoto)*

Left The Swingeing Sixties: John Profumo in the raiments of a Privy Councillor. The Profumo Affair of 1963 was a turning point at which British political culture began to look a little less hidebound. *(Popperfoto)*

Right The Happy Hypocrite: Ivor Novello and Vivien Leigh, 1936. *(Popperfoto)*

Above Thrown to the lions: Harold Davidson, former vicar of Stiffkey, performs at an amusement park in Skegness, England. He was mauled to death a short while after this photo was taken, more sinned against than sinning. *(Popperfoto)*

Right Novelist and thinker H. G. Wells, pictured at home in 1939, was the seemingly unlikely cause of an attempted suicide. *(Popperfoto)*

Above A scene in Rennes during the court martial of Captain Alfred Dreyfus (*left*). In anti-Semitic turn-of-the-century France, tempers ran high and troops were needed to keep order. *(Popperfoto)*

Poor Oscar: a fresh-faced Wilde at Oxford in 1878.
He sought out tragedy, and found himself.
(Popperfoto)

Then there was the matter of Kirk's release on Saturday 17 September. Kirk admitted that he had been unrestrained when Joyce and Keith had driven him back to London. Arriving, they had stopped off in Haymarket to withdraw money from the American Express office. Then they had wandered around Trafalgar Square and had had lunch in the Hard Rock Café on Piccadilly. At no time had Kirk either tried to escape or sought aid from passing policemen. Why?

'Because they were taking me back to Epsom,' Kirk shrugged.

Under Elgrod's questioning, Kirk confirmed that the reason he had ceased to see Joyce in Utah was because they had indulged in pre-marital sex, and his bishop had forbidden Kirk to associate with, much less marry her.

Was it true, Elgrod asked, that following this enforced breakup, Kirk had received a letter from a firm of Provo solicitors, acting on Joyce's behalf, informing him that she was pregnant, that she intended to have the child and would file legal proceeding against him if he failed to acknowledge paternity and marry her? Kirk conceded that this was true, but he had done nothing because he believed Joyce had been lying about the positive pregnancy test.

'She told me she was pregnant just three days after we [originally] had intercourse,' Kirk said to underline Joyce's overoptimistic eagerness to be in the 'blessed state.' He had been unsurprised, he went on, when the pregnancy failed to develop and he did not believe Joyce's claim to have had a miscarriage. He believed she had simply invented the baby to try to force marriage on him.

Following his appearance in the witness box, Kirk Anderson did not return to the court, although his fellow Mormon representatives were always there in force.

The case defence council Stuart Elgrod presented to the presiding magistrate emphasized that Joyce and Kirk had been lovers and, if Kirk had been less in thrall to his faith, would probably have been man and wife. However, under pressure from his religious superiors, Kirk had been forced to abandon the pregnant Joyce and go abroad. Over the following year, Joyce had tirelessly sought out her lover and, when she discovered his location in England, had hurried to be reunited with him. He had gone *willingly* to Devon with Joyce and her friend Keith May. All three had regarded the trip as a rescue from a heartless religion, not a kidnapping.

The evidence of Kirk's willingness to go with Joyce, Elgrod continued, was seen in his total failure to try to escape and his readiness to have sex with her. The chains, ropes and manacles were nothing more than bondage sex toys: a little unorthodox to the old-fashioned and prudish perhaps but, after all, this was 1977. Sexual experimentation was hardly a rarity in British or American society.

Unfortunately, after they had returned to London, Kirk's fear of excommunication from the Mormon Church had overcome his happiness at being reunited with Joyce. Instead of facing up to his religious superiors and insisting that he and Joyce were not going to be forced apart again, he had cravenly filed a claim of kidnapping and sexual assault against her.

'It is quite clear, from what we know, that any further relapse by Mr Anderson would result immediately in his being sent home and excommunicated,' Elgrod said in conclusion. Certainly the Church of the Latter Day Saints and their chosen beliefs were not standing trial, he stressed, but the magistrates should take the strictness of the Mormon way of life into account when considering how it had impacted on the events of the immediate case.

Elgrod ended on a Shakespearian note with a modified line from *Hamlet*: 'Methinks the Mormon doth protest too much.'

If Kirk Anderson had been a rather unimpressive figure in court, the same could not be said for Joyce McKinney. While wearing the sort of sober clothes that emphasized her claim still to be a deeply religious person – if not a Mormon any more – she still managed to show off the good looks and strong personality that had helped her win the title of Miss Wyoming three years earlier.

She had a rounded, pert face, a broad, winning smile and a slightly up-turned nose, all surmounted by surprisingly dark brown eyes for someone who claimed that her honey-blonde hair was totally natural. She made the same claim for her apparently gravity-defying breasts. As she was being led back to the police van to be returned to Holloway Prison, tabloid journalists shouted bawdy compliments. She paused, presented her full profile to the photographers and, indicating her upper body, shouted: 'All mine!'

Neither Joyce nor Keith May gave evidence, because the defence chose not to call them. (In fact it is rare for a defendant to give evidence, unless called upon to be examined by the prosecution. It is a legal truism that the most dangerous witness to a defence case is the defendant themselves, as they rarely make a perfect impression on judge or jury.)

However, following her defence lawyer's summing-up, Joyce announced that she would like to read a prepared statement to the court. The magistrates said that this would be allowable, if it was not too long, and Joyce made her way to the witness stand with an ominously thick folder in her hand. Printed on the folder cover – in Joyce's now easily recognizable handwriting – were the words: 'THE GREATEST LOVE STORY EVER TOLD.' It was noted that Stuart Elgrod did not look happy about the new turn of events.

Taking out fourteen pages of closely handwritten script, Joyce launched into what she plainly meant to be her big scene (she had already started to write the film script of her version of events, and meant to insist that she should play herself when Hollywood producers competed to buy the rights to her story).

She began by describing her earlier life, speaking quickly in a Deep South accent that her British listeners sometimes found hard to follow. She described herself in far from humble tones – stressing her accomplishments at university, as a beauty queen and as an amateur actress. She even mentioned her IQ score at the age of nine: 'Nine points above that of genius. I'm not saying this just to toot my own horn.'

She then moved on to her conversion to Mormonism and her pilgrimage to Utah. There, she said, she had soon become deeply disillusioned. Staying in the halls of residence of the Brigham Young University, she had been horrified to see Mormon girls drinking alcohol and ogling pictures of naked men. The young male Mormons were, she said, even worse: 'The missionaries, whom I expected to be spiritual enough to be prospective husbands, were wolves.'

'I didn't expect this at all,' she went on. 'I was in a state of cultural shock. I prayed for a very special boy who would come into my life. . . and that is where Kirk comes in.'

Joyce went on to describe her first meeting with Kirk in more or less the same details he had given previously, with one exception – she was clearly nettled at his statement that he had originally been drawn to the charms of her car, rather than herself – 'I would like to say that he did not propose marriage to the car; he proposed marriage to me,' she commented tartly.

It was Kirk who had first suggested marriage, Joyce continued, not she. She had asked him: 'Honey, are you sure you can support me?' To which she said the nineteen-year-old had enthusiastically replied: 'Honey, I'd work five jobs to support you.'

'To a woman this means something,' Joyce read on, 'these are pretty heavy promises. He even promised to give me a rock [a diamond on their engagement ring] so big it would make my hand sag.

'Believe me,' she stressed, 'after fighting off guys for twenty-four years, I wouldn't just give myself to a man unless he'd made some pretty heavy promises and marriage plans.'

On a rather plaintive note, Joyce added: 'We even had our [prospective] children named. They were to be called Gabriel Kirk and Joshua Kyle.'

Concerning the pre-marital sex she had with Kirk in Utah, Joyce said that 'any physical desire I felt was an indirect result of the real spiritual and mental love I had for him. A love he *encouraged*.'

She added, perhaps rather cattily: 'I cannot say I ever got any pleasure out of sexual relations with Kirk – I was too busy trying to satisfy *him*.'

As to the sinfulness of even pleasureless sex before marriage, Joyce had decided that God had forgiven her: '[Making love with Kirk] was the most special commitment of my life. It had made me his wife in God's eyes.'

Unfortunately, Kirk had not seen the matter in the same light: '[for him] it was a quick thrill. Something we call casual – something to cover up to his bishop and his mother.'

On the subject of Kirk's attempts to escape the righteous wrath of his church and family, Joyce said: 'This isn't the first time he's accused me of raping him. He told the same story in Utah. A friend of his told me that he said to his mother: "Mom, she did everything I just lay there. I didn't have anything to do with it." '

After his interview with his bishop, Kirk and many of the Mormons of Provo had ostracized her, Joyce said. People crossed the street to avoid her, her car was dented by a vandal with a crowbar, and she started to receive anonymous phone calls at night, threatening both her and her unborn child.

As to the public rows she had with her former lover, Joyce described herself invariably getting the better of 'scared little boy' Kirk. At one point, when meeting with him and his mother to discuss Joyce's pregnancy, Kirk had shouted 'Fuck you!' at her. She described herself calmly replying: 'That's what you did dear, and that's why we're in this mess.'

Kirk at that time, Joyce insisted, was sheltering behind the skirts of his matriarchal mother, and allowed his excessive love for her to eclipse his proper feelings for Joyce and their unborn baby. When Joyce lost her temper with him at one point, calling him a 'son-of-a-gun,' Kirk had shouted: 'Don't call my sweet mother names!'

(Joyce seems, like many people, to have thought of 'son-of-a-gun' as a very mild expletive, but perhaps Kirk knew it's actual derivation. It's a naval insult from the age of sail used to describe the bastard of a low-price prostitute – those women who would come on board a ship in port to do business with members of the crew between two guns on the cannon deck.)

However, according to Joyce, matters soon became much more serious than mere childish name-calling. She claimed that two men attacked her, knocked her down and kicked her in the stomach. That trauma, she said, coupled with her fragile emotional state was what had caused her to miscarry the baby.

'I believe the spirit of Kirk's child is still living as much as you or me,' Joyce read to the court through her tears. 'And I believe I can still mother him one day.'

Joyce did not believe Kirk was behind the assault and insisted that he still loved her.

'If I did not have faith in his love for me, I could not have flown half-way round the world with my wedding band and my trousseau in my suitcase to see him.'

However, turning to the alleged kidnapping itself, Joyce was predictably scathing of Kirk's version of events. She and Keith May had carried guns, she admitted, but only to frighten off any Mormons who tried to stop them leaving. Kirk had guessed that the handguns were fake the moment he saw them. Climbing into the car of his own volition, Kirk had grinned at Joyce and said: 'Hi, pintsize. Are you going to fight the whole Mormon army?'

The drive down to Devon had been an escape from the grasping control of the Church of the Latter Day Saints, not a kidnapping, Joyce then insisted. She positively scoffed at the idea that Kirk had been dragged away and held against his will.

'I picked a romantic little honeymoon cottage because I wanted to get away from the smog of Los Angeles. You should have seen the place when we walked in. There were presents everywhere for him and his slippers under the chair. I had a solid, eighteen-carat gold ring for him. It cost me over £1,000, but I wanted him to have the best. I just loved cooking for him, fixing his favourite meals and massaging his back.

'We made love several times at the cottage,' she read on, 'If he didn't like it, why didn't he just walk up to the people next door and say: "Excuse me? There's a girl in the cottage next door and she's kidnapped me! She's there making my favourite meals and baking me chocolate cake, giving me a better back rub than my mother and making love with me!"

'Why didn't he do that?' she demanded, 'because nobody would believe him. They'd think he was a fool.'

Concerning his claim of sexual assault, Joyce was positively scornful.

'A woman raping a man? Him eighteen stone and me eight stone? Come on! Whom is kidding whom? His claim that he was unwilling makes me laugh!

'I was supposed to be play-act the part of a beautiful woman who had him in her love prison. He laid down on the bed for me and let me tie him up. I did so by myself [not with the help of Keith May] and put fake stage blood on him.

'Yes, I tore off his pyjamas and it was : "Oh! You sexy tiger!" But I acted the whole scene out for him. The whole works on *his* request.

'If he was so unwilling, then why was he lying there grinning like a monkey? Why was he moving his hips with me?

'I said, "Honey, does that feel good? Do you like it like this?" And he goes 'Phew! Hot!'

Perhaps noting the court's reaction to her intimate statements, Joyce apologized to the bench, suddenly as demure as any southern belle from *Gone with the Wind*: 'It sure embarrasses me to tell things like this. But it has to be told.'

She then continued with her reading: 'At this point I think I should explain sexual bondage and Kirk's sexual hang-ups.

'Kirk was raised by a very dominant mother. He has a lot of guilt about sex because his mother over-protected him all his life. When we make love he has to have all the lights out and wash up afterwards. He believes truly that sex is dirty.

'Kirk has to be tied up to have an orgasm. I co-operated because I loved him and wanted to help him. Sexual bondage turns him on because he doesn't have to feel guilty. The thought of being powerless before a woman seems to excite him.'

She continued shyly: "I didn't have to give him oral sex, but I did do it, at his request, because he likes it.

'It was just amazing,' she added, apparently off-the-cuff and in a tone of wonder, 'he just kept going and going. . .'

Then she returned to the main theme: her defence against the charges.

'He's had all kinds of temper tantrums after sex. I guess putting me in prison is an extension of those tantrums.'

Speaking for over an hour, Joyce painted a picture of herself deeply in love: 'I loved him so much that if anybody had tried to shoot him, I would have stepped in front of him and stopped the bullet.'

Unfortunately, according to her, the object of her love was a young man with severe sexual hang-ups and a fear of his church that could lead him even to frame the woman he loved: 'My little priest is quite sexually frustrated. But as soon as the ropes hit his wrists, he attained sexual satisfaction. . . It saddens me now to think of the things he did at the cottage to make it look like a kidnap.'

Her summing up was a plea to the court that would have done credit to Scarlett O'Hara: 'This man has imprisoned my heart with false promises of love and marriage and family life. He has cast me into prison for a kidnap he knows he set things up for. I don't want anything more to do with Kirk. He does not know what eternal love is.

'All I ask is that you do not imprison me any longer. Let me pick up the pieces of my life. I ask you to let me out of prison so I can get a counsellor to help me get over the great emotional hurt I feel inside.'

Again in floods of tears, Joyce made a final plea for mercy before leaving the stand: 'My father has a bad heart and this may be the last Christmas I spend with him.'

The bemused magistrates took very little time, however, to decide that it would take a full trial at the High Court to winnow the truth out of such a bizarre case. Nevertheless, Joyce's pleas had moved them enough to allow the release of both Joyce and Keith May on bail. Joyce's bail was paid by her father – a poor man who had to mortgage his house to get the money, a circumstance that could not have helped his heart condition.

The newspapermen trying to follow the story were, if anything, more confused after Joyce's lengthy statement. On the one hand there was Kirk Anderson, who claimed that an experience that most men his age would have leapt at was, to him, a terrible ordeal. On the other was the attractive Miss McKinney, who claimed to have spent her life savings of $17,000 tracking, 'rescuing' and pampering a man who returned the compliment by having her thrown in jail. Certainly most sympathy lay with Joyce, as Kirk had not been hurt in any non-spiritual fashion, but that didn't mean that her story was taken at face value. She was a little too much of a drama queen – a demure southern rose one minute, a roistering girl-of-the-world the next – to be wholly believed.

Then there was the mysterious Keith May who, so far, had remained silent. An educated Californian in his mid-twenties, he did not, on first sight, seem the type to cross the globe to help two other people find true love, whether enforced or not. Throughout the preliminary hearing Joyce had sat next to him and held his hand. The pair's affectionate body language clearly indicated that there was some sort of a close bond between them – but, the pressmen wondered, just how far did it go?

However, such uncertainties certainly made for good news copy, and an unrehearsed comment Joyce had made off-the-cuff during her statement to the court had especially the lowbrow British tabloids in a fever. Describing the depth and passion of her love for Kirk, Joyce had said that, for him, she would 'have skied down Mount Everest in the nude with a carnation up my nose.'

Now she was out in comparative freedom, the papers were frantically competing to buy her exclusive story (most of which would have to be printed after the up-coming trial to avoid the ever present British *sub judice* laws). The editor of the *Sun* was said to be especially keen to pay Joyce to pose for the paper's 'art' photo on page three.

Specifically, he wanted her on a fake mountain, wearing nothing but skis and a carnation – although presumably he did not want her to push the latter up her nose. Joyce – in full religious maiden mode – indignantly refused the offer, insisting that she could never pose nude, whatever the payment. She *was* interested, however, in selling her story. . . to the highest bidder.

Meanwhile, some journalists had spotted the main hole in Joyce's story. She came from a poor family and gave her profession as 'model'. If so, where had she amassed the small fortune of 17,000 dollars that had paid for her pursuit of Kirk?

Most of the two years since her split-up with Kirk in Utah had been spent, according to Joyce, in Los Angeles, California. Journalists from the *Mirror* newspaper (The *Sun's* main competitor in the British tabloid market) headed for LA, mainly in the hopes of finding photographs of Joyce 'modelling' – however demurely – to scoop the *Sun*. They realized that some such pictures had to exist if Joyce had indeed made her money as a model.

Interviews with several of Joyce's friends and acquaintances in California initially confirmed her story – she had certainly been looking for Kirk and had told everyone who would listen that she feared the retribution of the Church of the Latter Day Saints. She had also apparently saved herself for her lost love – refusing all offers of dates and, as far as anyone knew (or would admit) never having sex with anyone.

The *Mirror* journalists had all but given up on finding any salacious gossip about Joyce when a chance encounter led them to the man who was looking after Joyce's belongings, car and dog while she was away.

Steve Moskowitz casually admitted that both he and Keith May were in love with Joyce, but she had made it plain that her heart belonged to the missing Kirk. When asked if he was also holding Joyce's modelling portfolio,

Moskowitz handed over several sheets of black and white contact proofs. Most of the tiny pictures showed Joyce in various respectable modelling costumes – a cowgirl, a lady aviator, a bride etc. – but there were also several of her naked, prancing through a field, apparently representing Eve in the Garden of Eden. As if this were not enough of a scoop, Moskowitz then casually asked why, if they wanted naked pictures of her, the journalists hadn't asked the porno magazines Joyce had posed for?

It turned out that, far from being too moral ever to pose naked, Joyce had been photographed for magazines with titles like *Chopper, Hogtie, Knotty* and *Bound to Please*, sometimes in positions that were virtually gynaecological. Strangely, although most of the pictures were sado-masochistic hardcore – involving Joyce pretending to be tortured by other women – she maintained her fidelity to Kirk in one respect: there were no pictures of her engaged in actual sex.

The *Mirror* journalists, perusing the magazine back-issues at the publisher's down-at-heel office, were also interested to note that although Joyce *was* a natural blonde – as she had claimed – tell-tale scars visible in certain pictures were clear evidence that her vaunted breasts had, in fact, been enhanced by surgery.

However, even lowering herself to hardcore pornography did not explain how Joyce had made over 17,000 dollars in a little over a year. The answer again came from her friend Steve Moskowitz.

When asked about the money he laughed and told the journalists: 'Hell! The way Joy spent money tracking Anderson, 17,000 dollars wouldn't have gotten her to the airport.'

He then showed them an advert in the *LA Free Press* (nicknamed the *FREEP*):

Gorgeous Former
'Miss USA'
Contestant Desires Work!
Beauty Brains and Talent! –
THE BEST GAL IN THE FREEP

(PhD in Drama/Film, former model, actress & state beauty queen, 38-24-36, a slim sweet Southern Blonde) – How would you like her to leisurely bathe you, lovingly blow-dry/style your hair, then give you a delicious nude massage on her fur-covered water bed? ($100) – or try her 'Fantasy Room' – (Your fantasy is her speciality! – S&M, B&D, escort service, PR work, acting jobs, nude wrestling/modelling, erotic phone calls, dirty panties or pictures, TV, charm school fantasies etc.) Mail your Fantasy to

'JOEY'

P.S.- 'Ah love shy boys, dirty ol' men and sugah daddies!'

The style of the advert – the confused wordiness and mix of egotism and worldliness – made the advert unquestionably the work of Joyce 'Joey' McKinney. But did the inclusion of the phrase 'escort service' (a euphemism for high-class prostitution) indicate that she had finally been fully unfaithful to her Kirk?

Steve Moskowitz was unequivocal in his denial. In fact, he said, when Joyce realized that some customers could not be satisfied with everything but full sex, she had brought in a female partner to perform that extra service. She could afford to, Moskowitz said – after all, the 'business' was making thousands every month.

Joyce did not read the *Mirror*'s subsequent revelation of her secret life in California – at least, not in Britain. She and Keith May skipped bail and escaped back to America via Ireland before the case could come to trial. She was eventually found guilty *in absentia* and ordered to serve a year in prison but, of course, never returned to undergo the token sentence.

Kirk Anderson had been sent back to Utah well before Joyce and Keith did their moonlight flit, but he was not excommunicated from the Church of the Latter Day Saints.

The usually taciturn Keith May made a comment to a British journalist shortly before skipping bail: 'This is a pretty strange country. If Joy had been busted in the US for doing what she did to Kirk, the only thing the cops would have done before they let her go was make sure they had her phone number.'

MCPHERSON, AIMÉE SEMPLE

THE MYSTERY KIDNAPPING

Aimée Semple McPherson – once described as 'the world's most pulchritudinous evangelist' – lost her immense following with dramatic suddenness after a farcical trial in which she was charged with 'a conspiracy to obstruct justice'.

She was born Aimée Elizabeth Kennedy, on a small farm in Canada, near Ingersoll, Ontario, on 9 October 1890. Her mother, a highly dominant woman, had been a Salvation Army lass until she married a devout farmer many years her senior. Aimée, like her mother, had a determined character, and there was a great deal of conflict between them in her childhood. Minnie Kennedy – later known as 'Ma' – found marriage to her elderly husband boring and frustrating and took it out on her family.

At the age of seventeen Aimée fell in love with a young English evangelist named Robert Semple and married him in spite of her mother's objections. Semple intended to become a missionary and apparently felt that she would make an ideal wife. She joined her husband in his evangelist activities in Chicago, then they went to England to see his parents. But when they arrived in Hong Kong, where he intended to begin his missionary work, Semple was stricken with fever and died in the English hospital. Aimée gave birth to a girl soon afterwards. The China mission provided funds to send her back to America.

She joined her parents, who had moved to New York, tried life on the farm in Canada, then returned to New York and married a grocery clerk named Harold McPherson, by whom she had a son. Marriage bored her and within eighteen months she was on the move again, following the only profession she knew – that of evangelist. In Canada, she attracted a crowd by standing on a chair at a street corner, her eyes closed and her arms raised in prayer. As the crowd waited in silent expectation, Aimée suddenly opened her eyes and yelled, 'Follow me!' and rushed to the revival hall. Once the crowd was in she shouted, 'Shut the doors. Don't let anyone out.'

For the next few years, it was a rather discouraging routine of travelling around the country in a battered old car with a tent in the back. Her mother joined her and took the collections. Aimée preached the literal truth of every word in the Bible and the personal return of Jesus Christ. Slowly, she acquired a following. She began to hire lecture halls. Then, in 1917, at the age of 27, she made the momentous decision to head for California. In her old car, with her mother and two children, she made her way slowly across the country.

Aimée was not, in fact, 'pulchritudinous'; her features were too heavy, and her legs were like those of a Welsh dresser (so she always wore long skirts). But by the usual standards of female evangelists, she was a welcome change.

Within a week of arriving in Los Angeles, she was able to rent the Philharmonic Auditorium, which held over 3,000 people. Suddenly she was a celebrity. The rich contralto voice could hold the multitudes. On a new wave of confidence, she travelled to Canada, New Zealand and Australia. It seems to have dawned on her that American sales techniques could be used to sell religion. Back in California, this time in San Diego, she scattered evangelical tracts from an aircraft and held meetings in a boxing arena.

It was in San Diego that Aimée suddenly became far more than a successful preacher. San Diego was full of old and retired citizens and the suicide rate and the statistics for mental and physical illness were far higher than in the rest of California. At an outdoor meeting in Organ Pavilion, in Balboa Park, a middle-aged paralytic rose from her wheel chair in front of 30,000 people and took a few halting steps. Suddenly, hundreds of people were hobbling towards the platform, tears streaming down their faces, praising the Lord and Aimée Semple McPherson. The next day, everyone in San Diego was talking about the miracle.

Aimée embarked on another triumphant tour of the Pacific coast. Then she realized it was time to stop moving around like a travelling showman. She would build a temple in Los Angeles. In 1923, Los Angeles was not the world's most sprawling city; it was still an enormous village, full of country folk. They welcomed the idea of an evangelical temple, and contributed generously. On 1 January 1923, trumpets blared, and Aimée unveiled the floodlit, electrically rotating cross that formed the heart of the Angelus Temple; by night it could be seen fifty miles away. The Temple, and Sister Aimée's house next door, had cost about $1½ million. The Temple had a seating capacity of 5,000, a broadcasting station, a theological seminary, an enormous organ, and a 'Miracle Room' full of discarded crutches. Groups of disciples engaged in non-stop prayer, participating in relays. Aimée, with a genius that owed something to Hollywood (and to which Billy Graham undoubtedly owes some of his own methods), held pageants with music, picture-shows of the Holy Land, and dramatized sermons, all accompanied by a vast choir. Her neighbour Carey McWilliams remarked felicitously that, 'Aimée kept the Ferris wheels and merry-go-rounds of religion turning night and day.' At the end of her sermons, she asked sinners to come forward to be saved; as the lights were lowered, and soft music soothed the audience, hundreds rose to their feet and moved down the aisles. Then Aimée would shout, 'Turn on the lights and clear the one-way street for Jesus,' and suddenly the music would turn into a brazen blare. Aimée was one of the earth's great showmen. For sheer entertainment her meetings surpassed anything that could be seen in the cinemas.

It was in 1925 that a new radio operator took over the Temple's radio station. His name was Kenneth G. Ormiston and he had a soothing, cultivated voice. At first, Aimée spoke to him only over the headphones; then they met by the Temple steps and and she drove him home to his wife. But soon Ormiston was no longer hurrying home to his wife once the programmes were over. Instead, he went to a room in the Ambassador Hotel, where Sister Aimée was waiting. In 1926 Aimée went on a visit to the Holy Land, financed by 'love offerings' from her followers. Ormiston was absent from California during this period, although it is not known for certain whether he travelled with Aimée. She was back in Los Angeles in May 1926, and continued her clandestine meetings with Ormiston in various hotels. On 14 May Ormiston rented a cottage in Carmel, told the landlord that he would be returning with his 'invalid wife', and went back to Los Angeles.

Four days later, Aimée disappeared. She had gone to the beach at Venice for a swim. She sat in a beach tent, working on sermon notes, and after a while, she sent her secretary off on some errand. When the secretary returned, Aimée had vanished. Her mother proclaimed from the steps of the Temple, 'She is with Jesus – pray for her.' For the next 32 days, her followers mounted a frantic search. Aircraft flew close to the waves; men in diving suits looked for her body on the ocean floor. Two followers committed suicide – a young man yelled 'I'm going after her' and leapt into the sea. Aimée's mother had flowers scattered from an aircraft on the spot. A collection of $36,000 was taken for a memorial.

On 27 May, a newspaper mentioned that Ormiston had also vanished; his wife had reported him missing. Further probing by reporters revealed that he had also been absent when Aimée was in the Holy Land. As all Los Angeles began to buzz with indecent rumour and speculation, Ormiston strolled into the search headquarters, denied all knowledge of Aimée's disappearance and vanished again.

The police of California began to suspect that there might be a connection between Aimée and Ormiston, and that if they could find one they would find the other. Suddenly the search was intensified. On the morning of 29 May Ormiston called at a Salinas garage, near Carmel, to collect his car; he was accompanied by a woman, and later that day, they registered as 'Mr and Mrs Frank Gibson' at a hotel in St Luis Obispo. That night, their car was stopped by a suspicious newspaper reporter. Ormond turned and headed back towards San Francisco. Five days later, on 23 June 1926, a resident of a cottage in Agua Prieta, just across the Mexican border from Douglas, Arizona, was awakened by a knocking at the door, to be confronted by a woman who claimed she had been the victim of a kidnapping. It was Aimée.

Her story was that she had been kidnapped by two men and a woman – Rose, Steve and Jake. She had been taken to a shack in Mexico and had eventually escaped. When she returned to Los Angeles, 30,000 people were waiting at the station and she was carried to her car through lanes of flowers. Her followers showed a tendency to forgive and forget, and the rest of the world might have done the same, if Aimée had not tried quite so hard to prove her innocence.

She kept asking what the police were doing to find the kidnappers and issued challenges over the radio. A grand jury declared that there was no evidence to indict anyone. Soon after that, someone tracked down her 'love nest' in Carmel. Ormiston, who was still in hiding, sent an affidavit stating that although he had stayed in the cottage with a woman who was not his wife, that woman was not Aimée. This seemed to be confirmed when a woman announced that the lady in question was her sister; Aimée publicly declared herself vindicated. But when the lady proved to be wanted by the police for passing bad cheques, the press once again showed a disposition to regard Aimée as an adulterous woman who had decided to brazen it out. Another grand jury was convened; this time, a follower of Aimée's vanished to the lavatory with a major piece of evidence – a scrap of paper found in the 'love nest' with Aimée's writing on it – and flushed it down the toilet. The grand jury was dismissed. Finally, Aimée was charged with conspiring with others to obstruct justice. She raised a 'fight the Devil fund' of $¼ million, explaining to her followers that she was being crucified by the forces of evil. The evidence against her looked overwhelming; chambermaids testified about her sessions in hotel rooms with Ormiston and the hotel registers left no doubt about it. She was identified as the 'Mrs McIntyre' of the Carmel 'love nest' and the cheque-bouncing lady who had supported Ormiston's story now admitted she had been paid by Aimée, who had carefully coached her in her story. And yet, in spite of all this, District Attorney Asa Keyes suddenly moved to dismiss the case against her – there was talk of a $30,000 bribe. (Keyes was later sentenced to prison for corruption in office.) Aimée announced that the Lord had rescued her and settled down to writing her autobiography, *In the Service of the King,* in which she repeated the kidnapping story.

Soon after this, Aimée set out on another lecture tour; this time the subject was her own life and she expected her audiences to pay for admission. To her surprise, few people seemed inclined to do this. It was the same when she went on a European tour in 1928. The faithful continued to regard Sister Aimée as a saint and a wronged woman but the general public seemed to regard her with a cynical amusement. Her publicity stunts, her public quarrels (with her mother, among others) and her law suits began to bore even the American Press. She chartered a liner for a crusade to the Holy Land but only a hundred followers turned up. For this occasion, Aimée had her chestnut hair bleached to blonde; her mother was indiscreet enough to mention that she had also had her face lifted and this alienated more of the faithful than the kidnapping escapade. In 1931, she decided to ignore her own teaching on divorce – she had always insisted that no divorced person should remarry during the lifetime of the other partner – and married an overweight radio announcer named Dave Hutton. Two days after the wedding, another woman sued Hutton for $200,000 for breach of promise.

When the case was tried, Hutton was ordered to pay $5,000. But when she heard the news, Aimée fainted and fractured her skull on the flagstone of the courtyard. She went to Europe to recuperate. Hutton sent her a telegram: 'Take your time, honey . . . Daddy wants a well woman.' But she and Hutton never lived together again.

During the remainder of her life she was sued 55 times in the courts of Los Angeles for unpaid bills, broken contracts, slander and other charges. There were a number of successful suits by relatives of Temple followers who had left their money to Aimée. She was as flamboyant as ever and as she grew older, her style in clothes became increasingly girlish, but the world had ceased to be interested in her.

On the morning of 27 September 1944, Aimée Semple McPherson was found unconscious in her hotel room in Oakland, California, with sleeping capsules scattered around her on the floor; she died later in the day. It was never established whether she had taken an overdose deliberately or accidentally.

MACPHERSON, JAMES

THE OSSIAN SCANDAL

There appeared in Edinburgh in 1760 a small volume entitled *Fragments of Ancient Poetry, collected in the Highlands of Scotland and translated from the Galic or Erse Language.* The translator was one James MacPherson. To say the work created a sensation would be an exaggeration, but it aroused warm interest. The classical spirit of the age of Dr Johnson was gradually giving way to an exciting new attitude that would be called 'Romanticism'. Poets like James Thomson and William Cowper were observing that nature was beautiful and the novel – virtually invented by a printer called Samuel Richardson less than twenty years earlier – was teaching a new generation to daydream. The world of mountains and mists and heroic simplicity of these 'fragments of ancient poetry' struck an immediate chord in the heart of all true Scots. It was almost an implicit criticism of the kind of stilted, artificial stuff that had passed for literature in England for the past half century.

James MacPherson, the son of a poor farmer, was only 24 at the time; he had studied divinity at Aberdeen and Edinburgh and was now working as a schoolmaster, being too young to become a minister. He had become a friend of a poet called John Home, whose play *Douglas* was popular and who had published a poem called 'The Highlander' two years earlier.

Now Home and other friends – like Hugh Blair and Dr Alexander Carlyle of Inveresk – urged him to go on a tour of the Scottish Highlands to gather more poetry. Blair had written the introduction to the *Fragments,* in which he had stated that these disjointed pieces were part of a longer epic. MacPherson was oddly reluctant; he pleaded lack of money. Whereupon some of his new friends invited him to a special dinner and proposed to raise enough money to send him to the Highlands. Since they included a distinguished peer – Lord Elibank – the poor farmer's son found it hard to refuse. A subscription was raised and more than £100 subscribed – the philosopher Hume was a donor. Armed with letters signed by distinguished people, James MacPherson set off for the Highlands. He was accompanied on his first journey by a relative, Lachlan MacPherson, who helped him to take down recitations in Gaelic. He later made a trip to Mull and the coast of Argyll and returned with still more transcriptions and manuscripts. Since he was not a Gaelic scholar, friends helped him to translate these. Finally, there appeared in 1762 a lengthy work called: *Fingal, an Ancient Epic Poem in Six Books, together with Several Other Poems composed by Ossian, the son of Fingal.*

It was this that made MacPherson famous, not simply in Britain, but all over Europe. It sold out and immediately reprinted. It was translated into German, French, Spanish, Italian, Dutch, Danish, Russian, Polish and Swedish. The Prince of Sweden was even named after Ossian's son Oscar and eventually succeeded to the throne as King Oscar I. MacPherson went to London and became a literary lion.

The Ossian poems were written in a kind of rhymical prose which had a certain bareness and wildness that produced an effect like music. With its tales of heroic warriors, queenly maidens and 'battles long ago', it often brings to mind Tolkien's *Lord of the Rings* – particularly those appendices written in the style of the old sagas. MacPherson set out to create a mood of nostalgia:

A tale of the times of old! The deeds of days of other years!
The murmur of thy streams, O Lora! brings back the memory of the past. The sound of thy woods, Garmallar, is lovely in mine ear . . .
Who comes from the land of strangers, with his thousands around him? The sunbeam pours its bright stream before him; his hair meets the wind of his hills. His face is settled from war. He is calm as the evening beam that looks from the cloud of the west, on Cona's silent vale . . .

The English were less enthusiastic about Ossian than the rest of Europe. After the rising of 1745, the Scots were not popular. Critics like Samuel Johnson had a certain vested interest in the highly civilized 'classical' style of the 'age of reason'. Johnson was contemptuous; when Boswell asked him if any modern man could have written Ossian he replied, 'Yes, sir, many men, many women and many children.'

Fingal presented some baffling historical anomalies. Fingal was supposed to be king of a state called Morven, on the west coast of Scotland; he lived in the third century AD, at the time of the Roman emperors Severus and Caracalla. But the poem is about a Viking invasion of Ireland. When the Irish hero Cuchulan is routed, Fingal rushes to help him and expels the Vikings. The Vikings, however, did not invade until the middle of the eighth century AD. Moreover, as a learned clergyman called Warner pointed out in a pamphlet soon after *Fingal's* appearance, the original of the Scottish hero Fingal is the Irish hero, Finn MacCool. It is unlikely that Finn ever saw a Roman in his life yet Ossian has him fighting the Romans in Scotland. As to Cuchulain, he was some three centuries earlier, at the time of Christ. While it is true that a few distortions might have crept into poems which, according to MacPherson, had been recited down the centuries by Gaelic bards, it seems unlikely that the bards would have committed such a howler as making an eighth-century Viking meet a first-century Irishman.

Two years after *Fingal*, MacPherson produced another Ossian epic called *Temora*. Purely as literature, this was much inferior to *Fingal*, being altogether more bombastic. Hume wrote to Blair that most people took it for 'a palpable and impudent forgery'. MacPherson had written a lengthy introduction to *Temora* and made the mistake of including a specimen of the original Gaelic poem; experts soon pointed out that it contained several modernisms.

There were other anomalies. MacPherson's earliest find was a poem called 'The Death of Oscar', and it gave a completely different version of the Oscar legend than the one based on Irish tradition. In MacPherson's version, Oscar kills his friend Dermid in a quarrel over a girl. There were many variants of the original legend but all of them have Dermid dying at a boar hunt from a poisoned bristle. It seemed highly unlikely that Ossian had produced a different version. MacPherson recognized the force of the argument and suggested that there were two Oscars, but this was also denied by Irish scholars.

In 1773, Dr Johnson travelled to Scotland with Boswell; his *Journey to the Western Isles* appeared in 1775, and contained some scathing words about Ossian which led MacPherson to write to the publisher and demand that they should be removed. He even sent Johnson an announcement to insert in the book; Johnson ignored him. When MacPherson sent him a challenge, he bought himself a large, stout stick. MacPherson's publisher had an announcement printed in the newspapers, declaring that MacPherson had deposited the originals of the Ossian poems in his own shop in 1762 for anyone to examine and that he had even tried to raise a subscription to publish them in the original Gaelic but without success. This story was disingenuous; the 'manuscripts' MacPherson had deposited were his own transcriptions of Gaelic poetry and would have proved very little.

Johnson, like most critics, was willing to accept that Ossian was not pure invention. There were many genuine fragments of ancient poetry there, as MacPherson's fellow collectors, who had accompanied him on his journeys to the Highlands, could testify. But there was no original 'epic'. MacPherson had stuck fragments of Gaelic poetry into his own composition as he felt inclined.

The clash between Johnson and MacPherson was the talk of literary London and Johnson's criticisms eventually led most people to conclude that Ossian was largely MacPherson's own composition. One of MacPherson's original patrons, David Hume, practically admitted as much when he described how MacPherson had visited him before his journey to the Highlands and had outlined the plot of *Fingal*.

MacPherson still had his supporters. One of these, William Shaw, set out for the Highlands in 1778 to gather materials for a Gaelic dictionary and to attempt to prove that the Gaelic legends of Ossian were genuine. It was his intention to submit any material he found to a minister or justice of the peace, so no one could question it later. He spent six months travelling around the Highlands, plying old gentlemen with snuff and whisky and persuading them to recite any fragments of Gaelic poetry they could recall. But although he heard many legends and fairy tales, there was no trace of the story of Fingal or Temora as told by Ossian. He continued his search in Ireland and met with little success. Then, finally, it dawned on him that MacPherson had been lying all along and that the poems were his own compositions. He published an *Enquiry into the Authenticity of the Poems ascribed to Ossian* and it added fuel to the flames of the controversy. MacPherson himself chose to remain silent which most people construed to mean that he had nothing much to add.

MacPherson had no reason to regret Ossian, even if he had been led into concocting it by the admiration of noble patrons. It laid the foundations of a prosperous career. He spent two years in Florida as secretary to the governor, wrote a history of Great Britain and Ireland that was mainly a glorification of the Celts and an attack on the English, translated the *Iliad* into Ossianic prose, and caused a scandal with a continuation of Hume's *History of England* in which he accused some of the most illustrious families of treachery and treason. He secured a place supervising the newspapers on behalf of the Court, moved into a house in Westminster, and bought another in Putney. Towards the end of his life – he died in 1796 – he became a Scottish landowner and built himself a mansion overlooking the River Spey. He left a considerable sum of money, some of which went to support five illegitimate children whom he had fathered on five different mothers. He was buried, at his own request, in Westminster Abbey.

After his death, at the age of 59, a commission of enquiry was set up by the Highland Society to try to settle the question of the authenticity of the poems once and for all. Their report in 1805 repeated what was already known: that there were many fragments of 'Ossianic' poetry around in the Highlands but no continuous epics such as *Fingal* or *Temora*. But in 1886–7, a series of articles in the *Celtic Magazine* by Alexander Macbain established beyond all doubt that the author of the Ossian poems was ignorant of Celtic history, that the life portrayed in the poems was totally unlike that known historically about the period, and that the Gaelic fragments quoted by MacPherson to prove their authenticity were a translation from MacPherson's English version, not vice versa. Finally, he pointed out that MacPherson's early poem, The Highlander', published four years before *Fingal,* bore a close resemblance to the Ossian poems. MacPherson had tried hard to suppress this later, without success.

Whether a fraud or not, the Ossian poems exercised a tremendous influence on a whole generation and led to the creation of the Romantic movement in literature.

MAXWELL, ROBERT

THE STRANGE DOWNFALL AND DEATH OF A 'TYCOON'

The story behind the drowning of publishing baron Robert Maxwell on 5 November 1991, is still a mystery. Since his giant publishing empire had literally collapsed under him, it may well have been suicide. But then, Maxwell was so widely detested that there was inevitably speculation whether it might actually have been murder. Accident seems the least likely of the three.

Ian Robert Maxwell was born in Slatinske Doly, a Ruthenian village on the Czech-Romanian border, on 10 January 1923. His real name was Jan Ludvik Hoch, and his family were poor Jewish peasants, Mechel Hoch and his wife Hannah. Maxwell once claimed that he had not owned a pair of shoes until he was seven years old, and this may well be true. The child's original name was Abraham Lajbi, but by the time Maxwell was born, his birthplace had changed its position from Hungary to Czechoslovakia, and the Czechs insisted on the change of name.

Because the orthodox Jewish community disliked the emphasis on Christianity in the local school, they organized their own education system, so Maxwell learned Hebrew, and proved to be a brilliant linguist who picked up languages easily. This ability was to launch him on his career as an entrepreneur.

When Hitler invaded the Sudetenland in late September 1938, Ruthenia became Hungarian yet again. Since the Hungarian leader, Admiral Nicolas Horthy, was an anti-semite, and was forcing young Jews into labour battalions, Maxwell's parents decided to send him to Budapest. His progress during the war is unrecorded, but the Czech unit in which he was fighting was evacuated to Liverpool on the fall of France. Most of Maxwell's family perished in concentration camps.

Maxwell joined the Pioneer Corps, learned English with ease, and changed his name to DuMaurier. Always charming, he impressed the brigade commander of the Sixth Battalion of the North Staffordshire Regiment and was transferred to Intelligence. In France after D-day, now calling himself Jones, he was promoted to Second Lieutenant, and it was his Brigadier, Carthew-Yourston who suggested that he should change his name to Robert Maxwell. In Paris he fell in love with Elizabeth Meynard, and married her.

He fought with distinction at Paarlo, on the Belgium-Dutch border, and received the military cross for his bravery in leading his platoon in counter-attacks on the Germans. It was Montgomery himself who presented the medal. The end of the war saw him in Hamburg, where his position as one of the few Intelligence officers who spoke nine languages, including Russian and Polish, made him invaluable to the British. He served in the Allied Control Commission working as a captain in the Public Relations and Information Services Control, which meant that, in effect, he became a kind of censor, who had to be approached by anyone wishing to publish books or newspapers. A man named Arno Scholtz applied for a licence to publish a newspaper to be called *Der Telegraf*, which was granted, and it soon became the best known in Berlin. Maxwell and Scholtz became close friends, and it was Scholtz who introduced Maxwell to Ferdinand Springer, the head of Springer Verlag, a publishing company specializing in science – they even published Einstein. Soon Maxwell became the British and American distributor for Springer, and bought a publisher called Pergamon Press for £13,000. By now, Maxwell had moved back to London. With a fellow Czech named Low-Bel, he bought German newspapers for sale to prisoners of war in Britain.

Springer was delighted to be distributed by this brilliant young man, whose official position meant that he could circumvent the many regulations imposed by the occupying forces. This was the beginning of Maxwell's enormous fortune.

Soon, Pergamon Press became the most prominent scientific publisher in Britain and, by 1957, was publishing over a hundred books and journals a year.

In 1964, Maxwell was elected to the UK Parliament as a Labour member. But Maxwell was never a popular Member of Parliament. He lacked the kind of tact required to be a good politician. Soon he was widely disliked for his boorishness and his obvious determination to make an impact. His relations with the Soviet Union were extremely close, partly because Pergamon published so many Soviet scientific journals.

It was in May 1968, travelling by train from Moscow to Kiev, that he was approached by Zaloman Litvin, a Jewish officer in Soviet military intelligence, who had also been a Soviet spy attempting to steal America's atomic secrets. He brought Maxwell to Moscow, where he was taken to meet Yuri Andropov, head of the KGB. Russia at the time was angry about the 'Prague Spring', the attempt of the Czechs to gain a certain freedom from the Russian yoke. Alexander Dubcek was enormously popular, and the Soviets anticipated having to use force to bring him to heel. They wanted Maxwell's help in persuading the British Parliament to accept this. And that is exactly what Maxwell did. When, on 26 August 1968, Russian tanks rolled into Prague and the Czech bid for freedom was crushed, Maxwell stood up in the House of Commons and gave an influential speech, underlining the importance of continuing détente with the Soviets. He carried the day, and Labour's protest to Moscow was feeble.

It was in 1969 that Maxwell's financial methods suddenly became the subject of harsh criticism. The American company, Leasco, made a takeover bid for Pergamon Press, but the accountants concluded that Pergamon's accounts were fraudulent, and the takeover panel described Maxwell as a liar. The Department of Trade and Industry declared that Maxwell was not fit to run a public company. In 1970, Maxwell was defeated in the General Election, and ceased to be the Member of Parliament for Buckingham.

Maxwell now demanded a favour in return for his support of the Soviets. He needed them to bail Pergamon out of trouble. So the Soviet Union agreed that Pergamon should publish biographies of communist leaders, which would be published in huge editions of 50,000 each. According to Tom Bower, in *Maxwell: the Final Verdict*, Maxwell deceived the KGB and Leonid Brezhnev about the number of copies published. The subsidy from Russia never appeared in Pergamon's accounts.

With the aid of the Communist Bloc, Pergamon was again showing a healthy profit by 1974. And at this time, Maxwell began to show signs of that almost manic desire to add to his empire – the passion that was finally to bring him down – by buying the British Printing Corporation (BPC) in 1981, then the Mirror Group Newspapers in 1984. BPC, which was on its last legs when Maxwell took it over, had soon been revived by immense injections of cash borrowed from the banks, who were deeply impressed by Pergamon's success.

The *Daily Mirror* was also having problems when Maxwell bought Mirror Group Newspapers in 1984. Tom Bower has pointed out that Maxwell was jealous of Rupert Murdoch's success, and went out of his way to try and impress him. In February 1991, Maxwell rang Murdoch and declared: 'We're two big publishers – we should talk.' Accordingly, Murdoch went to see Maxwell in Maxwell House, making it clear in advance that he only had exactly forty minutes to spare. Maxwell apparently spent the whole forty minutes boasting about his worldwide diplomacy, his intimate relations with the Kremlin, and with the Government of Israel. At the end of forty minutes, Murdoch asked: 'Is there anything else we need to talk about?' 'No,' said Maxwell. And as Murdoch went down into the street, he exclaimed: 'What was all that about? He's ludicrous.'

It could have been this desire to rival Murdoch that brought about Maxwell's downfall. He bought the American publisher, Macmillan, for $2.6 billion, which was generally regarded as paying over the odds, and bought the Official Airlines Guide for $750 million. He also bought the Berlitz Language School and then the New York *Daily News*.

Maxwell's obituary in the *Encyclopedia Britannica Yearbook* summarizes the problems that he brought on himself:

The recession and high interest rates reportedly intensified his financial woes ... In 1991, to generate cash, Maxwell floated Mirror Group Newspapers on the London Stock Market and sold part of Pergamon to a Dutch publisher. Nonetheless in May 1991 he acquired the financially troubled New York *Daily News* and was a willing front-page hero. Maxwell continued to shuffle businesses in and out of both a family trust and holding company, which he had incorporated (1984) in Liechtenstein, and a Gibraltar-based operation he opened in May 1991.

It adds: 'The value of Maxwell's vast holdings was impossible to pin down, but it became clear that his debts exceeded profits.' In fact, all his life, Maxwell had shuffled profits in and out of holding companies, so that it was difficult to pin them down. Says John Canning: 'Huge misappropriations of funds, most disgracefully from the Mirror Group Pension Fund, had taken place; the Byzantine structure of his financial empire with its interlocking complex of private and public companies, made it fiendishly difficult to track down the missing money now estimated at £2 billion.'

The only thing that seems clear is that Maxwell had spent far too much money, and was about to be engulfed by his debts.

On the morning of 31 October 1991, Maxwell flew from Luton in his Gulfstream jet to join his yacht, *The Lady Ghislaine*, at Gibraltar. He was suffering from a heavy cold. They set sail at four o'clock that afternoon. Two days later, the yacht put into harbour at Funchal, and Maxwell went for a swim and visited a casino. On Sunday they went on to Tenerife, and the captain, Angus Rankin, reported that Maxwell was in a good mood throughout the cruise, swimming, relaxing, working and taking endless telephone calls. If he was suicidal, he certainly did not show it.

Nevertheless, Maxwell had a great deal on his mind during those last few days. Since the previous November, his companies had been in trouble. The Maxwell Communications Corporation had been forced to try and raise money, and the international banks were worried. His youngest son, Kevin, had been trying to persuade various possible backers that the financial squeeze was only temporary. The truth was that his father was on the edge of bankruptcy. When Credit Suisse turned down a loan of £50 million, Kevin Maxwell told their representative, Julie Maitland, 'We can provide ample security for the loans.' But the share certificates offered for security were registered in the name of Bishopsgate Investment Management, a private company established by Maxwell to manage nine pension funds of his 23,400 employees. These contained about £727 million. So, in fact, Maxwell was borrowing money from his employees without their knowledge.

Moreover, Kevin offered Julia Maitland 500,000 Berlitz shares, owned by Maxwell's public company, as security for this deal. In effect, the Maxwells were using money that belonged to the public company for their own private purposes.

Maxwell had another problem. The American investigative journalist, Seymour Hersh, had alleged in his book, *The Samson Option*, that Maxwell was working for the Israeli Secret Service, Mossad, and had been responsible for the betrayal of the man who had blown the whistle on Israel's secret nuclear weapon. He was Mordechai Vanunu, a technician who had taken photographs of the Dimona nuclear facility, and sold them to the *Sunday Times*. When Vanunu went to London, the day before the photographs were published, he was entrapped by a beautiful Israeli secret agent and lured to

Rome, where he was drugged, kidnapped, and taken to Israel. There he was sentenced to eighteen years' imprisonment. Hersh alleged that Vanunu's address in London had been betrayed to Mossad on Maxwell's orders by the *Daily Mirror's* foreign editor. Maxwell, declaring that the whole thing was a 'ludicrous invention', issued a writ for defamation. But when two Members of Parliament mentioned the accusation in the House of Commons, they were protected by Parliamentary privilege, so that every newspaper was able to publish the allegations.

Maxwell's New York *Daily News* was also doing badly, its circulation having sunk to the level (720,000) which would allow advertisers to demand refunds. Maxwell asked one of the executives to massage the circulation figures upwards, but he had refused.

As Maxwell's yacht continued south, Kevin Maxwell rang from London to say that 55 bankers were telephoning for reassurances about their loans. Lloyds, to whom Maxwell owed £166 million, flatly turned down a request for a further 10 to 20 million.

The Credit Suisse, however, lent Maxwell a further £12.8 million, secured by shares that Julia Maitland believed to be owned by Maxwell. Kevin had to exert all his considerable charm to soothe various other bankers from Sumitomo, Salamons, Bank of Nova Scotia, Citibank and Swiss Bank, and managed to get some of the loans rescheduled. Another bank, Goldman Sachs, was also badgering Maxwell for repayment, and when Maxwell had telephoned the bank a month before that last trip, a lawyer there had flatly declined to see Maxwell, saying 'I'm not interested – our only interest is in being paid.' Maxwell demonstrated his determination and persuasive power by walking into the bank and talking them into accepting a payment of £5 million a week.

As Maxwell's yacht departed, the *Financial Times* was about to publish a report revealing that his debts were double those that he publicly acknowledged. Goldman Sachs decided to start selling Maxwell shares. And on the afternoon of Tuesday 5 November 1991, Maxwell's company shares were suspended on the Stock Exchange. Kevin rang his father on his yacht to tell him about this, and that the Swiss Bank was threatening to call in the Fraud Squad.

At 11:10 on the morning of Tuesday 5 November, a call from New York was put through to Maxwell's stateroom. When there was no reply, Captain Rankin went down to investigate and found the cabin door was locked. He entered with the master key and found it empty. Maxwell's nightshirt was on the bed.

A search of the ship failed to disclose his presence, and at 11:30 am, the captain phoned Kevin Maxwell to tell him his father had disappeared.

Hours later, a Spanish air-sea rescue helicopter winched the body of Robert Maxwell aboard – all 22 stone of him. It was naked, and had been floating face up. An autopsy the following day, carried out by Doctor Carlos Lopez de Lamela, Doctor Maria Ramos and Louisa Garcia Cohen revealed little water in Maxwell's lungs, a graze on his forehead, and a cut behind his ear. The result was a finding of natural death – apparently there was no sign of a heart attack. But the autopsy reports also revealed that he had a chronic lung disease and a heart ailment. Maxwell's body was flown to Jerusalem, where he was buried.

The tone of British obituaries was at first respectful. Maxwell was referred to frequently by his nickname of 'Cap'n Bob', and no one seemed to have any doubt that, piratical or not, he was a remarkable man. But when the plundering of the pension funds became apparent, the tone changed completely. Maxwell was suddenly seen for what he was – a crook on a gigantic scale.

In due course his two sons, Kevin and Ian, and two directors, went on trial for fraud. At the trial in 1995, Kevin's defence was that his company had been plunged into bankruptcy by the City. (Kevin Maxwell had himself gone bankrupt for £406 million.) Kevin and Ian Maxwell and Larry Trachtenberg were all found not guilty.

How did Maxwell die? A widely held opinion is that it was suicide, but another possibility, mentioned by John Canning in a book on unsolved mysteries, is that he may have been murdered. Photographs of Maxwell's body taken during a final post-mortem before he was interred show that he was badly bruised. A French pathologist who examined the evidence said that it was probable that Maxwell had suffered a violent blow to the back of the head with a weapon. Canning points out that if, in fact, Maxwell was an agent for Mossad, and also an arms dealer, he might have been targeted by many Arab organizatons. 'The slackly guarded, high-profile tycoon in the slow-moving *Lady Ghislaine* would not have been a difficult "hit" for a group of determined assassins.'

But Tom Bower writes:

Distillation of the pathologists' opinions leads towards the most reliable conclusion. Feeling unwell, the deceased had been on deck for fresh air. Stumbling, probably from a minor heart attack, he had fallen backwards, passing under the steel cord or over the rail and, as he had twisted to grab it, had hit the side of his head against the boat. In double agony, he had lost his grip and dropped into the sea. There he died, some time later, from exhaustion or a heart attack.

However, in November 2002, a book by two investigative journalists offered the most astonishing solution to the mystery so far: that Maxwell was murdered by an Israeli hit team. The book, called *The Assassination of Robert Maxwell: Israel's Superspy*, is by Gordon Thomas and Martin Dillon. They cite various Israeli sources, the reporters state that, as he realized that he was close to ruin, with debts of £2.2 billion, Maxwell approached Mossad, the intelligence service (for which he had worked), imploring them to exert their influence with banks in Israel and, if possible, in London and New York, to provide him with money. After an increasing number of desperate phone calls, he was told that it was impossible: providing that kind of money was simply not in their remit. 'But he refused to heed the spy chiefs' implicit warning not to involve them in his personal disaster', claim Thomas and Dillon.

Maxwell now made his major mistake; he attempted to apply pressure by threatening to reveal all he had done for Mossad and Israel. What he wanted was £400 million.

At that point, Mossad decided that Maxwell had to die. So the assassination was arranged.

It is not surprising that Maxwell seemed cheerful when he set out in his yacht. He believed that an Israeli team was coming on board *The Lady Ghislaine* in the early hours of the morning to give him a bank draft for £400 million.

That evening, Ian Maxwell made a speech on his father's behalf at the Anglo-Israeli Association in London. It had gone down well. And when Ian ended the phone conversation: 'See you tomorrow, dad,' Maxwell responded: 'You bet.'

At 4:25 that morning Maxwell was seen standing on the after deck by the second engineer, Leo Leonard; he was staring out at the lights of the Gran Canaria. From where he was standing, the security cameras could not have picked him up – which is probably why he often chose that spot to urinate over the side. Seeing Leonard, Maxwell asked him to turn up the air conditioning in his cabin, and Leonard went below to carry out the order.

According to Thomas and Dillon, during a trip ashore a few hours earlier, Maxwell had received a call telling him that the packet he was expecting would be delivered on deck between 4 and 5 am.

Then, say the authors, a dinghy came alongside from a nearby yacht; it contained three men in frogmen's suits. They used rubberized grappling hooks to come silently on board. One removed a syringe from a rubber pouch on his belt. Within seconds, the assassin had plunged the syringe into Maxwell's neck behind his right ear. It contained a deadly nerve toxin. Maxwell's unconscious body was lowered into the sea, and within minutes, the assassination team was back on board their own yacht.

When a young Spanish pathologist, Dr Maria Ramos, helped perform the post mortem, she noted the tiny puncture behind the right ear – it looked like a mosquito bite. Lacking other evidence, the Spanish team finally decided that death was probably due to heart failure.

This version of Maxwell's death invites a few obvious doubts. Would not Maxwell be suspicious to be told that three frogmen were coming aboard simply to deliver a bank draft? Surely there were simpler ways of handing it over than all this cloak and dagger stuff? And would the Israeli secret service have murdered one of their country's major benefactors? (The answer to that is, sadly, yes – Mossad is known as one of the most ruthless intelligence organizations in the world.) And what could Maxwell have said that would have embarrassed Mossad so deeply that they wanted him dead? The answer to that question has probably been buried with Maxwell.

It has to be admitted that this story certainly provides us with a convincing account of why and how Robert Maxwell died.

MAYERLING AFFAIR, THE

DOUBLE-SUICIDE IN A HUNTING LODGE

The suicide of Archduke Rudolf of Habsburg after killing his eighteen-year-old mistress has been described as the greatest royal scandal of modern times.

If Rudolf had lived, he would have presided over a collapsing empire. The dynasty of the Habsburgs had dominated Europe for seven hundred years. But by the end of the nineteenth century, it had spread itself too far; it had too many ill-assorted subjects and great social changes were ripping apart the old fabric. Subject nations wanted their independence. The 1848 revolution had made the Emperor Franz Joseph determined to resist all change but it was like trying to hold on the lid of a pressure cooker by manual force.

Franz Joseph was a rigid disciplinarian, who rose at 4 a.m. to work on state papers; his life was one of exact routine. His empress, Elizabeth, was beautiful and sensitive and she found the atmosphere of her husband's court – dominated by her mother-in-law – impossible to stomach; she spent most of her time travelling over Europe, permanently dissatisfied.

Her eldest son Rudolf had his father's obstinacy and his mother's sensitiveness. Born in August 1858, he became an army officer and took pride in the number of his sexual conquests, entering their names in a ledger – red for aristocrats, black for commoners. He grew bored with seduction and flirted with left-wing ideas. Later, he wrote newspaper articles that revealed he had considerable literary talent. He was indeed highly intelligent.

It seems conceivable that at some point he contracted venereal disease. What is certain is that he contracted the rich dilettante's disease of boredom and a sense of meaninglessness. 'He seemed to doubt the validity of everything he did', says one commentator. His father declined to allow him any taste of responsibility. At 23 he was married to the seventeen-year-old Princess Stephanie of Belgium, a silly, selfish, empty-headed girl, who bore him a daughter. Rudolf became increasingly depressed and listless, and began to take morphine. When the German emperor inspected Franz Joseph's army in 1888, he protested that the infantry ought not to be in the charge of an incompetent like Rudolf; he was removed – one more blow to his self-esteem. To some brother officers he made the surprising proposal of a suicide pact, which they failed to take seriously, although it was reported to the police.

His relationship with his father became increasingly bitter. He began to plot, in a rather half-hearted manner, his father's downfall. His friend Count Stephen Károlyi was a Hungarian patriot and he planned to speak in the Hungarian parliament against granting funds to Franz Joseph's army. Rudolf seems to have agreed to a hare-brained scheme of Károlyi's to oust Franz Joseph and put him on the throne. (It might, in fact, have saved the Austrian empire if it had ever happened, since Rudolf's liberal tendencies may have defused the tensions.) A butler reported that the emperor bitterly upbraided his son for disloyalty.

Maria Vetsera was an attractive teenager of Greek extraction, whose mother had married into the minor Austrian nobility. She caught a few glimpses of Rudolf in society and decided she was passionately in love with him. Through her friend, Countess Marie Larisch, who was Rudolf's cousin, she succeeded in being presented to him in the Prater in Vienna. Rudolf was not one to turn down the opportunity to accept a girl's virginity when it was offered; the two became lovers in 1888. By this time he was already brooding on suicide.

On 28 January 1889, Rudolf received a telegram from Budapest. As he threw it aside he was heard to mutter, 'It has to be. There is no other way.' He spent the day writing farewell letters, then set out for his hunting lodge at Mayerling. He had arranged to meet Maria on the way; that morning, she slipped away from her mother and made off in a carriage sent by Rudolf. It seems likely that she had already agreed to the suicide pact. They met at an inn.

Rudolf had arranged a hunting party at his lodge and various friends were also there. But on 29 January 1889, he protested that he had a cold and stayed indoors. That evening, he dined with Count Hoyos, while Maria stayed upstairs. When Hoyos left, Rudolf's valet, Loschek, entertained them by singing for them. They both wrote farewell letters – Maria told her sister: 'We are both going blissfully into the uncertain beyond ...' They then discussed whether they preferred to die by poison or a bullet and decided on the revolver. Maria noted this decision on an ashtray. They went up to the bedroom where Rudolf shot Maria immediately. He himself waited until six in the morning, when he went downstairs and told Loschek to prepare breakfast. He returned to his room, drank a glass of brandy, and shot himself in the head. The bodies were discovered a few hours later.

Franz Joseph was deeply shocked by the news, and the empress broke down when she read Rudolf's farewell letter. At first the court insisted that Rudolf had died of heart failure but the truth could not be held back for ever. There was a wrangle with the Cardinal Secretary of State, Rampolla, as to whether Rudolf could be buried in consecrated ground as he had committed suicide. Eventually he was laid to rest in the Capucin Crypt in Vienna. Maria's naked body was thrown into a woodshed immediately after she was discovered and was not recovered for two days.

It is still not clear why Rudolf killed himself and why he, a Catholic, chose to die with the murder of Maria Vetsera on his conscience. The answer to the latter question may be that he was a physical coward and wanted someone else to die with him. He was probably not in love with Maria for he had spent the night before leaving Vienna with a prostitute named Mizzi Kaspter. It seems conceivable that she was as anxious to die with the man she adored as he was to have someone to die with him. He may even have felt he was conferring a favour on her by involving her in the suicide pact – after all, he was heir to the throne and she was a nobody.

In 1983, ex-Empress Zita, the last survivor of the Habsburg monarchy, caused a sensation when she announced that the double-suicide was really a political murder. She claimed that she had received this information from her husband, Emperor Karl, and from Prince Rudolf's sisters, Archduchess Gisela and Archduchess Marie-Valerie and her aunts Archduchess Maria Theresa and the Duchess Marie-José. 'I have recorded precisely everything that was told to me under the seal of deepest sympathy. I intend to publish these documents which are among my personal papers when the time is right.' According to the ex-Empress, Prince Rudolf was assassinated because of his republican sympathies and because he had made many political enemies. In a cloister built out of part of the hunting lodge, Carmelite nuns in a silent order still pray day and night for the 'three dead' of Mayerling. Why three, rather than two, remains another mystery; according to some, Maria Vetsera was expecting Rudolf's child.

The Empress points out that an enormous amount of documentation has disappeared from the state archives, including a 2,000-word telegram which the Emperor sent to Pope Leo XIII arguing that in spite of the official suicide explanation, his son had a right to a Christian burial. This telegram has also disappeared from the Vatican archives.

In September 1898, the Empress Elizabeth was stepping into a boat at Geneva when she was stabbed to death by a young anarchist named Luigi Lucheni. There were those who felt her death was a release. Since Rudolf's suicide she had been wandering all over Europe like an unhappy shade.

Rudolf was succeeded as heir to the throne by his cousin, Archduke Franz Ferdinand. It was the assassination of the archduke and his wife at Sarajevo on 28 June 1914 that precipitated World War I, and brought about the final destruction of the Austrian Empire.

NOVELLO, IVOR

THE RED ROLLS-ROYCE SCANDAL

In April 1944, a year before the end of World War II, newspapers all over England carried headlines: Famous Actor Jailed For Petrol Offence. Ivor Novello, Britain's most famous matinée idol, had been sentenced to two months' imprisonment for an offence that amounted to fraud.

Ivor Novello was born David Ivor Davies in Cardiff, Wales, the son of an accountant and a music teacher. He was taught singing by his mother and proved to be brilliantly gifted. At the age of ten he took first prize for singing at a National Eisteddfod and his soprano voice won him a singing scholarship to Magdalen College, Oxford. He wanted to become a composer and conductor. His first song was published when he was sixteen, and was performed – without much success – at the Royal Albert Hall in London with Novello as accompanist. His first successful song, 'The Little Damozel', appeared when he was seventeen, and was soon being sung by every soprano in the country. At this time, he also moved to London, supported by a modest income from his songs. He became famous at 21, in 1914, with the song 'Keep the Home Fires Burning', which became almost a second national anthem during World War I. The singer, John McCormick, earned £20,000 from his recording of this song alone.

During the war Novello served in the Royal Naval Air Service but after two crashes he was transferred to the Air Ministry. There, in 1916, he wrote half the music for a show called *Theodore and* Co. produced by the actor George Grossmith. His fellow composer was Jerome Kern. The show ran for eighteen months at the Gaiety.

After the war, Novello was asked if he would act in a film *The Call of the Blood* which was filmed in Rome. It was an immense success. Novello had exactly the right kind of romantic good looks for a silent screen star and acting ability was hardly required – although he had his share of that too. In the 1920s he was a film star, an actor-manager, a composer and a playwright. People argued whether he or John Barrymore had 'the world's most handsome profile'. He starred in Hitchcock's 'first true film' *The Lodger* in 1926 – it has become a classic of the silent cinema. But it was in 1935 that he achieved a new dimension of fame with *Glamorous Night,* a combination of drama and musical with lavish spectacle. His formula was escapist romance and it was exactly what the audiences of the 1930s craved. *Careless Rapture* (1936) and *The Dancing Years* (1939) repeated the success. When World War II broke out in 1939 he had a luxurious flat in the Aldwych and a country home near Maidenhead. He was driven around in a red Rolls-Royce inscribed with his initials in black.

As the petrol shortage increased, it became increasingly difficult for Novello to travel from London to his country home for the weekend. His secretary wrote to the Regional Transport Commissioner's office to request extra petrol for him to drive to Maidenhead on the grounds that he needed to spend the weekends there writing his plays. The application was twice turned down. Just before Christmas 1942, Novello went into his dressing room where there was a crowd of admirers and asked despondently, 'Anyone want a Rolls? Mine's no good to me.'

Among the admirers in the room was a dumpy, middle-aged woman who had adored Novello from afar for years and gradually managed to get herself accepted among his retinue. He knew her as Grace Walton but her real name was Dora Constable. She now told Novello that she might be able to solve his problem. She was, she said, the secretary of the managing director of a firm with an office at Reading. She suggested that she might be able to apply for a special licence if the car was transferred to her firm for 'war work'. All this was arranged by Novello's secretary. The car was formally transferred into the firm's name; the firm even took over the insurance policy. Then Dora Constable wrote to the Regional Transport Commissioner to ask for a licence to 'facilitate speedier transport by the managing director and his staff between our many works and factories'. A few weeks later she collected the permit and handed it to Novello. He was effusively grateful and gave her a pair of earrings that had belonged to his mother, who had recently died.

Whether the firm actually made use of the initialled Rolls-Royce is not clear. Novello's biographer Peter Noble implies that it did, and that Novello then simply used the car 'from time to time' to take him from London to Maidenhead. But if this is so, then it is difficult to see why the firm was shocked to discover that it was supposed to be the owner of Ivor Novello's Rolls-Royce. For this is what happened in October 1943, almost two years after Novello had received his permit. The managing director of the firm rang Novello and asked him to come to his office. On arrival, he learned that his admirer was not called Grace Walton but Dora Constable, and that she was not the managing director's secretary but a filing clerk. The firm knew nothing whatever about the deal with the Rolls-Royce.

Novello realized that he could be in serious trouble. Not long before, the bandleader Jack Hylton had been fined £155 and sentenced to two weeks in jail for a similar petrol-rationing offence. (In the event the jail sentence was quashed.)

Novello decided against a cover-up – he felt it was not his fault. He informed the authorities what had happened and so did the firm. An inspector from the Fuel Ministry caine to see him and Novello rather ungallantly put all the blame on Dora Constable, saying it was her idea and that he had no suspicion that he was doing anything illegal. This, of course, was nonsense; he knew he was using a false permit for his petrol. His waspishness backfired. When his remarks were repeated to Dora Constable, she replied indignantly that Novello was being unfair. He had known exactly what he was doing and even made various suggestions about the transfer. 'He was willing to do anything crooked as long as he had the use of the car.'

With a statement like that, the authorities had to act. On 24 March 1944, Novello was summoned to appear at Bow Street Court. He went to pieces and protested, 'The suggestion of my conspiring with a person of this woman's type is repugnant. But it was too late. On 24 April 1944, he stood in the dock at Bow Street alongside Dora Constable. His self-pitying remarks were quoted to the magistrate. The managing director of the firm went into the witness box and admitted, 'Novello was deceived as completely as I was.'

Novello gave one of his worst performances in the witness box. He was muddled and panic-stricken, and he gave the unfortunate impression that he was trying to unload the blame on to Dora Constable. The judge was an old-fashioned gentleman and there can be no doubt that Novello's attempt to dodge the blame revolted him. Dora Constable was fined £50 with £25 costs. Novello was fined £100. But, added Mr Justice McKenna, 'that would obviously be no punishment for a man like you, so I sentence you to eight weeks' imprisonment.' Novello was granted bail, pending an appeal. Shattered and stricken, he staggered from the court.

Two months later, on 16 May 1944, the appeal was heard at the London Sessions courthouse. The Chairman of the appeals committee was Mr Eustace Fulton who had quashed Jack Hylton's prison sentence. This time he was not in such a lenient mood. When Novello's secretary Fred Allen said that he had no suspicion there was anything wrong about the car transaction, 'otherwise I wouldn't have touched the damn thing', Fulton rebuked him for the use of 'damn'. Allen stammered nervously and Fulton snapped, 'Oh, get on!' The defending solicitor said, 'I am sorry your Lordship shows signs of impatience.' The judge snorted, 'I have shown every patience.' It did not bode well for Novello. And in spite of some distinguished character witnesses – Sir Lewis Casson, Dame Sybil Thorndike, Sir Edward Marsh – the most Fulton would concede was that Novello's sentence was perhaps too long and halved it to four weeks. As Novello left the court he turned and flung open his arms 'in a gesture of infinite despair'.

Novello was not a good prisoner. Although the authorities at Wormwood Scrubs leaned over backwards to treat him kindly – he was placed in charge of the prison choir – he almost went insane with despair and he plunged into extravagant self-pity. When he was released on 13 June 1944 he looked thin and haggard. A week later, he returned to the stage in *The Dancing Years* and was cheered by a sympathetic audience who delayed the start of the show by ten minutes. His biographer Peter Noble is nevertheless convinced that the jail sentence should be regarded as a tragedy. Novello died seven years later of a heart attack at the age of 58. He was to write three more successes after his prison sentence: *Perchance to Dream, King's Rhapsody* and *Gay's the Word*. Noble believes the sentence shortened his life. In *Scales of Justice*, Fenton

Bresler speculates that the prison sentence also cost Novello the knighthood that crowned the careers of most of his successful theatrical contemporaries.

Yet for the objective observer, it is hard to feel too much pity for Novello. His own behaviour was almost certainly responsible for the prison sentence. The obvious self-pity, the attempt to lay the blame on his admirer, who showed altogether more dignity when she decided not to testify, undoubtedly produced a mood of impatience in both judges. They probably felt that he was a spoiled brat who deserved a rap on the knuckles. Novello's real problem was that his life had been an almost unbroken run of success and until he was middle-aged he always had his adored mother to give him approval and moral support. The result was that he never really grew up. He was prone to self-pity and self-dramatization. He once told Peter Noble, 'I have a suspicion that Fate has a sense of humour, and a rather malicious one. Fate says, "Ah, that boy's had a success. He is getting a bit above himself. Now for a few slips!"' A little more of this attitude might have averted the prison sentence or at least made it more bearable.

NOYES, JOHN HUMPHREY

THE ONEIDA COMMUNITY – PROMISCUITY JUSTIFIED BY THE SCRIPTURES

To his disciples, John Humphrey Noyes was an inspired prophet and a great spiritual leader but to most of his contemporaries he was a libertine whose doctrines of free love and 'complex marriage' were a danger to the community. There were many strange religious communities in America in the nineteenth century: the Shakers (so called because they went into convulsions of religious ecstasy that made them shake all over), the Ephrata, the Rappites, Zoarites and many others. Most of these were 'Perfectionists' – that is, they rejected the notion that man is a miserable sinner as unnecessarily pessimistic and taught that, through Divine Grace, man can achieve perfection. The Shakers believed that God is both male and female by nature, so women were as important as men in their religious rites, many of which looked like orgies. But the Shakers taught the importance of strict chastity.

The 1830s and 1840s were a time of tremendous religious revivals in America, to such an extent that one portion of New York State was known as the Burnt Over Region because the fires of revivalism had burned so fiercely there. Men like Hiram Sheldon, Erasmus Stone and Jarvis Rider preached their gospel in the cotton village of Manlius and their converts adopted the name of the Saints. One of the subjects that fascinated them was whether the old marriage vows would still be binding when the New Heaven and New Earth arrived. (Most of the great religious revivals were based on the conviction that the Day of Judgment was just around the corner.) It was John Humphrey Noyes who provided a startling and controversial answer to that question.

John Humphrey Noyes was born at Brattleboro, Vermont, the son of a Congressman; he studied law, then divinity. He was a man of considerable magnetism and remarkable intellect and he seems to have spent the two years following his conversion (at the age of twenty) in religious broodings and wrestlings. He found that he simply could not accept that he was a miserable sinner. Then, when he was twenty-two, the answer suddenly revealed itself to him in a blinding flash of revelation. Reading the Gospel of St John, he could see clearly that Jesus had announced the Second Coming within one generation of his own lifetime – that is, in the year AD 70. But if Jesus had already come to earth, then the Kingdom of God was already here. In that case, why was there so much sin on earth? The answer must be because people were unaware of the Second Coming. This, Noyes could now see and explained why he himself could never feel that he was a sinner. He wasn't. He was already saved. All he had to do was to live according to the gospels and nothing could go wrong.

The Bible said that in heaven there would be no marriage or giving in marriage. The Shakers also accepted this and for them it meant an obligation to celibacy. Noyes did not agree. Sex is obviously necessary to continue the race. What the Bible meant was obviously that all men were married to all women and vice versa. In *The Battle Axe,* the newspaper of the Perfectionists, he published in 1837 a letter in which he explained that 'at the marriage supper of the Lamb . . . every dish is free to every guest.' Sexual intercourse is one of the best things of life – men and women were intended to 'reflect upon each other the love of God'. Sexual shame was a consequence of the Fall, so all the Saved should now abandon it. Men and women should have sex together just as they felt inclined, regarding it as a sacrament.

At the age of 23, Noyes returned to his home in Putney, Vermont, and preached his views; he converted a number of his own family. He married the daughter of the State Governor and one of his disciples, J.L. Skinner, married his sister. In 1840, Noyes and a number of disciples founded the Putney Community, which consisted of seven houses and a store on five hundred acres of fertile land. They spent the afternoons in manual labour to support themselves and the rest of the time in debate, prayer, reading, and teaching various subjects, including Latin, Greek and Hebrew.

Meanwhile, Noyes continued to brood on the problems posed by his doctrines of 'free love'. In 1846, he saw the answer. The problem with sexual intercourse was that it often produced unwanted results in the form of children. Mrs Harriet Noyes had produced five babies in six years and four had been stillborn. The answer was simple. Men and women should have full sexual intercourse, with orgasm taking place in the vagina only when they wished to produce children. For the rest of the time, the man must teach himself continence – not abstention. He could place his penis in the vagina but he must exercise severe self-discipline not to have an emission. It was a method that would later become known as the *karezza,* a term invented by Dr Alice Bunker Stockham of Ohio. Noyes pointed out that this method *'vastly increases* pleasure' (his italics). This doctrine was complemented by the notion of 'complex marriage' – that every man should regard all women as his wives and vice versa.

Noyes was not a man to keep his ideas secret – religious prophets seldom are – and he preached 'male continence' (i.e. the *karezza)* and 'complex marriage' quite openly. His neighbours were naturally outraged at what they took to be a public rejection of all decency. (Even nowadays, a community with these ideas would probably have a hard time of it if they lived in the vicinity of a small town.) There was public outrage and the following year, Noyes was indicted on a charge of adultery. He decided that his great vision was too important to be destroyed by a few bigots. Fortunately, some of his disciples had already set up a community near Oneida Lake, about sixty miles away, with 23 acres of land. In 1847, Noyes and his disciples moved there and set up the Oneida Community.

What followed was a typical American success story – success preceded by disappointment and hard work. There were only two log houses, a log hut and an old sawmill; the disciples were obliged to sleep in garrets and outhouses for another twelve years. There were many hardships until an inventor called Sewell Newhouse joined the community; he saved it from bankruptcy by inventing a steel trap which the community proceeded to manufacture. They made travelling bags, satchels, preserved fruit and silk, and their workmanship made them widely known. They acquired more land and more people joined them. Two years after the community was formed, another branch was started at Brooklyn, and then others at Wallingford, Newark, Putney, Cambridge and Manlius. By 1878 there were over three hundred members. They had built a large brick house in which they all lived. They had factories, offices, a school, a carpenter's shop, barns and stables. The Mansion House – the main building – was centrally heated, with baths and labour-saving kitchens. The community also employed over two hundred workers from outside and treated them well.

The aspect that has chiefly interested posterity was the sexual innovation. Any man could propose love-making to any woman (or, indeed, vice versa) and she was free to reject him. Oddly enough, direct courtship was not allowed – a man who wanted to sleep with a woman had to approach her through the intermediary of a third person. What 'male continence' (or *coitus reservatus)* meant in practice was that the man put his penis into the woman's vagina, then they lay still for anything up to an hour and a quarter. The woman was allowed to climax but the man was not expected to do so – even after withdrawal – Noyes denounced Robert Dale Owen's idea of *coitus interruptus* as 'Male incontinence plus evasion'. The male was supposed to stay in the woman until he lost his erection and this was believed to obviate any frustration and nervous tension. Noyes claimed that his community had a far better record of less nervous illness than the outside community while failing to recognize that there may have been other explanations for the situation.

As a system of sexual and moral hygiene 'complex marriage' seems to have been highly successful. Boys lost their virginity soon after puberty, girls somewhat later. An older person of the opposite sex was generally chosen to initiate the young – one of the aspects of 'complex marriage' that horrified the 'outside world' which felt a mixture of envy and moral indignation at the idea of a middle-aged man or woman being allowed to deflower a fifteen-year-old. One visitor wrote: 'The majority of the old women are hideous and loathsome in appearance and it seems to me the most horrible fate in the world to be linked with them.' But Noyes himself, as the father of the community (he was even known as Father Noyes), naturally had a wider freedom of choice than most – after the age of 58 he fathered eight children. It is not clear whether this was accidental or intentional. The community practised eugenics – which Noyes called stirpiculture – and at one stage, 24 men and 20 women were selected for an experiment in selective breeding. But 'accidents' also happened – on average one every eighteen months.

Accounts of the community make clear that it was not a sexual free-for-all. The women dressed modestly, looking rather like the Chinese in long white trousers covered by a skirt. Any tendency by a couple to fall in love was regarded as selfish and 'idolatrous', and was discouraged by the system of 'mutual criticism', which usually meant that the person to be criticized was summoned before a committee, who then detailed his or her faults. People often requested mutual criticism just as someone today might go to a psychiatrist. One historian of the movement, Mark Holloway in *Heavens on Earth* (1951) has recorded that it was also used successfully to cure physical ailments, demonstrating that Father Noyes also understood about psychosomatic illness. There was one case in which 'mutual criticism' went further: when William Mills, a man in his early 60s – with an unattractive wife – tried to initiate more than his share of teenage virgins with the aid of sweets and alcohol, and as a result was hurled unceremoniously into a snowdrift.

Close attachments among children were also discouraged as selfish, which caused a certain amount of heartache. Otherwise, the children had an enviably pleasant time. They were allowed to sleep as late as they liked in the morning and there were dances, plays, pantomimes and other forms of entertainment for them. Nor were they deprived of parental affection. A mother weaned her child, then placed it in the Children's House where, until the age of three, it spent the daylight hours. After that children also spent the night there but parents could visit them as often as they liked and take them for walks. They left the Children's House at fourteen, when they were ready for sexual initiation and to join the adult community.

The adults also had a pleasant time of it once the community was well-established. Most members were supervisors rather than workers and they could change their jobs to avoid monotony. Times of meetings, amusements and meals were also changed for the same reason. There was fishing, hunting, boating and swimming at Oneida Lake, twelve miles away, and they could visit other communities.

The only real problem was the attitude of the outside world. The American constitution allowed for religious freedom but flagrant sexual immorality was quite another thing. One of the community's chief enemies was Professor John W. Mears, of Hamilton College, who denounced it as 'a Utopia of obscenity'. The Presbyterian Synod of Central New York appointed a committee of seven to investigate the activities of the community but was unsuccessful in destroying it. Eventually, the community began to decay from within. Many younger members thought that Noyes's religious doctrines were absurd; some were even agnostics (Noyes allowed members to study Huxley and Darwin). Noyes wanted to retire and appointed his agnostic son, Dr Theodore Noyes, to take his place but this caused dissension. Some members of the community even sided with the puritanical Dr Mears. Noyes finally slipped quietly away from Oneida and moved to Niagara Falls in 1876 at the age of 65. It became clear that if Oneida wanted to survive, it would have to stop outraging the outside world with its sexual freedom. 'Complex marriage' was abandoned; the alternatives offered were celibacy or marriage and most preferred marriage. But to try to suppress 'complex marriage' was tantamount to removing one of the main foundations of the community. 'The Community sank step by step into its own Dark Ages,' says one historian. The old generosity of spirit vanished, so that 'it was almost impossible to borrow a hammer from one's next door neighbour'. In 1881, the Oneida Community was reorganized as a joint stock company, and 'communism' was abandoned. Children were still educated free until they were sixteen, then they were given $200 to give them a 'start in life'. 'An arid commercialism' replaced the old communal spirit and the community began to split up. Yet the original Oneida branch remained commercially successful.

Noyes died in 1886 still believing firmly that the community had been ordained by God; praise and violent criticism continued long after his death. One English visitor had described him as 'a tall, pale man, with sandy hair and beard, grey, dreamy eyes, good mouth, white temples and a noble forehead.' But the secularist Charles Bradlaugh was to describe him as 'singularly unloveable, with his protruding, stuckout lower lip, his tired satyr-like leer . . . an eccentric goatish half-inch stripe of beard running from ear to ear.' Yet 53 young women had once signed a resolution declaring that they belonged to him as 'God's true representative', and that they were perfectly happy for him to decide which of the male members of the community were to father their children. It cannot be denied that Noyes was one of the most remarkable visionaries to come out of America in the nineteenth century.

PAYNE, CYNTHIA

THE 'SEX-FOR-LUNCHEON-VOUCHERS' SCANDAL

In April, 1980, dark-haired Mrs Cynthia Payne, was jailed for eighteen months for keeping a disorderly house in Ambleside Avenue, Streatham, in south London. She was a middle-aged lady christened 'Madam Sin' in a play on names by the popular Press. Her sentence was reduced on appeal to six months, of which she served only four – to the chuckles of the public at large, most of whom found more to laugh at than lecture in the scandalous goings-on at her suburban establishment.

Male clients there paid £25 a time for luncheon vouchers which were traded in for sex plus 'generous helpings' of food and drink. Customers and scarlet women broke the ice at Madam Sin's over a glass or two of wine and sandwiches in rooms furnished with fitted carpets. At the subsequent court-hearing, even the prosecution was moved to admit that it was 'a well-run brothel'. Down in the kitchen, Mrs Payne nailed her colours to the mast with a sign which proclaimed: 'My House Is CLEAN Enough To Be Healthy . . . And DIRTY Enough To Be Happy.' It all sounded so genteel, more of a mini-scandal than any outrage on morality.

Mrs Payne, who was 46 at the time of her arrest, revealed that she numbered several vicars, barristers, an MP and a peer of the realm among her regular customers. Clutching their luncheon vouchers, they whiled away their nervous first moments in Ambleside Avenue at a bar in the conservatory, decorated with red fairy lamps and a stuffed parrot perched in a gilded cage. Later the girls – described by Mrs Payne as 'dedicated amateurs' mostly, housewives out to make a little pin-money – received £6 for each voucher they handed in. There were more than fifty men present when police raided the house. Later, while Mrs Payne was detained elsewhere, a man of 74 who gave his name as Squadron Leader Robert Smith, Retd., acted as caretaker and took journalists on conducted tours.

In March 1983 the name Madam Sin featured in more newspaper headlines when renewed activity was reported at the house in Ambleside Avenue. This time, however, no luncheon vouchers were issued, while Mrs Payne was quoted as saying, 'I'm doing it for love.' She told a *News of the World* reporter, 'These days neighbours sometimes see a lot of cars parked outside my house, and say "Oh, so you're at it again, are you, Cynthia?" Alas, I'm no longer in business . . . but I feel I'm still doing a service, even though I'm not making a living out of it. It's like real, genuine welfare work.' She harked back briefly to the good old luncheon-voucher days, 'I'd like to think that I'll be remembered for running a nice brothel. . . not one of those sordid places like they have in Soho. I should have been given the OBE for what I did for the country.'

POLANSKI, ROMAN

THE RAPE CASE

Roman Polanski's life as a successful Hollywood film director came to an end abruptly one day in 1977, when he was arrested and charged with drugging and raping a thirteen-year-old girl.

Polanski's own version of what happened is told in his autobiography *Roman* (1984).

Polanski was the enormously successful director of films like *Repulsion* (1965), *Rosemary's Baby* (1968) and *Chinatown* (1974).

In 1977, Polanski was doing a photographic assignment for *Vogue*. It was Polanski's own idea to do a feature on some adolescent girls. A friend suggested a thirteen-year-old girl, the daughter of an aspiring actress. Polanski drove out to the house one afternoon, and was introduced to her. They drove up into the hills, where Polanski took some photographs. He noticed a bruise on her neck, and she told him that it was a love bite, given to her by her boyfriend, with whom she admitted having spent the night in her mother's house when he was sleeping on the settee, and she went and joined him.

The next time Polanski filmed her was in a house belonging to the film star Jack Nicholson. On the way there, Polanski asked her when she had first had sex, and she admitted casually that it was at the age of eight, with a boy down the street.

He decided to take some shots in the jacuzzi. He snapped photographs of the girl naked in the water, drinking a glass of champagne. After that, Polanski dived into the swimming pool. When he got out, the girl and he dried one another 'then, very gently, I began to kiss and caress her. After this had gone on for some time, I led her over to the couch.

'There was no doubt about her experience, and lack of inhibition. She spread herself and I entered her. She wasn't unresponsive. Yet when I asked her softly if she was liking it, she resorted to her favourite expression: "It's all right."'

Afterwards, he drove her home, and showed her mother the photographs he'd taken. She seemed to like them. But later, the friend who had first mentioned the girl rang up to say that the mother was furious and thought the photographs were 'horrible'. Polanski was puzzled, since the mother herself had seemed to like them.

The following day, about to leave his hotel lobby, he was accosted by a man who showed him a badge and told him he was from the Los Angeles Police Department. He said that he was arresting him for rape.

In an interview with Martin Amis which took place in 1979 in Paris, Polanski remarks that when he was being driven to the police station the car radio was already talking about his arrest. 'I thought, you know, I was going to wake up from it. I realised, if I had *killed* somebody, it wouldn't have had so much appeal to the police, you see? But ... fucking you see, and young girls. Judges want to fuck young girls. Juries want to fuck young girls – *everyone* wants to fuck young girls! No, I knew then that this is going to be another big, big thing.'

At the trial, Polanski was found guilty of having sex with a minor, and allowed bail to go and direct a film for Dino de Laurentiis in Tahiti, *Hurricane*. In fact, he never made the film, but instead went to Paris, the city of his birth.

Roman Polanski had been born there on 18 August 1933; his father Ryszard Polanski (who also called himself Liebling) was a painter and plastics manufacturer. His Russian wife, like her husband, was Jewish. Because of a rising anti-Semitism in France, the family returned to Poland in 1937. But when the war broke out, they were confined to the Polish ghetto in Krakow, and were there until 1941, when both his parents were thrown into concentration camps. His father had cut the wire around the ghetto and pushed Roman out, telling him to run away. Later, Roman saw his father being marched away, in a column of other Jews. When Roman tried to speak to him, his father hissed: 'Push off.'

His father had made plans for Roman's survival in case he himself was arrested. A couple named Wilk would take him in and look after him. They were reassured by the fact that Roman did not look Jewish.

Polanski's mother, who was pregnant, would die in a gas chamber in Auschwitz. His father survived the war, dying in 1984.

From the beginning, Roman had been obsessed by films. He was given pocket money by the Wilks, and since the cinema was cheap, was able to see a great many of the pre-war classics. Out of the tea caddy he found on a rubbish dump, he tried to make himself a movie projector. Soon after that, Roman was sent out of the city to live in the country with a poor peasant family, where he learned something about farming and the care of cattle. He returned to Krakow, but during one of the last German air raids, was blown through a lavatory door by a German bomb. And at the age of sixteen, he had a close brush with death when he was persuaded to enter a bunker by a man who began to beat him over the head with a rock. With blood pouring from his head, he succeeded in escaping. The man was arrested later, and proved to have committed three murders.

The Russians entered Krakow, and although they were capable of rape and a great deal of thieving, they were kind to children, and in the famine which followed the German withdrawal, organized soup kitchens. And one day, his father returned from the concentration camp. He had been well fed by the Americans, and looked tanned and healthy.

Back at school, Polanski continued to see as many films as possible – he saw Olivier's *Hamlet* twenty times, and then went on to read all Shakespeare's plays in Polish.

Polanski became a child actor by accident. There was a weekly radio programme called *The Merry-go-round,* which went out from Krakow, and one day, the public was allowed in to visit the studio. Polanski was asked what he thought of the programme, and said he thought it was awful. Asked if he could do any better, he proceeded to recite a peasant monologue, which led to his being hired on the spot. Polanski went on to get the lead role in a play about a boy who was a regimental mascot. When the play was presented in Warsaw, Polanski won a cash award, which was shared out among the cast.

His drawings led to his acceptance in the school of fine art, while his stage experience brought an offer of a part in a film being made by some Lodz film students. After this, Polanski applied for a place in the Krakow Drama School but was rejected because of his size. This was a disaster, because unless he could get into some kind of educational establishment, he would be called up to do his National Service, and any hope of an acting career would be over. Fortunately, at the last moment, he received a phone call from a cameraman he knew, telling him that a director called Andrzej Wajda was making his full-length feature film, and had a part for Polanski. It was a film with a Communist ideology content, but Wajda's realism turned *A Generation* (1954) into a masterpiece of realism, which made his reputation.

Polanski spent the next five years at the Lodz Film School, and made a number of short films that immediately revealed his talent – *Two Men and a Wardrobe* begins with two men staggering out of the sea carrying a wardrobe. This won a prize at the 1958 Brussels World Fair. Short films that followed, *The Fat and the Thin* and *Mammals* showed strong surrealistic influence, and increased his reputation. He also married for the first time. His wife, Barbara, was an exceptionally beautiful actress, and in 1959, they went to Paris, hoping that she would have a film career. Although her lack of knowledge of French was an obstacle, she finally landed a small part as an *au pair* girl. They managed to stay on in Paris by borrowing money.

They returned to Poland, and here at last Polanski's career took off with his film *Knife in the Water* (1962) a drama of sexual rivalry in which a young couple pick up a hitchhiker and invite him for a weekend on their yacht. This full-length film already contains the essence of Polanski – a certain obsessive, subjective quality, and the Polish film critics predictably hated it – its message was not sufficiently optimistic and socially committed. It nevertheless gained a prize at the Venice Film Festival, and brought Polanski a degree of international recognition. It was even nominated for an Oscar, which Fellini eventually won with his film 8½.

Polanski was now bankable, but was finding it extremely difficult to raise the money to make a film that was to be about two gangsters on the run who get trapped on an island. (This finally became *Cul de Sac.*) But in London, he was approached by a group who ran a Soho Cinema Club which specialized in mildly pornographic movies. This was the 'Compton Group', and it was they who offered Polanski to finance a cheap horror movie made in black and white. Polanski decided he could probably make something worthwhile out of it, and although the Compton Group became desperate as he overran his budget as well as his time with his careful and precise scene setting, *Repulsion* (1965) was an instant success. It is about a beautiful and neurotic girl who is terrified of sex, and who murders her boyfriend and then her landlord. There is little dialogue, and the action seems curiously unmotivated, but the film has undoubted power.

It made him enough money and reputation to be able to persuade the same group to back his film about the two gangsters. The shooting of *Cul de Sac* on the Scottish island of Lindisfarne was something of a disaster, and Polanski's description in his autobiography *Roman* is brilliantly funny. Unfortunately, the film left the critics completely bewildered, and was a commercial flop.

The same thing, unfortunately, applied to his next film *The Fearless Vampire Killers* (1967), a spoof of *Dracula* which showed an extraordinary lapse of judgement – at that time audiences wanted to be scared by vampires, not to make fun of them. The star was the beautiful blonde Sharon Tate. Issued in America as *Pardon Me, Your Teeth Are In My Neck*, it deservedly flopped, although Polanski protests that it was so hacked and changed that he felt ashamed of it. (His original version became a cult success in later years.)

But as soon as he read Ira Levin's novel *Rosemary's Baby*, about a young couple who become involved with a group of devil worshippers, he was instantly gripped by it. Again, there were problems in the making, and at one stage he was almost sacked because he was taking too long and overrunning the budget. Nevertheless, the film justified the care he put into it, and was a box-office hit. It made the reputation of Mia Farrow as an actress, but also broke up her marriage with Frank Sinatra, who wanted her to work on a film he was making, *The Detective*, and had her presented with divorce papers when she refused to walk off the set.

By this time, Polanski was married to Sharon Tate, the actress who had played in *The Fearless Vampire Killers*.

In February 1969, the Polanskis rented a house off Benedict Canyon from Terry Melsher, the impresario of the Beach Boys. Two of their friends looked after the house during their frequent absences: Wojtek Frykowski, who had worked on films with Polanski in Poland, and the coffee heiress Abigail Folger.

On the evening of August 8, 1969, Sharon Tate, who was eight and a half months pregnant, was giving dinner to her house-sitters and to a former lover called Jay Sebring, a fashionable hair-stylist. Three people entered the house – a man and two women, who were followers of the paranoid 'messiah' Charles Manson. They saw Frykowski asleep on the settee; then he woke up and asked 'Who are you?' and the man answered, 'I am the devil, and I'm here on the devil's business.' They proceeded to tie his hands with a towel. One of the women, Susan Atkins, was sent upstairs to see how many people there were in the house, and glanced into Abigail Folger's bedroom. Abigail, high on MDMA, gazed back at her and smiled.

When Susan Atkins reported to the man, Tex Watson, that there were three more people upstairs, he ordered her to bring them down. She did this by threatening them with a knife. Sebring tried to grab Watson's gun, and was shot through the lung. Then Watson looped the length of a long nylon rope they had brought round Sebring's neck, and threw the other end over a beam; he then tied it round the necks of the other two women. Frykowski succeeded in running into the garden, but Susan Atkins pursued him and stabbed him in the back. Indoors, Watson shot Frykowski twice then beat him over the head with the jammed gun. The two women were struggling to free themselves, and Abigail Folger got as far as the garden before she was also stabbed several times by Susan Atkins. Then Watson, Susan Atkins and a third woman, Patricia Krenwinkel joined in stabbing the pregnant Sharon Tate to death. Sixteen wounds were later found on her body. Susan Atkins dipped a towel in Sharon Tate's blood and daubed the word 'pig' on the living room door.

Polanski was in London when he heard the news by telephone. He was so dazed that he began banging his head against the wall and had to be held back by film star Warren Beatty, and part-owner of the Playboy Club, Victor Lownes. Completely shattered, Polanski flew back to Los Angeles. There the general theory seemed to be that these four victims, together with a youth called Stephen Parent, who had been visiting the houseboy when he was shot by Watkins, were generally believed to have been high on drugs, and their death was attributed to some quarrel with drug dealers. Polanski himself was even asked to take a lie detector test to make sure that he had no connection with the murders. Most of the newspapers and magazines drew attention to the similarity of the murder scene and Polanski's own films.

Manson's killers had gone on to commit another murder the following evening – a supermarket owner called Leno LaBianca and his wife Rosemary. This time Manson himself was present; he went into their bedroom and tied them up, then ordered his followers to go in and kill them. All were high.

Two and a half months later, in October, Manson and his followers were arrested – but not for the murders. The 'family' were living on a deserted farm in Death Valley, and had been charged with destroying a bulldozer by setting it on fire, an act of gratuitous drugged-induced vandalism. They were also suspected of murdering a musician named Gary Hinman. In prison, Susan Atkins confided to her cellmate that she had taken part in the Sharon Tate killings. The Manson family went on trial in 1970, and were condemned to death, although the sentences were subsequently commuted to life imprisonment. Watson was tried separately and charged with seven counts of murder, and he was also sentenced to death, although it was commuted.

Polanski had been about to make a film called *The Day of the Dolphin* at the time of the murders, but when he encountered problems with the film company, United Artists, he decided to drop it; in any case, he had no heart for work

In an attempt to forget the tragedy, Polanski went to make a film in Italy called *What?* He describes this as: 'A ribald Rabelaisian account of the adventures of a fey, innocent girl, wholly unaware of the sort of company that surrounds her in a weird Riviera villa inhabited exclusively by phallocrats.' In spite of having Marcello Mastroianni in the lead, this flopped. And so did a subsequent film of *Macbeth*, written by Polanski and the critic Kenneth Tynan. Critics generally felt that it was too realistically bloody and violent. But his next film, *Chinatown* (1974), a superbly made detective story in the tradition of Raymond Chandler and Dashiel Hammett was perhaps his greatest success so far, and is regarded by many as his best film. It received six academy award nominations.

His next venture was a French film called *The Tenant*, in which Polanski himself played the lead, a Polish-born bank clerk whose mental stress leads to transvestism and suicide. Badly received at the Cannes Film Festival in May 1976, it received harsh reviews, one critic saying that it was like *Repulsion* with Polanski in the part of Catherine Deneuve, but not as good.

It was while in France that Polanski received an invitation to be the guest editor of the Christmas 1976 issue of *Vogue*, and it was this that led to the disastrous encounter with the Californian nymphet that caused Polanski to flee to France, and make his home in Paris.

Polanski's next film, shot in France, was Thomas Hardy's *Tess* (1979). The heroine was played by Nastassia Kinsky, the daughter of actor Claus Kinsky, with whom Polanski had had a relationship since 1975, when she was fifteen. The shooting, as usual, took far longer than intended, and went wildly over budget. The four-hour film, finally cut to three, received its premiere in Germany, where it was hatcheted. The three-hour version was successful in France, but was unable to find an American or British distributor. An attempt by Coppola to edit it and make it more 'acceptable' failed to appeal to Polanski. But eventually, a warm review by Charles Champlin, critic of the *Los Angeles Times*, calling it the best film of the year, finally led Columbia to agree to distribute it, whereupon it was a considerable success, and finally justified Polanski's faith in it.

By any standard, Polanski's career has been vertiginous. While undoubtedly one of the most brilliant film directors of his time, his obsessively subjective approach has prevented him from gaining the wide audience appeal that he deserves. Perhaps the reason can be found in the first sentence of his autobiography *Roman*: 'For as far back as I can remember, the line between fantasy and reality has been hopelessly blurred.'

PROFUMO AFFAIR

THE MINISTER AND THE RUSSIAN SPY

Few if any politico-sex scandals in British history have titillated the public's imagination as much as the Profumo-Christine Keeler affair of the so-called 'swinging 60s'. It centred on a real-life situation which, on the face of it, seemed so absurd as to sound more like a plot for some particularly bawdy West End farce; one in which John Profumo, MP, Her Majesty's Secretary of State for War, took turn and turn about in call-girl Christine Keeler's bed with (among others) Captain Eugene Ivanov, the assistant Soviet naval attache in London and, allegedly, a Russian spy bent on gathering nuclear secrets from any resultant pillow talk.

So seriously was the possibility taken that a judicial inquiry was appointed and charged, among other things, with considering '. . . any evidence there may be for believing that national security has been, or may be, endangered . . .' And, if that were not enough, the affair also had racial undertones, arising from the trial and imprisonment of two of Miss Keeler's former lovers, both West Indian. The resultant scandal was sparked off by her disappearance on the eve of the first trial, in which she was due to appear at the Old Bailey as chief witness for the prosecution; instead she was discovered, by the Press, in Spain. As all Britain laughed behind its hand, questions were asked in Parliament. After first strenuously denying allegations of any impropriety in his dealings with Miss Keeler, War Minister Profumo later resigned – when he had confessed that he had lied to the House, the Cabinet and the Prime Minister about their relationship. Soon there was talk in the foreign press of 'widespread decadence' in British public life, while the most scurrilous and salacious rumours (never substantiated) began to circulate at home of sexual orgies in upper-crust circles, attended by 'The Man in the Mask' – always naked, carrying a whip, and popularly supposed to be another Tory cabinet minister. This particular rumour gained such credence that it became common gossip in pubs, clubs and homes throughout the country.

Then came tragedy, when Dr Stephen Ward – osteopath, talented portrait-artist, procurer of women for his rich and famous friends (who all deserted him after his arrest) and a central character in the whole Profumo Affair – committed suicide during his own Old Bailey trial, in July 1963. Ward took an overdose of barbiturates when the court adjourned for the night after part-hearing the judge's summing up, and died in hospital without knowing the verdict. Miss Keeler herself was later jailed for committing perjury at the trial of the second of her two West Indian former lovers. Finally, a year after the resignation in October 1963 of Prime Minister Harold Macmillan, on health grounds, the Tory party was beaten at the polls after more than twelve years in power; a defeat, said the pundits, which was hastened by the odium of the Profumo Affair.

At the time the scandal began, 'Dr' Stephen Ward – he was an osteopath, not a medical practitioner – had for several years rented a cottage *orné*, on peppercorn terms, at Cliveden, the country estate owned by his friend Lord Astor. Ward's guests were allowed use of the swimming pool and it was there that he introduced Christine Keeler to both Mr Profumo and Captain Ivanov in the summer of 1961. Unconfirmed reports that Profumo, the husband of actress Valerie Hobson and a wealthy man in his own right, was competing with Ivanov for Miss Keeler's favours were already circulating in Fleet Street by mid-1962. Only *Queen* magazine dared, however, to hint at the incredible situation that was said to be developing. It printed a brief but barbed reference to a chauffeur-driven Russian Zis limousine arriving at an unnamed lady's front door, just as a government chauffeur-driven Humber pulled away from the back. That flat was in Wimpole Mews in central London, provided by Stephen Ward at nominal rent for Christine Keeler's use. But since no identification was made, the article caused no great stir beyond a privileged readership.

Then on 14 December 1962 a West Indian called Johnny Edgecombe was arrested after firing a revolver at the door and window of the flat. Inside were Christine Keeler and a friend, Mandy Rice-Davies, likewise destined soon to become a household name. They rang Dr Ward at his consulting rooms nearby and he called the police. On 14 March 1963 Edgecombe stood trial at the Old Bailey. The charges included one of attempted murder and another of wounding 'Lucky' Gordon, a fellow West Indian who had supplanted him in Christine Keeler's affections. Chief prosecution witness Keeler failed to appear; unknown to the court she was in Spain. However, no request was made for a postponement and of the two women present in the flat at the time of the shooting, only Miss Rice-Davies gave evidence. Edgecombe, who had previous convictions, was found not guilty of attempted murder, or of wounding Gordon, but guilty on a lesser charge, of possessing a firearm with intent to endanger life. For this he was sentenced to seven years' imprisonment and the scandal now moved into the open.

Two national newspaper reporters who had refused to name their informants to the Vassall (spy) Tribunal were already in jail, so Fleet Street, although fully aware of Mr Profumo's association with Christine Keeler, was obliged to proceed cautiously. It, therefore, printed stories about the Edgecombe trial and its missing prosecution witness, alongside apparently unconnected stories concerning John Profumo. *The Sunday Pictorial* printed an exclusive interview with Dr Stephen Ward, in which he said: 'Now it looks as though somebody – no doubt a loyal friend – has spirited her away . . .'

Who that 'loyal friend' may have been and what if any were his motives, has never been established. In his official report, Lord Denning, who had examined the bank accounts of both Mr Profumo and Dr Ward, found no evidence to suggest that either man had assisted her in leaving the country.

However, on 22 March *Private Eye* published a mock 'report' under the byline 'Lunchtime O'Booze' which read:

Mr Silas Jones, a West Indian immigrant of no fixed abode, was today sentenced at the Old Bailey to twenty-four years Preventive Detention for being in possession of an offensive water-pistol. The chief 'witness' in the case, gay fun-loving Miss Gaye Funloving, a 21-year-old 'model', was not actually present in Court. She has, in fact, disappeared. It is believed that normally, in cases of this type, a Warrant is issued for the arrest of the missing witness.

Parties. One of Miss Funloving's close 'friends', Dr Spook of Harley Street, revealed last night that he could add nothing to what had already been insinuated. Dr Spook is believed to have 'more than half the Cabinet on his list of patients'. He also has a 'weekend' cottage on the Berkshire estate of Lord—, and is believed to have attended many 'parties' in the neighbourhood. Among those it is believed who have also attended 'parties' of this type are Mr Vladimir Bolokhov, the well-known Soviet spy attached to the Russian embassy and a well-known Cabinet Minister.

Resignation? Mr James Montesi, a well-known Cabinet Minister, was last night reported to have proffered his 'resignation' to the Prime Minister, on 'personal grounds'. It is alleged that the Prime Minister refused to accept his alleged 'resignation'. Mr Montesi today denied the allegations that he had even allegedly offered his alleged 'resignation' to the alleged 'Prime Minister'.

That night, outspoken Socialist MP Colonel George Wigg – no friend of Mr Profumo's and with whom he had already clashed in the House on another unrelated matter – addressed the Commons as they debated the affair of the two reporters jailed by the Vassall Tribunal. Colonel Wigg said,

There is not an Honourable Member in the House, nor a journalist in the Press Gallery, nor do I believe there is a person in the Public Gallery, who in the last few days has not heard rumour upon rumour involving a member of the Government Front Bench. The Press has got as near as it can – it has shown itself willing to wound, but afraid to strike. This all comes about because of the Vassall Tribunal. These great Press Lords, these men who control great instruments of public opinion and power, do not have the guts to discharge the duty that they are now claiming for themselves. That being the case, I rightly use the privilege of the House of Commons – that is what it is given to me for – to ask the Home Secretary, who is the senior member of the government on the Treasury Bench now, to go to the Dispatch Box – he knows that the rumour to which I refer relates to Miss Christine Keeler and Miss Davies and a shooting by a West Indian – and, on behalf of the government, categorically deny the truth of these rumours. On the other hand, if there is anything in them, I urge him to ask the Prime Minister to do what was not done in the Vassall Case – set up a Select Committee, so that these things can be dissipated and the honour of the Minister concerned freed from the imputations and innuendoes that are being spread at the present time

Home Secretary Henry Brooke refused to pick up the gauntlet, while Mr Profumo himself was not in the House. He was, however, informed of what had happened and promptly made a personal statement to the Commons. The 'personal statement' is a device used by MPs, including Ministers, for a variety of reasons (including the denial of rumours, repeated under the cloak of Parliamentary privilege). By tradition, the speaker is never questioned about a personal statement so that he in turn becomes honour-bound to tell the truth, the whole truth, and nothing but the truth. To betray this mutual trust is to commit political *hara-kiri*. Mr Profumo made his personal statement with his wife watching from the Stranger's Gallery, and himself on the Front Bench flanked by Prime Minister Harold Macmillan and Iain Macleod, the Leader of the House.

He said,

> I understand that my name has been connected with the rumours about the disappearance of Miss Keeler. I would like to take this opportunity of making a personal statement about these matters. I last saw Miss Keeler in December 1961 and I have not seen her since. I have no idea where she is now. Any suggestion that I was in any way connected with or responsible for her absence from the trial at the Old Bailey is wholly and completely untrue. My wife and I first met Miss Keeler at a house party in July 1961 at Cliveden. Among a number of people there was Dr Stephen Ward, whom we already knew slightly, and a Mr Ivanov, who was an attaché at the Russian Embassy. The only other occasion that my wife or I met Mr Ivanov was for a moment at the official reception for Major Gagarin [the first man in Space] at the Soviet Embassy. My wife and I had a standing invitation to visit Dr Ward. Between July and December 1961, I met Miss Keeler on about half-a-dozen occasions at Dr Ward's flat, when I called to see him and his friends. Miss Keeler and I were on friendly terms. There was no impropriety whatsoever in my acquaintanceship with Miss Keeler. Mr Speaker, I have made this personal statement because of what was said in the House last evening by the three Honourable Members, and which of course was protected by privilege. I shall not hesitate to issue writs for libel and slander if scandalous allegations are made or repeated outside the House.

Later that day the Minister and his wife were photographed at the races in the company of the Queen Mother. Press reaction was restrained, although

The Guardian declared: '. . . only the most compelling evidence to the contrary could warrant any suspicion now, after such explicit statements from Mr Profumo. . . . They ought to end the talk.' Christine Keeler, found at last by the press in Spain, said somewhat obliquely, 'I have nothing to be ashamed of; I know that now.' When she returned to Britain, the only penalty she incurred was to forfeit the £40 recognizance put by the Court on her duty to appear as witness at the Edgecombe trial. Mr Profumo himself made good the threat he had uttered earlier in the Commons, by commencing actions for libel against *Paris Match* and *Tempo Illustrato* magazines. (He gave the £50 out-of-court settlement paid by *Illustrato* to charity.) 'Dr' Stephen Ward said on television that Mr Profumo had told the truth about Miss Keeler; to all intents and purposes it seemed as if the 'scandal' was no more than press invention. And yet it stubbornly refused to die down.

On the night of 18 April 1963, Christine Keeler complained to the police that she had been attacked by 'Lucky' Gordon as she left a woman friend's house in London. He was arrested and bail was opposed. One week later Mandy Rice-Davies was arrested at London airport *en route* to Majorca and charged with possessing a forged driving licence. The licence enabled her to drive the Jaguar car given to her on her seventeenth birthday by slum landlord and racketeer, Peter Rachman. (In her memoirs, *The Mandy Report*, published in 1964, Miss Rice-Davies claimed that the real reason for her arrest was to persuade her to make a statement concerning Stephen Ward. She then gave evidence at his trial, which began on 22 July 1963.) Also in 1964, author and broadcaster Ludovic Kennedy wrote in his book *The Trial of Stephen Ward* that: '. . . [Ward] felt, naively perhaps but not altogether unreasonably, that as he had done his best to protect the Government's War Minister, the Government might do their best to call their dogs off him. He wrote to the Home Secretary, his local MP Sir Wavell Wakefield, and the Leader of the Opposition, Mr Harold Wilson. To Mr Wilson he wrote: "Obviously my efforts to conceal the fact that Mr Profumo had not told the truth in Parliament have made it look as if I myself have something to hide. It is quite clear now that they must wish the facts to be known, and I shall see that they are . . ."'

Copies of some of the letters Ward wrote were also sent to the press and further questions were tabled in the House. The Prime Minister thereupon instructed Lord Dilhorne, the Lord Chancellor, to investigate. Meanwhile Johnny Edgecombe's appeal had been dismissed; now it was 'Lucky' Gordon's turn to stand trial at the Old Bailey. This time Christine Keeler was present to give evidence. Gordon claimed that she had been pregnant by him when she went to Spain. As he attempted to talk matters over with her on her return, she fell over her suitcase and so caused the injuries she had sustained. Miss Keeler denied the pregnancy allegation and protested so vehemently when Gordon said she had given him a venereal disease that the judge ordered her from the court. Gordon, who dismissed his counsel and then conducted his own defence, asked for a number of witnesses to be called, including John Profumo and Stephen Ward. Neither was called. Only two men (said by Gordon to have been in the flat as Miss Keeler left) were sought but could not be found. Gordon was found guilty and sentenced to three years' imprisonment. A few weeks later, that sentence was quashed and he was freed. In his book *The Profumo Affair, Aspects of Conservatism,* author Wayland Young wrote: 'Six weeks later the Lord Chief Justice, having heard some new evidence which was not made public, upset the verdict and released [Gordon]. But already on the second day of the trial the whole grumbling, menacing mess of happenings and rumours of happenings had been lifted to the level of a duly constituted scandal by the resignation of the Secretary of State for War . . .'

After telling his wife the full story of his association with Christine Keeler, Mr Profumo had cut short their holiday in Venice, returned to England and resigned both as Minister and MP. The interchange of letters between himself and the Prime Minister revealed that he had committed the unpardonable sin of lying to Parliament when he made his personal statement.

John Profumo wrote:

Dear Prime Minister,

You will recall that on 22 March, following certain allegations made in Parliament, I made a personal statement. At the time rumour had charged me with assisting in the disappearance of a witness, and with being involved in some possible breach of security. So serious were these charges that I allowed myself to think that my personal association with that witness, which had also been the subject of rumour, was by comparison of minor importance only. In my statement I said that there had been no impropriety in this association. To my very deep regret I have to admit that this was not true, and that I misled you, and my colleagues, and the House.

I ask you to understand that I did this to protect, as I thought, my wife and family, who were equally misled, as were my professional advisers. I have come to realize that, by this deception, I have been guilty of a grave misdemeanour and despite the fact that there is no truth whatever in the other charges, I cannot remain a member of your Administration, nor of the House of Commons. I cannot tell you of my deep remorse for the embarrassment I have caused to you, to my colleagues in the Government, to my constituents, and to the Party which I have served for the past twenty-five years.

Yours sincerely,
Jack Profumo.

To which Mr Macmillan, then on holiday in Scotland, replied:

Dear Profumo,

The contents of your letter of 4 June have been communicated to me and I have heard them with deep regret. This is a great tragedy for you, your family, and your friends. Nevertheless, I am sure you will understand that in the circumstances, I have no alternative but to advise the Queen to accept your resignation.

Yours very sincerely,

Harold Macmillan.

The Times commented acidly: 'There can be few more lamentable documents in British political history than Mr Profumo's letter of resignation. In his reply the Prime Minister says: "This is a great tragedy for you, your family, and your friends." It is also a great tragedy for the probity of public life in Britain . . .'

If that was undeniable, the moral question was now overtaken by a more sinister aspect of the affair: had the national security been put at risk by Mr Profumo's conduct? It was clear that he had laid himself open to possible blackmail, but even before the Commons could debate the matter Mr Michael Eddowes, a former solicitor and member of the Thursday Club, published the contents of a letter he had written earlier to the Prime Minister. In it Mr Eddowes claimed he had warned MI5 in March 1963 that Miss Keeler had told him Ivanov had asked her to find out from Mr Profumo the date on which nuclear warheads were to be delivered to West Germany. (Christine Keeler herself maintained later the suggestion had come from Stephen Ward, not Ivanov, and had not been intended seriously: nor had she put any such question to the War Minister.) However, the disclosure came at a time when everything Miss Keeler said, or did, or was said to have done, was news. Her 'Confessions' were appearing weekly in the mass-circulation *News of the World*. She was said to have turned down an offer of £5,000 per week (for twelve weeks) to compère a cabaret show called 'Turkish Delight'. Against all the backcloth of rumour and known scandal there was also talk in political circles of more threatened Cabinet resignations, even a move to oust Premier Macmillan.

The highly responsible *New York Times* declared that: 'A political crisis even more profound than the storm over Suez which blew Anthony Eden out of office and brought Prime Minister Macmillan to power is now shaking Great Britain to its foundations. The Suez crisis forced a change in Conservative Prime Ministers but left the Conservative Government intact. The present crisis threatens to end the twelve-year rule of the Conservative party . . .'

During the Commons debate – which was held while Stephen Ward was awaiting trial – Mr Macmillan revealed that Ward had called on his Private Secretary on 7 May of that year, in the presence of an MI5 officer. During the course of his complaints, 'Mr Ward let drop the remark that Mr Profumo had not told the truth' (in his personal statement). Later, when the Lord Chancellor began his inquiries, he learned that '. . . Christine Keeler had told the police on 26 January (1963), while they were questioning her about the Edgecombe affray, that Stephen Ward had asked her to discover from Profumo the date on which certain atomic secrets were to be handed to West Germany by the Americans – this was at the time of the Cuba crisis – and that she did not put this question to Mr Profumo . . .' The Prime Minister added, 'I think it very unfortunate that this information was not given to me, but the head of the security service, in considering these reports, did not take that as of great importance.'

Ironically, the then head of MI5 was Sir Roger Hollis, who was himself later accused by some of his senior officers of being a Soviet agent. (There was another 'spy' connection, unknown at the time. On 22 July 1963, the day on which Ward's trial began at the Old Bailey, an exhibition of his drawings opened in London. Among his portraits of the famous were some of members of the Royal Family. As the trial proceeded a mysterious caller who declined to give his name bought the lot for £5,000 – paid in cash, with £5 notes. He was later identified as Professor Anthony Blunt, then Keeper of the Queen's Pictures. Another year was to pass before he confessed to being a long-term Soviet agent.

At the lower court hearing, the magistrates found that no *prima facie* case of brothel keeping had been made against Dr Ward; by the time his Old Bailey trial began, the Crown had further decided to leave two abortion charges on the file. Ward pleaded not guilty to five counts of poncing and procuring. On the seventh day of his trial, held in the Bailey's famous No. 1 Court and packed to capacity throughout, proceedings were adjourned before the judge had completed his summing-up. Ward was allowed home on bail. After sending for a *Daily Express* reporter, to whom he confessed that he was afraid of the outcome, he later took an overdose of barbiturates. For the ensuing three days he hovered between life and death at St Stephen's Hospital. Meantime the trial continued. He was found guilty on two counts (of living off the immoral earnings of three prostitutes, including Christine Keeler and Mandy Rice-Davies), not guilty of the other three. Dr Ward died before he knew the verdict or could appear before the judge for sentence.

However, he left several suicide notes, including one each to his trial judge and both leading counsel, as well as Lord Denning, who had been appointed by the Prime Minister to inquire into the whole Profumo Affair. He also wrote thanking a prostitute named Ronna Ricardo for having told the truth at the trial and directed that she should be paid £500 from his estate. (She had retracted much of the evidence she gave earlier at the magistrates court, claiming she was under police pressure.) To prostitute Vickie Barrett, another Crown witness, he wrote: 'I don't know what it was or who it was that made you do what you did. But if you have any decency left, you should tell the truth like Ronna Ricardo. You owe this not to me, but to everyone who may be treated like you or like me in future.'

Mr Wayland Young said apropos the Denning Report, which was published in September 1963,

> But many questions remain to worry the public. Was Ronna Ricardo telling the truth when she said she had been threatened by the police into giving false evidence? Why did Vickie Barrett break down when Ward died, confess to a journalist that she too had been lying, and then retract her confession? On whose instructions and with what right had Mandy Rice-Davies been forcibly kept in the country to give evidence against Stephen Ward? And, a question which seems to sum up the others, why did the police find it necessary to interview 140 people before they moved against Stephen Ward? How many people do they usually think it worth interviewing in order to prepare charges of poncing?

In general, Lord Denning found there had been no damage done to the national security, while he was 'satisfied' MI5 had not known in 1961 of Mr Profumo's affair with Christine Keeler (as Ward claimed). He confirmed, however, that MI5 knew in February 1963 about Miss Keeler's statement to the police, claiming that Ward had asked her to discover from the War Minister the date on which atomic secrets were to be handed to West Germany. 'They (the Special Branch Commander and a senior MI5 officer) decided there was no security interest involved such as to warrant any further steps being taken.' He was, however, critical of the government's failure to face facts and take the appropriate action. 'The conduct of Mr Profumo was such as to create, amongst an influential section of the people, a reasonable belief that he had committed adultery with such a woman in such circumstances as the case discloses. It was the responsibility of the Prime Minister and his colleagues, and of them only, to deal with this situation: and they did not succeed in doing so . . .'

Stephen Ward said, at his trial, of Christine Keeler, 'I don't think she ever had intercourse with Ivanov.' In his official Report, Lord Denning came to the same conclusion – although Miss Keeler, who should know, stated categorically in her book *Nothing but . . .* (with Sandy Fawkes, 1983) that, 'He gave me the kiss we had both been waiting for and we made marvellous, passionate love. He was gorgeous, so utterly masculine, we were for a while totally swept away . . .'

Whoever was telling the truth, Ivanov was the only one of the central characters in the Affair who got away scot-free. He simply stepped on a plane back to Russia. In December 1963 Christine Keeler was jailed for nine months for committing perjury at 'Lucky' Gordon's trial. Some thought it a stiffer sentence than she might have received for absconding and flying to Spain a second time. Stephen Ward was dead, while Mr Profumo disappeared from public view and has dedicated the rest of his life to running Toynbee Hall, the East End of London settlement and community workshop.

RAMPA, LOBSANG

THE 'THIRD EYE' HOAX

Some time in 1955, a man arrived at the office of the publisher Secker and Warburg in Great Russell Street, London, and managed to persuade its chairman, Fred Warburg, to see him. The man, who wore a tonsure, introduced himself as Dr T. Lobsang Rampa, and explained that he had written his autobiography and wanted Mr Warburg to publish it. He declared he was a medical doctor and produced a document, in English, which he said was issued by the University of Chungking. Mr Warburg agreed to look at the manuscript, which thereafter arrived in sections. It was a fascinating document describing how the young Rampa, child of wealthy parents, had been singled out by astrologers at the age of seven to become a monk and how he had trained in a monastery. At the age of eight, he had submitted to a brain operation to open the 'third eye' – the source of man's psychic powers. A hole was drilled in his forehead, then a sliver of very hard wood poked into this brain, so saw 'spirals of colour and globules of incandescent smoke'. 'For the rest of your life you will see people as they are and not as they pretend to be.' And Rampa saw, to his astonishment, that all the men in the room were surrounded by a luminous golden flame, the vital aura.

Warburg had his doubts; the details seemed authentic, but the style was curiously English and colloquial. 'I really did not think so much of kite-flying. Stupid idea, I thought. Dangerous. What a way to end a promising career. This is where I go back to prayers and herbs . . .' It didn't sound Tibetan. Various experts expressed contradictory opinions. But Rampa stood by his story of being a Tibetan. Warburg submitted him to a test: a few words of Tibetan. Rampa agreed that he could not understand it but explained that there was a perfectly good reason. During World War II he had been a prisoner of the Japanese, who had tortured him for information about his country; he had used his psychic powers to blot out all his knowledge of Tibetan.

Warburg swallowed his doubts and published, and the results vindicated his commercial sense. The book became a bestseller. It went into many languages and made Rampa a rich man.

A body of 'Tibetan scholars' was doubtful about its authenticity and hired a private detective, Clifford Burgess, to find out about Lobsang Rampa. What he discovered was that Rampa was in reality Cyril Henry Hoskins, a Devon man who now lived in Thames Ditton. Hoskins had been born in Plympton, near Plymouth, in 1911, and entered his father's plumbing business. He was apparently deeply interested in psychic matters and claimed to have been taken to China as a child. It seemed that Hoskins was given to fantasizing about China and things Chinese; a journalist on *Psychic News,* John Pitt, tracked down a couple who had known him when he was a clerk in

Weybridge and was told that Hoskins had claimed to be a flying instructor in the Chinese air force and had had an accident when his parachute failed to open. Later still, Hoskins changed his name to Carl Kuon Suo, called himself Dr Kuon, and claimed to have been born in Tibet.

Fred Warburg was understandably dismayed by these revelations but pointed out that he had published a note in the book saying that the author took full responsibility for all statements made in it. And he hinted at an alternative theory. 'But is the truth, the whole truth, out? . . . Did he believe his own fantasies? Was he, perhaps, the mouthpiece of a true Lama, as some have alleged?' Rampa/Hoskins was tracked down to a house outside Dublin, where he was living with a lady whom he had, apparently, seduced away from her Old Etonian husband. Rampa declined to be interviewed; so did the Old Etonian husband.

Quite undeterred by the furore, Rampa went on to write a second book, *Doctor From Lhasa* (1959), which was accepted by Souvenir Press. The publisher's note in this book acknowledged that *The Third Eye* had caused great contention but went on to state that the author's explanation was that he had been 'possessed' by the Tibetan lama Rampa since a blow on the head had caused mild concussion, and that Rampa now wrote his books through the author. Whatever the truth of the matter, the publisher added diplomatically, it is right that the book should be available to the public . . . *Doctor From Lhasa* continued the story where *The Third Eye* left off but is even more incredible. There is, for example, a chapter describing how Rampa jumped into an aircraft and, without any flying lessons, flew around for an hour or so, then brought the plane in to land.

Doctor From Lhasa revealed that Rampa had an audience who would believe anything he said. In a third book, *The Rampa Story*, he continued Rampa's autobiography from the point where he had left off at the end of the previous book – where Rampa was a prisoner of the Japanese and narrowly escaped execution – and described how he crossed into Russian territory, was imprisoned in the Lubianka prison in Moscow, then escaped, via Europe, to America. But the high point of the book is its seventh chapter, where Rampa described leaving his body and soaring to the astral plane, where his old teacher, the Lama Mingyar Dondup, was awaiting him. Dondup tells him: 'Your present body has suffered too much and will shortly fail. We have established a contact in the Land of England. This person wants to leave his body. We took him to the astral plane and discussed matters with him. He is *most* anxious to leave, and will do all we require . . .' Later, in London, Rampa is able to study the history of this Englishman in the Akashic record – the record on the 'psychic ether' of everything that has ever happened (Madame Blavatsky invented the phrase). Then Rampa goes to the Englishman's bedroom – in his astral body – and converses with the Englishman's astral body, agreeing to the swap. The Englishman tells him how he fell on his head and stood up to find himself standing by his physical body, connected to it by a silver cord. Then he saw a Tibetan walking towards him. 'I have come to you because I want your body . . .' And, after thinking it over, the unselfish Mr Hoskins decided that he had had enough of life anyway, and that he might as well hand over his body to someone who could make better use of it. The lama instructs him to climb the tree again and fall on his head in order to loosen the cord. Then a lama takes Hoskins by the arm and floats away with him to heaven, while Lobsang Rampa squeezes himself into the vacated body with a sensation of suffocating. Rampa finds himself confronted with such problems as riding a bicycle and claiming unemployment benefit. Life was difficult and painful until he met a literary agent and outlined the story of The Third Eye . . .

The book should end there, but there is more to tell. After finishing The Third Eye he has a heart attack, and he and his wife move to Ireland. (It is not clear why the climate of Ireland should be better for heart ailments than England.) There he wrote Doctor From Lhasa. But the task was still not completed; he had to go on and tell The Rampa Story. Driven out of Ireland by income tax problems, he moves to Canada. There he receives a telepathic message: he must go on writing and tell the Truth. 'Write it down, Lobsang, and also write of what could be in Tibet.' And he continues to tell a story of how Truth found it difficult to obtain an audience until he borrowed the coloured garments of Parable. After that, Truth was welcome everywhere. . . (This, presumably, is intended as a reply to people who claim that Rampa's Tibet is unlike the real place; he can always claim he is talking in parables.) The book ends with a nasty vision of an atomic rocket, launched from Tibet by the Chinese. 'Is it fantasy?' he asks. 'It could be fact.' The placing of the quotation suggests that it could refer to the whole Rampa story.

Rampa's explanations about his body swap must have convinced a fair number of readers, for he has gone on to produce several more books: Cave of the Ancients, Living With a Lama, You-Forever, Wisdom of the Ancients, and a book called My Visit to Venus in which he describes how he was taken to Venus in a flying saucer and spent some time studying the history of Atlantis and Lemuria in its skyscraper cities. (Space probes have since shown that Venus is too hot to support any form of life.)

It seems that Hoskins has constructed a story that cannot be disproved by the sceptics, since he has an answer to every objection. Yet there still remain a few matters that need explaining. Why did Hoskins tell his neighbours, a Mr and Mrs Boxall, in 1943 or 1944 that he had been a pilot in the Chinese air force? This was some years before his first 'meeting' with Lobsang Rampa. And why, in 1948, did he change his name to Dr Carl Kuon Suo, rather than to Lobsang Rampa? Of one thing we can be sure: Rampa would have no difficulty providing answers that would satisfy the faithful.

RUSSELL, BERTRAND

SEX LIFE OF A LOGICAL PHILOSOPHER

Bertrand Russell was a lifelong philanderer of whom one biographer wrote his 'private life was a chaos of serious affairs, secret trysts and emotional tightrope acts that constantly threatened, if never quite exploded into, ruinous scandal.'

Russell's father, Lord Amberley, was not quite so fortunate. At the age of twenty-two, his tutor recommended him to read a book on the overpopulation problem and four years later, Amberley took the chair at a meeting of the London Dialectical Society, in which he criticized the clergy for being opposed to the prevention of overpopulation and said that if women had more say in the matter they would be opposed to large families. Ten days later, the *British Medical Journal* repudiated birth control, and Lord Amberley, with 'indignation and disgust'. The *Journal,* and other organs that took up the attack, seemed to believe that Amberley was advocating abortion or infanticide. (Victorian delicacy made it hard for anyone to say openly what Amberley had advocated.) He was called a 'filthy, foulmouthed rake', and when he stood as a Liberal for Parliament, a placard of 'a scandalous and indecent character' was flourished at him. Understandably, he failed to gain the seat.

Russell was born in 1872. He tells in his autobiography how his father hired a tutor named Spalding to teach his elder brother science. The tutor was in an advanced stage of consumption but Lord and Lady Amberley decided that, although he ought to remain childless, it was unfair for him to remain celibate. So Lady Amberley gallantly offered Spalding the use of her own body to allay his frustration, 'though', adds Russell, 'I know of no evidence that she derived any pleasure from doing so.' This seems a naive remark; no woman, particularly the daughter of a peer, is likely to consent to allowing a young man to use her like a prostitute unless she has some sneaking admiration for him. The affair started soon after Russell was born. However, two years later, Lady Amberley died of diphtheria, and her husband, soon after, of bronchitis.

Russell was raised by a Presbyterian grandmother and brooded a great deal on his sinfulness. At fifteen he was 'constantly distracted by erections' and learned to masturbate. Then, at twenty, he fell in love with Alys Pearsall Smith, an American Quaker. At the same time he became involved with Alys's sister Mary, who had just left her husband. He later told intimate friends that he had had an affair with Mary. This seems to contradict the statement in his autobiography that until 1911 he had never had 'complete relations' with any woman. The solution may lie in the word 'complete'. As a child, Russell had fallen out of a carriage and hurt his penis and there is a suggestion that this induced periodic impotence. He mentioned later that he 'failed totally' to give his first wife a child. So he and Mary may have tried hard but failed to achieve any result.

Russell married Alys, who was five years his senior, and they seem to have been reasonably happy, in spite of her conviction that 'sex was beastly' and that 'all women hated it'. After some initial sexual problems, which he found 'merely comic', they seem to have overcome problems of mutual adjustment. Even so, Russell describes 'a day after three weeks of marriage, when, under the influence of sexual fatigue, I hated her and could not imagine why I had wished to marry her.' This is a highly revealing comment, which throws some light on the curious paradox of Russell's mental life. Intellectually he was brilliant, with a natural capacity for abstract reasoning. But he always seemed to handle emotional problems with a clumsiness that shows a total lack of imagination. This is why his writings, particularly on moral and social questions, often seem naive.

Russell was himself capable of recognizing this emotional inadequacy. When he began to work on his monumental *Principia Mathematica* with Alfred North Whitehead, he fell in love with Whitehead's wife Evelyn. She often suffered intense pain from heart trouble. One day Russell walked into the room to find her undergoing a severe bout of pain: 'She seemed cut off from everyone and everything by walls of agony, and the sense of the solitude of each human soul suddenly overwhelmed me. Ever since my marriage, my emotional life had been calm and superficial. I had forgotten all the deeper issues, and had been content with flippant cleverness. Suddenly the ground seemed to give way beneath me ...' The result was a sort of religious conversion, which turned him into a pacifist and, socially speaking, an idealist.

One day out bicycling, he suddenly realized he was no longer in love with Alys and that she irritated him profoundly. With typical unconscious cruelty, he decided he had better tell her so immediately. The poor woman was naturally shattered and went on clinging pathetically to him for several years, periodically begging him to come to her bed. (He did, but found it unenjoyable.)

Then one day he fell in love. He had been canvassing for his friend Philip Morrell, a Liberal candidate. In March 1911 he went to stay the night at the London home of the Morrells and found that his host had had to go elsewhere. He was entertained by Lady Ottoline Morrell, Philip's wife, who had red hair and a face like a horse. But both she and her house were intensely feminine and Russell was tired of Quaker plainness and flannel nighties. 'Making timid approaches, I found them to my surprise not repulsed. I found to my amazement that I loved her deeply and that she returned my feeling. ... For external and accidental reasons [he means presumably that she was menstruating] I did not have full relations with Ottoline that evening but we agreed to become lovers as soon as possible.'

The opportunity came when Russell went to visit her at her country house, Studland. Russell's dentist had told him he thought Russell had cancer and he describes how this knowledge heightened his happiness by giving it greater intensity. A specialist reassured him about the cancer and he and Ottoline remained lovers for five years to the fury of Alys and the disgust of Philip Morrell.

Russell, having embarked on a career of adultery, never looked back. In 1913, on holiday in Italy, he saw a young German woman sitting alone and induced one of the ladies in the party to invite her to join them. 'I made friends with the lady and we made an expedition into the country. I wished to make love to her, but thought that I ought first to explain about Ottoline. Until I spoke about Ottoline, she was acquiescent but afterwards she ceased to be so. She decided, however, that for one day her objections could be ignored.' In the following year Russell visited America, and met a surgeon's daughter named Helen Bradley in Chicago. He confessed to Ottoline that they had spent the day in the woods 'and I found that I care for her a great deal. It ended by our spending the night together and she will come to England as soon as she can.' Helen Bradley came to England with 'hopes and preparations for a honeymoon'; but Russell had already tired of her. Helen had to pour out her miseries to Ottoline, with whom she was staying. When Russell and Helen went together to Garsington – the Morrells' new country home – Helen could be heard knocking on Russell's bedroom door in the middle of the night; but he refused to open up. And back in London, Russell was making love to Ottoline in his new flat when Helen came and knocked on the door – and again received no answer. Meanwhile, Ottoline had introduced him to the beautiful Irene Copper Willis, a research assistant who worked with him on a political pamphlet. Russell made love to her, then wished that he hadn't for she was afraid of scandal and refused to go away with him. 'I do like people to be willing to shoot Niagara,' said Russell, conveniently overlooking his tendency to fall out of love with women when they were struggling in the water.

During World War I, Russell was dismissed from his lectureship at Trinity College, Cambridge, for his pacifist views. In 1916 his pacifism brought him into contact with a pretty twenty-year-old actress, Lady Constance Malleson, who was married to the actor Miles Malleson. When Russell had delivered a pacifist speech and received an immense ovation, they dined together and afterwards he went back to her flat – her husband was away – where they became lovers.

In 1915, Russell had bumped into T.S. Eliot in London – he had met him earlier in America (and Eliot had written a poem about him called 'Mr Apollinax'). Eliot was now about to marry a beautiful but rather unstable young lady named Vivien Haigh-Wood and they had nowhere to live. Russell offered to let them share his Bury Street flat. Apparently Eliot had no objection to Russell staying in the flat with Vivien when he himself happened to be away. Vivien seems to have preferred Russell to Eliot in many ways – Eliot was undervitalized (a doctor remarked that he had the thinnest blood he had ever come across). Even when the Eliots found their own flat, Russell would sometimes take Vivien out to dinner or lunch. He had decided that his relation with the Eliots should be purely 'paternalistic', but in 1918, he finally gave way and made love to Vivien. He told Constance Malleson that the experience was 'hellish and loathesome' and that he had to disguise his antipathy. He took the first opportunity of breaking with Vivien, who later went insane.

In 1919, Russell moved to Lulworth, in Dorset, for the summer. Among many visitors there was a personable young lady named Dora Black, a Fellow of Girton. She was also a campaigner for women's rights who was 'outspoken in her advocacy of greater sexual freedom.' She found Russell 'enchantingly ugly' and thought he looked like the Mad Hatter. The next time they met they talked about her aversion to marriage and he asked her what she wanted to do about children. She replied that they should be entirely the concern of the mother. Two weeks later there was a ring at her doorbell and Russell asked her if she could catch the 12:30 train to Lulworth on Monday. 'Am I to understand . . . ?' asked Dora breathlessly and Russell nodded. 'But I understand you are already in love with a lady?' Russell assured her it was all over. (In fact, it was to be another two years before he threw over Lady Constance.) Typically, halfway through their weekend, Lady Constance sent a telegram announcing her arrival so Russell informed Dora she would have to leave immediately . . .

In spite of this bad start, when he was offered a post at Peking University, it was Dora Black Russell decided to take with him. When they returned in 1921 she was pregnant. They agreed to marry but both insisted that they should retain their individual freedom. And when, in 1926, the Russells decided to start their own experimental school, one of the things they advocated was that free love should be allowed to the staff. Russell regarded the female staff as his private harem and thoroughly enjoyed himself. He explained to his staff that it was impossible for a man to know a woman until he had slept with her (a view also held by his contemporary Professor Joad.) 'He had no hesitation putting his beliefs to the test,' says Russell's biographer Ronald Clark, who also quotes him on the subject of his 'inability to restrain his abnormally strong sexual urges'. He had one fairly regular affair – a girl with whom he disappeared most weekends to his London flat, explaining blandly to his staff, 'As we both have to go to London it saves a chauffeur if we both go at the same time.' This can have fooled few of them, since Russell was in the habit of propositioning the more attractive females. One new teacher turned him down on her second evening at the school (he seems to have borne her no ill will). When Dora Russell was finally granted a divorce in 1935 the judge commented that Russell had 'been guilty of numerous acts of adultery . . . with persons in the household.' He added, 'in circumstances which are usually held to aggravate the offence,' implying that Russell did not confine his activities to 'dirty weekends' in London, but carried on under his wife's nose. Dora Russell describes how she had been spending a weekend with a young man in London when she received a note from the cook saying she must return home at once – she was refusing to let the governess come near the children because she had caught her sleeping with 'the Master'. 'Bertie had an aristocratic attitude to the servants', says Dora, recording that the cook had to go but that the governess, 'who was a charming girl', should stay on. Russell had by this time broken with Lady Constance Malleson after several attempts at reviving the affair that had ended in brief reconciliation. Russell remarked that philosophers in love 'are exactly like everybody else, except, perhaps, that the holiday from reason makes them passionate to excess.'

Russell had discovered that his ugliness – the prim but weak mouth, the receding chin, the large nose – made no difference where women were concerned; his fame was an aphrodisiac. Clark records that even as he approached sixty he was still endangered by 'an insatiable appetite for personable and intelligent young women'. There was, for example, the case of a Miss Joan Folwell, whom he met after addressing a political meeting in Salisbury. She was 21. Russell was a guest in the house of her parents and he asked her to read aloud an essay she had written. 'I then realized,' wrote Miss Folwell, 'that he was more interested in me than my writing.' Letters soon progressed from 'My Dear Joan (may I call you so?)' to 'My darling Joan', and after a short time he was inviting her to spend the night with him. 'My only fear is lest you may find me sexually inadequate, as I am no longer young . . . but I think there are ways in which I can make up for it. And I do want you dreadfully . . .' Problems intervened; he had to send her a telegram and cancel. Then he went to America but when he returned he renewed the pursuit. They met – the second time for dinner, the third to stay the night together. It had taken Russell three years to get her into bed. 'He was very tenacious . . . But the sleeping wasn't a success, so I gave him up.' More than forty years later, Miss Folwell recorded her conviction that Russell was largely responsible for the permissive society and that he would have hated it.

The marriage to Dora ended after she had had two children by an American journalist. Dora hired a pretty governess named Patricia Spence, known as Peter; inevitably, Russell became attracted to her and when Dora Russell's American journalist visited, they formed a *ménage à quatre*. Eventually, he and Patricia married but there continued to be other women. It made no difference whether they were already married or married to men with whom he was friendly – like Gamel Brenan, wife of his friend Gerald

Brenan, whom Russell pursued with customary tenacity for years. Then there was the young wife of a Cambridge lecturer, who moved into Russell's house with her husband to look after him when Patricia was in hospital after an accident. Although now in his mid-70s, Russell bombarded her with letters suggesting clandestine meetings in London or elsewhere. The philosopher Sidney Hook, who knew Russell well, records that the marriage with Patricia broke up when Russell declined to make a pledge of mutual fidelity. 'That was the last straw for Patricia who had suffered humiliation enough because of Russell's roving eye and affections.' Hook also recorded (in *Encounter,* March 1984):

> He volunteered confessions about his sexual powers, and related matters about which I would no more have enquired of him than I would of my own father. He seemed always on the prowl when attractive and vivacious young women were around and he assumed that my interest in extracurricular matrimonial activity was as keen as his own. On occasions I was rendered speechless by his unsolicited advice on how to 'make' a girl and what to do after one made her. 'Hook', he once advised, 'if you ever take a girl to an hotel and the reception clerk seems suspicious, when he gives you the price of the room, have her complain loudly, "It's *much* too expensive!" He's sure to assume she is your wife. . .' At another time when I commented on his remarkable memory, he mildly demurred and observed that it was not what it used to be. Seconds later, as if to illustrate his point, he turned to me and asked, 'Hook, what's been the most embarrassing moment of your life?' Without waiting for a reply from me, he went on, 'Mine was the failure to remember at breakfast the name of an attractive woman to whom I had made ardent love the night before. I really knew it, of course, but it came to mind too late!' Like George Bernard Shaw, Russell was apparently an eloquent vocaliser in his love-making ecstasies.

Hook offers some interesting insights into the paradox that was Bertrand Russell: the brilliant mind, the penetrating intellect, allied to a curious emotional immaturity. He lists the three things that prevent him from classifying Russell as one of the 'great minds who were also great human beings'. 'The first was Russell's vanity. He once told me that whenever he met a man of outstanding intellectual reputation, his first unuttered reaction was: "Can I take him or can he take me? . . ." There was more than a touch of exhibitionism in the riskless sit-downs of his last years, when he made well-publicized gestures to Ban The Bomb that were as futile as they were ill-advised.' The second trait Hook found unpleasant was Russell's greed. 'I was shocked to find what Russell was prepared to do for a little money. . . . He always seemed strapped for money and tended to blame it on Patricia's extravagance which seemed hardly plausible to me.' He cites an article

Russell wrote for a magazine called *Glamour* entitled 'What To Do If You Fall In Love With a Married Woman'. When Hook asked him why he did it, Russell replied, 'For fifty dollars.' The third trait Hook disliked was a certain cold-bloodedness. 'I reluctantly came to the conclusion that Russell's religion of truth overlaid a strong streak of cruelty.' He cites many examples, including Russell's treatment of Helen Bradley. 'Sensitive readers of Russell's autobiography will have been revolted by the cruelty of some of its pages, not only his account of his treatment of the infatuated young woman who followed him to England, but particularly by the reproduction of a letter from a harmless German savant who after making some contributions to the philosophy of mathematics had become insane. Publication of that letter was like jeering at a cripple.'

Dora Russell made the interesting comment, 'In love, too, Bertie was a perfectionist; the "spiritual" bond must exist, if it were broken then love might come to an end. In this, as in other matters, Bertie was not fully aware of his underlying motives; that spiritual bond might well mean that a wife must agree with him in every detail, so that she might be fully possessed.' It is the nearest she comes to admitting that Russell was an adept in self-deception.

SCHLIEMANN, HEINRICH

THE GREAT TROY HOAX

During his lifetime and for more than eighty years after his death, in 1890, the name of Heinrich Schliemann – 'the man who found Troy' – remained untainted by the slightest breath of scandal. The discovery in the late 1970s that he was, in fact, a pathological liar and a crook caused tremendous reverberations in the world of archaeology.

Heinrich Schliemann, the man who was to be described as 'the creator of prehistoric Greek archaeology', was born on 6 January 1822 at Neu-Buckow, Germany, the son of a country parson. It was from his father that young Heinrich first heard about ancient history. In his autobiography, he tells of the crucial event of his childhood: how, at the age of seven, he received for Christmas a copy of Jerrer's *Universal History,* with an illustration showing Troy in flames. Surely, reasoned the young Heinrich, walls so mighty could not have been destroyed? They must still be there . . .

His childhood was not happy. One of seven children, he was shattered by the death of his mother and by the scandal when his father took a maidservant as a mistress, and later when his father was accused of misappropriating church funds and dismissed (he was later exonerated). Heinrich and his father had many bitter arguments. At the age of fourteen, Heinrich became a grocer's assistant and had to work fourteen hours a day. Suffering from tuberculosis, he gave up his job and became a cabin boy on a boat sailing for South America; it was shipwrecked and he found himself eventually in Amsterdam. There he became a clerk, taught himself English and went on to learn nine foreign languages in six years. At the age of 24, he was sent to Russia as the chief agent of an Amsterdam merchant. In 1850, he sailed for America to claim the estate of his brother Louis, who had died in California. He records in his diary that he called on the President of the United States, Zachary Taylor, and had an hour-and-a-half's conversation with him, meeting his family and being treated with great kindness. Then he went on to Sacramento, where he set up an office to buy gold dust from the miners for the gold rush was at its height at that time. He amassed a fortune of $350,000 as a result. He noted in his diary that he was in San Francisco during the great fire of 1851. Back in Europe, he married a Russian beauty but she did not care for archaeology or travel and they eventually divorced. Schliemann visited Greece for the first time at the age of 37. Four years later, he was rich enough to realize the ambition of a lifetime and to become an archaeologist. He studied archaeology in Paris and travelled extensively in the Mediterranean area. In 1868 he visited Mycenae, in Greece – the home of Agamemnon – and propounded a startling theory that the royal tombs would be found within the ruined walls of the citadel, and not, as the Greek geographer Pausanius stated, outside the walls. Soon after this he was awarded his doctorate by the University of Rostock, writing his thesis, according to his autobiography, in classical Greek.

An old friend, Archbishop Theoclitus Vimbos of Athens, helped him find a Greek wife. A sixteen-year-old schoolgirl, Sophia Engastromenos, was selected for him; her parents agreed, and the couple was married. Her parents were much impressed by his tales, particularly the story about the fire of San Francisco.

Schliemann was convinced that Troy really existed and that it was no legend, as many scholars believed. Those scholars who accepted the existence of Troy – ancient Ilion – thought that it was situated three hours from the sea near Bunarbashi, on the Balidagh, in a mountain fastness. On the evidence of Homer, Schliemann disagreed – Homer's heroes had ridden between Troy and the coast several times a day. He decided that the site of Troy was probably a mound at a place called Hissarlik, an hour from the sea. He obtained permission from the Turkish authorities to dig there and started in 1871, with a gang of eighty men.

It must be admitted that, as an archaeologist, Schliemann does not rate very highly. His method was as subtle as a bulldozer. He simply ordered his men to cut a deep trench through the mound. He soon discovered that the mound contained several cities, one on top of the other. Convinced that ancient Troy must be the lowest, he ordered his workmen to dig straight down to it, destroying all the ruins above, including those of the city archaeologists now know to be the Troy of Homer. The city Schliemann thought was the Troy of King Priam was in reality many centuries earlier.

In the following year, Schliemann's workmen sliced the top off the mound. Many discoveries came to light, but so far, there was no sign of the gold that Homer talked about. At least he found structures he identified as the royal palace, the wall of the gods, and the ramp leading to the Scaean Gate.

By the spring of 1883 he was becoming worried; he had still found no gold and he had agreed to end the excavations in June. Then, one day in May he thought he glimpsed a copper vessel through a hole in a wall. What followed has been told in breathless detail by more than twenty biographers of Schliemann. Afraid that his workmen would make off with part of his find, he waited until they were eating, then asked Sophia to help him remove the 'treasure'. Indifferent to his danger for the wall above was made of loose masonry, he tore out the stones, aided by a large knife and, piece by piece, handed the marvellous gold objects – drinking vessels and jewellery – to his wife, who wrapped them in her shawl. Later, behind closed doors, Sophie was dressed in the jewels of Helen of Troy – Schliemann was later to take a photograph of her draped in the gold ornaments. In June he returned to Athens and finally announced his discovery of the treasure. It made him world famous. He was later to excavate Mycenae, where his guess about the situation of the tombs proved correct. He died in 1890, at the age of 68. Sophia survived him by forty years.

That is the story of Heinrich Schliemann, and it has been retold many times. Guides at Hissarlik still show fascinated tourists the spot where Schliemann discovered the treasure of Priam, only a few weeks before he was due to leave Troy for ever.

In 1972, William Calder, Professor of Classics at the University of Colorado, was asked to go to Schliemann's birthplace, Neu-Buckow, to give a lecture on the hundred-and-fiftieth anniversary of his birth. Studying the various biographies of the great man, he realized that about 90 per cent of their material came from Schliemann himself. As soon as he began to check source material, he discovered that Schliemann was rather less trustworthy than his admirers had assumed. Checking at the University of Rostock, Calder discovered that the doctoral thesis was not, as Schliemann had declared, written in classical Greek; it only had a short section in classical Greek and this was atrocious. Calder checked on the story about calling on the President of the United States and being kindly received; the reception at which Schliemann claimed he was presented to six hundred guests would certainly be mentioned in Washington newspapers. There was nothing whatever – Schliemann had invented it.

Calder's lecture about these saddening discoveries was read by David Trail, a classics professor at the University of California. In San Francisco, he was able to check the records of the bankers who had stored the gold dust that Schliemann had bought from the miners in Sacramento and found suggestions that Schliemann had systematically cheated them by sending them short-weight consignments. Checking Schliemann's account of the great fire of San Francisco, Trail discovered that Schliemann had quoted the wrong date – he gave it as 4 June 1851 when it had taken place on 4 May. Schliemann's papers are stored in Athens, and Trail checked the diary. The page with the account of the fire proved to have been glued in later. The page preceding it has an entry in Spanish, which continues on the following page. The account proved to have been culled from newspapers of the time.

Calder's opinion was that Schliemann was a pathological liar – a liar so convinced of his own romances that a lie-detector test would probably have indicated he was telling the truth. Even the story about seeing the pictures of Troy in a book he was given for Christmas proved to be an invention, fabricated later for Schliemann's book *Ilion*.

The diaries also revealed that there were doubts about the finding of the treasure. There was no entry for the discovery of the treasure; he speaks about it for the first time in an entry dated 17 June. In the published account, this entry is datelined from Troy. In the diary, 'Athens' has been crossed out and 'Troy' substituted. An entry that was a draft-account of the discovery for his German publishers fails to describe the treasure, with the exception of one gold cup, noted as having large handles and being shaped like a champagne glass, with a rounded bottom (the shape we would now describe as a hock glass). There is no such vessel among the treasure. The nearest to it is a kind of gold sauce boat with handles and the descriptions do not correspond. But Schliemann had unearthed many terracotta vessels that looked exactly like the 'champagne glass' he described. It seems that he simply invented the item in order to give his publisher a foretaste of the treasure.

Further investigation revealed that Sophia was not present at the time Schliemann claims he found the treasure. She was in mourning for her father in Athens and did not return to Troy. And although excavations continued for two weeks after Schliemann claimed to have found the treasure – giving him plenty of time to describe it – there is nevertheless not a single description in his diary. The inference is that he did not find any treasure – at least, not in the manner he described.

But where did the treasure come from? Trail's conclusion was that the 'treasure' was already back in Athens at the time Schliemann claims he discovered it. He was obliged by contract to share anything he found with the owners of the site, a Pasha and an American named Frank Calvert. What almost certainly happened is that Schliemann systematically cheated them, claiming he had found nothing, and smuggling his finds back to Athens – his letters often refer to objects that he failed to show to Calvert. In March, before the 'finding' of the treasure, a letter mentions sixty gold rings – precisely the number of rings in the treasure.

That Schliemann found something is proved by the testimony of his trusted overseer, Nicolaos Yannakis, who later told an English antiquarian, William Borlase, that he had been with Schliemann at the time of the find and not Sophia. And the find contained no gold or jewellery – only a quantity of bronze objects, found in a stone enclosure outside the city wall.

So why did Schliemann do it? Psychoanalysts who have considered the problem have talked about his relationship with his father – the admiration combined with fear and dislike that compelled him to seek fame so that he could finally feel he had outstripped his father. This may or may not be true. All that is certain is that Schliemann craved fame and applause – his lie about the meeting with the president reveals the desire to impress. 'We all bid for admiration with no intention of earning it,' says Shaw. In his own devious way, Schliemann set out to earn it. He wanted to believe that he had found Homer's Troy; to complete the triumph he needed to find King Priam's treasure. And if the treasure did not exist, then it had to be made to exist. Only in this way could Schliemann achieve the kind of celebrity he craved.

But although these revelations reveal Schliemann as a crook and a liar, they leave one part of his reputation untouched: that strange, intuitive genius that led him to dig in exactly the right place, first at Hissarlik and later at Mycenae. He may have been a confidence man, but he was still, in spite of everything, 'the creator of prehistoric Greek archaeology'.

SCOTLAND YARD

THE GREAT BRIBERY SCANDAL

Harry Benson, one of the most ingenious swindlers of all time, is remembered chiefly for his leading role in the great Scotland Yard scandal of 1877.

Benson was the son of a well-to-do Jewish merchant with offices in the Faubourg St Honoré in Paris. He had charming manners, spoke several languages, and liked to represent himself as a member of the nobility. Soon after the Franco-Prussian war of 1870–71, he approached the Lord Mayor of London, calling himself the Comte de Montague, Mayor of Châteaudun, seeking a subscription for the relief of citizens made destitute by the war. He collected £1,000 but his forged receipt gave him away and he was sentenced to a year in prison. He found prison life so intolerable that he attempted suicide by trying to burn himself to death on his prison mattress. He was crippled by it and had to walk with crutches thereafter.

When he came out of prison, Benson advertised for a secretarial position, mentioning that he spoke several languages. The man who answered his advertisement was a certain William Kurr, who specialized in swindles connected with racing. His crude method was to decamp hastily with his customers' winnings. The ingenious Benson soon convinced him that there were better and less risky ways of making a fortune. Members of the French aristocracy were the chosen victims. Kurr and Benson issued a newspaper called *Le Sport* which contained articles about racing translated from British newspapers. It also contained many references to a wealthy Mr G.H. Yonge, who was so incredibly successful in backing horses that British bookmakers always shortened their odds when they dealt with him. *Le Sport* was sent out, free, to dozens of French aristocrats interested in racing; they had no earthly reason for suspecting a prospective swindle.

One of the aristocrats who became a victim was a certain Comtesse de Goncourt. She received a letter from Mr Yonge of Shanklin, Isle of Wight, asking her if she would agree to act as his agent in laying bets. All she had to do was to send the cheque he would send her to a certain bookmaker; if the horse won, she would receive his winnings, which she would forward to Mr Yonge, and would receive a 5 per cent commission. Madame de Goncourt agreed to this arrangement and received a cheque for a few hundred pounds, which she posted off to the bookmaker in her own name. In due course, she received a cheque for more than a thousand pounds in 'winnings' and after she had sent this off to Mr Yonge, she received her £50 or so commission. It seemed a marvellously easy way of earning £50. What she did not realize was that the 'bookmaker' to whom she forwarded the cheque was simply another of Mr Yonge's aliases. When she had sent Mr Yonge several more lots of winnings and received several more lots of commission, she decided that he was obviously a financial genius and entrusted him with £10,000 of her own money to invest on her behalf. That was the last she saw of it.

Although Scotland Yard was a relatively new institution in the 1870s (it was established in 1829), its methods of crime-fighting depended a great deal on underworld 'narks' who betrayed fellow criminals. Police officers, then as now, were forced to cultivate the acquaintance of many criminals. It also meant that an underpaid police officer – in those days the salary of a detective was a mere £5 6s. 2d. a week – might be subjected to the temptation of accepting presents, favours and open bribes for protecting his own 'narks'. This may well be how a certain detective officer named John Meiklejohn became friendly with William Kurr and then began to accept money from him in exchange for not pressing his investigations into Kurr's earlier swindles. When Chief Inspector Nathaniel Druscovich, a naturalized Pole, confided to Chief Inspector Meiklejohn that he was in financial difficulties, Meiklejohn told him he knew a 'businessman' who could help him. The businessman was Benson and all he wanted in return for the £60 he 'lent' Druscovich was a little information – prior warning if the Yard intended to arrest him. Soon a third dectective had been drawn into the net – Chief Inspector William Palmer. Not long after this, Meiklejohn warned Kurr and Benson that the Yard was getting close. Meiklejohn's superior, Chief Inspector Clarke, had been tracking down sham betting offices and was hot on the trail of Gardner and Co., the name under which Kurr and his confederates had been operating.

Among these confederates was a man called Walters who belonged to a gang that Clarke had recently broken up. Now Benson wrote to Clarke from his pleasant home in the Isle of Wight – he kept a carriage, and had an excellent cook and many servants – saying that he had some interesting information about Walters. Unfortunately, he explained, he was crippled and could not come to Scotland Yard but if Clarke would be kind enough to come down to Shanklin. . . . In those days, policemen stood in awe of the aristocracy and were likely to treat a wealthy suspect with obsequious respect. So Clarke hurried down to Shanklin and was duly overawed by Mr Yonge's magnificent home. He was worried when Mr Yonge told him that Walters was going about saying that he had bribed Clarke and that he had in his possession a letter to prove it. Indeed Clarke had written Walters a letter; he was not a very literate man and he might easily have expressed himself in a way that could be open to false interpretation. Mr Yonge promised to try to get hold of the letter and he and Clarke parted on friendly terms. But Clarke than reported to his own superior that Yonge was a scoundrel. They had some correspondence and Yonge addressed Clarke as 'My Dear Sir and Brother' for they were both freemasons. They met several times and 'Yonge' later claimed he had given Clarke £50.

With this network of 'police spies', the Benson-Kurr gang should have been untouchable. But Benson now overreached himself. He wrote to the Comtesse de Goncourt saying that he had a marvellous and unique opportunity to invest a further large sum for her. The Comtesse had no more ready cash and she called on her lawyer, a Mr Abrahams, to ask him to turn certain securities into cash. Mr Abrahams took the precaution of contacting Scotland Yard and asking whether they knew anything about a certain Mr Yonge of 'Rose Bank', Shanklin. Druscovich, who was in charge of frauds connected with the Continent received the message and hastened to warn Benson that trouble was brewing. Scotland Yard had been asked by the Paris police to intercept letters containing money from various dupes – but the telegram containing this request was pocketed by Druscovich. Druscovich could see that he was playing a dangerous game; he would be expected to make an arrest soon. He begged the swindlers to remove themselves beyond his reach as soon as possible.

The gang, which included Kurr's brother Frederick, and two men named Murray and Bale, had put most of its ill-gotten gains into the safest place, the Bank of England. They could, of course, withdraw it without difficulty. The only problem about that was that English bank notes are numbered and for such a large sum of money, they would be numbered consecutively and would, therefore, be easy to trace. If the gang escaped to the Continent, they would be leaving a trail of bank notes behind them like a paperchase. Benson withdrew about £16,000 from the bank and hastened up to Scotland where he opened an account in the Bank of Clydesdale in Greenock; he also withdrew £13,000 in Bank of Clydesdale £100 notes. These had the advantage of bearing no number but they were still easily traceable. Benson was eating dinner with the manager of the Clydesdale Bank when he received a telegram from Druscovich warning him that he was on his way to arrest him. Benson fled, forfeiting the £3,000 still in his account at Greenock.

The detectives were rewarded with about £500 each (although Clarke does not seem to have been included). Meiklejohn immediately made the mistake of cashing one of his £100 notes and giving an office of the gang as his address. A week later he cashed another note with a Leeds wine merchant. The Leeds Police discovered this and since they were on the lookout for the gang sent a telegram to Scotland Yard. Druscovich intercepted the telegram and burned it.

Scotland Yard found it baffling that, in spite of all their efforts, the Benson gang had slipped through their fingers. The bribed detectives were still not suspected. Clarke's superior Williamson set it all down to sheer bad luck. In fact, most of the gang was now in hiding at Bridge of Allan in Scotland. When the Comtesse's lawyer Abrahams traced them to Scotland, Detective Officer William Palmer sent them a letter warning them to scatter.

It was Druscovich who was made responsible for rushing around the country to trap the swindlers. He met Kurr at the Caledonian Station in

Edinburgh and was offered £1,000 by him if he did not go to Bridge of Allan. Druscovich had to decline for he had been ordered to go to Bridge of Allan to collect certain letters that had been addressed to one 'Mr Giffard' at the Queen's Hotel. Mr Giffard was William Kurr.

Inevitably, the birds had flown by the time Druscovich reached Bridge of Allan. Williamson was understandably disappointed. He was astounded to learn that his subordinate Meiklejohn had been seen in the company of the swindlers at Bridge of Allan. This was surely the point when Scotland Yard had to smell a rat . . . But Meiklejohn explained that he had no idea he had been wining and dining with crooks. He had met Yonge by chance and believed him to be a perfectly respectable gentleman. Williamson accepted his story.

Now the gang found themselves with thousands of pounds in uncashable £100 notes and with no ready cash. Murray was sent off to cash a cheque at one of the banks in Scotland where they had opened an account; the police were waiting for him. Benson went to Rotterdam and tried to cash a note at his hotel but Scotland Yard had alerted the Dutch police and he was arrested. Druscovich passed on the news to Kurr who persuaded a crooked attorney named Froggatt to send the Dutch police a telegram signed 'Scotland Yard', ordering them to release Benson on the grounds that his arrest had been a mistake. It almost succeeded but the Dutch police decided to wait for a letter confirming the telegram, and this never came.

It was Druscovich, the expert on Continental crime, who was sent to Rotterdam to bring back Benson – and Bale, who had also been arrested there. There was nothing he could do about it except to look at them sternly and mutter under his breath that he would do his best. There was no opportunity to allow them to escape. Besides, his own position was now in danger. Williamson had now heard about the letter from the Leeds Police, telling them that Meiklejohn had cashed a £100 note there. He wanted to know if Druscovich had seen it. Druscovich denied all knowledge of it and he realized that any attempt to allow Benson to escape was now out of the question.

The swindlers finally stood in the dock and were found guilty. Benson received fifteen years and Kurr received ten. As soon as they reached Millbank Prison, they asked to see the governor and told the story of the corrupt detectives. A short time afterwards, Druscovich, Meiklejohn, Palmer and Clarke all stood in the dock – and, for good measure, the police had also arrested the crooked attorney Froggatt. Many letters from the detectives were produced, warning the crooks of the activities of Scotland Yard. Druscovich had also been seen talking to Benson and Kurr at St Pancras Station, London.

All except Clarke were convicted – the evidence against Clarke was inconclusive. Druscovich, Meiklejohn and Palmer all received two years' hard labour, the maximum sentence for conspiring to defeat the ends of justice.

Clarke was retired on a pension. Meiklejohn became a private detective. Palmer used his savings to become a publican. What happened to Druscovich is not known but he disappeared from sight; while Froggatt died in a workhouse.

The two principle swindlers still had many successful years before them. Benson and Kurr both received a third remission of sentence for good conduct. They teamed up again and slipped across the Atlantic where they became mining company promoters. Benson returned to Belgium and continued in business selling stock in non-existent mines. The Belgian police found out more about him from Scotland Yard and arrested him. Huge quantities of postal orders and cheques, apparently sent to him by gullible investors were found in his lodgings. He spent another two years in jail then moved to Switzerland. There he again set out to give the impression he was a wealthy stockbroker. He met a girl in his hotel, whose father was a retired general and surgeon of the Indian army. He persuaded the girl to marry him and induced the father to sell his shares and hand over the proceeds of £7,000 for 'investment'. Then he tried to disappear to America. His father-in-law managed to have him arrested at Bremen but decided not to prosecute when Benson gave back £5,000. Jewellery that Benson had given his fiancée proved to be made of paste.

His last great coup was in America. The singer Adelina Patti was arriving in New York for a tour. Benson, calling himself Abbey, bribed Customs officials to let him on the boat ahead of the Patti Reception Committee. He introduced himself to her as the head of the committee. When the committee arrived, he was deep in conversation with her and they assumed he was her manager. She left the boat on his arm. He then went to Mexico and sold thousands of bogus tickets of Patti concerts. He was arrested when he went back into the States and committed to the Tombs. Apparently, unable to face the prospect of another long period in prison, he leapt from a high gallery and fell 50 feet, snapping his spine. At the time of his death he was little more than forty years of age.

SHOLOKHOV, MIKHAIL

THE *QUIET FLOWS THE DON* PLAGIARISM SCANDAL

The most eminent Russian author to emerge since the Revolution in 1917 is undoubtedly Mikhail Alexandrovitch Sholokhov, born in the hamlet of Kruzhlino, on the banks of the Don, in 1905. Like Gorky, Sholokhov led a varied life – soldier, handyman, statistician, food inspector, goods handler, mason, book-keeper and finally journalist – before he hurtled to literary fame at the age of 23 with the first volume of *Tikhi Don, The Quiet Don* (translated into English as *Quiet Flows the Don*). When compared with the great Russian novels of the nineteenth century, it seems full of 'shock tactics' of the kind associated with cheap popular novels in England and the United States. The book begins with a scene in which the Turkish wife of a Cossack is trampled by a mob who believe her to be a witch. As a result she dies in premature childbirth. Shortly thereafter there is a description of how a seventeen-year-old girl is raped by her father and how her brother and mother then beat and kick him to death. Seductions, rapes and various forms of violence follow at regular intervals. But the nature writing is as fine as anything in the work of the novelist Turgenev.

Sholokhov's first book *Tales of the Don* appeared when he was only twenty. It is interesting to note in these tales of the civil war and shortly after that the village leaders are portrayed as isolated from the people; later, as he learned communist conformity, Sholokhov showed them integrated with the people.

Sholokhov began work on *Tikhi Don* when he was 21. When it appeared two years later – and became an instant bestseller – critics were amazed that anyone so young could write so powerfully; it eventually sold four and a half million copies before its fourth and final volume appeared fourteen years later. The later volumes are generally admitted to be inferior to the first. *Virgin Soil Upturned* (1932), about a collective farm, was a success in Russia but it is considered inferior to the earlier parts of *Tikhi Don*.

Soon after the first volume of *Tikhi Don* appeared in 1925, rumours began to spread around Moscow literary circles to the effect that Sholokhov was not the true author and that he had found the manuscript or a diary on which he based the book. In 1929, *Pravda* published a letter from a number of proletarian writers denouncing the 'malicious slander'. It even threatened prosecution. Nevertheless, Sholokhov was generally regarded as Russia's most important writer. In 1965 he was given the Nobel Prize for literature. By then, Sholokhov had become spokesman for the Soviet literary establishment, denouncing writers like Pasternak and Solzhenitsyn and taking an aggressively anti-intellectual stand that has caused young writers to regard him with distaste. This may be fuelled by envy for his lifestyle on a large estate at Rostov-on-Don, where he has a private aeroplane and theatre, and hunts regularly.

Alexander Solzhenitsyn, who was forced into exile in Zurich in 1974, brought out of Russia a number of documents about Sholokhov's work by a friend whom he identifies simply as 'D'. 'D', according to Solzhenitsyn, engaged in painstaking literary analysis of *Tikhi Don* but died before he could complete it. Solzhenitsyn explained that he could not reveal 'D's' real name for fear of reprisals against his family but he published the manuscript and appealed to western scholars to help complete the research.

'D's' textual analysis revealed two different authors of *Tikhi Don*: some 95 per cent of its first two volumes belong to the 'original author', while less than 70 per cent of the second two are his work. 'D's' scepticism was apparently aroused by the fact that the first two volumes which showed intimate acquaintance with pre-Revolutionary society in the Don region and described World War I and the Civil War were allegedly written by a young man between the ages of 21 and 23. Sholokhov was too young to have witnessed either war. Even the speed of composition seems incredible – a novel of well over a quarter of a million words had been written in two years. Yet it took another fourteen years to complete the remaining two volumes and the first part of *Virgin Soil Upturned*. Sholokhov seemed to have 'dried up'. His collected works, issued in honour of his 75th birthday in 1980, amounted to a mere eight volumes.

According to Solzhenitsyn, (introducing 'D's' book *The Mainstream of the Quiet Don*) the true author of *Tikhi Don* was a historian of the Don region, one Fyodor Dmitrievitch Kryukov, born in 1870, the son of a local 'ataman' (village leader). By the end of the nineteenth century he had achieved great popularity as a recorder of Cossack life and was elected to the state parliament (Duma). Solzhenitsyn believes he began writing his major work, *Tikhi Don*, in Petrograd during World War I. As a Cossack, he was opposed to the Bolsheviks who seized power in 1917 and fought with the army of the Don. When this collapsed, he retired to the Kuban and died there of typhoid at the age of fifty. 'D's' analysis of Kryukov's earlier works, which were never reprinted by the Soviet regime, convinced him that he was the true author of *Tikhi Don* and that as a journalist Sholokhov somehow came across Kryukov's manuscript and used it as a basis for his own book, deleting whole chapters where they did not suit his purpose and inserting material of his own. This, according to 'D', explains the unevenness of the style and various internal contradictions.

Understandably, the Soviet view is that Solzhenitsyn is merely concerned with slandering and undermining the greatest Soviet novelist. But if this is so, at least he has presented his evidence in full so it can be studied by literary scholars and experts who can decide on its merits.

SIMPSON, O. J.

THE MURDER TRIAL

Just after midnight on Monday 13 June 1994, a howling, blood-spattered Akita dog attracted investigation by neighbours of 35-year-old Nichole Brown Simpson. They found her lying dead in the garden of her luxurious Santa Monica condo in a partially enclosed area near the entry gate. Lying nearby was the corpse of 25-year-old Ronald Goldman, also murdered. Both had been dead for just over two hours.

Los Angeles Police scene-of-crime officers quickly reconstructed the events of the two murders from the available evidence. The angle of the wound indicated that Nichole Brown Simpson had been standing near and was probably conversing with the killer when he struck at her neck with a long-bladed weapon, nearly severing Nichole's head from her body and killing her almost instantly. The 25-year-old Goldman then struggled with the murderer and was stabbed and slashed over thirty times. The murderer then escaped.

Even from this sparse evidence the police could make some preliminary guesses: the killer was quite possibly known to Nichole Brown Simpson, as he had been standing close to her when he attacked – people, especially women, tend to keep over an arm's-length away when talking to total strangers. The killer was also almost certainly a man – to judge by the strength needed to make such damaging attacks on two unrestrained adults – a very strong man at that. Finally, although much more speculatively, there was the possibility that this was a crime of passion: a savage attack on an attractive woman and a young man who might have appeared, to the jealous killer, to be her lover. (In fact Ronald Goldman was a waiter from a nearby restaurant who was – as far as we know – simply returning a pair of dark glasses that Nichole had left there earlier that day.) All the initial evidence seemed to point to Nichole's ex-husband: football hero and movie star, Orenthal James 'O.J.' Simpson.

Before he fell under suspicion as a double murderer, O.J. Simpson's life had been a classic American success story. Starting his public career in American football in the 1970s, he was soon one of the most famous players in the game's history. Playing in the position of running back, the young O.J. displayed masterful dexterity, strength and, most of all, running speed – breaking several records, including the most touchdowns scored in a single season. Also, the fact that he was black and from a relatively poor background made him a living icon of the American Dream: that talent could take anyone, from any background, right to the top.

O.J. retired from professional football in 1979. In that year he also divorced from his first wife and, shortly thereafter, lost his young son in a tragic swimming pool accident.

Despite these personal misfortunes, O.J. maintained his public career and high popularity. His pleasant, affable demeanour made him a popular TV personality and he eventually branched out from the usual profession of retired sports heroes – sport commentary – to start a new career as an actor. His success in the role of an inept, accident-prone policeman in the hit comedy movie *The Naked Gun*, in 1988, made O.J. a hot property in Hollywood. He followed this with another acting success, playing a black man framed by a racist cop in *The Klansman*. O.J. also landed a lucrative advertising contract as the endorsing celebrity for Hertz car rental – in one TV advert for the company, O.J. was shown desperately running through an airport, trying to catch a departing plane. The irony of these TV and movie images was later to be much commented upon.

In 1985, O.J. Simpson married Nichole Brown. He had originally met her serving tables in 1977, when she was seventeen and still in high school. The simple fact that Nichole was white again seemed to highlight O.J.'s role as an icon of the modern American Dream: in this case, showing that prejudice against mixed-race marriages was a thing of the past (in the well-off part of Los Angeles, at least). However, all was not as perfect in the relationship as was shown in the glossy magazines.

Nichole complained to friends and family members that O.J. was violently jealous of her. She also showed them bruises that she claimed had come from beatings O.J. had given her for playfully flirting with other men. O.J. later denied ever having hit Nichole, insisting that the bruises had resulted from friendly games of 'wrassling', but the very fact that Nichole was making such claims indicated deep problems in the marriage.

Few friends of the pair were surprised, therefore, when Nichole filed for divorce from O.J. Simpson in 1992. She won a $433,000 cash settlement, plus $10,000 a month in child-support for their two children.

O.J. Simpson was in Santa Monica at the time of the murders – his house being only a few blocks from Nichole's – but he was not there when police called to inform him of the death of his ex-wife. He had caught a flight to Chicago at 11:45 pm – less than two hours after the killings.

A limousine, booked to take him to the airport had arrived at 10:25 pm, but the driver, Allan Park, failed to get any response when he rang the doorbell. Used to the often eccentric behaviour of LA's upper crust, Park went back to the limousine and waited.

At 10:56 pm Park saw a big man in dark clothes walk up the drive and enter Simpson's home. He assumed that this was O.J., though it was too dark to make a positive identification. A few minutes later O.J. opened the front door and told Park that he had been inside all the time, but had dozed off and had not heard the doorbell. They then drove to the airport and O.J. caught his flight to Chicago without incident.

The police tracked Simpson to the O'Hare Plaza Hotel the following morning. The officer assigned the difficult task of telephoning to inform a national hero that his ex-wife had been murdered, nevertheless noted that O.J. did not ask how, when or where Nichole had died – the usual questions immediately asked by a relative of a murder victim. O.J. didn't even ask if the murderer had been caught.

Homicide officers very gently questioned O.J. for about half an hour later that day. He denied any knowledge or involvement in the killings but was, at the same time, vague about his movements on the previous evening. The investigators failed to press him on these points.

Many people later thought the interviewers were too easy on Simpson. Follow-up questions were not asked and several obvious lines of enquiry were not pursued at all. This might have been because O.J. seemed to be emotionally shattered, and officers didn't want to upset him further, but his demeanour might also have been the behaviour of a guilty murderer. As any experienced homicide detective will testify, the first interview with a murderer is often the most important, as they may not have invented all the details of their false alibi and can be caught out and encouraged to confess.

The interviewing police did notice, however, that O.J. had a bandage on his left hand. He told them that he had a deep cut to the palm, but claimed not to remember where he got the wound. This was one of the key issues that investigators were criticized for not pursuing. O.J. later claimed to have cut his hand reaching into his Ford Bronco car on the night of the murders. He had reopened the wound, he said, when, stricken by grief at the news of Nichole's death, he had crushed a hotel water glass. The prosecution at his later trial claimed that this injury had actually been sustained during the murders.

Despite the obvious reasons to suspect O.J. Simpson's involvement in the double murder, the Los Angeles police continued to treat him with kid gloves – he was, after all, a popular celebrity and in fact had several close friends in the LAPD. This unwonted leniency was another bone of contention during the later trial, with many commentators concluding that this was evidence of special police treatment for rich and influential suspects.

The police allowed O.J. to remain free; an almost unheard of privilege for a person suspected of violent homicide. The normal procedure would have been to hold him for questioning until investigators had enough evidence to charge and arrest him or, if such evidence was not forthcoming, until they had to let him go under the *habeas corpus* rule. In fact, even after amassing enough evidence to issue a warrant for Simpson's arrest, the LAPD allowed him to remain at large until after Nichole's funeral. They simply asked the man they had charged with a savage double killing to hand himself in at his local police station at 10 the following morning.

Simpson failed to turn up. The police and Simpson's lawyer drove up to

O.J.'s house, but found it empty. However a note was discovered, written 'To whom it may concern', and phrased in such a way as to hint that O.J. had killed himself, but without actually saying so directly.

Any anxiety O.J.'s friends in the LAPD might have felt were soon allayed. O.J. was spotted being driven by a friend, A.C. Cowlings, on the nearby freeway in a white Ford Bronco. There followed a farcical 'slow-motion' chase in which dozens of police cars and several news helicopters followed the slow moving Bronco as it drove around the Los Angeles road system. Police negotiators talked to both men via mobile phone and Simpson eventually had himself driven to his home, where he was finally arrested. The car was found to contain a gun, $8,750, a passport and a false beard.

In their very first decision in the case – as to where the trial was to take place – the prosecution made what many believe to have been a bad tactical blunder. Normal procedure would have been to conduct the trial in the area in which the crime took place: Santa Monica. But the prosecutors instead asked for the case to be heard in downtown Los Angeles. They explained that the larger downtown courthouse would allow more members of the press and media to cover the trial and, rather selfishly, that the members of the prosecution team would also have less of a commute each day if the trial was not held in distant Santa Monica.

In fact, these reasons were almost certainly a cover for the real reason the trial was held away from affluent Santa Monica: the authorities' fear of race rioting.

Three years earlier, on 3 March 1991, four white LA police officers had stopped speeding black driver, Rodney King, and proceeded to hit him 36 times with heavy nightsticks, unaware that a horrified member of the public was filming them. Despite the unprofessional and conflicting reports of the incident filed by the officers and the apparently conclusive evidence of the videotaped beating, in April the following year a majority white jury acquitted all four officers. Downtown Los Angeles exploded into violent race riots. In the following 6 days 54 people were killed, 2,383 were injured, looters caused $700 million worth of property damage and the National Guard had to be called out. Given this very recent history in the city, prosecutors in the Simpson case could have been forgiven for erring on the side of caution.

A jury called in the exclusive and rich Santa Monica neighbourhood would almost certainly have a white majority. If such a jury convicted one of the most popular black men in the country, there might be serious repercussions. A downtown jury, on the other hand, would almost certainly be racially mixed – as it in fact was. Many commentators have suggested that the outcome of the case was influenced by the positive discrimination of the black majority jury.

Another prosecution mistake – also perhaps politically motivated – was to drop their option to call for the death penalty if Simpson were to be convicted. Many studies have shown that a so-called 'death qualified' jury is more likely to convict, because those that oppose the death penalty are automatically disqualified from capital punishment cases. People who are against capital punishment are statistically more prone to find defendants not guilty, whereas a jury of people who have all indicated their support of the death penalty are more likely to find a defendant guilty.

The 133-day 'trial of the century' followed, starting on 24 July 1995. There was unprecedented press coverage. TV cameras were allowed in the court by Judge Lance Ito, and from the beginning the often tedious courtroom developments got as much news coverage as the average major war. Asked how he intended to plead, O.J. Simpson replied emphatically: 'Absolutely 100 per cent not guilty.'

The prosecution's case was that Simpson was a jealous and abusive husband who had preferred to murder his estranged wife rather than see her with another man. He had, they said, confronted Nichole and Goldman after letting himself into her garden. O.J. had clearly planned to commit murder because he had brought a long-bladed weapon with him. After the killings he had made his way back to his own estate, hurriedly disposed of some, but not all, of the incriminating evidence, then had calmly caught a flight to Chicago.

The chief evidence for this theory – aside from numerous witnesses who had seen or heard O.J. threatening Nichole at one time or another – was the cut on Simpson's hand, dating from the night of the murder, and a pair of socks and a leather glove found in Simpson's home. They were stained with blood that DNA testing showed to belong to Nichole Simpson. Furthermore, blood found at the murder scene had been DNA tested and, the prosecution claimed, had been positively proved to be O.J. Simpson's.

Although a largely circumstantial case, few would have bet on Simpson's acquittal.

The prosecution first presented witnesses to O.J.'s willingness to kill Nichole and his predilection for marital violence. Nichole's sister, Denise Brown, described a family meal during which O.J. had grabbed Nichole by the crotch and said loudly: 'This is where babies come from, and this belongs to me.' Another time, she said, she had seen O.J. pick up Nichole and literally throw her against a wall.

Denise also described seeing O.J. at his daughter's school dance recital only a few hours before the double murder. She told the court that he looked 'scary' like a 'madman'.

Ron Shipp, a friend of Simpson, described how O.J. had told him once that 'I've had dreams of killing Nichole.'

Finally, and visibly disturbing to the jury, the prosecution played a tape of an emergency services 911 call made by Nichole. The eerie sound of the dead woman's voice filled the court, begging for assistance because her husband, O.J., had just beaten her and was threatening to do it again. O.J. himself could be heard shouting furiously in the background of the recording.

Next the prosecution offered evidence that O.J. Simpson had actually committed the murder. The limousine driver, Allan Park, testified to the apparent absence of O.J. from his home at 10:25 pm – approximately half an hour after the murders – and the arrival of the unidentified man who had looked like Simpson at 10:56 pm. He added that when O.J. had finally emerged from the house to go to the airport, he had been carrying a small black bag. Park offered to carry this bag along with the other luggage, but Simpson declined. O.J. was not carrying the bag when he checked onto his flight a few minutes later, and an airport staff member was called by the prosecution to testify that he had seen O.J. approaching a rubbish bin. The implication was that this was how Simpson had got rid of the murder weapon.

O.J. Simpson's house had not been empty on the night of the killing; there was a houseguest called Kato Kaelin staying there. He testified that he and O.J. had gone on a 'run for Big Macs and French fries' at around 9:30 pm. He had not seen O.J. again after they got back. Then, just before 11 pm, Kaelin had heard several loud thumps on his wall. Again, the prosecution wished the jury to infer that after the food run, Simpson had slipped out, committed the murders and had been crashing about when he got back, trying to deal with the bloody evidence of his crimes.

This final, possibly clinching proof – the physical evidence – was the concluding part of the prosecution case. First there was the wound on O.J.'s left palm. His vague explanations to the police could not hide the fact that the cut looked very like a knife wound, perhaps sustained during a frenzied attack.

Several technical experts testified that hair, clothing fibres and footprints found at the murder scene indicated Simpson's presence. There was also blood found there – DNA testing showed that only 0.5 per cent of the population could have deposited this blood; O.J. Simpson was one of this very select group.

The police had found a pair of bloodstained socks at the foot of O.J.'s bed and, even more damning, an extra large Aris Light leather glove, of a type Simpson was known to wear, was found at the murder scene. Another such glove – apparently the partner of the murder scene glove – was found soaked in blood, in a hallway of O.J.'s house. The likely inference was that O.J. had attacked his victims with only his right hand gloved (there was no cut to the palm of the left glove), had sustained the wound to his left hand, then dropped the left glove at the crime scene. He had accidentally dropped the blood-soaked right glove in his hall during his efforts to clean himself up to catch his flight to Chicago.

DNA testing pointed to a 6.8 billion-to-one likelihood that the blood on the gloves and socks belonged to Nichole Simpson Brown – she was probably the only person on earth with blood to match the samples.

Short of the murder having been videoed by a member of the public, the prosecution case could not have been stronger – at least, that is what numerous press commentators believed before the council for the defence began their attack on the evidence.

If the prosecution had gone about the trial as if Simpson were not a superstar – presenting the evidence concisely and plainly – they probably would have stood a better chance of winning a conviction. However, under the unnerving public spotlight, they decided to err towards excess and cross every 't' and dot every 'i'. They brought in so many witnesses – 72 in all – that the jury, not to mention the worldwide viewing public, apparently became tired, confused and not a little bored. A more direct and forceful case would have presented the fairly damning evidence much more effectively.

O.J. Simpson's defence team – dubbed the 'Dream Team' by the press, because they comprised some of the best lawyers in the country, including F Lee Bailey – sought to exploit the tired confusion of the jury to sow a seed of doubt. In this task they were given invaluable help by one of the prosecution's star witnesses: Officer Mark Fuhrman of the LAPD.

During the prosecution's questioning of Fuhrman – the officer who had found the glove in Simpson's house – he had been presented as a model policeman. The defence cross-examination, however, soon exploded this image. He was asked if he had ever used the 'N-word' (nigger) to which he immediately replied that the word had never passed his lips. The defence then played an audio tape – made while he was acting as an advisor for a TV show about the LAPD – in which Fuhrman not only used the 'N-word' with racist abandon, but also admitted to planting evidence to help secure convictions.

The Dream Team built much of their defence argument on Fuhrman's racial bigotry and admissions of evidence planting. The glove in Simpson's house, they insisted, had originally been at the crime scene with the other, but Fuhrman had dipped it in Nichole's blood and had transplanted it to O.J.'s hall. Presumably he also took a pair of O.J.'s socks back to the murder scene, dipped them in blood and then transported them back to be found under his bed. Predictably (and arguably with good reason) the prosecution objected repeatedly to this purely theoretic line of defence but, despite the lack of supporting evidence, Judge Ito allowed it to go into the record.

After their defeat over Officer Fuhrman, the prosecution attempted to win back the lost ground by getting O.J. to put on the gloves in front of the jury. This was another crashing mistake because the gloves were self-evidently too small for him. Visibly shocked and demoralized at the complete reversal of their attempted coup, the prosecution team later pointed out that a leather glove soaked in blood would have shrunk, but the damage could not be undone.

Even what might have been a case-winning stroke in other circumstances could not save the prosecution. When the defence called a doctor to state that, despite his bulk and golfing activity, O.J. was a martyr to arthritis (less a physique like Tarzan than of 'Tarzan's grandfather') the prosecution played a recent video in which O.J. was to be seen doing very vigorous exercises. At one point he even performed a number of punching movements while joking to the camera that this was one to try 'with the wife'.

In what could be called a dazzling display of smoke and mirrors, the defence team argued, with little or no supporting evidence, that there was a racist conspiracy to convict the innocent O.J. Simpson. They also presented character witnesses who swore to O.J.'s gentle nature and called their own forensic expert, Dr Henry Lee, who rubbished the DNA evidence of the prosecution's blood samples. Today his testimony can be seen to be far from incontrovertible, but in 1994 DNA profiling was still being questioned and the science was mistrusted by members of the general public. So Dr Lee's refutation of the prosecution evidence seems to have carried a lot of weight with the jury.

In the final summings-up, the difference between the prosecution and defence teams were thrown into sharp contrast. Prosecutor Marcia Clark spent much of her time attacking one of her own witnesses: Mark Fuhrman. He was the 'worst type' of cop – one you wouldn't want 'on this planet' – but Fuhrman's personal faults did *not* add up to proof of a criminal conspiracy to convict an innocent man nor, indeed, prove that O.J. Simpson was guiltless. The entire speech sounded defensive, even though her logic could not be faulted.

On the other hand, Johnny Cochran, for the defence, was anything but defensive. He too attacked Officer Fuhrman, comparing him to Hitler. From there Cochran proceeded to attack Hitler's racism and 'anti-religionism'. What this had to do with the murders of Nichole Brown Simpson and Ronald Goldman is unclear, but Cochran certainly managed to underline the dangers of white racism to a jury of which nine members were black. (Fellow Dream Team member Robert Shapiro later accused Cochran of 'not only playing the race card, but playing it from the bottom of the deck'.)

Cochran concluded by stressing that the jury should not convict if there was a shadow of a doubt in their minds. Echoing the moment when O.J. put on the gloves and showed they were too small (or shrunken) for his hands, Cochran repeated the litany: 'If it doesn't fit, you must acquit.'

The jury took just three hours to acquit O.J. Simpson on all charges.

In his post trial statement, O.J. Simpson insisted that he would dedicate the rest of his life to tracking down the actual killer of his ex-wife. He got little time to do this, however, as the bereaved families immediately filed a civil suit, demanding damages from O.J. for killing their loved ones (civil cases can only award financial penalties).

All over America, blacks were jubilant, while whites were stunned and enraged. This was reflected in the title of a book called *Outrage* by Vincent Bugliosi, the prosecutor in the Manson case, who defiantly subtitled the book *The Five Reasons Why O. J. Simpson Got Away With Murder*. He saw the major reason as Judge Ito's decision to allow the defence to play 'the race card'. And the cover blurb says: 'there were disastrous lapses in the prosecution's strategy which allowed damaging defense testimony to go unchallenged; prosecutors Clark and Darden failed to stand up to the abuses of Judge Ito, thereby hurting their credibility with the jury; the final summations were weakly constructed, listlessly argued, and, most unforgivably, inadequately prepared. The trial was a travesty of justice, a showcase of incompetence.'

In what is probably the best account of the case, *The Run of His Life – The People v O.J. Simpson,* by *New York Times* journalist Jeffrey Toobin, the author leaves no doubt that he regards Simpson as guilty, blaming his acquittal, like Bugliosi, on the incompetent prosecution. And he rules out totally the defence's attempt to show that the police planted evidence, pointing out that this would have been impossibly complicated.

Where Judge Ito in the criminal trial was often criticized for letting lawyers on both sides wander off the case into wild theories, Judge Hiroshi Fujisake, who sat on the civil proceedings, kept a tight ship. All attempts by O.J.'s defence team to suggest that their client was the victim of a huge, if unprovable, racist conspiracy were overruled by the bench. Only solid evidence was accepted onto the court record.

Some new evidence at the civil trial showed that O.J. Simpson had lied to police in one important matter – the footprints found around the murder victims. The prints of the murderer proved to have been made by a pair of size twelve Bruno Magli shoes. Simpson had denied ever owning such a pair of shoes, but pictures taken before the murders were found by the newspapers, clearly showing Simpson wearing Bruno Magli shoes of the type that had made the prints. Simpson's feet were also size twelve.

O.J. Simpson had not been called to give evidence in the criminal trial, but was forced to in the civil case. He made a bad impression on the stand, mumbling replies to questions and looking furtive.

After a deliberation of seventeen hours, the civil jury concluded that O.J. Simpson was guilty of the 'wrongfully caused deaths of Ronald Goldman and Nichole Brown Simpson'. He was ordered to pay compensatory damages of $8.5 million to the bereaved families and $25 million in punitive damages. This did not reduce him to a pauper because, under California law, he was able to set up a $25,000-a-month pension fund that could not be touched by any legal judgement against him.

Toobin points out that in the civil case, the only juror who thought Simpson innocent was a middle-aged black woman.

As a result of the case Simpson's contracts with Hertz Rentacar and NBC were cancelled. And although never formally expelled from the Riviera Country Club, where he played golf, he was informed that he would no longer be welcome there. A two-hour videotape interview with him about the murders was a commercial flop.

Then followed a lengthy legal battle over whether Simpson should have access to the two children he had had with Nichole Brown Simpson, which he won.

In America, as under most democratic legal systems, O.J. Simpson cannot be brought before a criminal court twice for the same crime without dramatic new evidence coming to light that calls for a verdict of mistrial on the first case. He is therefore likely to remain in legal limbo – found both guilty and not guilty of the murders.

It is perhaps indicative that, despite his promise to 'hunt down' his ex-wife's killer, O.J. Simpson has apparently done nothing substantial towards that end. It is also interesting that Johnny Cochran – the one man most responsible for getting O.J. acquitted in the criminal trial – is said, before he was assigned to the Dream Team, to have told a friend: 'O.J. is in massive denial, he obviously did it.'

SINATRA, FRANK

SWING WHEN YOU'RE SINNING

Francis Albert Sinatra was the only child of a reasonably well-off family in Hoboken, New Jersey. As a child he wore Fauntleroy suits, and was given anything he wanted. Even at the age of fifteen, he still played with dolls, while affectionate uncles kept him well supplied with candy. In fact, he was thoroughly spoilt, exploding into fits of rage when he was not allowed his own way – which helps to explain why he went on to become one of the most detestable individuals in twentieth century show business. When he lost his temper, which was not infrequently, he went virtually insane – on one occasion, he tried to hurl one of his retinue out of his private aeroplane in midair, and was only prevented from committing murder when others restrained him.

This kind of conduct has characterized many tyrants in history, including Ivan the Terrible and Adolf Hitler, but probably Sinatra is the only popular entertainer who can claim that distinction.

Sinatra was lucky. He was more than seventy years old when someone finally dared to tell the whole truth about him. This was the journalist Kitty Kelley, in a biography called *His Way*, and it is her version, rather than the many accounts by star-struck admirers, that will be followed in the following pages.

Francis Albert Sinatra was born on 12 December 1915, in an Italian and Irish neighbourhood in Hoboken. 'Everybody carried a twelve inch pipe then – and they weren't studying to be plumbers,' Sinatra later remarked. But, as we have seen, this attempt to portray himself as a tough, deprived kid was a myth he invented himself.

His father, Anthony Martin Sinatra (known as Marty) was physically a small man, born in Sicily, who started life as a bantamweight boxer. Sinatra's mother, Dolly, was an extrovert blonde, who dominated the family, and was known as a practising abortionist. She was born in Genoa.

When Sinatra was six, his uncle Babe – his mother's younger brother – got himself arrested for driving a getaway car after the driver of a Railway Express truck was shot to death. Dolly went to court every day, pretending to be Babe's wife, and holding a baby, which she had borrowed. She sobbed noisily, declaring that the baby needed his father, but the judge declined to be swayed, and sentenced Babe to fifteen years hard labour.

When prohibition arrived in 1919, Dolly Sinatra lost no time in becoming a bootlegger, adding to the family's already adequate income.

At the age of sixteen, Sinatra entered Demarest High School, but was expelled within a few months for being rowdy. He had always disliked school, and his teachers regarded him as lazy.

With no qualifications, there were not many jobs open to him. His mother got him a job on the local newspaper, the *Jersey Observer*, on which his godfather was the circulation manager. He worked on the delivery truck, heaving around bundles of newspapers for $12 a week. When the sportswriter on the paper was killed in a car crash, Sinatra's mother told him to take over the job and, accordingly, Sinatra went and sat at his dead colleague's desk, assuring the editor that his godfather had given him permission to be there. When his godfather admitted he knew nothing about it, Sinatra was fired. Both Sinatra and his mother were so furious that they never again spoke to his godfather. Dolly Sinatra had already pushed her husband into a job at the fire department by using political contacts at City Hall.

Dolly made so much money from her abortion practice that the family was able to move into a new house. It cost more than $13,000 – an astronomical sum when most houses cost less than a quarter of that sum. And although her son was out of work, Dolly Sinatra bought him a car in which he took out his first girlfriends. When he was seventeen, it was a girlfriend who suggested that he should form a band to play at school dances. The quartet, which they called the Hoboken Four, was a success, and Sinatra began doing vocals, inspired by the singer he admired most – Bing Crosby. His mother bought him a PA system, and when other local bands wanted to use it, Sinatra was usually allowed to sing. But since his voice was so light, most of his neighbours agreed that he was awful.

When he was twenty, Sinatra appeared in his first film, made in the New York Biograph Studios in the Bronx. He made-up with a black face and wore a top hat. And Dolly Sinatra, who had lobbied vigorously to get her son this job, invited the cast over for a large breakfast before Frankie drove them out to the studio.

The Hoboken Four appeared on stage in the Capitol Theater on 8 September 1935, in a talent competition, and walked away with first prize. The result was that they were signed up at $50 a week, and went on tour with other acts.

It was on this tour, when he was 23, that Sinatra became accustomed to adoring female fans, which enraged the other three members of the quartet. The result was that the skinny, undersized Frank was often beaten up. He finally got tired of it, and walked out on the quartet to return home.

He began taking elocution lessons, and one of his friends commented that he began to sound like an Englishman.

In 1938, while he was still 23, Sinatra was taken on as a singing waiter at a roadhouse called The Rustic Cabin – the pay was $15 a week. One of his fellow musicians later put it on record that 'he didn't seem to have any talent.' Nevertheless, Sinatra began to sing on the radio every Saturday evening.

It was at The Rustic Cabin that Sinatra became the subject of a dispute between two girls; Toni Della Penta who had been made pregnant by him not long before, but had had a miscarriage, and Nancy Barbato, a stonemason's daughter who was several years Sinatra's junior. After Toni had tried to tear off Nancy's dress, Sinatra sent Nancy away, and then told Toni that he had to marry Nancy because she was pregnant. Toni went straight to the police and swore out a morals charge against Sinatra – that he'd had sexual intercourse with her having promised her marriage. That was the first of two occasions when Sinatra spent time in jail on a charge of seduction.

Toni finally agreed to let Sinatra out of jail when he promised that his mother would apologize to her for treating her as her inferior. But after another screaming fight between Toni and Dolly, it was Toni who was arrested.

Probably to end this kind of thing, Dolly Sinatra pushed her son into marrying Nancy Barbato. This was on 4 February 1939, when Sinatra was 23. He was making $25 a week as a singing waiter, and Nancy was making $15 as a secretary.

Sinatra's first break came when the trumpeter Harry James heard him singing on the radio. James had just left the Benny Goodman band to set up on his own. James went along to watch him sing and said that he knew immediately that 'he was destined to be a great vocalist'. So in June 1939, Sinatra's salary suddenly increased to $75 a week. Harry James suggested that Sinatra should call himself Frankie Satin, but Dolly immediately vetoed that.

Sinatra's early recordings were not a success; his 'All or Nothing at All' sold a mere 8,000 copies. He was unhappy at the lack of acclaim, but cheered up when Harry James was booked into the Palomar in Hollywood. Unfortunately, this burned down before they got there. Another club accused the band of playing too loud, and they were thrown out when Sinatra was halfway through singing 'All or Nothing at All'.

Soon after that, when James's band was playing in Chicago, the band leader Tommy Dorsey slipped Sinatra a note asking him to meet him, and offered him a job at $125 a week. Sinatra did not hesitate. His replacement with Harry James was a singer called Dick Haymes, who became a film star.

Within a few months of working for Dorsey, Sinatra recorded a song called 'I'll Never Smile Again', and suddenly became famous – the record stayed in the hit parade for weeks.

The drummer, Buddy Rich, resented Sinatra's elevation, and the two became sworn enemies. On one occasion, Sinatra hurled a jug of iced water at Rich's head, and it shattered all over the wall, leaving pieces of glass stuck in the plaster. Finally, Dorsey fired Sinatra for two weeks, until he agreed to keep his temper.

Sinatra was finding it hard being a famous singer and a married man. Always highly sexed, he saw no reason why he should not take advantage of the dozens of teenage fans who literally swooned as he sang.

He went to Hollywood with the band and made his first film, *Las Vegas Nights*, for Paramount, in which he sang 'I'll Never Smile Again'. He had a major love affair with a blonde starlet called Alora Gooding, and they began to live together. Rita Maritt was fresh from a convent school when Sinatra seduced her at the age of sixteen. Another mistress was a socialite named Mary Lou Watts, whose father was an oil baron. It was Mary Lou who finally persuaded Sinatra to eradicate the last traces of New Jersey from his accent.

By 1941, Sinatra had displaced Bing Crosby as the top American vocalist.

Sinatra was driven by consuming ambition, particularly after he made a record with 'The Song is You' on one side and 'Lamplighter's Serenade' on the other. He played it over and over again, obviously amazed at his own vocal skill. Shortly after that, he gave Dorsey notice. Dorsey took it very badly indeed, feeling – rightly – that he had made Sinatra. Shortly afterwards, he agreed to let Sinatra go for $60,000.

The story went around that the Mafia boss Willie Moretti had called on Dorsey in his dressing room and waved a revolver at him. Both Dorsey and Sinatra denied this. Dorsey is quoted as saying of Sinatra: 'He's the most fascinating man in the world, but don't stick your hand in the cage.'

The first time Sinatra sang on his own at New York's Paramount Theater, his backing was Benny Goodman. The clarinettist had never heard of Sinatra, but as soon as the vocalist walked out on stage, the girls in the audience began to scream and Goodman, his arms raised to start the orchestra, looked over his shoulder and said: 'What the fuck was that?' Soon after that, Sinatra's new press agent, George Evans, hired plump teenage girls wearing bobby sox (ankle socks) to shriek as Sinatra sang. Evans's relentless publicity campaign made millions of males all over the world furious, and turned millions of women into fans. Bing Crosby had certainly never provoked this hysteria. Evans also made a great deal of the fact that Sinatra was a happily married family man, and got him to say things like: 'Nobody comes before my wife Nancy.'

Sinatra was now making larger sums than he'd ever dreamed of, thousands of dollars a week. But he accepted a mere $800 a week for an engagement at a New York nightclub, the Riobamber, taking third place in the billing – the two lead stars were paid twice that much. The nightclub was in trouble with dwindling audiences, but within days it was jammed to the doors for every Sinatra performance, and finally the other two stars were sacked so that Sinatra could take over on his own. His pay was also doubled.

When he returned to the Paramount Theater, screaming teenagers surrounded the building and broke down the doors. According to Nick Sevano, Sinatra's 'butler', the girls threw their bras and panties at him. 'They went nuts, absolutely nuts.'

Sinatra suddenly found himself the centre of a storm of criticism. From then on, almost every attack on Sinatra involved the word 'hysteria.' One doctor even said it was due to 'mammary hyperaesthesia.'

Nick Sevano also mentions that Sinatra showed an increasing tendency to fly off the handle. 'He'd just go crazy if things weren't done the minute he wanted them done.' In short, Sinatra was turning into a full-blown version of the spoilt child he had always been.

As criticism mounted that Sinatra, unlike most of his famous contemporaries, was staying well clear of the war, he finally decided that it was time to make a move. His preliminary medical showed him to be 1-A. But a month later he was found to be 4-F because of a tiny puncture in his eardrum.

Not long after that, Sinatra fired Nick Sevano, who had been with him for four years. Nancy Sinatra was irritated because Nick was going to Hollywood with his boss while Nancy had to stay in New York and look after their two children. One day, she saw Sevano going into Sinatra's bedroom and taking a ten dollar bill – which he needed to make some purchases that Sinatra had asked for. Nancy told Sinatra Nick was a thief. And she kept up the nagging until Sinatra agreed to fire him.

In Hollywood, Sinatra sang at The Hollywood Bowl with the backing of a symphony orchestra, and had to tell his teenage fans not to scream. He had a record audience. And by 1944, Sinatra was not only the most famous singer in America – he was the most famous singer in the world.

Soon after that, he became equally famous as a film star. His first film *Higher and Higher* drew huge audiences, even though one critic called it *Lower and Lower*. After that, Sinatra went on to make one of his best movies, *Anchors Aweigh*, with Gene Kelly.

Sinatra now decided to move out to California, and bought Mary Astor's huge estate in the San Fernando Valley. His mother Dolly was indignant because Nancy was also taking her sisters with her. But then, Dolly had become a social celebrity in New Jersey ever since her son achieved worldwide fame, so she had nothing to complain about.

When Roosevelt stood for re-election in the autumn of 1944, Sinatra supported his campaign, and gave $5,000 to it. When he performed in the Paramount Theater, begging the screaming girls to be quiet, one disgusted male member of the audience managed to hit him in the face with three eggs.

When, early in 1945, Sinatra again had to appear before the draft board to check on his health status, he was upgraded to 2-AF, which meant that there was a possibility he might after all be inducted into the army. As a result, there were headlines about girls threatening to commit suicide if Sinatra was drafted.

Comedian Phil Silvers thought of an interesting way to defuse some of the hostility. When he first appeared in front of troops in Italy, Sinatra was presented as the underdog, continually interrupted and slapped down by Silvers. The result was that a sympathetic audience begged Sinatra to sing 'Nancy With the Laughing Face', a song Silvers had written for Sinatra's four-year-old daughter Nancy.

Sinatra learned an interesting lesson – that a good way of defusing hostility was to make fun of yourself.

Soon after this, Sinatra discovered a new way of courting popularity. He began pleading against racial intolerance, and talking about the problems of juvenile delinquency. The discovery that the millionaire singer had a social conscience went down well with the music critics.

But Phil Silvers's wife remarked: 'He was a sincere liberal . . . but then he was always mean to the little people around him. He seemed to enjoy making people look little in front of others.'

One of the men Sinatra admired most was 'Bugsy' Siegel, the head of the Mafia on the West Coast. When Sinatra and Silvers saw Siegel in a restaurant where they were eating dinner, they stood up, saying: 'Hello, Mr Siegel. How are you?' 'They were like two children seeing Santa Claus', said Silver's wife. She added: 'Like Bugsy, Frank had a Mafia red-neck mentality.'

Sinatra was also not averse to demonstrating his power over women. When a group of his buddies were sharing an apartment where they held bachelor orgies, Sinatra arrived with Marlene Dietrich, took her by the hand, and led her past the card-playing men into the bedroom.

In Hollywood, Sinatra was getting a bad name for being temperamental. He often kept members of the MGM crew standing around all day long, and simply didn't show up. When a Hollywood columnist, Erskine Johnson criticized Sinatra, he got a telegram saying: JUST CONTINUE TO PRINT LIES ABOUT ME AND MY TEMPER – NOT MY TEMPERAMENT – WE'LL SEE THAT YOU GET A BELT IN YOUR VICIOUS AND STUPID MOUTH.

His temperament also caused problems with his wife Nancy. In October 1946 he walked out on her, and went to Palm Springs where he began seeing Ava Gardner and Lana Turner. It was Phil Silvers who engineered a public reconciliation in a Hollywood restaurant.

Closer ties with the Mob seem to have started in January 1947, when he renewed a friendship with the Chicago gangster Jo Fischetti, a cousin of Al Capone. 'Lucky Luciano' had been exiled to Cuba, and Mafia bosses from across the country were going to see him in Havana. Sinatra was invited to join them. Sinatra was photographed with Luciano, and with other gangsters, including Albert Anastasia, Carlo Gambino, Vito Genovese, Frank Costello and many others. 'Doc' Stacher, who controlled slot machines for the gangster Meyer Lansky, is quoted as saying: 'The Italians among us were very proud of Frank. They always told me they had spent a lot of money helping him in his career . . .'

Unfortunately, this publicity backfired on Luciano when a newspaperman – and later novelist – Robert Ruark denounced Sinatra for 'cavorting among the scum', which resulted in Luciano being arrested and sent back to Italy. It was from then on that Sinatra had the reputation of being mixed up with mobsters. Sinatra explained his position by saying: 'Any report that I've fraternized with goons and racketeers is a vicious lie. I was brought up to shake a man's hand when I am introduced to him without first investigating his past.' But on a visit to Naples, Sinatra gave Luciano a solid gold cigarette case inscribed: 'To my dear pal Charlie.'

Another columnist who took issue with Sinatra over his friendship with gangsters was Lee Mortimer, who, among other things, referred to Sinatra as 'Frank (Lucky) Sinatra'. In April 1947, in the Hollywood nightclub Ciro's, Sinatra saw Mortimer leaving with a female singer. At the front door, Sinatra's friends grabbed Mortimer – who was not a large man – while Sinatra called him 'a fucking homosexual' and hit him. Mortimer fell down and Sinatra's friends held him pinned to the ground while Sinatra continued hitting him.

A photographer called Nat Dallinger saw the fight and intervened. Sinatra and his friends finally backed off.

At two in the morning, Sinatra's West Coast publicity agent Jack Keller was awakened by a reporter, who told him that Sinatra had just hit somebody. After that, the phone went on ringing with enquiries from journalists. Then Sinatra knocked on Keller's door saying: 'Jeez, I think we're in trouble.' 'You bet your ass we're in trouble,' said Keller and hastily took Sinatra to the house of another of the entourage. There, Sinatra was instructed to ring up the newspapers and to tell them that the reason he attacked Mortimer was that he heard him saying to the lady he was escorting: 'There's that little dago bastard now.'

The next day, the newspapers reported that Sinatra had knocked Mortimer to the ground with one punch because Mortimer had referred to him as a dago.

Mortimer lost no time in swearing out a warrant for Sinatra's arrest charging him with assault and battery. The following day, Mortimer received two anonymous calls threatening him unless he dropped the charges.

Lee Mortimer worked for the newspaper tycoon William Randolph Hurst, and all Hurst's newspapers took up the case. When MGM attorneys discovered that it was untrue that Mortimer had referred to Sinatra as a dago, Lewis B Mayer ordered Sinatra to pay Mortimer $9,000 in damages and to apologize publicly.

Sinatra's publicity man George Evans tried to persuade the famous Hollywood columnist Louella Parsons to join the argument on Sinatra's side, but she refused. Eventually she relented, accepted a lunch invitation from Sinatra, and was predictably charmed.

The next problem was the Hurst press. But because he knew Hurst's mistress, the actress Marion Davies, Sinatra succeeded in getting invited to tea with Hurst, and the 84-year-old magnate, who was in failing health, was also charmed by him.

Nevertheless, Sinatra's next film, *Miracle of the Bells*, in which he played a catholic priest, received such bad reviews that Sinatra refused at first to go to the premiere in San Franciso.

His unpopularity made MGM decide to try and repeat the success of *Anchors Aweigh* by teaming Sinatra with Gene Kelly again. The first film, *Take Me Out to the Ball Game*, was a flop, but the second, Leonard Bernstein's *On the Town*, has become a classic.

But Sinatra's penchant for getting into trouble continued to make his private life unpredictable. His admiration for gangsters had led him to buy a couple of revolvers. One night in the autumn of 1948, Sinatra and Ava Gardner went out to a small place called Indio, in California, got drunk, and proceeded to fire off the revolvers in all directions. Again, it was the West Coast publicity agent Jack Keller who had to get them out of trouble. Sinatra and Gardner were in jail, but the police chief had recognized Sinatra, and taken care that the press did not find out. Keller rang up a friend who ran a hotel and asked him how much money he had in the safe. His friend said $30,000. Then Keller hired a plane and flew out to Indio. He sat down with the police chief and asked: 'Okay chief, how much to keep this quiet?' The chief thought that $10,000 would do for the moment – $5,000 for himself, $2,000 each for the arresting officers, and $1,000 to get rid of the hospital records of a man whose stomach had been grazed by a bullet. Keller paid it out, and then got the addresses of various storekeepers whose shops had been hit by bullets. He went around to all of them and offered to pay for their damage on the spot. They all accepted. But the man who had been grazed with the bullet was more difficult – he thought he might get more by taking it to court. He showed Keller the line made across his stomach by a bullet that had gone through his clothes. But finally he accepted $10,000 to keep quiet.

It was typical of Sinatra that he decided to fire Keller soon after this, for telling his East Coast publicity agent, George Evans, about the trouble; he ordered Evans to break the bad news. But Evans dug in his heels and refused. Whereupon Sinatra lost his temper and fired him too.

By this time, Sinatra was involved in a passionate affair with Ava Gardner. He had become totally obsessed by her. Unfortunately, she had the same fiery temperament as Sinatra, and the result was violent clashes. One of Sinatra's reasons for firing George Evans was that he'd strongly advised Sinatra to stop seeing her.

The consequences of firing Evans were disastrous. With no one around to ensure favourable items in the press, his appeal began to fade, and in the *Downbeat* poll of 1949, Sinatra was in fifth place for the first time in six years. Magazines began to pan his latest records, and film critics panned his latest film, *Take Me Out to the Ball Game*. When he made it, Sinatra had been assured that his name would appear above Kelly's. But by the time the second Kelly and Sinatra film, *On the Town* came out, Sinatra was so unpopular that the studio decided to give Gene Kelly top billing.

There was more bad publicity when Sinatra walked out on his wife,

Nancy, because she wouldn't give him a divorce. His ex-publicity agent George Evans prophesied that 'a year from now you won't hear anything about him. He'll be dead professionally.' Shortly after, Evans dropped dead of a heart attack. Sinatra went to his funeral, and seemed to be devastated. And as the publicity about Sinatra and Ava Gardner continued, Nancy Sinatra finally agreed to give him a divorce. As 'the other woman', Ava Gardner became almost as unpopular as Sinatra. But she remained defiant, telling even the studio publicity team to mind its own business. The studio became seriously angry after Sinatra's latest escapade. Ava Gardner had agreed to go to a party at the home of her former husband, bandleader Artie Shaw. Sinatra rang up and said he was calling to say goodbye. When she asked where he was going, she heard the sound of two shots. She rushed from the party, screaming, and went to the hotel where she and Sinatra were staying. He was in bed in his pajamas, with two bullet holes in the mattress. This was hastily exchanged for a mattress from another apartment, so that when the police arrived, they could find no trace of bullet holes. MGM insisted that Ava Gardner should leave for Spain immediately to start work on a film called *Pandora and the Flying Dutchman*.

MGM also decided to terminate Sinatra's contract a year before its expiry date, agreeing to pay him $85,000. But Nancy Sinatra's lawyer served the studio with a restraining order preventing them from paying the money until her maintenance suit was settled.

It began to look as if George Evans's prediction was coming true.

In Spain, Ava Gardner, irritated by Sinatra's failure to get a divorce from Nancy, began a highly publicized affair with her co-star, a bullfighter called Mario Cabre. On stage in a nightclub called The Copa, Sinatra's voice suddenly gave out completely, and when he opened his mouth, not a sound came out. The next day, The Copa announced that Sinatra had suffered a haemorrhage of the throat, but the truth was that it was purely psychosomatic – a form of hysteria.

He rushed to Spain, quarrelled with Ava Gardner, then returned to New York, where crowds of reporters wanted to know if it was true that he had run away from the Spanish bullfighter.

Sinatra's records were no longer selling, and his voice was beginning to fail. The Columbia Records engineers, who would often help out a singer by extending his notes in an echo chamber, were sick of his tantrums, and decided to do nothing. Sinatra signed a three-year contract with CBS for a weekly television variety show as well as a radio show, guaranteeing a quarter of a million dollars a year. But after thirteen weeks, poor ratings led CBS to cancel the show.

Finally, Sinatra was forced to beg his Mob contacts for nightclub jobs, and many of them obliged. Jo Fischetti, Al Capone's cousin, gave him work in Chicago. In return, Sinatra made a plane trip to Palm Springs with Fischetti to impress an automobile tycoon from whom Fischetti was trying to buy a franchise. Because of Sinatra, the deal went through, and the Fischettis were able to open car agencies run by the Mob in various cities.

Sinatra's affiliations with the Mob were again brought to public attention in 1950 in the nationally televised Kefauver hearings into organized crime. At one of these hearings, photographs of Sinatra and Lucky Luciano in Havana were shown to the cameras. Joseph L. Nellis, one of the committee's lawyers, reeled off a long list of the names of gangsters – Frank Costello, Jo Adonis, Longy Zwillman, Meyer Lansky, Bugsy Siegel – and Sinatra admitted that he knew them all and that 'those guys were okay'. But when asked whether he knew what business Lucky Luciano's friends were in, Sinatra claimed he did not.

He was divorced from Nancy in October 1951. A week earlier, he and Ava Gardner had taken James Mason – star of *Pandora and the Flying Dutchman* – and his wife Pamela out to dinner. There Ava decided that Sinatra was paying too much attention to a woman at a nearby table, and threw her six-carat diamond engagement ring across the room, shouting: 'Let's just call off this fucking wedding.' But they had made up the quarrel by the time of the wedding.

The trouble was that Sinatra was almost demoniacally possessive. He told her to turn down a part in Hemingway's *The Snows of Kilimanjaro*, because he wanted her with him in New York, and finally only allowed her to act in the film when the studio agreed to shoot her part in ten days.

Ava Gardner could be equally temperamental. One night when she was in the audience at a New Jersey nightclub, an ex-girlfriend of Sinatra's, Marilyn Maxwell, walked in. Convinced Sinatra was singing for Marilyn alone, Ava stormed out of the club, and flew back to California. It was one of dozens of such spats.

All this was reducing Sinatra to a nervous wreck. When he sang in his home town Hoboken, his voice was so bad that the audience booed and threw fruit.

It was Ava Gardner who finally gave her husband's career the boost it needed so badly. Sinatra had read James Jones's bestseller *From Here to Eternity*, and thought that he would be good in the part of Maggio, the good-natured little private who is beaten to death by a sadistic sergeant. Ava Gardner rang the wife of Harry Cohn, the head of Columbia Pictures, to ask if she could go and see her. When she was there, she begged her to help Sinatra get a screen test for Maggio. Mrs Cohn's pressure on her husband worked, although Cohn had earlier dismissed Sinatra out of hand. But he finally agreed to give him a screen test. When Sinatra didn't hear after many weeks, he decided to fly to Africa with his wife, who was going to play opposite Clark Gable in *Mogambo*.

There, for a week, the Sinatras raged at one another and fought, and Grace

Kelly, who was occupying the next tent, was shocked and told a friend: 'Ava is such a mess it's unbelievable.'

In the midst of this, the call for Sinatra's screen test came, and he went back to Hollywood. Handed the script, Sinatra said: 'I don't need this – I've read it many times.' The test was so good that the producer, Buddy Adler, knew immediately that Sinatra was the right man. However, Cohn was out of town, and so Sinatra went back to Africa. There he sank into total depression, and had to be cheered up by Clark Gable.

Fortunately for Sinatra, Eli Wallach, the actor Cohn preferred, demanded more money than Cohn was willing to pay. Cohn, torn between the two actors, finally asked his wife to look at the screen test and decide. She pointed out that Wallach was much too heavily built to play the skinny little Maggio, so the part finally went to Sinatra.

From Here to Eternity surpassed everybody's expectations. It was nominated as the best picture of 1953, and everybody in it was showered with praise – Montgomery Clift, Burt Lancaster, Donna Reed, Deborah Kerr – and of course, Sinatra. Everybody agreed that his portrayal of Private Maggio was a great performance – one critic said of it that Maggio's death scene was one of the best ever filmed.

Sinatra behaved himself, except during the conclusion of the filming in Hawaii. He wanted to play a drunken scene sitting down, while the director, Fred Zinnemann, wanted it done standing up. Montgomery Clift, who shared the scene, also wanted to do it standing up, according to the script. Sinatra burst into a flood of obscenity, refusing even to compromise by having the scene shot both ways. Somebody had to ring Harry Cohn, who was just sitting down to dinner with his wife, and who came over to the set and exploded with rage. Sinatra was told he was leaving on the next plane back to the US. Fortunately, by that time, the scene had been shot.

But although From Here to Eternity was the turning point in his career, the film had not yet been released when he went on a singing tour of Europe. An Italian audience booed him, he sang to half-full houses in Copenhagen, and in Malmö, Sweden, the press were so rude about his cutting short an open air performance in a park that the bad reviews decided Sinatra to cancel the rest of the tour.

Sinatra and Gardner went back to America separately, and the fights were now so frequent and so violent that by October 1953, MGM had announced that their marriage was over. On 18 November, Sinatra was found on the floor of an elevator with his wrists slashed. Finally, Sinatra was persuaded to see a psychiatrist – the same one who looked after Marilyn Monroe.

His luck as a singer began to change when he signed with a new company, Capitol Records, and was assigned Nelson Riddle as an arranger. It was Riddle's swinging arrangements that finally put Sinatra back on top. The invention of the long-playing record was also a break for Sinatra, because it enabled him to build up a mood over a whole side instead of being restricted to single songs.

But in Spain, where she was making *The Barefoot Contessa* with Humphrey Bogart, Ava Gardner was now having an affair with the famous bullfighter Dominguin, and was suing for divorce from Sinatra. Sinatra took it all very hard, and spent his nights playing cards and getting drunk. After the divorce, which came through in 1956, Sinatra told a friend that one of the insults Ava Gardner threw at him was that he was a 'goddam hoodlum and a gangster'.

Now his career was revitalized, Sinatra proceeded to prove her right by buying a stake in the Sands Hotel in Las Vegas, where he was among an impressive line-up of gangsters. The New Jersey mobster Joseph 'Doc' Stacher, who ran the Sands, admitted that Sinatra had been drawn in to attract the 'high-rollers'. For the next thirteen years, Sinatra made an enormous income from the Sands.

One of the first completely frank assessments of Sinatra appeared in *Look* magazine. It was by a journalist called Bill Davidson, and the first article, 'Talent, tantrums and torment', infuriated Sinatra so much that he threatened to sue the magazine for more than $2 million. The second article told the truth about Sinatra's upbringing in Hoboken – that he was not, as he liked to pretend, some poor slum kid, but a spoilt mama's boy. The third article talked about Sinatra's sex life, and his obsessive promiscuity. (There was a saying in Hollywood that the definition of a square was a hat check girl who hadn't been to bed with Frank Sinatra.) Sinatra finally dropped the case.

After the death of Humphrey Bogart from throat cancer in 1957, Sinatra began dating his wife, Lauren Bacall. After he proposed and she accepted, they went to a restaurant on Sunset Boulevard and when a girl came to their table asking for autographs, Sinatra told Bacall to put: 'Betty Sinatra'. The result was that 24 hours later, headlines proclaimed that they were going to get married. When Bacall rang Sinatra long distance to Miami, he was upset and said: 'We'll have to lay low for a while, not see each other.' That was the last time Bacall heard from him. She was shattered by the public humiliation.

Sinatra was making more money than ever before, but a weekly show for BBC television was dropped after 26 weeks because of what was described as Sinatra's 'arrogance'. Sinatra's attitude to the shows was casual, his attitude to the other actors patronizing, and his refusal to rehearse insulting to everybody else in the show.

Sinatra had developed a group of friends who often appeared with him on stage in Las Vegas, consisting of Dean Martin, Peter Lawford, Sammy Davis Jr, Joey Bishop and actress Shirley Maclaine. They were known as the Rat Pack, a name that Lauren Bacall had coined for the group around Humphrey Bogart which had included Sinatra. But when Davis said in an interview in Chicago that, although Sinatra could be the kindest and most generous man in the world, he also 'does things there are no excuses for', he was suddenly excommunicated. He had said it in Chicago, where Sinatra's most admired mobsters lived. After two months of refusing to talk to Davis, Sinatra finally forgave him.

But because of his friendship with the Mob, Sinatra was about to face the biggest humiliation of his life.

Sam Giancana was the Chicago Mob boss who succeeded Tony Accardo when Accardo stepped down. Where Accardo had been quiet and retiring, Giancana loved publicity and enjoyed displaying his power publicly. His various rackets brought him in up to $50 million a year. Sinatra worshipped him, and was always eager to perform in Giancana's nightclubs. He would finish his act by singing 'My Kind of Town', as a tribute to Giancana. Says Kitty Kelley in His Way, 'Each had something the other wanted. For Frank it was the power derived from associating with an underworld capo; for Giancana it was the opportunity to enrich Mafia coffers by using the biggest entertainer in Hollywood as a draw.' And she quotes singer Eddie Fisher as saying: 'Frank wanted to be a hood. He once said "I'd rather be a don of the Mafia than president of the United States."'

Giancana often visited the Sands in Las Vegas, but because he was one of eleven criminals who were not allowed in any casino in Nevada, Sinatra had to keep him hidden in his dressing room.

Because Peter Lawford, the British film star and long time member of the Rat Pack, was married to Patricia Kennedy, the sister of the man who would become president, Sinatra agreed to support Kennedy's campaign. But he thought that he could do something that would be even more valuable. He went to Sam Giancana and suggested that if he could do something to help Kennedy win, Kennedy would almost certainly turn down the pressure on the Mafia. Kennedy's brother Robert had served on the McClellan Committee senate hearings, whose aim was to expose Mafia involvement with the Teamster's Union headed by Jimmy Hoffa, which was heavily involved with the Mob. Robert Kennedy had exposed corruption in fifteen Unions and fifty corporations. The implication was that if the Mob would help Kennedy into power, his brother would show less hostility to the Mob.

Accordingly, Giancana used his Mafia connections to swing the Black Wards in Chicago. Kennedy carried the state of Michigan by only 8,858 votes.

In fact, Kennedy won the election by the skin of his teeth – a mere 118,000 votes out of the 68 million cast.

Sinatra believed that after Kennedy became president, he would become an honorary member of the Kennedy clan.

Unfortunately, Sinatra had left out of account the fact that Robert Kennedy had sworn to break the power of the Mafia. So when Kennedy appointed his brother Attorney General, Giancana and his friends felt that they had been stabbed in the back – not only by Kennedy, but by Sinatra.

Sinatra had another reason for feeling that Kennedy 'owed him'. Throughout their acquaintance Sinatra had kept him supplied with a stream of women, probably including Marilyn Monroe, who had a chalet in the Sinatra-owned club Cal-Neva at Lake Tahoe. In *His Way*, Kitty Kelley quotes a lawyer on Bobby Kennedy's staff: 'We are out front fighting organized crime on every level, and here the President is associating with Sinatra, who is in bed with all these guys.'

Robert Kennedy asked the lawyer for a memorandum with all the facts, and three reports on Sinatra were prepared detailing his association with ten leaders of organized crime in America.

The president was due to stay with Sinatra at his Palm Springs home in March 1962; Robert Kennedy rang Peter Lawford to ask him to break the news to Sinatra that Kennedy was cancelling. Sinatra had spent a lot of money preparing his home for Kennedy's visit, building extra cottages for the secret service men, installing 25 extra telephone lines, and building a heliport. When Sinatra was told that the president would be staying with Bing Crosby – a Republican supporter – instead, Sinatra exploded into a screaming rage, and began to demolish the helipad with a sledgehammer. After that he declared himself a Republican supporter. But his failure to deliver on his promises of immunity brought him into considerable disfavour with the Mob.

The evidence now seems to suggest that it was the Mob that was responsible for Kennedy's assassination in Dealey Plaza, in Dallas, on 22 November 1963. Amateur film footage of the shooting taken by a man named Abraham Zapruder shows Kennedy's head jerking violently backwards as the bullets hit him, although Lee Harvey Oswald, the man believed to be the assassin, was actually behind Kennedy on the sixth floor of the Texas Book Depository. On the other hand, an assassin hidden on the grassy knoll, which Kennedy's car was approaching at the time of the shots, would have been in the ideal position to hit him. A young soldier named Gordon Arnold was watching the president's motorcade from the top of the grassy knoll when a bullet whizzed past his ear; it came from behind a fence on the knoll, where a man claiming to be a secret service agent had forbidden Arnold to go a few minutes earlier. As Arnold dropped flat, another shot sounded from behind him.

The man who organized the assassination was almost certainly Sam Giancana.

It was only revealed later that Sinatra had been Kennedy's pimp, and that Sam Giancana and the president had actually shared one mistress – Judith Campbell (who would later write a book about her affair under the name Judith Campbell Exner).

In fact, before the assassination of Kennedy, Robert Kennedy had already ordered that Giancana should be closely shadowed by the FBI. Even on the golf course, Giancana was followed by federal agents. He finally became so angry at this lack of privacy that he actually sued the FBI, and won.

It was in 1962 that Marilyn Monroe tried to commit suicide at Cal-Neva, and was rushed to hospital just in time, to have her stomach pumped. (She would die a few days later from another overdose – a reason for suspecting that the stories that she was murdered may lack substance.)

Giancana spent a great deal of time at Cal-Neva, in spite of the fact that he was a mobster. And Sinatra himself was behaving more and more like a mobster. A cocktail waitress called Toni, who had been Sinatra's mistress, married Deputy Sheriff Richard E. Anderson in March 1962. On 30 June 1962, Anderson came late to pick up his wife, and was standing in the Cal-Neva kitchen talking to the dishwashers when Sinatra came in and asked him what he was doing there. A fight developed, and Anderson punched Sinatra so hard that Sinatra was unable to sing for the rest of that week.

Two weeks later, on 17 July 1962, Anderson and his wife were on their way to the Crystal Bay Club for dinner, driving along Highway 28, not far from Cal-Neva, when a maroon convertible drove towards them at top speed. Anderson's car went off the road and hit a tree, killing him immediately. Toni suffered multiple fractures. The maroon car did not stop, and the Sheriff investigating the accident could not determine what had happened.

Recounting the story in *His Way*, Kitty Kelley leaves little doubt that she thinks Sinatra was behind the death of Anderson.

The FBI reported Giancana's presence at Cal-Neva to the Nevada Gaming Control Board. When Ed Olsen, head of the Control Board, rang Sinatra to ask about Giancana, Sinatra asked him to dinner. Olsen refused, and suggested meeting in his office. Sinatra was soon screaming down the phone 'Don't you fuck with me.'

Olsen decided to issue a complaint, accusing Sinatra of violating Nevada's gambling laws, and trying to intimidate the chairman himself, as well as offering bribes to agents who had been in Cal-Neva in the course of duty.

When Sinatra failed to answer these charges within fifteen days, as the complaint specified, the board revoked his gaming licence.

Giancana was so angry with Sinatra's behaviour that he broke off his friendship. 'That bastard and his big mouth. All he had to do was keep quiet, let the attorneys handle it. . . but no, Frank has to get on the phone with that damn big mouth of his and now we've lost the whole damn place.'

When Sammy Davis happened to see Olsen he took him aside to say: 'That little son of a bitch, he's needed this for years. I've been working with him for sixteen years and nobody's ever had the guts to stand up to him!'

In May 1964, when Sinatra was filming in Hawaii, his life very nearly ended prematurely. On the afternoon of Sunday 10 May 1964, he was on the beach with several friends he had invited, including a powerfully built actor named Brad Dexter. Sinatra went into the sea with Ruth Coch, the wife of his executive producer. They were both dragged further out by a riptide, and Dexter was in the house collecting drinks when someone shouted that Sinatra was drowning. When Dexter swam out to them Sinatra gasped 'I'm going to die – I'm finished. It's all over.' And although Dexter shouted at him that nobody was going to die, Sinatra seemed to have given up. Finally, lifeguards reached them with surfboards, and got them back to land.

Sinatra's reward was to draw Dexter closely into his private circle of friends.

But Dexter was shocked by the way that Sinatra could explode. Sinatra had a black valet called George Jacobs, and Sinatra treated him as if he was a black slave. When, after inviting Dexter to dinner, Sinatra lost his temper about the spaghetti and threw it in George Jacobs' face, Dexter said: 'That was a very unkind thing to do.' George Jacobs calmly wiped the spaghetti off his face, and went back to the kitchen.

In due course, both George Jacobs and Brad Dexter would be victims of Sinatra's paranoia.

When the young actress Mia Farrow determined to marry Frank Sinatra, she was unaware of what she was taking on. In 1965, at the age of nineteen, she was selected to play Alison in the television serial *Peyton Place*, which was being filmed in Hollywood. She had a taste for older men – such as Yul Brynner and Kirk Douglas – and instantly fell for Sinatra when she saw him on the set of *Von Ryan's Express*. She was wearing a transparent gown, and had undoubtedly decided to make a play for Sinatra. When she saw him about to leave for Palm Springs in a jet plane which only had room for three, she asked why she hadn't been invited, and Sinatra lost no time in issuing an invitation. That is how their affair began.

Typically, it was only after Dexter had told Sinatra that he did not approve of the marriage because the thirty-year age gap was too great, that Sinatra began throwing things, then grabbed the telephone and told one of his lieutenants in Las Vegas to get a marriage certificate. Dexter said later: 'Mia's doom was sealed.' The two were married in Las Vegas on 19 July 1966.

As with Ava Gardner, conflicts soon developed because Sinatra did not want Mia to work. When producer David Susskind reluctantly gave her the part of the mute in *Johnny Belinda*, Sinatra had him threatened by the Mob, and a friendly gangster warned Susskind not to go to either Las Vegas or Miami. Susskind later described Sinatra as 'an ill-bred swine who operates on the level of an animal.' When the executive vice-president of the Sands, Carl Cohn, stood up to Sinatra one night and retaliated against his violence by hitting him in the face, splitting Sinatra's upper lip and knocking the caps off two of his teeth, people in Las Vegas suggested that Cohn should be elected mayor.

Kitty Kelley has an amusing paragraph contrasting Sinatra and Mia

Farrow: 'He drank Jack Daniel's; she smoked marijuana. He got drunk; she got stoned. He gave her diamonds; she wore wooden love beads. . .'

In the autumn of 1967, Sinatra was about to begin a film called *The Detective* and wanted Mia to star in it. He wanted her to begin work immediately. She said she couldn't, because she was working on Polanski's *Rosemary's Baby*. And when he ordered her to walk off the set and come and join him, she flatly refused.

Like a spoilt child, Sinatra would not be thwarted. He called his lawyer Mickey Rudin and told him to draw up divorce papers. These were presented to Mia Farrow as she was about to begin shooting a scene in *Rosemary's Baby*. She was understandably shattered, as Sinatra had intended her to be – when he gave orders, everybody had to jump.

The night before the decree was granted, Mia Farrow was in a nightclub called the Daisy when Sinatra's valet, George Jacobs, walked in with his date. Mia danced with him a couple of times, and there was an item about it in a newspaper. The result was that when George Jacobs returned to Palm Springs, Sinatra refused to speak to him, and told Mickey Rudin that he was to be fired.

Brad Dexter, the actor who had saved Sinatra from drowning, was dropped in the same abrupt way when he made some objection to Sinatra's desire for change in a film Dexter was directing. Later, when somebody mentioned Dexter to him, Sinatra said 'Who's that?'

When Lyndon Johnson announced in 1968 that he would not seek a further term as president, the democratic senator Hubert Humphrey announced his candidacy. So did Senator Robert Kennedy, the enemy of the Mafia. Sinatra lost no time in declaring himself for Humphrey – he was still determined to try and get a foot in the door of the White House.

But most of Sinatra's show business friends – like Shirley MacLaine and Sammy Davis – were supporting Robert Kennedy. And yet again, the question of Sinatra's Mob connections came up when a number of Humphrey's friends pointed out to him that Sinatra had been known as a friend of Lucky Luciano, Sam Giancana (who had been shot to death in 1967), and other mobsters. When a story about Sinatra's Mob connections appeared in the *Wall Street Journal*, Sinatra was enraged, and cancelled his appearance at the Democratic Convention lunch.

Sinatra's support made no difference anyway; Humphrey lost the presidential election to Richard Nixon.

The publication of Mario Puzo's novel, *The Godfather*, in 1969 raised the whole question of Sinatra's Mafia connections again. The singer Johnny Fontane, whose career is almost floundering when the godfather intervenes to make sure he gets a part in a Hollywood movie, is fairly obviously based on Sinatra. Sinatra saw Puzo in a Hollywood restaurant, and screamed abuse at him.

When the New Jersey State Commission on Crime summoned Sinatra to testify about the Mafia, Sinatra sued, claiming that the Commission was unconstitutional. He lost the case and appealed to the US Supreme Court, who also turned down his case. But when Sinatra eventually testified in front of the Commission – at midnight (to avoid reporters) on 17 February 1970, he lied as usual about his connections, claiming that he had no knowledge of Sam Giancana's reputation as a member of Cosa Nostra (the Mafia) or of Lucky Luciano's.

When governor Ronald Reagan of California announced in 1970 that he was a presidential candidate, Sinatra once again outraged his friends by deciding to support him, and TV host Steve Allen wrote Sinatra a letter accusing him of supporting Reagan as a way of getting revenge on the Kennedy family. Sinatra did not reply.

In 1971, Sinatra announced that he intended to retire from show business and take a long rest. His films were getting poor reviews, and his records selling badly.

To everyone's amazement, Sinatra decided to support Nixon for re-election in 1972. Sinatra had also been for some time a friend of vice president Spiro Agnew and when Nixon was re-elected, Sinatra at last had his wish to get his foot in the door of the White House.

Things soon went wrong for Agnew when he was accused of taking bribes and was forced to resign in order to avoid criminal prosecution. But Sinatra stood by his friend, lending him $200,000 to pay back taxes.

In 1973, Sinatra decided he'd had enough of retirement, and announced his re-entry into show business. But a big television special failed to attract a large audience. His public performances were still full of the old Sinatra personality, and his ability to mesmerize an audience, but he was also showing a tendency to paranoia in his addresses to the audience, with violent attacks on journalists – particularly female journalists, about whom he said many crude and downright nauseating things.

When the German press attacked Sinatra for his gangland connections, Sinatra cancelled his tour of Germany. In England he was better received, but Prince Charles said he was distressed by the 'creeps' (Sinatra's bodyguards) and 'Mafia types.' And Prince Charles also noted that Sinatra could be 'very nice one minute and . . . well, not so nice the next.'

In Australia, Sinatra found himself immensely unpopular with his attacks on the press. And went on to talk about female journalists as 'hookers'.

The next day, the leader of the Labour Party in New South Wales asked who Sinatra thought he was, and a Member of Parliament made some unkind references to Sinatra's 'goons'. And when the Stagehands Union refused to work, Sinatra's tour came to an abrupt end. The Waiter's Union refused to serve him, so he could no longer get room service at his hotel. Airport workers refused to refuel his plane until he apologized. Sinatra's lawyer Mickey Rudin had to step in and negotiate with the unions about a public statement that would satisfy everybody.

In America, newspapers observed with satisfaction Sinatra's humiliation.

Back in America, Sinatra displayed the same paranoia about journalists whenever he stopped singing to talk to an audience, and in Toronto, he even made the critics pay for their own tickets.

By this time, he was married again – to Barbara Marx, ex-wife of Zeppo Marx, who was a former model. Her boss at the time said: 'Barbara is not very intelligent, but she's beautiful, she's sweet, and she's incredibly patient.' These were obviously qualities that Sinatra needed in a wife. She put up with his insults, and even his violence – in the South of France he slapped her so hard that she could not come out of the hotel room for two days.

In 1976, Sinatra was back in trouble again for his relationship with the Mob. In Tarrytown, New York, the Mafia built the Westchester Premier Theater, but it was bankrupt within a year as a consequence of the Mafia habit of taking money from the till. Federal agents taped a phone conversation that revealed the involvement of the New York Gambino crime family in the theatre, and the result was an investigation. One of the exhibits that came up at the trial was a photograph of Frank Sinatra posing with a number of mobsters, including Carlo Gambino, Jimmy Fratianno and Paul Castellano.

Fratianno co-operated with the prosecution when he learned there was a Mafia contract on his life, and described how he had gone to see Sinatra in Palm Springs and told him that his crime family needed a favour – some benefit performances by Sinatra at the Premier Theater. Sinatra agreed to four performances and Fratianno told him, 'if ever there's anything we can do for you, just say the word.'

Fratianno then claimed that Sinatra's secretary had telephoned to say that Sinatra wanted one of his former bodyguards murdered because the bodyguard had written articles in the *National Inquirer,* and there were rumours that he was writing a book about Sinatra.

This plan apparently fell through because no one quite knew where to find the ex-bodyguard. But the incident offers an insight into the kind of 'favours' Sinatra expected from the Mob.

During a three-year hearing, Sinatra's name was frequently mentioned in connection with gangsters, and Sinatra responded, as he had throughout his life, by stepping up his charitable activities.

Reagan had lost in his first bid for the White House, but in 1980 he campaigned again, and again, Sinatra supported him. This time, Reagan won, and became president in January 1981. Sinatra, naturally, became a favoured visitor of the White House.

Kitty Kelley's unauthorized and frank biography of Frank Sinatra, *His Way,* caused the predictable explosion of rage, but the book became one of the bestselling biographies of all time, and Sinatra was finally presented to the American public as he really was, and not simply as he wanted to appear. He in turn accused her of using items from newspapers and magazines without checking her facts. But undoubtedly, the basic facts she gives about Sinatra's foul temper and violent behaviour are accurate.

After the appearance of Kitty Kelley's book, Sinatra had ten more years to live. He retired to his magnificent home in Beverly Hills, surrounded by his wife and children – Tina, Nancy and Frank Jr. His career as a performer was now over, his voice little more than a croak, but the rewards and tributes continued to pour in.

When Congress proposed to bestow its gold medal on Sinatra in January 1997, Kitty Kelley wrote a number of articles denouncing the nomination.

By 1996, it was clear that Sinatra's health was failing, and when he was hospitalized in November, there were rumours that he was being treated for pneumonia and heart problems. In January 1997, he was in hospital again, this time for a minor heart attack.

He finally died of a heart attack on 14 May 1998, at the Cedars-Sinai Hospital in Los Angeles.

THORPE, JEREMY

THE LIBERAL LEADER AND THE MALE MODEL

The trial of Jeremy Thorpe, leader of the British Liberal Party, on a charge of conspiracy to murder was the greatest political scandal in England since the Profumo case (*see* page 248). The charge was that Thorpe had incited three men – who stood beside him in the dock – to murder the former male model Norman Scott, with whom Thorpe was alleged to have had a homosexual affair.

Until the Scott case, the career of John Jeremy Thorpe, born on 29 April 1929, had been an unbroken success story. The son of a Conservative Member of Parliament, he was educated at a private school in Connecticut (during World War II), then at Eton College and Oxford University. He was obviously a man of driving ambition and became President of the University Liberal Club, then the Law Society, and finally – the most coveted post of all – of the Oxford Union, the debating society whose presidents have often become distinguished politicians. He was called to the bar in 1954 and contested the North Devon constituency as a Liberal in the following year. His flair for politics was obviously great, and he conducted his campaign 'with all the panache of an American congressional campaign', in the words of his biographers (Lewis Chester, Magnus Linklater and David May, in their book *Jeremy Thorpe, A Secret Life*). The same biographers quote various Oxford contemporaries of Thorpe to the effect that he could be too ruthless in achieving his aims and was capable of 'cutting corners'. This first political campaign ended in failure, but he cut the Tory majority in half. When he contested the seat again in 1959, he won by 362 votes. He made an immediate impact on the House of Commons with his wit and oratory. There was only one small cloud on the horizon: in March 1960, a routine security check into his background concluded that he was believed to have homosexual tendencies – at that time, homosexual activity was a criminal offence. It was also in 1960, on a visit to a riding stable in Oxfordshire, that Thorpe made the acquaintance of the man who was to be his political downfall, Norman Josiffe, later to be known as Norman Scott.

Josiffe, eleven years Thorpe's junior, was the child of a broken marriage and was emotionally unstable. The most important thing in his life was his pony. At the age of sixteen he was found guilty of larceny and placed on probation. In the following year he became a riding instructor. By this time he was having severe emotional problems: he was subject to crying fits and was in the habit of inventing tragic stories about his background to arouse pity. A doctor prescribed tranquillizers and he was admitted to a clinic. In 1961 he took an overdose of Largactil and had to be rushed to hospital. It was when he came out that he recalled Jeremy Thorpe's remark that if ever he was in difficulties, he should feel free to look him up at the House of

Commons. Josiffe went there on 8 November 1961, and had an interview with Thorpe. Afterwards, they went down to Oxted, in Surrey, where Thorpe's mother had a house. According to Josiffe, their homosexual affair began that night.

Josiffe alleged that on the way to Oxted, Thorpe asked if he would mind being introduced as a member of a television camera crew, with whom he would be travelling abroad the next day. At Mrs Thorpe's house, Josiffe signed the visitor's book with a false name. That night, when Josiffe was in bed, Thorpe visited him with a book by James Baldwin, the homosexual novel *Giovanni's Room*. Later, he returned to Josiffe's room in a dressing gown and pyjamas, and sat on the bed. 'He said I looked like a frightened rabbit . . . he just hugged me and called me "poor bunny" . . . he got into bed with me.' Thorpe went out to get some vaseline which he put on his penis. Then he put a towel on the bed and made love to Josiffe, with Josiffe as the passive partner. According to Josiffe, when Thorpe left, 'I just lay there with my dog . . . crying.' But although Josiffe declared that he did not enjoy being sodomized, ('I just bit the pillow and tried not to scream'), the affair continued apace. Josiffe was given a job on the staff of Len Smith, a Liberal Party official, and moved into a small service flat near the House of Commons where, according to him, Thorpe went to make love to him. They went down to Mrs Thorpe's house four or five times. They would meet in the Reform Club and go to a Chelsea restaurant for dinner. Josiffe went down to Devon with Thorpe at Christmas and while their hosts were walking in the garden, Thorpe made love to Josiffe in the bathroom.

Problems began to arise. A Mrs Ann Gray accused Josiffe of stealing her suede coat and when the police wanted to question him, Thorpe insisted on the interview taking place in his office in the House of Commons, explaining that he was 'more or less' Josiffe's guardian since Josiffe had lost both parents. Soon after, Josiffe moved to a position with a farming family in Somerset, and Thorpe wrote him a letter in which he told him that he could 'take the Ann Gray incident as over and done with'. The letter concluded: 'Bunnies *can* (and *will*) go to France.' There was a postscript: 'I miss you.'

But when Thorpe began to look into the matter of Josiffe's 'lost' parents and discovered that they were both alive and well, the relationship began to cool – at least, on his side. There was the additional problem that the farming family found Josiffe too nervous and highly strung. Josiffe moved to the home of a Dr Keith Lister and when the doctor wrote Thorpe a letter enquiring about the young man's background, he was told rather brusquely that he should consult Josiffe's parents, whose addresses were enclosed. But Thorpe continued to help Josiffe and sorted out a problem about his national insurance card.

Unfortunately, as Thorpe seems to have found himself losing patience with the 'bunny', Josiffe decided he was in love with Thorpe. When Josiffe's dog Tish killed Dr Lister's ducks, Josiffe was asked to leave. He tried confessing his 'sins' to a Catholic priest but was refused absolution unless he broke off his association with Thorpe. Josiffe felt himself torn in several directions at once and began to feel increasingly bitter. One day, in a fit of wild self-pity, he began talking to a young lady about his plan to kill Thorpe and commit suicide. The result was that Josiffe was interviewed at the Chelsea police station in December 1962, and began a statement: 'I have come to the police to tell you about my homosexual relations with Jeremy Thorpe. ...' The police took the 'Bunnies will go to France' letter and another, and these ended up in the file of the Assistant Commissioner of Police. The police made no attempt to follow up the allegations about the homosexual affair. Josiffe soon went to Ireland to take another job involving horses. When a West End outfitter, Gieves Ltd, wrote to Thorpe asking payment for a pair of silk pyjamas that Josiffe had ordered on his account, Thorpe refused to pay, and said he had no idea of Josiffe's present whereabouts. It was obviously his fervent wish never to hear from Josiffe again.

It was not to be. In 1964, Josiffe contacted Thorpe to ask for his help in getting a job on the Continent. Thorpe advanced him the money to go to Switzerland. Josiffe went there, disliked the job, and returned promptly without his luggage. With exemplary patience, Thorpe offered to help him retrieve the luggage. By now, Josiffe had upgraded himself; he called himself the Honourable Lianche-Josiffe and declared that his father, who had died tragically, was a peer of the realm. He also claimed that his wife had died in a car crash. He went back to Ireland, ran into more employment problems and finally wrote Jeremy Thorpe's mother a letter telling her in some detail about his homosexual affair with her son, and alleging that he felt himself shamefully mistreated. Mrs Thorpe passed the letter on to her son.

Thorpe was worried and his reaction was to confide in a fellow Liberal MP, Peter Bessell, the Member for Bodmin. Bessell's political career had been, in some ways, as meteoric as Thorpe's own, and Thorpe had helped him in the crucial campaign. Bessell listened sympathetically and then flew off to Dublin, carrying a legal letter threatening Josiffe with a libel suit. He met Josiffe and found him, on the whole, likeable. Bessell told him firmly that he could not believe that there had been a homosexual relationship with Jeremy Thorpe and asked if he had any proof. Josiffe replied that he did – that there were letters from Thorpe in the luggage that was still in Switzerland. Bessell promised to help him retrieve this. Bessell's secretary finally located the luggage and sent it on to Dublin. When it arrived, Josiffe telephoned Bessell to report that the letters from Jeremy Thorpe were missing ... Bessell was less concerned than he might have been; he was on the verge of bankruptcy and all his efforts were directed at borrowing $15,000 or so. Eventually, with some help from Jeremy Thorpe, he succeeded.

In 1966, the Labour Party won the Election, dashing the hopes of the Liberal leader, Jo Grimond, for a pact with the Labour Party. Grimond decided to resign. To many Liberals, Jeremy Thorpe was the obvious choice as a replacement. He had proved himself a brilliant fundraiser and had become party treasurer. There were many who felt he was too lightweight, that for all his charm and eloquence, he lacked the qualities of a future Prime Minister. And, regrettably, there were also rumours about his sexuality – largely the result of Bessell's inclination to gossip. A 'Stop Jeremy' movement was formed among Liberals. But it made no difference and Thorpe was elected leader of the party in January 1967 by a unanimous vote of the executive. He was 37.

Meanwhile, Josiffe had changed his name to Norman Scott and had found work as a male model. Three months after Thorpe became leader, Josiffe-Scott wrote to Peter Bessell explaining that he wanted to go to America but had burned his passport during the 'upset' over Jeremy – could Bessell help? Josiffe also lacked insurance cards, which meant he could not apply for unemployment benefit. In August 1967, Josiffe came to London and Bessell arranged to pay him a 'retainer' of between £5 and £10 a week until he could either find a job or obtain another passport. There was, of course, no reason why Josiffe should not apply for a new passport and insurance card. But he had come to the conclusion that Jeremy Thorpe should have put insurance stamps on his old card and this was the basis of yet another grudge.

Bessell was not sure that it would be a good idea for Josiffe to go to America. Although homosexuality had ceased to be a criminal offence in England in July 1967, there was still a stigma attached to it. If Josiffe accused Thorpe of being a homosexual in England, Thorpe could sue him for libel, and since Josiffe now had no proof that he had known Thorpe, Thorpe would undoubtedly win. In America, Josiffe could say anything he liked, and the results could be embarrassing for everyone, including Bessell, who had business interests there. And as far as Thorpe was concerned, this was certainly no time for a scandal. Many Liberals were dissatisfied with him; his style of oratory had become dull and pompous, and some fellow party workers felt he was too dictatorial.

In May 1968, Jeremy Thorpe married 29-year-old Caroline Allpass, whom he had met through a friend named David Holmes, a businessman who became his honorary deputy. While he was on honeymoon, there was an attempt to unseat him as Liberal leader and he had to rush back to London. All this aroused sympathy for him and the threat temporarily receded. But Scott remained a menace in the background. And sometime in the autumn of 1968, according to the prosecution case, Thorpe began to consider seriously the idea of killing Scott. In December, he and Bessell had a discussion in the House of Commons just before the division bell rang. When Bessell said it seemed to be impossible to find Scott a job in America,

Thorpe replied, 'In that case we have got to get rid of him.' Bessell asked, 'Are you suggesting killing him off?' and Thorpe answered, 'Yes.'

In May 1969, Thorpe had a temporary respite from his worries about Scott when the latter married. But his relief was short-lived. Scott and his wife had moved to a Dorset cottage and she was pregnant. Soon cash was short and although an emergency insurance card was issued, so that the expectant mother could claim maternity benefit, Scott became increasingly angry and hysterical. He rang Jeremy Thorpe's house in Devon, and found himself speaking to Caroline Thorpe. He poured out his story to Caroline who was understandably shocked. Scott also rang Bessell, threatening to give his story to a Sunday newspaper; Bessell did his best to soothe him. Eventually, Scott's marriage came to an end when he confessed to his wife that, during her absence, he had been sleeping with a former boyfriend. Once again, Thorpe was in the firing line.

Matters began to come to a head when Scott's wife sued him for divorce in the autumn of 1970. Both Bessell and Thorpe knew what that could mean. Anything a man says in a court of law is 'privileged' – he cannot be sued for libel. Both knew Scott well enough to believe that he would seize his opportunity to denounce Thorpe. But denounce him for what? For having 'seduced' him in 1961? But a seduction involves two people and besides, Scott had since become a practising homosexual. Scott was, in fact, trumping up a number of absurd and hysterical charges against Thorpe. Thorpe's increasing irritation and desperation were justified. These were undoubtedly increased by the personal tragedy that took place soon after the summer election of 1970 (which Labour lost to the Conservatives.) On 29 June, Caroline Thorpe set out to drive to London from Devon. Near Basingstoke her car struck an oncoming lorry and she was dead by the time she reached hospital. Later gossip asserted that Scott had gone to Thorpe's house the previous day and told her the full story of the homosexual affair, and that this was preying on her mind. Scott flatly denied this story. But it does seem likely that Thorpe's problems with Scott were preoccupying her mind on that last journey.

The next time Scott put on the pressure, he received an irritable rejection. With Bessell's help, Scott had moved to Talybont, in Wales. He decided to start a horse-training school and asked Bessell to help him with money. But Bessell had serious troubles of his own; his own money worries were enormous and he was struggling to avoid bankruptcy. He finally announced that he was unable to help him. Scott persuaded a new friend in the village to write to Thorpe, explaining that Scott's financial situation was now critical. A reply from Thorpe's personal assistant replied that he did not know a Mr Scott but that if he was the same person as Mr Josiffe, then Mr Thorpe was under no obligation to him.

Scott now persuaded another gullible acquaintance, a Mrs Gwen Parry-

Jones, to write to a local Liberal MP, Emlyn Hooson, to say that a certain well-known Liberal had shamefully wronged a young man of her acquaintance. Hooson thought that the MP referred to was Peter Bessell. A meeting was arranged between Scott and Liberal MP David Steel who was shaken to learn that the accused man was Jeremy Thorpe. Hooson's reaction, when he was told, was 'Thorpe must go'. But when Thorpe learned about this, he protested angrily. Scott, he said, was an unbalanced young man whom he had helped in earlier days and who had concocted this whole absurd fantasy. Four Liberal MPs now interviewed Scott; one of them openly accused him of blackmail. Scott walked out indignantly. He began telling his story to the press: 'I was deeply in love with Jeremy. I thought our idyllic friendship would last forever. But he discarded me. That's why I loathe him now.' (Hooson was to say, 'I formed the strong impression that Norman Scott had a definite fixation about Jeremy Thorpe, somewhat in the manner of a jilted girl . . .') But the newspapers declined to touch it.

In March 1973, Thorpe married the former concert pianist Marion Harewood. At about this time, Scott attempted suicide by slashing his wrists. In the autumn of that year, he met Thorpe's Tory opponent Tim Keigwin and told him the long, sad story. Clearly, he had no intention of fading into the background. And when, in the following year, Edward Heath called his emergency election in an attempt to break the miners' strike, Thorpe began to feel that Scott was a ticking time-bomb that would blow up the Liberal Party. Scott no longer had Thorpe's own letters but he had all the letters from Peter Bessell, which constituted strong evidence for his claims – after all, why should Bessell have paid him several hundreds of pounds unless there was a guilty secret somewhere? It was certainly not Bessell's guilty secret – Bessell's own extra-marital affairs were strictly heterosexual. The result was that Thorpe's friend David Holmes paid Scott £2,500 for the 'Bessell file'. Thorpe was re-elected with an increased majority. But the Election was otherwise a tie, in which the Tories lost their majority. For a while it looked as though Heath would propose a Liberal–Tory pact and Thorpe would at last attain some real political power. It was not to be, but the long discussions at 10 Downing Street were an indication of Thorpe's crucial political importance.

Meanwhile Scott had spent most of the £2,500. He was living in squalor in a cottage on the edge of Exmoor, taking various drugs and drinking heavily. He was now convinced that his life was in danger and that he had been a fool to part with the Bessell file. He even started to institute proceedings to recover it from the well-meaning doctor who had acted as intermediary with David Holmes. (In fact, Holmes had burned Bessell's letters.) Odd incidents terrified Scott. He alleged that a helicopter landed near his remote cottage and two men came and knocked on his door and that he stayed quiet until they went away. A man who claimed to be a foreign journalist, interested in his story, arranged an appointment in a hotel lounge in Barnstaple. Scott went along with his briefcase and was called to the telephone by the journalist, who said that he had to cancel the appointment because Mrs Margaret Thatcher had been appointed head of the Conservative Party and he had to rush to London. When Scott had finished the telephone conversation, he found his briefcase was missing. A week later he was beaten up by two assailants as he came out of a pub in Barnstaple. Then a man who called himself Peter Keene came to see him and told him he was in great danger because a hired killer was on his way from Canada to assassinate him. Scott was too nervous to go with Keene to meet the unknown benefactor who, according to Keene, was trying to protect him. However, he agreed to meet him in the centre of Combe Martin on 24 October 1975. Scott decided to take his Great Dane along.

'Keene' was a junior pilot officer with British Airways called Andrew Newton. They met at a hotel, as arranged, and Newton persuaded Scott to drive with him to Porlock, where he had business. They could discuss the 'assassin' on the way. Newton left him in Porlock for an hour, then collected him with apologies for being late. Scott was now beginning to feel at ease with 'Keene'. Newton seemed to be driving very badly and explained that he was tired. Scott offered to drive. On the edge of the moor, Newton stopped the car, Scott got out and ran through heavy rain to the driver's side of the car. As he arrived there, he found the door open and Newton standing outside the car. The Great Dane, Rinka, was barking excitedly. 'This is it,' said Newton, producing a Mauser pistol. He shot the dog through the head, then placed the gun against Scott's head, saying, 'It's your turn now.' Scott froze, terrified. But the gun seemed to have jammed; Newton was swearing loudly. Scott began to run over the moor, then decided it was useless to run away and went back to his dog. Newton pointed the gun at him again and said, 'Fuck it.' He jumped into his car and drove away. Soon after, another car drove up and Scott flagged it down. Its occupants included an AA scout who contacted the police for Scott.

Newton was easily traced: a suspicious landlady had noted the number of his car the first time he came to see Scott and it proved to have been hired from a firm in Blackpool. Newton was arrested and told the police that Scott had been trying to blackmail him, and that he had shot the dog to 'scare him off'. In due course, Newton was sentenced to two years in prison – he served slightly more than a year.

In January 1976, Norman Scott was charged with defrauding the Department of Health and Social Security of £58.40. On 29 January, he finally did what he had been threatening to do for so many years. In court in Barnstaple, he blurted out that he was being hounded because he had once had a homosexual relationship with Jeremy Thorpe.

Now the story was out. Inevitably, Thorpe promptly denied it. He told the Liberal chief whip, Cyril Smith, in confidence, that Scott was a common blackmailer and that he had been blackmailing Bessell about an affair he was having with his private secretary. Bessell had been persuaded to write a letter to this effect – it would explain the sums of money he had paid to Scott over the years. But Bessell had been told that his 'confession' would only be used in a case of extreme emergency. When away in America a friend told him on the telephone that the letter had been leaked to the press; Bessell's first reaction was to deny it. Thorpe telephoned him and persuaded him to withhold his denial for a few days. 'Peter, I'm begging for time.'

But by now the Press felt they had an important story. The Prime Minister, Sir Harold Wilson, added a new dimension of scandal to it when he proclaimed his belief that sinister forces from South Africa were behind the attack on the Liberal leader – Thorpe being an outspoken opponent of apartheid. From Thorpe's point of view, this intervention was less than helpful, for it led investigative journalists to probe deeper than ever into his own background. A 'Get Rid of Jeremy' movement began to snowball – one of its supporters was the now disillusioned Peter Bessell, who was living in Oceanside, California, where he had fled from his creditors. Finally, Thorpe had to give way. On 10 May 1976, he sent in his letter of resignation as party leader.

For another year, the scandal again became dormant; it began to look as if, in spite of losing his position as party leader (he was succeeded by David Steel), Thorpe was going to survive politically. But in April 1977, Andrew Newton was released from prison. He felt that someone owed him something for his year of discomfort and began trying to sell his own story to the press. On 19 October 1977, the scandal exploded again when the London *Evening News* came out with a headline: 'I Was Hired To Kill Scott. *Exclusive.* Gunman tells of incredible plot – a murder contract for £5,000.' The newspaper had paid Newton £3,000.

A week later, Thorpe gave a press conference in which he read aloud a statement giving his own version of his relationship with Norman Scott. He admitted asking Bessell to act as his intermediary with Scott but insisted that he had no knowledge of the purchase of the 'Bessell file' for £2,500. He added: 'As far as Mr Bessell is concerned, it is my considered opinion that if he had credible evidence to offer, he should have gone to the police rather than the press.' This was virtually a declaration of war on the man who had helped him so much.

Matters now came quickly to a head. The Director of Public Prosecutions had to decide whether to prosecute. By now, the newspapers had sniffed out what they called 'The South Wales Connection' – the allegation that Newton had been hired to kill Scott by two businessmen from Port Talbot, Wales – John Le Mesurier, who ran a discount carpet firm, and George Deakin, who had made a fortune from one-armed bandits. On 2 August 1978, warrants were issued for the arrest of Jeremy Thorpe, David Holmes, John Le Mesurier and George Deakin. On 20 November, the four men appeared in court in Minehead, the nearest court to the place where Norman Scott's dog had been shot. The magistrate had to decide whether there was a case to answer. The chief witness was Andrew Newton, with his assertion that he had been hired to kill Scott. The story that emerged was that in October 1974, David Holmes had gone to visit an old friend, John Le Mesurier, in Port Talbot, and was introduced to George Deakin, the one-armed-bandit king'. At the third or fourth meeting, Holmes mentioned that a friend was having trouble with a blackmailer. Could Deakin find someone to frighten this man? Deakin in turn went to a friend called David Miller, who ran a printing shop in Cardiff; it was Miller who recommended his friend Andrew Newton. Newton had at first been promised £15,000 to frighten Scott; this was later dropped to £10,000, then to £5,000. When Newton came out of prison in April 1977, he was summoned to a lonely moorland road by Miller and Le Mesurier and given his £5,000. A private detective hired by Miller roared past in a car and photographed the transaction – Miller was hoping he might sometime sell his story to the press.

This, then, was the background to how Newton came to shoot the dog. (Newton insisted he had no intention of killing Scott and that he had deliberately pointed the gun away from him before pulling the trigger a second time.) The magistrate decided that all this amounted to a conspiracy to murder. The trial of the four men opened at the Old Bailey on 8 May 1979.

All four – Thorpe, Holmes, Le Mesurier and Deakin – pleaded not guilty. The counsel for the prosecution, Peter Taylor, QC, told Norman Scott's story of how he had been seduced by Thorpe and the gradual breakdown of their relationship. According to Scott, the affair with Thorpe had continued for five years and he had frequently come back from Ireland to have sex with Thorpe. The turning point in the relationship came when Scott wrote to Thorpe's mother, telling her that he and Jeremy had been lovers for the past five years.

The most startling evidence came from Peter Bessell on day four of the trial. He described acting as intermediary between Thorpe and Norman Scott, then went on to tell of the day in the House of Commons in 1968 when Thorpe had first suggested 'getting rid' of Scott. They had then discussed various methods of disposing of Scott's body – it could be buried, dropped in a river, concealed in the rubble of a new motorway. When Bessell mentioned the tin mines in his Cornish constituency, Thorpe took him by the shoulders and exclaimed, 'That's it!' The body could be dropped down an empty mineshaft. Bessell said he thought killing was immoral and Thorpe replied, 'It's no worse than shooting a sick dog.'

A few months later, according to the prosecution, Bessell and Holmes attended another meeting in the House, and this time, Thorpe proposed that Holmes should pose as a reporter and invite Scott to Plymouth. On the way he could get him drunk in a pub, kill him in a lonely spot and dispose of him. Bessell remarked that shooting Scott would be noisy and messy. 'In that case,' said Thorpe, 'it will have to be poison. You can slip it into his drink, David, in a pub.' Holmes said it might be awkward if Scott dropped dead off his bar stool. Bessell said, 'You can apologize to the landlord and ask for directions to the nearest mineshaft.' Thorpe snapped, 'This is a serious matter.'

According to Bessell, they regarded Thorpe's murder plans as something of a joke. In any case, they were dropped when Scott got married. But Thorpe anticipated more trouble from Scott, and began to discuss luring him to America to kill him in some remote place.

In 1971, Holmes and Bessell met in New York to discuss a 'charade' that would convince Thorpe they meant to kill Scott. Holmes bought a toy pistol that would fire plastic pellets a few feet so he could report he had acquired a murder weapon. Holmes telephoned Thorpe from New York to explain that the plan had failed because Scott had not turned up.

The prosecution told the story of how Andrew Newton had been hired and how he had asked Deakin privately, 'I understand you want somebody bumped off?' Newton was apparently not particularly competent and went to Dunstable instead of Barnstaple. He contacted Holmes, who explained he would be happier if Scott vanished from the face of the earth. Newton described how he tried to lure Scott to the Royal Garden Hotel in Kensington and had gone there with a chisel hidden in a bunch of flowers – he intended to kill Scott with the chisel in a hotel room. But Scott failed to show up. Finally, Newton described how he had contacted Scott under the name of Peter Keene and had taken him for the drive that ended in the death of the dog. He again insisted that he had only pretended that the gun had jammed. It was for this abortive attempt that he was paid £5,000.

Where had this money come from? It was part of the prosecution's case that it had been syphoned off from Liberal Party funds, supplied by a millionaire named Jack Hayward, who had been a generous benefactor of the Liberals. After the 1974 Election, Thorpe had written to Hayward, explaining that he needed £50,000 for election funds, but that it would be best if he could have two cheques, one for £40,000 and one for £10,000. The £40,000 went into the Liberal funds; the £10,000 into an account on Jersey belonging to Thorpe's friend, and the godfather of his son, Nadir Dinshaw. Dinshaw sent the money on to David Holmes; in March 1975 the procedure was repeated, and a further £10,000 went to Holmes via Dinshaw. (The latter was dubious about the proceeding but was reassured by Thorpe that it was all perfectly above board.)

When the prosecution had finished presenting its case, things looked very black for the accused. The evidence that Thorpe had wanted Scott 'disposed of' had been precise and circumstantial. But when the defence presented its case, things began to look better. In the witness box, Peter Bessell agreed that he was hoping to make a great deal of money from a contract with a newspaper; if Thorpe was convicted, the total payment would be £50,000; if not, only £25,000. The defence's inference was that Bessell had good reason to want to see a conviction. Bessell was made to admit in court that he had 'disappeared' in 1974 to escape his creditors. It also emerged that the prelude to this disappearance had been an unsuccessful plot to swindle Jack Hayward of $½ million. Thorpe had been heavily involved in this scheme according to Bessell. In a brilliant cross-examination, George Carman QC succeeded in conveying a strong impression that Bessell was a swindler and a habitual liar.

He was equally impressive with Norman Scott. He scored a vital point when he made Scott admit that he had been boasting about a sexual relationship with Jeremy Thorpe before he went to see Thorpe in the House of Commons for the first time. Scott admitted that he had been mentally ill at the time and was suffering from a delusion. The implication was obvious: that Scott might have invented the whole story of his sexual relations with Jeremy Thorpe. And even if he hadn't, he had gone to the House of Commons with the idea of an affair in his mind – so the story of being dragged unwillingly into homosexuality by Thorpe must be untrue. This admission may well have been the turning point of the trial.

Scott made a thoroughly bad impression in court – one of a hysterical neurotic who had persecuted a public man out of malice. The impression made by Andrew Newton was equally bad. He began by admitting that he had lied on oath at his original trial for shooting the dog. Carman pressed him to admit that he had been hired simply to 'put the fear of God' into Scott and not to kill him. Newton disagreed but by the time he had finished giving his evidence, his general credibility was also badly dented.

Of the four accused, George Deakin was the only one who chose to go into the witness box. He insisted that he had merely helped to find someone to frighten a blackmailer and that he had been totally incurious about who was being blackmailed. He denied any subsequent involvement in intimidating Scott – he had been named as the man who had gone to Barnstaple to steal Scott's briefcase.

The prosecution and defence took five days to summarize their cases. Thorpe's counsel emphasized that the fact he had chosen not to go into the witness box did not prove him guilty. He had a perfect right to remain silent. The summing up by Mr Justice Cantley was, on the whole, in favour of the accused. He was scathing about the credibility of the prosecution witnesses and he also emphasized that the refusal of Thorpe, Holmes and Le Mesurier to go into the witness box should not be regarded as evidence of guilt. When he spoke of Bessell the judge further emphasized that his evidence about Thorpe's 'ultimate solution' to the problem of Scott was uncorroborated.

When he spoke of Scott, he obviously found it impossible to hide his distaste. He spoke of his 'hysterical, warped personality', and described him as an accomplished liar and a crook. He pointed out that the 'Bunnies can go to France' letter might be seen as evidence of a homosexual relationship or it might not. It was possible that when Scott first went to see Thorpe at the House of Commons, he had blackmail in mind. 'He is a fraud. He is a sponger. He is a whiner. He is a parasite. But of course, he could still be telling the truth. It is all a question of belief.'

When the jury retired, they were divided six to six for and against acquittal. An hour later, they were two to ten in favour of acquittal. By the following day, only one man held out for a guilty verdict. Finally, after two days, that one man was convinced. On Friday, 22 June 1979, the four accused filed back into the dock. The foreman read out the verdicts of acquittals for all the four. Thorpe looked rigid and stunned. Then he tossed the three cushions he had been sitting on over the side of the dock and leaned forward to embrace his wife.

The authors of *Jeremy Thorpe, A Secret Life,* add one curious footnote to the case. The turning point had probably been Scott's admission that he had boasted about a sexual relation with Thorpe even before he went to the House of Commons. The authors traced Scott's psychiatrist and asked about this. The psychiatrist, Dr Anthony Willems, assured them that this was not true; Scott had discussed his sexual fantasies very fully during his treatment, in the days before he went to meet Thorpe in the House. But Thorpe's name had never been mentioned. So Scott had, in effect, unnecessarily undermined his own case – another example, as the authors point out, of his being his own worst enemy.

TRESTRAIL, COMMANDER MICHAEL

THE FIRST PALACE HOMOSEXUAL SCANDAL

The summer of 1982 was a torrid time in Britain for Palace scandal and none of it to do with the Royal Family, except by association. On 19 July of that year, at a time when Scotland Yard was already in sackcloth and ashes over the intruder-in-the-Palace fiasco Her Majesty's personal police bodyguard, Commander Michael Trestrail, MVO, resigned because he was found to be a promiscuous homosexual.

Commander Trestrail was 51 years old and would normally have expected to serve for a further six years. He had successfully passed a positive vetting check only four months earlier, following a change in security procedure. His resignation was announced to a shocked House of Commons by Home Secretary William Whitelaw, after Trestrail's association with a male prostitute named Michael Rauch had been reported to Buckingham Palace by a Fleet Street newspaper.

Yorkshire-born Rauch, aged 38, had known the Queen's bodyguard since he was a detective-sergeant. According to newspaper reports, they continued their homosexual affair after Trestrail's promotion and appointment to the Royalty Protection Group. Rauch was said to have visited him at Buckingham Palace, as well as at his flat in Teddington, Middlesex. The two men were also alleged to have holidayed abroad together. The Commander broke off the association when Rauch tried to blackmail him and after reading press reports of the intruder-in-the-Queen's-bedroom scandal, Rauch attempted to sell the story of his relationship with Trestrail to a Fleet Street newspaper for a reported £20,000. Instead, the newspaper reported the matter to Buckingham Palace and Rauch was interviewed by Scotland Yard detectives on 17 July 1982.

Shortly after the Commander's resignation, his solicitor, Sir David Napley, said his client wished to express his 'deep sorrow' for the embarrassment he had caused both the Royal Family and the Force, 'towards whose service his only objective has been to devote himself, including ensuring the safety of Her Majesty'. Questions arising from the failure of the positive vetting system were tabled in the Commons but a Security Commission chaired by Lord Bridge of Harwich found that: 'If a man in a public position leads a secret double-life and succeeds, as Trestrail did for so long, in maintaining a total and effective separation between the two sides of his activities, this must present the positive vetting investigator with an almost impossible task . . .' Lord Bridge added that there was no connection, 'direct or indirect', between Commander Trestrail's resignation and Fagan's break-in at Buckingham Palace. His report did reveal, however, that the Palace had twice previously been warned that Trestrail might be a homosexual and, therefore, a security risk. These warnings came from a fellow police officer (referred to only as 'X') soon after Trestrail joined the Royalty Protection Group, but were ignored. Although the positive vetting check in April 1982 also failed to uncover his double-life, the Commander resigned immediately he was confronted with Rauch's evidence.

The Commission decided that neither his association with Rauch, nor a series of other secret liaisons over the years had breached security, even though Rauch made one attempt to blackmail him. Security at the Palace 'was not put at risk. Commander Trestrail carried out his duties as Queen's Police Officer loyally and efficiently, but led a secret double-life in that he indulged in promiscuous homosexual activities, mostly with prostitutes.' He also met casually with other homosexuals, especially when he had been drinking. Lord Bridge said that Trestrail, who had been aware of his homosexuality from teenage years, had been reluctant to acknowledge it to himself and sought to repress it. 'In the result, the occasions of his homosexual activity have been spasmodic and infrequent, separated by intervals of "months", according to his own account . . .' Even when he had been drinking and felt unable to control his urge, '. . . there was no breach of security, and in my judgment, security was not put at risk . . .'

Only two of the homosexuals with whom he consorted knew he was the Queen's personal bodyguard. Rauch, whom he knew as 'Michael Pratt', was one; the other was a Spaniard from the Canary Islands he met in Hyde Park. The report said Rauch had tried to blackmail him (for £2,000) two or three years earlier, but 'nothing came of it and the two did not see each other again.' Of 'X's' warnings the report commented: 'On hearing of Trestrail's resignation, X very properly communicated with Scotland Yard, volunteered a statement and in due course gave evidence before me. The substance . . . was . . . that twice after Trestrail's joining the Royalty Protection Group (X) reported to Commander Perkins, who was then the Queen's Police Officer, his suspicion that Trestrail was a homosexual. According to X, Commander Perkins simply brushed the matter aside, telling X in effect that it was nothing to do with him.' Commander Perkins was now dead and Lord Bridge took the view that while X was a completely honest witness, he was unable to provide Commander Perkins with hard evidence to back up his suspicions.

The Report criticized the media for its 'singularly unpleasant publicity' about the scandal, but found that the authorities were right to accept Commander Trestrail's resignation. He had clearly laid himself open to blackmail, while, 'Doubts as to the soundness of his judgment, and public opinion with regard to indiscriminate promiscuity would, in any case, have made it impossible for him to continue.' Lord Bridge also said that the Metropolitan Police were unable to provide him with an authoritative account of how its officers were selected for service with the Royal Protection Group. Apart from routine steps to ensure that they were not known criminals or security risks, no special checks on character or background were made.

Michael Trestrail, the son of a Cornish greengrocer, and a slim, balding man who accompanied the Queen on overseas tours as well as domestic engagements, was seconded to the Royal Protection Group in 1966. He was made a member of the Royal Victorian Order eleven years later. On his resignation in 1982 he was paid a lump sum of £25,000, plus a (reduced) pension of £600 a month. Male prostitute Michael Rauch was later found dead in his hotel room in Notting Hill Gate, after taking an overdose of drugs. He was said to have died penniless. An unnamed friend was quoted as saying, 'No one wanted to know him because he had betrayed Michael Trestrail and embarrassed the Queen. The gay community loathed him . . .'

VOIGT, WILHELM

'THE CAPTAIN OF KOPENICK'

The story of the bogus 'Captain of Kopenick' made all Kaiser Wilhelm's Germany rock with laughter. On the morning of 17 October 1906, a troop of ten soldiers, headed by a sergeant, was marching through Tegel (now in West Berlin). Suddenly, a man in a captain's uniform stepped in front of them and roared, 'Halt!' The captain was a plump man with a drooping moustache, in his late 50s. He inspected the squad, then ordered the sergeant to accompany him to Kopenick, a dozen or so miles away, where he had official business at the town hall. Being Prussians, they obeyed without question. When they arrived at Kopenick, the captain gave them a mark each and told them to fall out for the midday meal. After their meal, he lined them up outside the town hall and set guards at the doors, ordering them to keep callers from entering. Then he marched the remaining seven men into the building, set some of them as guards on stairs and in corridors, and marched into the mayor's office. The captain informed the mayor that he was under arrest. Then he demanded to be shown the cash box with the municipal funds. It contained 4,000 marks which he confiscated, after carefully counting them.

The captain ordered his men to lead the prisoner away, while a soldier was told to requisition three vehicles. Into the first two of these, the soldiers and the mayor were ordered; their destination was a police station some fifteen miles away. The captain and the cash box entered the other cab. It was this cab that failed to arrive at the police station. It took more than two hours of confusion and mutual recriminations before it dawned on the police and the mayor that they were victims of a hoax.

The 'captain' was an old lag named Wilhelm Voigt, who had spent 27 of his 57 years in jail. He had walked into a pawn shop, shortly after his release from his latest spell in prison, and purchased the second-hand captain's uniform. It is not clear whether the robbery was planned, or whether it was a spur of the moment decision as he saw the soldiers marching through Tegel.

The news of the comic-opera robbery spread round the world. Even the kaiser is said to have roared with laughter when he heard about it and said, 'Such a thing could only happen in Germany.' From the description, it didn't take the police long to identify the captain as Voigt. While all the Berlin police searched for him, the city was flooded with picture postcards of the exploit showing the trembling mayor standing before the ferocious captain, while another showed Voigt winking and smoking a fat cigar. The newspaper *Berliner Tageblat* said that he ought to be rewarded, not punished, for teaching the Germans a lesson.

Voigt was arrested ten days later in his room in a Berlin slum. Most of the

4,000 marks were still unspent. He was sentenced to four years in jail but this was later reduced to twenty months – on the direct intervention of the kaiser, it was whispered.

Voigt came out of prison in 1908 and discovered that a dramatist called Kalnberg had written a successful play called *The Captain of Kopenick*. Voigt requested, and received, a free seat for a performance of the play.

The case had political echoes. In 1910, Herr von Oldenburg-Januschau, a fire-eating right winger, defended Prussian militarism against the dangerous liberalism that seemed to be undermining the country. He declared, 'It must always be possible for the German Emperor and King of Prussia to tell the nearest lieutenant: take ten men and close down the Reichstag (parliament).' This sentiment backfired as comedians all over Germany parodied the statement. After the exploit of Wilhelm Voigt, Prussian authoritarianism was no longer treated with quite the same respect.

WATERGATE

THE US PRESIDENTIAL SCANDAL

At 1 o'clock in the morning of 17 June 1972, a young black security guard named Frank Wills, who worked in the vast Washington complex of shops and offices that included the Watergate Hotel, noticed that the spring catch of a door into a basement garage had been 'taped' back – that is, a piece of sticky tape had been stuck over the catch to prevent it from closing. Clearly, whoever had done it was no professional burglar, for a professional would have placed the tape vertically down the edge of the door, where it could not have been seen when the door was closed, not horizontally, as this was. He removed the tape – locking the door – but when he came back from eating a cheeseburger at the Howard Johnson motel across the street, the lock was taped again. So whoever had done this was not only no professional; he was also stupid enough not to realize that in replacing the tape, he was alerting the security guard that an intruder was still in the building.

He called the police. A three-man patrol arrived, and found that locks on the sixth floor had also been taped. This floor contained the temporary office of the Democratic National Committee, the ruling body of the Democratic Party. And as the police moved from room to room, they trapped, and then arrested, five men hiding behind a desk. What was happening soon emerged when the leader of the five admitted – after offering a false identity – that he was James McCord, security co-ordinator for the Campaign to Re-elect the President, (CRP – known to Democrats as Creep) i.e. Richard Nixon. His co-burglars were carrying electronic gear for bugging phones, and large sums of money in hundred dollar bills – presumably their 'wages'. They were – it emerged later – intending to tap the phone of Larry O'Brien, chairman of the Democratic National Committee. The other burglars had all worked for the CIA, the foreign Intelligence service, and three had been involved in the abortive invasion of Cuba in 1961.

Clearly, someone was up to 'dirty tricks' – although, looking back on it from several decades later, we might be forgiven for feeling that no very serious crime had been committed. However, the Republicans had most certainly been caught with their trousers down, and the Democrats can hardly be blamed for playing it for all it was worth. Which is exactly what they did. And although Nixon was, in fact, re-elected in November 1972, the clamour continued until he was forced to resign in August 1974.

But to return to 17 June 1972: when the burglars were arrested, two more men, Howard Hunt and Gordon Liddy, the planners of the operation, were in a room in the Watergate Hotel; warned by a look-out, they lost no time in fleeing. Hunt was an ex-CIA agent, while Liddy, an ex-FBI man, was finance counsellor of the CRP.

At the time the news of the arrests was reported, President Nixon was in the Bahamas. His Chief of Staff, Bob Haldeman, was in Florida. John Mitchell, former Attorney-General and now Director of the CRP, was at a fundraising event in Los Angeles. John Dean, counsel of the president, was in the Philippines. Only the President's Domestic Policy Adviser, John Ehrlichman, was in Washington.

Liddy rang his own immediate boss, Jeb Magruder (who had authorized the break-in) in Los Angeles. Magruder was appalled. He had never liked Liddy – who had a hair-trigger temper – and now groaned: 'Oh God, why didn't I fire that idiot when I had the chance?' But he now made a serious mistake. He told Liddy to approach Richard Kleindienst, the new Attorney-General, and ask him to get the burglars out of jail. This involved the assumption that Kleindienst was a mere catspaw of the president, and when Liddy approached him at his golf club, he was furious, and rang the prosecutor handling the case to tell him that the burglars were to be treated like anybody else.

Back in Washington, Bob Haldeman began the cover-up operation by ordering that various documents be shredded. Hunt was ordered to get out of town, and flew to Los Angeles. John Dean, however, declined to throw a briefcase full of evidence into the Potomac, and so managed to emerge from the case with his reputation more or less intact.

The day after the break-in, John Mitchell issued a statement that the burglars were not operating with the consent of the White House, and that the CRP deplored what had happened. Four days later, the president himself stated that the White House had no involvement in the incident.

This was plainly absurd; on whose behalf was the Democratic Headquarters being bugged, if not the president's?

While the burglars were awaiting trial, newspaper investigation revealed that $114,000 had been paid into the account of one of the accused, Bernard Barker, and the signator of a traceable cheque (most of the money was 'laundered') said it was a $25,000 campaign contribution paid to the CRP. This seemed undoubted proof that the burglars were linked to the CRP. So as the press stepped up the pressure – two young reporters on the Washington Post, Carl Bernstein and Bob Woodward, were told to devote their full time to investigating everyone connected to the break-in – the White House's problem was damage limitation.

Within a week or so, the investigators heard the name Gordon Liddy, who was supposedly involved in an organization known as 'the Plumbers', or White House Special Investigations Unit, a kind of 'dirty tricks' squad who were paid by money siphoned off from campaign contributions to the CRP. In mid-September 1972 Liddy and his co-conspirator Howard Hunt were also arrested.

What the CRP did not know was that someone in their own ranks had turned traitor, and was passing information on to Woodward and Bernstein.

His identity is still a secret, but he became known as 'Deep Throat' (after a famous pornographic film of that period). More than anyone else, Deep Throat was responsible for the White House's accumulating problems.

But why should the White House want to organize a burglary in June 1972, when Nixon was well ahead in the polls?

The problem had begun in 1971, when a former government employee named Daniel Ellsberg, a passionate opponent of the war in Vietnam, released to the press various classified documents about the Vietnam war. Ellsberg was clearly in the wrong, since he had broken his oath of secrecy; but in that atmosphere of anti-war demonstrations, he received widespread support from liberals. Lyndon Johnson had been driven out of the White House by the anti-war movement, and one result was a conservative backlash that brought Nixon to power.

In June 1971, the *Washington Post* began publishing the 'Pentagon papers', and two weeks later received support from the Supreme Court on grounds of freedom of the press. Liddy and Hunt had been sent to California to try and dig up information showing Ellsberg to be of unsound mind, and they organized a break-in at the office of Ellsberg's psychiatrist Dr Fielding. When John Ehrlichman, Nixon's Domestic Policy Adviser, heard about it, he lost no time in ordering this line of approach to be discontinued. But Nixon, feeling himself under siege from liberals and leftists, began to show signs of paranoia; he even ordered a phone tap on Henry Kissinger, his own National Security Adviser. Watergate sprang from this atmosphere of paranoia and mistrust. The 'Plumbers' were founded to investigate White House leaks.

By the autumn of 1972 Nixon heartily wished he had never heard of Watergate, his opponents had no intention of letting him off the hook.

Nixon decided that more of the CRP team had to be thrown to the wolves. On 30 April 1973, he broadcast to the nation, admitting that there had been a cover-up – although he had not been involved himself – and he now wished to announce the resignation of Haldeman and Ehrlichman, 'two of the finest public servants it has been my privilege to know.' He also announced the resignations of John Dean and Richard Kleindienst. John Mitchell resigned, giving as his reason that his wife had left him.

It was all, of course, too late. The media had smelt blood and the American public was delighted to be entertained with this escalating political scandal. If Nixon had jumped off the roof of the White House, everybody would have been disappointed that the show had finished so soon.

In fact, there were fresh developments on the day of Nixon's broadcast, when Judge Matthew Byrne, presiding over the Ellsberg trial in Los Angeles, ordered Ellsberg to be released, on the grounds that the 'conduct of the government' had precluded a fair trial. He also revealed that he had been offered the directorship of the FBI, the implication being clearly that he was being offered a bribe to find Ellsberg guilty.

Just as Nixon must have felt his fortunes were hitting rock bottom, there was an even greater disaster. On 17 July 1973, Alexander Butterfield, a Haldeman aide, told the Senate Investigation Committee that for the past two years, Nixon had been taping all phone conversations in the White House. This meant that there was taped evidence about whether or not Nixon had ordered the Watergate break-in.

Understandably, the Committee wanted those tapes. Equally understandably, Nixon was determined to hang on to them. (His aim in making them had apparently been to provide material for a future book on his presidency, and he regarded them as his personal property.) He claimed 'executive privelege'.

The ensuing struggle was bitter. Nixon offered a 'summary' and the Committee declined. And when some of the tapes were handed over, on 21 November 1973, no one was surprised when one of them proved to have an eighteen and a half minute gap in a conversation between Nixon and Haldeman. Nixon's secretary admittted that she had 'accidentally erased' five minutes, but that left thirteen and a half minutes unaccounted for.

Now everyone was asking: can an incumbent president be indicted and brought before a grand jury – perhaps even sent to jail? More tapes were demanded and reluctantly handed over, Nixon protesting that all this would 'irreparably damage the presidency.' In July, the Supreme Court ruled against him. And in late July, the Judiciary Committee voted that the president should be impeached, accused of conduct 'designed to obstruct justice'.

Shown by the tapes to have directed the FBI agents away from the White House, Nixon was forced to admit that he was involved in the cover-up, and this cost him his support in Congress. In the country itself, his popularity had dwindled from 61 per cent to 27 per cent since the election. He resigned the presidency on 9 August 1974. His vice president Gerald Ford (who had taken over from the disgraced Spiro Agnew, forced to resign through a tax-evasion scandal) became president on 6 December 1974.

Although Ford had stated that he would not interfere with the indictment of Richard Nixon, he in fact granted him a full pardon a month after assuming office on 6 December 1974. His own popularity rating instantly dropped from 71 per cent to 50 per cent, and the slump undoubtedly played a part in his electoral defeat by Jimmy Carter in 1976.

A suggestion that all the Watergate conspirators should be pardoned encountered universal hostility. Haldeman would serve eighteen months, and write a bestselling book, *The Ends of Power.* Ehrlichman also served eighteen months. Charles W. Colson, a senior White House aide (who had threatened that after Nixon won the election, the administration was going to 'shove it in' to the *Washington Post*, received seven months. (In fact, challenges of the Post's ownership of two Florida TV stations had caused the *Washington Post* stock to drop by 50 per cent.) John Dean would serve four months for conspiracy (but his book *Blind Ambition* was also a bestseller, and plus a television presentation, made him a millionaire). Jeb Magruder was in jail for seven months and became a born-again Christian. John Mitchell served nineteen months.

As to the original 'Watergate seven', Gordon Liddy was sentenced to 'not less than six years and eight months, and not more than twenty years.' (He served 52 months in jail, the longest of all). Hunt was sentenced to thirty-five years, of which he served thirty-three months. The 'Miami four' (Eugenio Martinez, Bernard Barker, Virgilio Gonzales and Frank Sturgis) were sentenced to forty years each, but in fact served between twelve and fifteen months each. McCord served four months.

Nixon's reputation saw a slow but steady rise for the remaining twenty years of his life (he died on 22 April 1994); a series of television interviews with David Frost showed him in a sympathetic light, while television programmes about his life underlined his real political achievement. In retrospect it is difficult to maintain the view of Nixon as 'the man who shamed a nation'.

WELLS, H. G.

THE LOVE LIFE OF A LITERARY DON JUAN

As a lifelong seducer of women, H.G. Wells was the subject of a great deal of scandalous gossip – Arnold Bennett recorded in his journal, perhaps with a touch of envy, that Wells openly displayed photographs of his various mistresses on the mantelpiece. However, the gossip never reached the general public; perhaps the nearest thing to an open disclosure was a malicious story of M. P. Shiel called 'The Primate of the Rose' in which Wells is represented as a popular but mediocre journalist-philosopher whose self-esteem depends upon sexual conquest. (Wells had once stretched the truth in the opposite direction when he described Shiel as 'a flaming genius'.)

Wells was the son of a gardener and a maidservant. He experienced a great deal of poverty during his childhood in Bromley, Kent, where his father ran an unsuccessful crockery shop; his mother deserted the family when he was thirteen and became housekeeper in a country mansion. 'Bertie' (as he was known) was apprenticed to the drapery trade, which he hated as much as Dickens hated the blacking factory, and he ran away at the first opportunity. (His mother forced him to return just as promptly.) He became a schoolmaster, gained a scholarship to the South Kensington School of Science, had a few articles accepted, and became a writer. (His first book was a textbook of biology.) He came near to dying of tuberculosis, married his cousin, and slowly achieved success. But during the period when he was struggling to make a living, his marriage broke up, and he ran away with one of his students, Amy Catherine Robbins. Unfortunately for Wells, who was sexually insatiable, Catherine was only mildly interested in lovemaking, so he remained sexually obsessed with his first wife. (In his autobiography, he even admits to going over to see her a few years after their separation and imploring her to give herself to him again; she refused.)

Soon after marrying Catherine in October 1895, Wells was unfaithful for the first time. He was alone in the house with a Miss Ethel Kingsmill, to whom his wife was teaching the retouching of negatives. 'I forget by what excuse Ethel Kingsmill flitted from her retouching desk upstairs to my study. But she succeeded in dispelling all the gloomy apprehensions I was beginning to entertain, that lovemaking was nothing more than an outrage inflicted upon reluctant womankind. ... The sound of my returning aunt's latch-key separated us in a state of flushed and happy accomplishment.' Wells had been virtually sex-starved up to the age of thirty but he set out to make up for it in the remaining fifty years of his life.

In the posthumously published postscript to his autobiography (*H. G. Wells in Love*, 1984), Wells describes how it was the renewal of acquaintance with a childhood friend, Sidney Bowkett, who had become an actor, that converted him from a romantic attitude towards women into a determination to 'get' them. Bowkett boasted about his own conquests.

The first girl Wells tried to 'get' was apparently a teenager named May Nisbet, the illegitimate daughter of a journalistic colleague, E.F. Nisbet, who had died suddenly. Wells paid the girl's school expenses and invited her to his house at Sandgate for holidays. He describes her as a 'gawky and rather sullen girl' of fifteen or sixteen, to whom he was not particularly attracted until 'one day upon the beach at Sandgate she came down towards me wearing a close-fitting bathing dress; instantly she seemed the quintessence of sunlit youth to me, and I was overwhelmed with a rush of physical desire ...' He goes on to say, 'I never gratified that physical desire', and then adds, rather puzzlingly, 'I made love to May Nisbet, but quite vaguely and inconclusively ...' But this inconclusive love affair aroused a desire 'that had to be assuaged'.

He met a writer named Violet Hunt at some literary gathering, who experienced 'the same restless craving for the clasp of an appreciative body as myself'. They became lovers. 'There were one or two other *passades* about this time.' One was with Ella D'Arcy, who wrote short stories in *The Yellow Book*; another was Dorothy Richardson, a schoolfriend of Catherine Wells, whose mother had committed suicide, and who had become a dentist's receptionist. 'For me, it was a sensuous affair, for Dorothy was then a glowing blonde. ... But a vein of ego-centred mysticism in her had always made her mentally irritating to me; she seemed to promise the jolliest intimate friendship; she had an adorable dimple in her smile; she was most interestingly hairy on her body, with fine golden hair, and then – she would begin intoning the dull clever things that filled that shapely, rather large, flaxen head of hers; she would lecture me on philology and the lingering vestiges of my Cockney accent, while there was not a stitch between us.' Dorothy Richardson later gave an account of her love affair with Wells – calling him Hypo Wilson – in a volume of her autobiographical novel *Pilgrimage (Dawn's Left Hand)*. He also recalls a woman from Australia who had read *Kipps* and asked him to come to her lodgings, and a black prostitute in America with whom he talked literature after their lovemaking.

In 1901, a book called *Anticipations,* containing Wells's vision of the future, was a considerable success, and Wells was invited to join the Fabian Society, a socialist group run by Sidney Webb, Bernard Shaw, Graham Wallas and Hubert Bland. Bland, who looked the typical English gentleman, with his monocle and bristling moustache, was himself an incorrigible Don Juan. He was married to Edith Nesbit, the writer of children's books, and his wife's best friend, Miss Hoatson, also lived with them. When Miss Hoatson announced that she was pregnant, Edith was warmly sympathetic until she found out that her husband was the father of the baby. She ordered Miss Hoatson out of the house but Bland threatened to go too so they continued as a *ménage à trois*. In due course, Bland turned to seducing his daughters' schoolfriends. Then, according to Wells, he began to contemplate incest with Rosamund, his illegitimate daughter, a 'dark-eyed sturdy girl'. Wells decided that the best way to save Rosamund was to seduce her himself. Bland found out his intention before this was accomplished and was furious, while Edith Nesbit wrote letters to Catherine Wells denouncing her tolerance of her husband's affairs. 'Rosamund was hastily snatched out of my reach.'

Wells was becoming a leading figure in the Fabian Society, challenging Shaw and the 'old guard' for leadership. His heady teachings about sexual freedom inspired a number of young ladies with ardent admiration. One of these was Amber Reeves, a teenage student at Cambridge, who was the daughter of two Fabians, Maud and Pember Reeves. Maud Reeves encouraged the development of a friendship between Wells and her daughter, a pretty, dark-haired girl. They used to go for long walks and discuss social questions. Wells called her Dusa (short for Medusa). One day, Amber told Wells she was in love and when Wells asked 'With whom?', she hurled herself into his arms. Wells was never one to decline an invitation to lovemaking. They stripped and climbed into bed although without lovemaking. In Soho shortly thereafter, Amber surrendered her virginity – probably in one of the hired rooms that Wells had learned about from Violet Hunt. They spent some days together in a lodging at Southend while Amber was supposed to be with friends in Epping and then Wells took a room in London where they could spend a day together every week or so. He describes how they would snatch opportunities for lovemaking on country walks and how they obtained the key of a church belfry from the sexton and made love in the room below the bells.

Wells told himself that this was the ideal situation for a writer: Amber, the mistress, Jane (as he called his wife), the understanding mate, and his work. Amber told her mother about the relationship and Maud Reeves did her best to be broad minded. (For some reason, this always seems to be easier for the mother of a seduced girl than for the father.)

Soon Amber Reeves became aware that she was pregnant. Her father had to be told and this was done by a young man called Rivers Blanco White, who was in love with Amber himself, and wanted to marry her. Pember Reeves 'became all that an eighteenth-century father should be', declared his intention of shooting Wells and made the whole affair a public scandal – at least, among the Fabians.

Wells was greatly torn. His ideal *ménage à trois* was turning into a nightmare and there was no doubt that for Amber, the ideal solution would have been for Wells to divorce Jane and marry her. But Wells was too fond of his home and children. The worst of it was that he was physically addicted to Amber. Wells installed her in a chalet in Le Touquet and rushed over to see her as often as possible. Finally, he told her that the best solution would be for her to accept the offer of marriage from Rivers White. She was shocked and indignant. Wells left her. On her way back to England on the Channel packet, she attempted to jump overboard but was saved by a steward. Finally, exhausted, she agreed to marry Rivers White.

Beatrice Webb, a leading Fabian, was particularly outraged by Wells's conduct and began writing poison-pen letters to other members of the Society who had teenage daughters, warning them to keep them out of Wells's reach. One of these letters was sent to Sidney Olivier, a member of the 'old guard' who had four pretty daughters. Olivier liked Wells and showed him the letter saying, 'Here's something that will make you laugh.' Wells was furious and wrote the Webbs a letter so full of abuse that it made Sidney Webb recognize that his wife was running the risk of a libel suit. Beatrice ceased to write the poison-pen letters but continued her campaign verbally. She was even more outraged to learn that Wells was a frequent visitor at the cottage at Woldingham, in Surrey, in which the young married couple had settled. Rivers White must have been either an admirer of Wells or a singularly weak man, for he allowed Wells to live with them in a *ménage à trois* for several weeks. Wells and Amber still contrived to meet after she had had the baby, a daughter, and in later life, she and Wells and Rivers White once again resumed an open friendship. Wells remarks in his autobiography that, 'I do not see much of Blanco White because I find him sententious and argumentative in an unimaginative way. I prefer . . . to entertain her alone. I take her to a theatre or opera at times or we dine at a restaurant . . .'

His wife's attitude was equally accommodating. Wells implies that she was perfectly happy to see her husband having affairs with other women. 'Jane was wonderful. She betrayed no resentment, no protesting egotism. She had never seen or felt our relationship as being primarily sexual. . . . She had always regarded my sexual imaginativeness as a sort of constitutional disease; she stood by me patiently, unobtrusively waiting for the fever to subside. Perhaps if she had not been immune to such fevers, I should not have gone astray . . .' This, at all events, was Wells's rationalization. Unfortunately, we have no direct insight into how Jane Wells felt about it. We only know that she died of an abdominal cancer in 1927.

Wells further scandalized the Fabians by publishing a novel called *Ann Veronica*, which had been written during his affair with Amber, about a girl who proposes to her college teacher that she should become his mistress. Every reviewer in London knew that Ann Veronica was Amber Reeves and it seemed that Wells was flaunting his immorality. The reading public was shocked at the idea that a 'nice' young, middle-class girl should offer her virginity to her teacher and that he should accept it. The chorus of outrage made *Ann Veronica* something of a bestseller. There was further trouble two years later with Wells's novel *The New Machiavelli*, about a politician who deserts his wife for his mistress – the mistress was again clearly based on

Amber Reeves. (There was also an acid portrait of the Webbs.) When the book appeared, after being turned down by several publishers, it was banned by a number of book sellers and libraries but the controversy did the sales no harm.

It was as well that Jane lacked the proprietorial temperament. After the break with Amber, Wells set himself up in a flat in Candover Street and tried to get the 'fever of Amber' out of his blood by sleeping with as many young women as possible. One of these was Elizabeth von Arnim, a successful authoress who had left her German husband, the Count von Arnim, because he wanted to keep her in a perpetual state of pregnancy. She had called on the Wellses at Sandgate, was apparently fascinated by Wells's reputation as a lady-killer, and became his mistress at the first opportunity. They went abroad together several times and made love on the pine needles at her villa near Montana. While he was still having an affair with her, he met another young woman who showed an immediate inclination to become his mistress. Her name was Cicely Fairfield; she wrote under the name of Ibsen's heroine, Rebecca West. She had attacked one of Wells's books and he asked her to come and see him. She spent a weekend with Wells and his wife. The next time they met, 'face to face with my book-shelves, in the midst of a conversation about style or some such topic, and apropos of nothing, we paused and suddenly kissed one another.' She went to see Wells at his flat in St James's Court and they became lovers. 'It was our second encounter and she became pregnant.' Rebecca declined to have an abortion, so Wells rented a villa at the seaside town of Hunstanton and persuaded her to go there. In due course a son, Anthony West, was born. Rebecca made a series of moves from place to place but it was only after an unpleasant episode in a house at Leigh-on-Sea, when it dawned on her that an unmarried mother was regarded with contempt even by the servants, that she decided to replace Jane as Wells's wife. Jane's reaction was simply to pass the word round that Rebecca was behaving badly. When this got back to Rebecca, she gave way to violent emotions that thoroughly alienated her lover. He flatly refused to divorce Jane and marry her. So the stormy relationship dragged on until, after World War I, it gradually broke apart. In the biography of his father, Anthony West suggests that she was a mythomaniac – not so much a liar as a person who totally believed her own fantasies.

In 1923, Wells's private life almost became public property. A 'pretty young woman with a face like the *Mona Lisa*' came to see him from Vienna, to tell him about what was happening in Austria. She also asked if she could translate Wells's *Story of a Great Schoolmaster,* which provided a further excuse to see Wells. One day when Jane was absent 'she passed rather suddenly and skilfully from an intelligent appreciation of my educational views to passionate declarations. . . . I hate to snub an exile in distress, and she was an extremely appetising young woman . . .' He was soon forced to recognize yet again that there is probably no such thing as a love affair without 'strings' attached. She bombarded him with letters about her adoration and Wells gave way and 'assuaged her sufferings on various occasions'. One weekend she came down to Felsted, near Easton, where Wells was living, and asked him to call one afternoon to meet her hosts. When Wells called, he found her alone for the hosts had gone away, leaving her in charge of the house. She was wearing a tea gown and nothing much besides. ' "This must end," said I, "this must end," – allowing myself to be dragged upstairs.'

She went back to Austria for a while and when she returned, Wells had decided it was time to call a halt to the affair. He instructed his maid that if she called he was not at home. One evening he was about to leave his Whitehall Court flat to go to dinner when the woman called and a temporary housemaid let her in. Wells went into his study and found her lying on the hearthrug, naked except for a waterproof – which she had opened – and her shoes and stockings. It is a proof of how far she had exhausted Wells's patience that he declined the invitation and went to summon the hall porter. While his back was turned, she produced a razor, and slashed her wrists and armpits. Two policemen were summoned and she was taken off to Charing Cross Hospital. The carpet was covered with blood. Wells realized that this was the kind of story that could ruin him if it got into the newspapers. He had recently published his bestselling *Outline of History* and was planning a further two immense volumes covering biology and sociology. How could readers take him seriously if the sight of his name conjured up visions of a woman wearing only shoes and stockings lying with her legs apart on a hearthrug? Fortunately, Wells knew two of the leading press barons, Lord Beaverbrook and Lord Rothermere. He telephoned them and explained the problem. They gave orders to all their newspapers that Wells had ceased to be news for the next few weeks. And apart from a couple of brief mentions in other newspapers, the affair was suppressed. Later, Wells learned that the woman made a habit of trying to commit suicide in front of lovers who had decided to get rid of her – she had learned how to cut her veins without bleeding to death. On his seventieth birthday, Wells had a friendly note from her, she was now happily married, and met her without unpleasant repercussions.

Yet Wells never seemed to learn by experience. It was at about this time that he started yet another affair with a woman who was to cause him endless trouble – Odette Keun. The telephone rang and a woman's voice explained that she had come from Grasse to see him; she asked him to come to her hotel. She had been writing to him for several years and made it clear that she wanted him to become her lover so Wells knew what he was letting himself in for. 'I found myself in a dimly lit apartment with a dark slender young woman in a flimsy wrap and an aroma of jasmine.' She told him that he was all she had to live for. ' "If you feel like *that,*" said I . . .' And in writing of the episode, Wells makes the acute observation: 'This sort of free gift is one that no one should accept.' He was beginning to suspect at last that this kind of bait usually had a fish-hook attached.

But not soon enough. Odette Keun proved to be his biggest mistake so far. She was highly intelligent but aggressive, emotional and quarrelsome. Anthony West says that her 'profound seriousness was masked . . . by a rather childish desire to shock and by a degree of sexual exhibitionism.' She liked to repeat the story of her 'seduction' of H.G. in mixed company. Fortunately, she was unable to obtain a visa to come to England, having had differences with the British authorities in Constantinople, so Wells was able to keep his life with her apart from Jane and his family. He built a house for her in the South of France and had inscribed over the fireplace: Two Lovers Built This House. (Wells told Charlie Chaplin, who visited him there, that he had had it removed and restored several times, after each violent quarrel.) But he soon began to find her an intolerable nuisance. She began by regarding him as a kind of superman. 'My god-like quality diminished with every freedom I gave her. . . . The danger of losing me, which had had the most salutary influence on her behaviour at the beginning of our liaison, seemed to have passed altogether.'

Wells tells a typical story of her craving to shock. A highly respectable Englishman, Sir Wilfred Grenfell, was dining with them and Odette was hoping he was going to invite her to Labrador, where he was in charge of various missions. The conversation turned to Casanova, and Sir Wilfred asked vaguely, 'Now let me see – what exactly did Casanova do?' Wells saw an ominous brightness in Odette's eyes and knew there was nothing he could do about it. 'She told him in a word.' An awful silence fell. Wells hastily intervened with more general information. Odette was not invited to Labrador.

Wells was sick of her by 1928. But it was not until 1933 that she gave him the excuse to break with her, by opening a letter from a woman friend who was not a mistress, but who began her letter 'Darling'. Odette threatened to tell the woman's husband. Wells told her that if she opened his letters, he was finished with her. But when he started to write the postscript to his autobiography in 1934 he had to admit: 'So Odette is receding out of my life down a *diminuendo* of parting shots.' The 'parting shots' were violently abusive letters which, according to Wells, were Odette's normal way of letting off steam.

Ironically, the only woman Wells really loved deeply in the last years of his life refused to marry him. She was Baroness Moura Budberg, whom Wells had first met in St Petersburg in 1914. He met her again in 1920 when he went to Russia to visit Lenin; she was now the secretary of Maxim Gorki. Wells learned later that, because of her connection with a British secret agent,

Bruce Lockhart, she had been blackmailed by the secret police into working for them and spying on Gorki. She decided to tell Gorki the truth; the result was that he became her protector. When Wells was in Moscow she became his official interpreter. 'I fell in love with her, made love to her, and one night at my entreaty she flitted noiselessly through the crowded apartments in Gorky's flat to my embraces.'

In 1929, at a time when Odette was making his life a misery, Moura turned up at a lecture Wells gave in Berlin, and he decided instantly that he was in love with her. In 1932, Odette exploded when Wells told her he expected to see Moura at a writers' conference in Dubrovnik and told him that if he went, he need never come back. Wells seized on the excuse to leave their home in the South of France for ever. Even his discovery that Moura was still a Russian spy made no difference to his feelings. But he went through a crisis of misery and jealousy when he discovered that she had been staying with Gorki at a time when she wanted him to believe she was at her home in Estonia. By the time he wrote about her, in the postscript of his autobiography, in 1934, he had decided that 'she does not cheat deliberately. It is just her easy way with fact. . . . Like a child she believes a thing as she says it . . .' Their relationship lasted, on and off, until Wells's death in 1946.

WILDE, OSCAR

'ONE MUST SEEK OUT WHAT IS MOST TRAGIC'

Oscar Wilde's father, Sir William Wilde, was a constant subject of Dublin gossip and scandal. Known as 'the Wilde knight', he was reputed to be the father of many illegitimate children – Bernard Shaw said he had a child in every farmhouse. In 1864 (when Oscar was ten), a libel case against his wife, Lady Jane Francesca Wilde, turned into a trial of Sir William, a leading physician, on a charge of raping a female patient.

Lady Jane had written a furious letter to a Dr Travers, Professor of Medical Jurisprudence at Trinity College, accusing his daughter of blackmailing Sir William and disseminating a pamphlet accusing him of 'an intrigue' with her. The daughter, Miss Mary Josephine Travers, decided to sue; she wanted £2,000 damages.

When the case came up on 12 December 1864, the prosecution lost no time in informing the jury that 'the particulars ... are of so shocking a description that I wish to God it had devolved upon some other counsel to present them ...' Having cured Miss Travers of ear trouble, Sir William had lent her books and money, bought her bonnets and dresses, taken her to lectures and exhibitions, and finally raped her in his consulting room. (One lady fainted and had to be carried out of the courtroom.) She had gone to him to be treated for a burn on her neck and in the course of the treatment had fainted. She had awakened to realize that, alas, she was no longer a maid. Sir William had urged her to keep this quiet. Miss Travers had gone to Lady Wilde to complain but had been treated with scorn. She had attempted suicide with a dose of laudanum (opium) but had recovered. To redress her wrongs, she had printed the pamphlet accusing Sir William of taking advantage of her. When Miss Travers was called to the witness box, the judge told the ladies in the gallery that any who wished to do so might leave; no one did. Then the prosecution asked the question, 'When you were unconscious was your person – er – violated?' and Miss Travers replied, 'It was.'

But the cross-examination was damaging. Why, Miss Travers was asked, did she accuse Sir William of violating her after administering chloroform? Miss Travers agreed that it had not happened like that but could give no excuse for printing a false version. Then Sergeant Sullivan, in Sir William's defence, went in for the kill. Had the alleged assault happened on other occasions? Blushing, Miss Travers admitted that it had. She explained that Sir William had led up to it with 'rudeness and roughness'. But the jury must have found it a little odd that a girl who had been raped while unconscious should give the rapist the opportunity to do it several times more – even with rudeness and roughness. The jury returned to say that they found Lady Wilde's letter libellous, which implied that her husband was guilty, but they awarded Miss Travers only one farthing in damages. The Wildes had to pay the considerable costs. Oscar should have learned from the example of Miss Travers that it can be dangerous to accuse someone of libel; it can lead to embarrassing counterclaims.

Oscar Wilde was born on 16 October 1854. At seventeen he won a scholarship to Trinity College, Dublin. There he came under the influence of the remarkable Professor of Ancient History, the Reverend John Pentland Mahaffy. It was from Mahaffy that Wilde picked up his passionate love of the classics, particularly those of ancient Greece. At this time, Wilde's sexual inclinations were basically heterosexual, with a mild touch of ambivalence, such as may also be noted in Lord Byron. And, as with Byron, his intellectual and emotional appreciation of Mediterranean pederasty laid the foundations for his later development.

At Trinity, and later at Oxford, Wilde was brilliant rather than hardworking. He had the typical charm of those born under Libra. At Oxford he came under the influence of John Ruskin, who taught him to appreciate painting and architecture, and Walter Pater, who taught that the basic aim of life is to live with 'a hard, gem-like flame' and who revived Victor Cousin's phrase 'Art for art's sake'. Pater confirmed Wilde in that intellectual elitism he had picked up from Mahaffy, the feeling that the true aristocrats of this world are the men of brilliance and imagination. And when, at the age of 23, he accompanied Mahaffy on a tour of Greece, the experience confirmed his conviction that beauty is the only ultimate value.

In his last year at Oxford, Wilde wrote to a friend: 'I'll be famous, and if not famous, I'll be notorious.' And when he went to join his mother in London – his father had died – he decided to become both at once. His elder brother Willie, who had become a journalist, introduced him to editors, and Wilde published some poems. He fell in love with the famous beauty Lily Langtry, mistress of the Prince of Wales, and wrote her a number of poems. When a volume of verse failed to bring him fame, he announced that a revolution in dress was more important than a revolution in morals, and began to call attention to himself with a velvet coat edged with braid, knee breeches and black silk stockings. He was one of the first great modern experts in the art of self-publicity. By 1880, he was being regularly satirized in *Punch*. In the following years, W.S. Gilbert portrayed him in *Patience* as the mediocre poet Bunthorne. Gilbert no doubt thought he was being cruel but Wilde was delighted with the notoriety it brought him. This led to a request to go on a lecture tour of America. Wilde arrived in New York with the typical comment, 'I have nothing to declare but my genius.' He was not particularly fond of America. Later, when he heard that Rossetti had given someone the money to go to America he commented, 'Of course, if one had enough money to go to America, one wouldn't go.'

In 1883, after a lecture tour of Scotland, he announced his engagement to

Constance Lloyd, daughter of an Irish barrister, a beautiful and sweet-natured girl. They were deeply in love and on the morning after his wedding night, Wilde strolled in Paris with his friend Robert Sherard and described his sexual pleasures with embarrassing detail. Two sons were born of the marriage.

It was about two years after his marriage that Wilde made a shattering discovery. At Oxford he had contracted syphilis from a prostitute and had been 'cured' with mercury treatment (which had discoloured his teeth). Now he learned that the spirochaetes were still in his bloodstream. With modern treatment he would have been cured in a weekend. As it was, he felt that he had to give up sex with Constance. At about this time he met a seventeen-year-old youth named Robert ('Robbie') Ross, who was amusing, cultivated and amiable. Ross later claimed that he was the first male Wilde had been to bed with.

Success was slow in arriving; early plays like *Vera, or The Nihilists* and *The Duchess of Padua* failed to make an impression. He was literary critic for the *Pall Mall Gazette,* and he became the editor of a magazine called *The Lady's World* (renamed *Woman's World*). He wrote short stories, children's stories, poems and essays. Finally, in 1891, when he was 37, *The Picture of Dorian Gray* appeared and caused a degree of public outrage that he must have found highly satisfying. In the following year, *Lady Windermere's Fan* went on at the St James's Theatre and finally made Wilde rich as well as famous.

In the year of *Dorian Gray,* Wilde met a handsome young aristocrat of 22, Lord Alfred Douglas, son of the Marquess of Queensberry (responsible for the Queensberry Rules in boxing). Soon they were inseparable, dining in expensive restaurants, spending weekends at country houses, attending art exhibitions and first nights. Inevitably, they slept together, although Douglas later insisted that there was no sodomy – only mutual masturbation and a certain amount of oral sex. 'Bosie' (as Wilde called Lord Alfred) was himself a pederast and preferred boys to older men. The French novelist André Gide has described how Wilde and Douglas were responsible for his own downfall. For years he had been struggling against his homosexuality. In Algiers, he discovered that Wilde and Douglas were staying in the same hotel – he had met Wilde in Paris. Before they set out for the evening, Douglas remarked to Gide, 'I hope you are like me. I have a horror of women. I only like boys.' Wilde told the 'vile procurer who came to pilot us through the town' that he wanted to see some Arab boys and added 'as beautiful as bronze statues'. But a brawl broke out in the café the procurer took them to and they went home disappointed. Soon after, Douglas went off to Blidah, where he was hoping to buy an Arab boy from his family (in fact, the boy ran away with a woman). Wilde took Gide out for another evening in the Casbah, and in a little café, a beautiful Arab youth came and played on a flute for them. Then Wilde led Gide outside and whispered in his ear, 'Dear, would you like the little musician?' and Gide, his voice choking, answered, 'Yes.' Later, the youth came to a hotel room and Gide wrote: 'My joy was unbounded, and I cannot imagine it greater even if love had been added.'

Back in London, Wilde met Alfred Taylor, an upper-class young man who had spent his way through a fortune. Taylor was a homosexual who liked to dress as a woman; he burned incense in his dimly lit apartment and spent his days picking up young men – many of them telegraph boys of the kind who figured in the Cleveland Street scandal (see page 83) – and taking them back to his room for sex. The first youth Taylor picked up for Wilde was a twenty-year-old named Sidney Mavor – known in his own circle as Jenny. The following evening, Wilde took Taylor, Douglas and 'Jenny' to dinner at Kettner's and afterwards Wilde and Mavor went to a hotel room together. It emerged later that Wilde's idea of sex was to have the boy seated on his knee, while he fondled his genitals and occasionally indulged in oral sex. Wilde would tell them to imagine they were women and that he was their lover, which suggests that his role was fundamentally masculine and dominant. He disliked obviously feminine youths – he commented once that having sex with coarse, masculine types gave him a feeling of 'dining with panthers'. His appetite seems to have been enormous – he told Beardsley once that he had had five messenger boys in one evening and had kissed them all over their bodies. 'They were all dirty and appealed to me for that reason.'

Some time in 1893, Douglas gave a suit of clothes to an unemployed clerk, who found in the pockets a number of letters from Wilde. The result was an attempt to blackmail Wilde. 'A very curious construction can be put on that letter,' said the blackmailer, to which Wilde replied, 'Art is rarely intelligible to the criminal classes.' When the blackmailer said he could get £60 for the letter from a certain man, Wilde advised him to go and sell it immediately. The astonished blackmailer relented and gave Wilde the letter back for nothing – an example of Wilde's extraordinary charm, which was based upon a fundamental kindliness.

Unfortunately, a copy of the letter fell into the hands of the Marquess of Queensberry who was particularly outraged by the sentence: 'it is a marvel that those rose-red lips of yours should have been made no less for music of song than for the madness of kisses.' Queensberry was an eccentric Scottish aristocrat – in The Trial of Oscar Wilde Montgomery Hyde calls him 'arrogant, vain, conceited and ill tempered', and says that he was probably mentally unbalanced. One day when Queensberry saw Wilde and his son dining together at the Café Royal, he allowed himself to be persuaded to join them, and was dazzled by Wilde's charm, and told 'Bosie' afterwards that he could understand why he loved him. The 'rose-red lips' letter seems to have changed his mind and he wrote a furious letter ordering Douglas never to see

Wilde again. Douglas replied with a telegram: 'What a funny little man you are.' Queensberry began to haunt the restaurants where Wilde and Douglas dined, threatening to thrash Wilde. One afternoon, the Marquess came to Wilde's house to order him to stop seeing his son. Wilde ordered him, and his bodyguard, out. Queensberry continued to persecute Wilde. He tried to get into the theatre on the first night of *The Importance of Being Earnest*, but was kept out by police. On 18 February 1895, he left his card at Wilde's club, the Albemarle, with a note written on it: 'To Oscar Wilde, posing as a somdomite' [*sic*]. When he received it two weeks later, Wilde decided to sue. He went to see a solicitor, Charles Humphries, and assured him that the accusation of being a sodomite was untrue. (He may well have felt he was being honest – he was not, as we know, inclined to sodomy.) Humphries agreed to prosecute.

The first trial proved a disaster for Wilde. His old schoolfellow Edward Carson was defending. Wilde was brilliant and amusing in the witness box but when Carson declared in court that he would prove that Wilde brought boys to the Savoy Hotel, it was obvious that Queensberry had done his homework – or paid private detectives to do it – and the prosecution realized it would have to withdraw or suffer defeat. The Marquess was acquitted.

Now Wilde's friends begged him to flee the country. Homosexuality was a criminal offence. Wilde refused and there was undoubtedly a touch of masochism in his refusal. In fact, he seemed to identify himself with Christ and to believe that he had to live out a tragic destiny. ('One must always seek what is most tragic', Wilde had told Gide.) On the day the Marquess was acquitted, a warrant was issued for Wilde's arrest, on a charge of committing acts of indecency with various male persons. Taylor, who had refused to betray Wilde, was also charged with him. This, Montgomery Hyde insists, was unfair to Wilde, since the case against Taylor was a great deal stronger than that against Wilde. The second trial lasted from 6 April to 19 April 1895. The judge's summing up was in Wilde's favour – at least, he urged the jury to take into account every possible doubt of Wilde's guilt. The jury failed to reach an agreement. For the next three weeks Wilde was out on bail.

The third trial began on 20 May 1895, and this time, Taylor was tried separately. He was soon found guilty of indecent acts with males. Then Wilde stepped into the dock. Again, a succession of working-class young men described being taken back to Wilde's room. Sodomy sometimes took place; more often, mutual masturbation and fellatio. Wilde was again brilliant and amusing in the box but seldom convincing. Finally, as everyone by now expected, Wilde was found guilty on every count but one. He and Taylor were sentenced to two years' imprisonment with hard labour.

Wilde was taken to Reading jail. Standing around on the station platform he remarked to the guard, 'If this is the way Her Majesty treats her prisoners, she doesn't deserve to have any.' But the old sparkle had gone. The experience of prison almost drove Wilde insane. He wallowed in self-pity and wrote a long letter – in fact, a short book – to Alfred Douglas, accusing him of his ruin. It was later published, in an expurgated version, as *De Profundis*. His hard labour consisted in picking oakum (that is unpicking old ropes for caulking boats). He served every day of his sentence and was finally released on 19 May 1897.

The desire to write had vanished. 'Something is killed in me,' he told Robbie Ross. Constance Wilde died in a nursing home in Genoa after an operation to correct a spinal injury, soon after reading Wilde's long poem *The Ballad of Reading Gaol*. Wilde went to Dieppe, where he bumped into the poet Ernest Dowson, who persuaded him to go to a brothel. Wilde did not enjoy it. 'The first in these ten years – and it will be the last,' he told Dowson. 'It was like cold mutton.' He lived in Paris under the name of Sebastian Melmoth – borrowing the name from the Gothic novel *Melmoth the Wanderer* by Maturin – and died in poverty in a cheap hotel on the Left Bank on 30 November 1900, telling a friend who came to see him, 'I am dying beyond my means.'

WISE, THOMAS J.

THE 'FIRST EDITIONS' SCANDAL

In 1932, two young London booksellers, John Carter and Graham Pollard, were intrigued to discover that both had been investigating the same curious bibliographical problem. They decided to pool their information. The problem concerned certain rare pamphlets by John Ruskin and other Victorian writers. In the notes to their complete edition of Ruskin, his editors, Cook and Wedderburn, had asserted that certain pamphlets were undoubtedly forgeries. The reason they said was that the text of the pamphlets, which were supposed to be 'first editions', was that of later revised editions of Ruskin, not of earlier ones.

But there were many other pamphlets that puzzled Carter and Pollard – more than fifty. For example, there was a pamphlet of *Sonnets by E.B.B.* (Elizabeth Barrett Browning) dated 'Reading 1847'. These were the famous *Sonnets from the Portuguese,* and there is a romantic story of how Mrs Browning came shyly down to breakfast one morning and slipped a sheaf of papers into her husband's pocket, then ran back to her room, terrified of his verdict on her poetry – on which, of course, he was able to reassure her. What was slightly puzzling about this 'first edition' of the sonnets was that they were printed at Reading. Why should the Brownings send them all the way to England when they could have had them printed more easily in Italy, where they were living?

The answer to this question had apparently been provided by the eminent literary critic Edmund Gosse, who, in turn, had had it from some 'unnamed friend'. Gosse said that the poems had been sent to Mrs Browning's friend Mary Russell Mitford and that she had arranged the printing. By the 1920s, a few copies that had been kept back by Miss Mitford were selling to collectors for as much as $1,250 each.

It was while they were trying to find out how the copies had come on to the market that the investigators came upon the name of the eminent bibliographer, Thomas J. Wise, who had published a bibliography of the works of Elizabeth Barrett Browning. He told how the copies had been given to a doctor friend, who had in turn sold them to Browning collectors.

Carter and Pollard decided to call chemistry to their aid. They had the paper of the 1847 pamphlet analysed and discovered that it was made of wood pulp, which had not been used in paper-making until the early 1880s. The type itself also afforded a clue in the form of the f's and j's which were of a kind known as 'kernless font'. In this font no part of the type projects beyond the rest of the letter (as with the curled top of an f or the curled tail of a j). Research revealed that these had not been introduced into the type in which the 1847 pamphlet was printed until 1880.

But if the pamphlet was a forgery, who was responsible? The first task was to try and track down the printer. The pamphlet bore no printer's name but the detectives were lucky enough to stumble on another pamphlet in exactly the same type. It was of a poem by Matthew Arnold and this was not a forgery but an ordinary collector's facsimile reprint of the first edition. In the back, they found the address of the printer: Richard Clay and Son, a respectable London firm. But there the trail petered out. Clay and Sons told the investigators that their records before 1911 had been destroyed in a fire so they had no way of finding out who commissioned them to print the 'E.B.B.' pamphlet.

Carter and Pollard went on to study many more pamphlets by the famous such as George Eliot, Tennyson, Swinburne, Thackeray and Matthew Arnold; they found more forgeries. It seemed that the 'forger' usually took a poem or article from the works of the literary celebrity, had it reprinted as a pamphlet, and explained on the title page just how it had come to be printed before the genuine 'first edition'.

When two similar pamphlets had been questioned years earlier, Thomas J. Wise had pointed the finger of suspicion at two deceased bibliophiles, Richard Herne Shepherd and John Camden Hotten. Wise, who was now in his seventies, was so universally respected that it seemed unlikely that he could be the forger. Yet Wise was a friend of Gosse and could have been the source of Gosse's story about the Browning pamphlet. Wise had also been closely connected with both the Shelley and the Browning Societies and had often commissioned reprints of their first editions. If such a man asked the printers to run off a pamphlet by Ruskin or Elizabeth Barrett Browning, they would do it without the slightest suspicion.

Again and again the investigators came upon Wise's name in connection with pamphlets that proved to be forgeries. Eventually, they traced the source of supply of many of the pamphlets. The man who had launched them upon the rare book market was an antiquarian bookseller named Herbert Gorfin. At first the investigators suspected that Gorfin was the forger but when they interviewed him, his shock convinced them that he had no idea he had been selling fakes. He gave them full access to his records. Just as they had expected, it became clear that Gorfin had bought hundreds of copies of forged pamphlets from Thomas J. Wise.

Carter and Pollard now went to visit Wise, an ailing man of 73. He stonewalled; he had no idea how it had happened – his memory was rather poor. They told him they intended to publish their evidence and asked for his side of the story. Wise said he would try to find records of the sales. But they heard no more from him and, in 1934, Richard Clay and Company issued *An Enquiry into the Nature of Certain Nineteenth-Century Pamphlets*, which pointed the finger at Wise. They stopped short of accusing Wise of the forgery and pretended to believe that he was the victim of some unknown master forger.

Wise, meanwhile, had offered to buy all the remaining pamphlets from Gorfin at a good price – £400 on condition he declared he had received the pamphlets from another noted bibliographer, now deceased, called Harry Buxton Forman. Gorfin accepted the offer of the £400 but declined to support the Forman story.

Publication of the book about the forgeries caused a sensation far beyond the world of rare books and reporters rushed to interview Wise. He was evasive. In letters to *The Times Literary Supplement* he insisted that the pamphlets had come from Harry Buxton Forman but Gorfin denied this story. Carter and Pollard now told Wise that unless he stopped trying to pin the blame on Forman, they would tell the story of his attempt to persuade Gorfin to lie about it. Wise subsided into silence; he died in 1937, three years after the exposure, still refusing to admit his guilt.

Why did he do it? In his chapter on Wise in *The Scholar Adventurers* (1950), Richard D. Altick suggests that it was because he was himself an obsessive book collector, who started life as a clerk in an essential-oils firm. When he began to have a hand in the printing of facsimile editions of Shelley and Browning, he realized how easy it would be to sell reprints as originals. Later in life, he made such a success of the essential-oils business that there was no need for him to carry out the forgeries. Altick also cites some evidence that suggests Wise was telling at least half the truth when he accused Forman. The men seem to have known one another in the 1890s and Wise commented in a note to Forman: 'We print *Last Tournament* in 1896, and want "some one to think" it was printed in 1871.' *Last Tournament* was proved by Carter and Pollard to be another of the forgeries.

BIBLIOGRAPHY

Alexander, Marc *The Outrageous Queens* (Frederick Muller, 1977)

Altick, Richard D. *The Scholar Adventurers* (The Free Press, New York and Collier-Macmillan, 1960)

Anger, Kenneth *Hollywood Babylon* (Dell Publishing New York, 1975)

Barkeley, Richard *The Road to Mayerling* (Macmillan, 1959)

Barrow, Andrew *International Gossip* (Hamish Hamilton, 1983)

Blythe, Ronald *The Age of Illusion* (Penguin Books, 1963)

Bresler, Fenton *Scales of Justice* (Weidenfeld & Nicolson, 1973)

Bryan III, J. and Murphy, Charles J.V. *The Windsor Story* (Granada, 1979)

Chaplin, Lita Grey with Cooper, Morton *My Life with Chaplin* (Bernard Geis Associates, USA, 1966)

Chapman, Guy *The Dreyfus Case* (Rupert Hart-Davis, 1963)

Clark, Ronald W. *The Life of Bertrand Russell* (Jonathan Cape and Weidenfeld & Nicolson, 1975)

Connolly, Cyril *The Missing Diplomats* (The Queen Anne Press, 1952)

Cullen, Tom *The Prostitutes' Padre* (Bodley Head, 1975)

De Mille, Richard *Castaneda's Journey* (Capra Press, USA, 1976); *The Don Juan Papers* (Ross-Erikson, USA, 1980)

Evans, Christopher *Cults of Unreason* (Rampa, etc) (Harrap, 1973)

Fryer, Peter *Mrs Grundy* (Corgi Books, 1963)

Harris, Frank *Oscar Wilde* (Constable, 1938)

Harrison, Michael *London By Gaslight 1861–1911* (Peter Davies, 1963)

Higham, Charles *Errol Flynn: The Untold Story* (Granada, 1980)

Holland, Vyvyan *Oscar Wilde: A Pictorial Biography* (Thames & Hudson, 1960)

Holloway, Mark *Heavens on Earth* (Dover Publications, New York, 1966)

Hyams, Joe *Bogart and Bacall, A Love Story* (Sphere Books, 1976)

Hyde, H. Montgomery *The Cleveland Street Scandal* (W.H. Allen, 1976)

James, Robert Rhodes (Ed.) *Chips, The Diaries of Sir Henry Channon* (Weidenfeld & Nicolson, 1967)

Kayser, Jacques, *The Dreyfus Affair* (William Heineman, 1931)

Keeler, Christine with Fawkes, Sandy *Nothing But* (New English Library, 1983)

Kennedy, Ludovic *The Trial of Stephen Ward* (Gollancz, 1964)

Leighton, Isabel *The Aspirin Age 1919–1941* (Simon & Schuster, New York, 1949)

Mackenzie, Jeanne and Norman *The Time Traveller, The Life of H.G. Wells* (Weidenfeld & Nicoloson, 1973)

Mayersberg, Paul *Hollywood, The Haunted House* (Allen Lane and The Penguin Press, 1967)

Messiter, Ian *The Judgement* (Michael Joseph, 1981)

Middlemas, Keith and Barnes, John *Baldwin* (Weidenfeld & Nicolson, 1969)

Noble, Peter *Ivor Novello, Man of the Theatre* (Falcon Press, 1951); *The Fabulous Orson Welles* (Hutchinson, 1956)

Noyes, John Humphrey *Strange Cults and Utopias of 19th-Century America* (Dover Publications, New York, 1966)

Ramsaye, Terry *A Million and One Nights* (Frank Cass 1954)

Ray, Gordon N. *H.G. Wells and Rebecca West* (Macmillan, 1974)

Rees, Goronwy *A Chapter of Accidents* (Chatto & Windus, 1972)

Schulberg, Budd *Moving Pictures: Memories of a Hollywood Prince* (Souvenir Press, 1982)

Watkins, Glenn *Gesualdo* (Oxford University Press, 1973)

Welcome, John *Cheating At Cards* (Faber and Faber, 1963)

Wells, G.P. *H.G. Wells In Love* (Faber and Faber, 1984)
White, T.H. *The Age of Scandal* (Penguin Books, 1962)
Yallop, David A. *In God's Name* (Jonathan Cape, 1984)
Young, Wayland *The Profumo Affair, Aspects of Conservation* (Penguin, 1963)

INDEX

FROM ATLANTIS TO THE SPHINX

Colin Wilson

The compelling argument of Colin Wilson's bestselling book is that thousands of years before ancient Egypt and Greece held sway, there was a great civilisation whose ships travelled the world. Whereas we have no way of seeing the universe as a whole, these 'old ones' possessed some knowledge system that offered a unified view of the universe, which was then passed on to descendants who escaped to Egypt and South America. It was this knowledge system – alien to modern man – that enabled them to move stones weighing a thousand tons.

From Atlantis to the Sphinx sets out to reconstruct that ancient knowledge. In a fascinating exploration of the remote depths of history, here is a groundbreaking attempt to understand how these long-forgotten peoples thought, felt and communicated on a universal plane.

'A *tour de force* and a wonderful study of human perception that will be talked about for years to come.'
Robert G. Bauval, author of *The Orion Mystery*

Non-Fiction/History
0 7535 00647
£7.99

THE DEVIL'S PARTY

Colin Wilson

When David Koresh perished in the compound of the Branch Davidians at Waco, Texas, along with over seventy others, the event made headline news around the world. How did one man persuade these people to give up everything to follow him; to give up their daughters to be his 'wives', and ultimately, to give their lives to try to protect him? Was Koresh a con man exploiting his followers, or a man who truly believed he was the Messiah, leading his chosen people to the Promised Land?

Colin Wilson looks at the troubled history of charlatan messiahs, taking as a starting point the most famous 'prophet' of recent times. But Koresh was neither the most excessive of cult leaders, nor was he the most misguided. Others trod the path before him, and Wilson looks at the lives of cult leaders from the earliest days of Christianity, through the stories of, among many others, the 'Rev' Jim Jones – some nine hundred of his followers died 'committing suicide' – and Jeffrey Lundgren, who tried to back his claim to be a Mormon prophet by brutally killing an entire family.

Wilson goes on to consider what it is that makes these messiahs believe they are who they claim to be; and why there are those prepared to follow them – a messiah is nothing without someone to believe in him. What starts out as a study of self-delusion and powermania, leads Colin Wilson into an exploration of the human psyche, as he untangles the history of the charlatan messiahs and explores their world view.

Non-Fiction/History
0 7535 0502 9
£7.99

ESPIONAGE: SPIES AND SECRETS by Richard M. Bennett

Foreword by James Bamford with a Preface by David Shayler

Failure to defend against recent terrorist outrages has drawn unprecedented public attention to modern-day global espionage, from the US government's involvement in the politics of the Middle East, Europe and Africa, to the surveillance of their own citizens by governments throughout the western world. This compelling reference resource contains over 500 entries covering every aspect of modern-day intelligence-gathering and counter-terrorism, along with a comprehensive overview of its history. Global in scope, *Espionage* focuses in particular on developments in the field of intelligence since the end of the Cold War:

- Governmental failure to foresee recent terrorist attacks
- Counter-terrorism, including the growth in commercial terrorism
- Electronic and communications surveillance
- Illegal activities by the intelligence services from around the world, including assassination, smuggling and torture
- Terminology and equipment explained

With entries on individual spies, politicians and diplomats, from the players to the patsies, and profiles of the key historical events and scandals from the history of spying, *Espionage* is the ultimate guide for journalists, researchers and anyone with an interest in this highly topical, controversial and chilling subject.

Praise for *Espionage*:

'*Espionage* offers insights into this new era, where the threat lies not in hostile governments, but in highly sophisticated organisations like the al-Qaeda network.' *New Statesman*

'A fascinating read and an excellent source of reference.' *Military Illustrated*

'Easily one of the best popular encyclopedias ever written on the subject of intelligence . . . laced with gems throughout . . . a must buy.' *Eyespy*

'Helpfully covers the ground and will be useful to journalists and spies alike.' *Diplomat*

'Spook anoraks will devour this.' *Soldier*

Reference/History
Published in paperback 7 August 2003
07535 0830 3
£10.99

ELITE FORCES: THE WORLD'S MOST FORMIDABLE SECRET ARMIES

Richard M. Bennett, with a Foreword by Barry Davis BEM

The invincible reputation of specialist military units such as the USA's Delta Force, Israel's IDF and of course Britain's SAS, has grown steadily in recent years. Thanks to a number of campaigns and successful anti-terror operations, from London's Iranian Embassy siege in 1980 to their crucial role in Afghanistan following 11 September 2001, it's now assumed that special forces are ideal for our world of small, localised conflicts – and especially George W. Bush's war on terror.

With a capacity for fast, covert response that regular battle orders do not have, elite forces represent the future of conflict for governments everywhere. But their operations often raise the issue of democratic accountability, by making it possible for a government to conduct a successful military campaign to completion without reference to a legislature and without a declaration of war. As well as presenting stories of individual heroism, *Elite Forces* takes a look at operations of dubious legality; examines how deserved the reputations of each elite forces unit is; and takes an objective look at what happens when things go wrong, as they have most famously during the Gulf War of 1991, and in America's disastrous intervention in Somalia in 1993.

- Over 500 compelling entries which cut through the myth and the secrecy surrounding modern-day special forces
- Comprehensive overviews of the history, selection and training procedures, and orders of battle, of every major elite fighting force in the world today
- Packed with hair-raising examples of individual heroism, endurance and courage in adversity
- Fully up to date to include the impact of 11 September 2001 on the world of special forces
- Explores the hidden links between elite forces and governments, intelligence organisations and business, and their controversial lack of accountability
- Examines how new technologies have come to the aid of the elite soldier

It is the first book of its kind to examine all aspects of the overlap between elite forces and the hidden worlds of intelligence and counter-terrorism, and takes an objective look at the secret, controversial role of special forces and 'freelancers' in covert, deadly operations around the world. Fully up-to-date, it examines their relevance to the global fallout from 11 September 2001. *Elite Forces* is both a compelling, revealing and occasionally shocking read, and an authoritative and easy-to-use reference source.

Published in hardback 6 February 2003
1 85227 974 5
£18.99